JUDITH MILLER
ANTIQUES
HUNTER'S GUIDE
TO EUROPE

JUDITH MILLER
ANTIQUES
HUNTER'S GUIDE
TO EUROPE

MARSHALL PUBLISHING • LONDON

A Marshall Edition
Marshall Editions Ltd
The Orangery, 161 New Bond Street,
London W1S 2UF
www.marshallpublishing.com

First published in the UK in 2001 by
Marshall Editions Developments Ltd

Project Editor Caroline Ball
Project Art Editor Flora Awolaja

Editors Wendy Dear, Anna Fischel,
Nicola Munro, Anna Southgate
Managing Editor Julie Brooke
Art Director Dave Goodman
Editorial Director Ellen Dupont
Editorial Coordinator Gillian Thompson
DTP Manager Lesley Gilbert

Picture Research Jessica Curtis,
Frances Vargo
Proof Reader Marion Dent
Indexer Hillary Cooper
Map Illustrator Carrie Hill
Illustrations Linden Artists
Production Angela Couchman,
Nikki Ingram, Anna Pauletti
Main Contributors Joan Gannij, Jennifer
Leonard, Michael Ramscar, Verite Riley
Collins, Anne-Marie Sapstead, Simon
Smith, Mrinalini Srivastava, Bryan Wilder,
Roger Williams, Deborah Williamson

A CIP catalogue record for this book is
available from the British Library

ISBN 1-84028-334-3

Jacket credits
Photograph of Judith Miller by Adrian
Weinbrecht. Jacket front: tl Robert Harding
Picture Library, tc Michael Jenner, tr
Michael Jenner, bl AJ/AL, bc GR, br
PC/A&J; jacket back lRobert Harding
Picture Library, c Robert Harding Picture
Library/Maurice Joseph, r Britain on View.

Originated in Singapore by
Chroma Graphics

Printed and bound in Portugal by
Printer Portuguesa

CONTENTS

INTRODUCTION

When I started collecting "old" plates as a student at Edinburgh University in the late 1960s, I had absolutely no idea where this hobby would lead. As my interest grew I began to scour shops in other areas; when I went home to the Scottish Borders, or to visit friends in Dundee, Newcastle, London and then Copenhagen and Paris. What a joy to find new hunting grounds! The thrill of the chase, the opportunity to stumble across the unexpected, became an added delight to that of travel. Even a dull trip could be exciting thanks to a foray into the world of antiques and collecting.

The Antiques Hunter's Guide to Europe was born out of more than one missed opportunity. There is nothing more frustrating after an exciting trip to a foreign city, or one in your own country, than to be told by a well-meaning friend that you have missed quite simply the best – yet little known – museum, antiques shop or area. To enjoy this book you do not need to be an antiques devotee, you do not need to be an avid collector, just someone with a passion for the past.

This book is a personal selection – after 30 years of hunting, these are the cities, areas, museums and shops I have enjoyed, with some emphasis on the antiques the area is famous for (although their home city may not be the cheapest place to buy them). A few of the shops mentioned have absolutely nothing to do with the world of antiques, but are just too good to miss. If you do venture into any of the shops included, remember that while the dealers will be delighted to help prospective buyers, they do have a living to make.
Happy hunting!

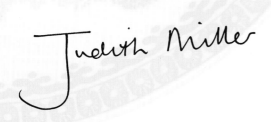

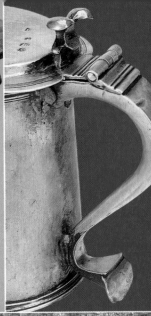

GREAT BRITAIN
& IRELAND

THE ANTIQUES LANDSCAPE

One of the great joys of antiques hunting anywhere in Great Britain and Ireland is that antiques or bric-a-brac shops can be found in almost any town or village and that, every weekend, local fairs – even rural boot fairs – can yield unexpected treasures from all over the world.

Until a century or so ago, at a time when international trade and home manufacturing were beginning to boom, the British Isles was at the hub of the largest empire on earth. Younger sons would ship off to India, China or Africa with the army or civil service and would return from their travels with exotic "trinkets" – which could be anything from an elephant's foot to a priceless Oriental vase – that would then be handed down through the family, their worth not always recognized. At the same time, it was part of the polishing of a young gentleman's education to spend a year or more on the Grand Tour around Europe (see Florence, page 242), in order to learn about art and to forge connections with the "right" types of European families. They, too, brought back souvenirs. The exquisite items that filled the great houses were copied by local craftsmen in less precious materials (porcelain figures copied in earthenware, for instance) for clients among the rising – and acquisitive – middle class, who had gained their money from trade and commerce.

The first Toby jug is credited to Ralph Wood (1715–72), one of several Staffordshire-based potters. These beer jugs often had hats which doubled as detachable lids.

The Industrial Revolution took off first in Britain, and processes such as steam power gave manufacturers a huge initial advantage over foreign competition. In the potteries, in and around Stoke-on-Trent, families such as Wedgwood, Doulton and Spode became household names; cotton from across the

Atlantic joined local wool to bring the mill-owners of Lancashire and Yorkshire vast wealth, and ports from London to Liverpool, Bristol to Belfast, received riches from the Empire.

With such a diverse trading background, it is impossible to know what you will find today, and this has made it very difficult to select which towns and areas to include. I have chosen my own favourite haunts, but would have wished for more space to talk about the great house-clearance sales in north Wales, my favourite shops in Co. Cork or the best hunting grounds of the north-east. Long ago, I caught the bidding bug and love to visit local auction houses. I always try to get to the preview, usually a day or two beforehand, to examine everything on offer at my leisure and (a vital rule!) decide what my price limit will be. The buzz and excitement of the fast-falling lots – at a country sale the auctioneer can get through well over 100 lots an hour – is part of the fun of buying at auction. Even if you're not able to attend, you can leave a sealed bid with the auctioneer or the clerk, who will bid on your behalf.

From the Scottish Highlands to Devon and Cornwall, and from East Anglia to the west of Ireland, there are treasures on every high street. Museums and country houses throughout the British Isles contain the most wonderful antiques and collectables. Although best known for the more traditional antiques, Great Britain and Ireland have a rapidly expanding market, particularly in many of the larger cities, for more unusual collectors' items, and high quality modern limited editions.

The exquisite panels and carving on this mid-17th-century oak chest betray late-Renaissance influences.

SCOTTISH BORDERS

An area of dramatic natural beauty, of historic houses and delightful villages, but for me it is home – where my whole journey into the world of antiques began.

Galashiels: statue of a Border Reiver patrolling on horse

THERE IS A MYSTICAL CHARM IN THE LANDSCAPE of the Scottish Borders, and, as my Dad used to say, "You can take the girl out of the Borders, but you can't take the Borders out of the girl" and so I'd like immediately to admit a bias: to me there is nowhere quite so beautiful, unspoilt and historic as the Scottish Borders. The sense of history is always with you: the wild moors with memories of the Border Reivers (the Scottish and English clans who plundered each other's territories in the 15th and 16th centuries), the forests which still ring with the shouts of royal hunting parties, the spiritual echoes of historic houses such as Traquair, Paxton House and Floors Castle, and my home area where the majestic Tweed meanders past the Eildon Hills. It is a wonderful area for antiques hunters as you never know what you are going to find. As the Scottish comedian and actor Billy Connolly so aptly put it, "The Scottish Borders looks more Scottish in appearance and atmosphere – it is what people think the Scottish Highlands look and feel like."

ABBOTSFORD REVISITED

Abbotsford is the first historic house I ever visited and has remained one of my favourites. Sir Walter Scott moved to the Cartley Hill farmhouse in 1812, enraptured by the views of his beloved River Tweed. He renamed the house Abbotsford and rebuilt it extensively between 1818 and 1822. The oak-panelled library has a spectacular crenellated ceiling and contains 9,000 rare books – and don't miss the study where Scott wrote his novels. After your visit, head into Melrose, one of the most charming Border towns, to see **Melrose Abbey**, built between the 14th and 16th centuries, when it was the richest abbey in Scotland. It is a truly romantic sight.
● **Abbotsford**. Tel: 01896 752043
● **Melrose Abbey**. Tel: 01896 822562

Abbotsford House, the home of Sir Walter Scott and, inset, the study

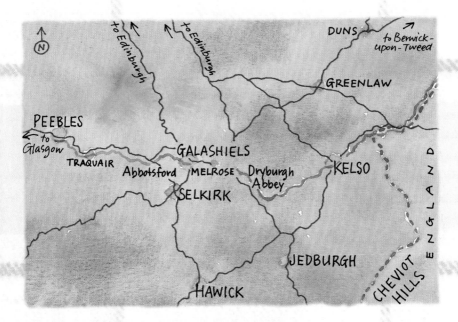

SHOPPING

The real joy of antiquing in the Borders is dropping into antique shops in any of the towns and villages you pass through – you are sure to turn up a surprise. Local dealers are often called to house clearances and you can never tell what little "sleeper", or unrecognized treasure, you may come across.

Silver box c.1839 with Abbotsford depicted on the lid

When I drive over the border my first stop is often:

R&M Turner Antiques, 34–36 High Street, Jedburgh (01835 863445) for a really great selection of items, with nine showrooms of furniture, clocks, ceramics and silver.

Also search out **The Caddy Mann** (see Restaurants) for sustenance and a good selection of general antiques.

In Peebles look in on **Veteran Antiques** and **Tubbecke** in the High Street, and **South Park Antiques** in Caledonian Road.

Take a walk along the High Street in Innerleithen to **The Glory Hole** (No 29), **The Last Century** (No 34) and **Keepsakes** (No 96). And pay a visit to **Robert Smail's Printing Works** to see a survival from the Victorian era.

Kelso is known for antiquarian booksellers and 20th-century first editions. **Border Books** in Palma Place and **McGregor's Book Store** in the Square are both good hunting grounds.

After visiting Abbotsford you could go on to Melrose and drop into **Waverley Antiques** in Scotts Place.

Something Different

At **Selkirk Glass** there is a special viewing area from where you can watch glass being made. Peter Holmes, who owns the glassworks and trained under Paul Ysart, is a major name in Scottish glass and has produced a large number of exceptional designs. Look out in particular for Peter's own limited edition paperweights which have become highly collectable.

● **Selkirk Glass**, Dunsdale Haugh, Selkirk. Tel: (01750) 20954

WHERE TO EAT AND DRINK

Caddy Mann Restaurant
Mounthooly Farm, near Jedburgh
Tel: (01835) 850787
An award-winning restaurant serving local produce – and traditional home baking. Best of all, you can buy the antiques that furnish it.

Wheatsheaf Hotel
Main Street, Swinton, Berwickshire
Tel: (01890) 860257
The restaurant here serves fantastic local seafood and game (the best in the area, I think).

WHERE TO STAY

Castle Venlaw Hotel
Edinburgh Road, Peebles
Tel: (01721) 720384. Fax: (01721) 724066
An 18th-century castle hotel with 24 rooms.

Dryburgh Abbey Hotel
St Boswells, Melrose
Tel: (01835) 822261. Fax: (01835) 823845
This is where I had tea with my parents when I was a little girl. Built around 1845, it is in a magnificent setting on the banks of the Tweed.

Woodlands House Hotel and Restaurant,
Windyknowe Road , Galashiels
Tel: (01896) 754722. Fax: (01896) 754892
A Victorian Gothic mansion with 18 rooms and wonderful food.

LONDON

For the antiques lover, London is one of the great hunting grounds. There are specialists in just about every type of antique and an amazing array of fascinating objects to suit every pocket and taste.

St Stephen's tower, home of Big Ben

LONDON'S HISTORY STRETCHES back 2,000 YEARS, to the Roman invasion of AD43. Londinium, as it was then called, became an important trading centre with the Thames as its main highway. The city quickly grew in size and status and in AD200 a defensive wall was built around the area now known as "The City". Sections of this and other Roman remains can still be seen today.

London's prosperous past is evident in the wealth of magnificent royal, ecclesiastical, civic and domestic buildings that give this capital city its unique character.

The exclusive Burlington Arcade, off Piccadilly, which opened in 1819

During the Victorian era, London reinforced its position as a world centre of art and culture with a profusion of museums and galleries emphasizing the nation's achievements, wealth and power as rulers of a vast empire.

London has been described as "the whole world in one place" and it is true that wherever you go you can see evidence of its rich multicultural and historical heritage, which is also reflected in the diversity of antiques that can be found here. Antiques shopping in London ranges from the rarified elegance of the Burlington Arcade in the exclusive Bond Street area to the hustle-bustle of London's many street markets. But do remember that London is a vast, sprawling city and you will have to plan your days carefully to get the most out of your visit.

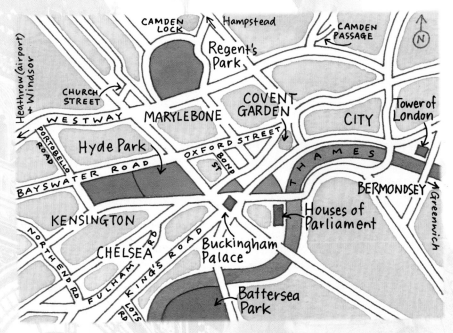

AUCTION HOUSES

London's major auction houses have regular general antiques sales, and also hold periodic auctions of more specialized antiques.

Bonhams & Brooks, Montpelier Street, SW7 or 65-69 Lots Road, SW10. Tel: (020) 7393 3900.

Christie's, 8 King St, St James's, SW1. Tel: (020) 7839 9060.

Christie's South Kensington, 85 Old Brompton Rd, SW7. Tel: (020) 7581 7611.

Phillips, 101 New Bond St, W1. Tel: (020) 7629 6602.

Phillips, Bayswater, 10 Salem Rd, W2. Tel: (020) 7229 9090.

Sotheby's, 34–35 New Bond St, W1. Tel: (020) 7293 5000.

Toby jug, first made in the early 18th century

QUICK GUIDE TO ANTIQUES

Whether you want to make a major investment or just love rummaging through bric-a-brac, London is an antiques lover's wonderland. Try the markets first, even for high quality pieces, as most dealers have excellent stock and the knowledge to go with it.
● **Camden Passage, Portobello Road** and **Bermondsey** are the biggest and best-known markets, but they do attract very large crowds.
● The many antiques shops in **Kensington Church Street**, the **West End** and **Fulham** have merchandise of the highest quality.
● There are bargains to be had if you are prepared to venture further afield to places such as **Hampstead** and **Greenwich**.

ANTIQUES FAIRS

Antiques fairs are held in a number of London venues throughout the year. Be sure to check listings on arrival.

Look out for:
● **Kensington Town Hall,** Horton St, W8, holds a huge antiques fair every autumn.
● **Chelsea Town Hall,** Kings Rd, SW3, has three antiques fairs a year: spring, summer and autumn.
● The National Hall, **Olympia,** Hammersmith Rd, W14 holds the Olympia Fine Arts and Antiques Fair each spring, summer, winter.
● **Fulham Town Hall,** Fulham Broadway, SW6, holds an annual 20th-century Decorative Antiques Arts Fair.
● **Alexandra Palace,** Wood Green, N22 holds antiques fairs all year round in its Great Hall, with the two largest events taking place in spring and autumn.

An auctioneer taking bids from the floor at a Christie's fine art auction

CHELSEA & FULHAM

Fashionable Chelsea and Fulham provide a fertile hunting ground for antiques collectors and, although these areas are expensive, experts often offer good value. Chelsea's King's Road is one of London's most famous streets – where Mary Quant designed the first mini-skirt.

Shop front of Chelsea's Antiquarius

EXPLORING CHELSEA AND FULHAM

This is the area that gave birth to the swinging '60s in London, but it is also where J.M.W. Turner painted and Oscar Wilde wrote. Many of the houses here have huge windows designed to bring light to artists' studios, a reminder of the area's more bohemian days in the 19th century

Try to fit in a visit to the **Chelsea Physic Garden**, first planted in 1673 for the study of medicinal plants and now also a centre for garden design. Nearby is the **Royal Hospital**, founded by Charles II in 1682 as a home for old soldiers. Set in formal gardens, this imposing building was designed by Sir Christopher Wren (who also designed St Paul's Cathedral). The Chelsea Pensioners (as they are known) can often be seen out and about in their distinctive scarlet coats and three-cornered hats. The annual Chelsea Flower Show is held here in May.

Rare Chelsea peach-shaped dish carrying red anchor mark, 1753

● **Chelsea Physic Garden**, 66 Royal Hospital Road, SW3. Tel: (020) 7352 5646.
● **Royal Hospital**, Royal Hospital Road, SW3. Tel: (020) 7730 0161.

SHOPPING

Antiquarius (131–41 King's Road) is an antiques hunter's heaven in the heart of Chelsea. This quality indoor market has a multitude of stands selling a wide range of antiques. Nearby Sydney Street is dominated by the Oosthuizens.

Pieter Oosthuizen (Unit 4, Bourbon-Hanby Antiques Centre, 151 Sydney Street) stocks Art Nouveau ceramics and Boer War memorabilia while **Jacqueline Oosthuizen** has a selection of Staffordshire figures, animals, cottages and Toby jugs. Around the corner, her shop at 23 Cale Street has a larger selection of the above, and some excellent 19th- and 20th-century jewellery. **Rogers de Rin** (76 Royal Hospital Road) specializes in Wemyss ware and collectables from the 18th and 19th centuries. English furniture from the 17th to early 19th centuries is stocked by **Apter Fredericks** (265–267 Fulham Road).

If you take the time to walk along the top end of the King's Road into New King's Road, you will find a wealth of interesting shops. **Rupert Cavendish Antiques** (610 King's Rd) has a mix of Gustavian, Biedermeier, Empire and Art Deco furniture and 20th-century paintings. Next door at 608, **Daphne Rankin** with Ian Conn stock Oriental ceramics. At **David Martin-Taylor Antiques** (558 King's Rd) there's classic furniture, as well as more unusual items. For a very wide choice of furniture and objects from different dealers under one roof, try **The Furniture Cave** (533 King's Road), then stroll on to **Lunn Antiques** (86 New King's Road) to find bed linen, nightdresses and christening robes. Just off the Kings Road, at 71 Lots Road, is **Lots Road Galleries**, a marvellous auction house with a seemingly inexhaustable supply of interesting furniture and objects. The galleries are open seven days a week; auctions are held on Mondays.

Fine mahogany inlaid Carlton House desk, 1890–1910

In Fulham itself don't miss the showroom of **Julia Boston** (The Old Stores, The Gasworks, 2 Michael Road) whose specialities include tapestry cartoons, works of art from the 16th century onward and furniture from the 18th and 19th centuries. **Birdie Fortescue Antiques** (Studio GJ, Cooper House, 2 Michael Road) has an extensive selection of 18th- and 19th-century French fruitwood furniture. Phone for an appointment (01206 337957/07778 263467).

Knightsbridge dealer **Norman Adams** (8–10 Hans Road) has a large stock of 18th-century English furniture, 18th-century clocks and barometers, mirrors and *objets d'art*.

Not far away is the St James's area of SW1. Head for Bury Street in particular. The shop of **John Bly**, at No 27, specializes in 18th- and 19th-century English furniture, silver, glass, porcelain and paintings. Just a few doors away at No 37 is **Albert Amor**, with a small stock of 18th-century English ceramics, including a selection of early Worcester and blue and white porcelain. **The Silver Fund** (40 Bury St) has a vast range of Georg Jensen silver and other antique silver items. Sculpture lovers should wander to the nearby shop of **Robert Bowman** (8 Duke Street) where they will find works in bronze, marble and terracotta dating from the early 19th century onwards. You can also find antique sculpture at the showroom of **Crowther of Syon Lodge** (77 Pimlico Road), in addition to garden statuary and architectural antiques. **The Parker Gallery** (28 Pimlico Street) stocks historical prints, English paintings and ship models. **Hotspur** (14 Lowndes St) has English furniture from the late 17th to the early 19th centuries.

Bone china George VI Coronation mug. These are rarer than those made for Edward VIII, who abdicated

COMMEMORATIVE WARES

When people think of London they usually think of the royal connection, and for antiques lovers who are interested in Britain's royal heritage what could be more fun than tracking down commemorative wares? This huge collecting area includes anything made to mark a historical event, but royalty predominates, with births, deaths, weddings and coronations all immortalized in ceramic form.

There is no shortage of commemorative ware in London, and the most valuable pieces predate the coronation of Queen Victoria (see Hope and Glory, page 19). Most pieces date from the mid-19th century, when improved methods of transfer printing let potters make less expensive souvenirs.

Lots Road, a fashionable auction house that often attracts celebrities to its sales

20TH-CENTURY COSTUME JEWELLERY

The term "costume jewellery" was coined in the early 20th century and refers to items of jewellery made with non-precious materials. During the last 100 years an astonishing quantity of such jewellery was produced, often delightfully quirky and making imaginative use of materials. Today good quality pieces have become highly desirable. Some collectors focus on a particular era or style, such as Arts and Crafts, Art Deco, Ethnic, 1960s "Space Age" and Op Art, or, my personal favourites, 1940s Retro and Romantic-Historical. Look out for pieces by leading couturiers such as Coco Chanel, Elsa Schiaparelli, Christian Dior and Paco Rabanne. Also sought after are upmarket pieces by makers such as Trifari, Joseff of Hollywood and Miriam Haskell. Beware of fakes, and check that a piece you like is in good condition. For a great choice at fair prices visit **Cristobal** at Alfie's Market (see page 21).

Top: Art Deco birds, 1925, with diamonds, rubies, sapphires and emeralds. Centre: Scandinavian retro brooch, 1940s. Bottom: decorative camel brooch by Joseff of Hollywood

KENSINGTON & PORTOBELLO

This is an area of smart streets, splendid stuccoed houses with pillared porches, stylish squares and elegant shops selling everything from designer fashion to desirable antiques. It's also home to some wonderful museums.

The Arab Hall at Leighton House

- **Leighton House**, 12 Holland Park Road, W14. Tel: (020) 7602 3316.
- **Natural History Museum**, Cromwell Rd, SW7. Tel: (020) 7942 5000.
- **Victoria & Albert Museum**, Cromwell Rd, SW7 2RL. Tel: (020) 7942 2000.
- **Science Museum**, Exhibition Rd, SW7. Tel: (0870) 870 4771.

Ruby glass jug, 1870–80

ROYAL KENSINGTON

Kensington acquired its Royal status when William III decided to move to Nottingham House (later Kensington Palace) in 1689, in what was then the village of Kensington. The palace, former home of Diana, Princess of Wales, is still a mecca for tourists. Several members of the Royal Family have apartments here and the **Royal Ceremonial Dress Collection** is open to the public. Exhibits, which go back to the 18th century, include clothes worn by the Royal Family as well as the ceremonial robes of officials and dignitaries.

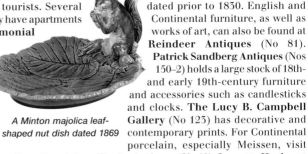

A Minton majolica leaf-shaped nut dish dated 1869

Nearby, the magnificent Leighton House is also well worth a visit. It was built for Victorian painter and sculptor Frederick Leighton as a home, studio and public art gallery, and is now a museum of Victorian art. The centrepiece is the exotic Arab Hall with its gilt mosaic frieze depicting mythological scenes, designed as a showcase for Leighton's extensive collection of pottery and tiles from the Middle East. The house also has a fine collection of paintings by Leighton.

Then, of course, there is Museum Mile, with the **Natural History Museum** (highlights include a 26-m (85-ft) *Diplodocus* skeleton) and the **Victoria & Albert Museum**, the world's largest museum of decorative arts. The **Science Museum**, provides a fascinating insight into Western technology and science.
- **Royal Ceremonial Dress Collection**, Kensington Gardens, W8. Tel: (020) 7937 9561.

KENSINGTON CHURCH STREET

Running between Notting Hill Gate and High Street Kensington, Kensington Church Street is the first port of call in West London for serious antiques collectors.

Eddy Bardawil (No 106) has a good selection of English furniture in mahogany, walnut and satinwood, in addition to mirrors, brass and tea caddies dated prior to 1830. English and Continental furniture, as well as works of art, can also be found at **Reindeer Antiques** (No 81). **Patrick Sandberg Antiques** (Nos 150–2) holds a large stock of 18th- and early 19th-century furniture and accessories such as candlesticks and clocks. **The Lucy B. Campbell Gallery** (No 123) has decorative and contemporary prints. For Continental porcelain, especially Meissen, visit **Davies Antiques** (No 40). **Jeanette Hayhurst Fine Glass** (No 32a) is wonderful for decanters, drinking glasses, perfume bottles and art glass, in addition to ancient pieces.

Crystal displayed in Kensington Church St

A pair of Staffordshire figures, c.1810

Collectors of commemorative china should head for **Hope and Glory** (No 131a), while early English pottery enthusiasts (for creamware, Staffordshire animals and tiles) must visit **Jonathan Horne** (No 66b/c). **Richard Dennis** (No 144) features British studio pottery including Martin, Doulton and Pilkington, as well as contemporary ceramics. Modernist silver specialists, the **Fay Lucas Gallery** (No 50), also stock signed 20th-century furniture and antique military and sporting jewellery. Porcelain expert **Simon Spero** (No 109) stocks enamels and water-colours in addition to 18th-century English porcelain. Clock collectors should visit **Raffety** (No 79), specialists in carriage clocks and barometers, English longcase and bracket clocks from the 17th and 18th centuries.

Kensington Church Street Antiques Centre is home to a group of shops dealing in a wide range of antiques. One of the most interesting is **Nicolaus Boston Antiques**, which specializes in maiolica. For those with an eye for glassware, try **Nigel Benson**, who carries a large selection of 20th-century pieces at affordable prices.

Just off Church Street is **Valerie Howard** (4 Campden Street) who has a wonderful collection of Mason's and English Ironstone china, French faience from Quimper and Rouen and an eclectic selection of mirrors.

NOTTING HILL GATE

This is one of London's most fashionable areas and the shops round here offer a great mix of old and new. Branching off from the Portobello Road Market are various side streets selling designer clothing, antiques and the latest in fashion for the home. At the bohemian end of Notting Hill, in Ladbroke Grove and Golborne Road, there are lots of little antiques shops where you may well pick up a bargain. A large array of brass, copper, pewter and paktong is offered by **Jack Casimir** (23 Pembridge Rd). At **The Coach House** (189 Westbourne Grove), there are four separate dealers selling a wide range of interesting antiques including naive and maritime paintings, colonial and campaign items, treen, equestrian accessories, Islamic and Egyptian Revival objects and tribal art. English pottery, porcelain and glass from the 18th and 19th centuries and Dutch Delft are sold at **Mercury Antiques** (1 Ladbroke Rd).

Early 19th-century enamelled étui

PORTOBELLO MARKET

The Portobello Road is the world's largest antiques market, with over 1,500 dealers selling every conceivable type of antique and collectable. The street market, held from 5.30am every Saturday, tends to offer merchandise from the cheaper end of the market while the more expensive items are in the street-side arcades and galleries, which are open every day except Sunday. Most arcades have specialist shops and these are fantastic places to browse. More than 200 individual dealers can be found at the **World Famous Portobello Market** (No 177). Antiques on offer include antiquities, bronzes, ivory statues, jade, precious metals, dolls, silver and plate, drinking vessels, stamps and coins, costumes and golfing accessories. Silver dating from the 17th to the 19th century is stocked by **Schredds of Portobello** (No 107) in addition to 18th- and 19th-century Wedgwood.

Garrick D. Coleman (No 75) stocks a great selection of conjuring and magic accessories, glass paperweights and chess sets from the mid-18th to the late 19th century. At the same address, **June and Tony Stone Fine Antique Boxes** live up to their name, with a superb selection of 18th- and 19th-century boxes, including rare tortoiseshell and ivory tea caddies. For accessories, furniture and stonework from further afield, visit **David Wainwright** (No 63) who stocks Eastern items dating from the 15th century onwards.

SHOPPER'S TIP

You can buy some good-quality antiques in Portobello, but you really must have some expertise if you want to pick up a bargain. Most of the traders here are experts – some with many years' experience – and they know their stock inside out. If they do not have exactly what you want, they will usually be able to direct you to someone who does.

WEST END & MARYLEBONE

Among the designer fashion shops and exclusive galleries around Bond Street are many excellent and reputable antiques dealers, while Marylebone is home to one of my favourite antiques centres, Alfie's.

A corner of Gray's Antiques Market, just off Bond Street in London's West End

GRAYS ANTIQUES

Grays Antiques is one of London's largest indoor antiques markets, housed in a listed 19th-century terracotta building, with a diverse range of jewellery, fine antiques and collectables. Don't be put off by the glamorous appearance of some of the stalls at the entrance. Prices are generally competitive (and you may even find the odd bargain) and there is plenty for the enthusiastic collector. Look out for **David Bowden's** display of 18th- and 19th-century Chinese snuff boxes. **Arca** has a good selection of Asian, Oriental and Islamic art, and delightful inlaid wooden boxes.

In the basement, alongside the many jewellery stalls, are some more unusual collections including **The Thimble Society** with its delightful selection of bone bobbins and antique thimbles commemorating historical events. Also here is **Wheatley Antiques**, which specializes in Chinese ceramics.

A little further down the street is **Grays Mews**, housing even more stalls, with toys and ancient artifacts the speciality here. Take a look at **Peter McAskie**'s 20th-century toys and **Wheels of Steel** with its collection of model train sets

Dinner plate with "tobacco leaf" design, Qianlong period c.1770; George II silver chocolate pot, 1742

dating back to the 1920s. **Fellner & Sellers** has a fine collection of Victorian china dolls, and **Another Dimension** specializes in original props from the movies.

● **Grays Antiques**, 58 Davis Street, W1. Tel: (020) 7629 7034.

PLACES TO VISIT

A must-see for all art lovers is **The Wallace Collection**, described by one writer as "a little Louvre Museum". It is certainly one of the most impressive small museums in the world and one of the city's best-kept secrets. It was put together by four generations of Marquesses of Hertford and was eventually bequeathed to the nation by the widow of Sir Richard Wallace, illegitimate son of the fourth Marquess.

The first Marquess was a patron of the painter Sir Joshua Reynolds, the second bought the house which is itself part of the collection, the third had a taste for 17th-century Dutch painting and 18th-century Sèvres porcelain (some of the world's finest pieces of Sèvres are displayed), but it was the fourth who really expanded the collection, by buying anything in Europe that caught his fancy. During the French Revolution he acquired works by Fragonard, Boucher, Watteau and Lancret although they were unfashionable at the time, along with pieces of sculpture and furniture. His son collected Renaissance gold and maiolica from Italy. Alongside all this are portraits by Rembrandt, Titian, Gainsborough, Rubens, Van Dyck and Canaletto. The armour and weaponry collection in the basement is the finest outside the Royal Armouries (now housed in Leeds).

Not far away is **Spencer House**, the ancestral home of the late Diana, Princess of Wales. With its classic Doric façade, it is one of the very finest examples of 18th-century elegance in London. Inside there are gilded state rooms, including the Painted Room which was the first room in Europe to be completely decorated in the Neo-classical style. The gardens have recently been renovated to reflect the style of the house.

At the **Sherlock Holmes Museum** the fictional Victorian detective's rooms are full of memorablia – for an added touch of authenticity you can even have a guided tour from "Holmes' housekeeper".

● **The Wallace Collection**, Hertford House, Manchester Square, W1. Tel: (020) 7935 0687.

● **Spencer House**, 27 St James Place, SW1. Tel: (020) 7499 8620.

● **Sherlock Holmes Museum**, 221B Baker St, NW1. Tel: (020) 7935 8866.

BOND STREET AREA

The Bond Street Antiques Centre (124 Bond St) houses 27 dealers who stock a wide range of antiques with an emphasis on jewellery. For silver, go to the **Bond Street Silver Galleries** at Nos 111–112, where 20 dealers offer high quality pieces. More silver can be found nearby at **John Bull** (No 139A).

Tompion & Banger bracket clock with ebonized case, c.1708

Just around the corner is **Halcyon Days** (14 Brook Street), which sells Georgian and Victorian enamels, perfume bottles, treen, papier-mâché, tôle and objects of vertu. Lovers of Oriental antiques should visit **Gerard Hawthorn** (104 Mount Street). Just a short walk from Bond Street, this tantalizing shop has ceramics, enamels, jade, lacquer, bronzes, paintings and textiles dating from 2000BC to 1960. On the same street is **The O'Shea Gallery** at No120A, specializing in maps, prints, atlases and illustrated books from the 15th to the 19th century, and **Stair and Company** (No 14) who stock 18th-century English furniture, works of art, mirrors, chandeliers, barometers, clocks and needlework. Just off Bond Street, **Wartski** (14 Grafton Street) deals in 18th-century gold, silver, jewellery, Fabergé and Russian art. **Bernard J. Shapero Rare Books** (32 St George Street) deals in modern literature and antiquarian books and prints.

MARYLEBONE

Alfie's Antique Market houses more than 180 dealers on four floors. Look out for **Beth Adams'** selection of the decorative arts. Collectors of toys, clocks, watches, cameras or entertainment memorabilia must visit **Collectors World**. **Cristobal** offers a fabulous, yet affordable, selection of jewellery and accessories from the 1920s to the 1960s. Art Deco items and glass, lighting, chrome from 1925 to the 1960s can be found at **Geoffrey Robinson**.

Across the road from Alfie's are a number of individual dealers that are worth dropping in on. The **Gallery of Antique Costume and Textiles** (2 Church St) has a huge selection of textiles, particularly curtains, items of needlework, English quilts, brocades, velvets and clothing from the first half of the 20th century. Victorian, Edwardian and reproduction desks, as well as writing tables, bureaux, chairs, filing cabinets and roll tops, can be found at **Just Desks** (No 20), and **Beverly** (No 30) focuses on the decorative arts and is a must for collectors of Art Nouveau and Art Deco.

● **Alfie's Antique Market**, 13–25 Church Street, NW 8. Tel: (020) 7723 6066.

Regency mahogany sofa table with crossbanding in satinwood, c.1825

VICTORIAN LITERARY LONDON

The Sherlock Holmes Museum, an impressive recreation of the fictional detective's Baker St home

The house where Charles Dickens wrote some of his best-known novels is now a museum and looks exactly as it did in his day, complete with first editions (48 Doughty St, WC1. Tel: (020) 7405 2127). The 18th-century British writer Samuel Johnson was passionate about London, famously claiming that "the man who is tired of London is tired of life". His home and workplace, built in 1700, has been restored to its original condition and is open to the public (17 Gough Square. Tel: (020) 7353 3745). While you're in the area why not pop round the corner to his favourite pub, Ye Olde Cheshire Cheese.

ISLINGTON & CAMDEN

Camden Town has an eclectic mix of shops and there is a lively street scene, including a sprawling market. Neighbouring Islington is more gentrified, with some stunning Georgian architecture.

French opaline glass jug in "rose pompadour", c.1845

SHOPPING

Plan your visit to Islington on either a Wednesday or Saturday when there are more antiques outlets trading.

The first place to head for is Camden Passage, a charming 17th-century flagstoned street that has become an "antiques village" in the heart of London. Situated at the Angel, Islington, it comprises smart shops, malls and regular outdoor markets. Here you will find everything from whole suites of Art Deco

Camden Passage antiques market. (Right) Doulton foot warmer

furniture to precious 18th-century glass to tiny silver thimbles. On Wednesdays and Saturdays the stalls lining the passage deal in all manner of antiques and collectables, while on Thursday there is a thriving book market. Most of the shops are open throughout the week. Look out for **Linda Gumb** (9) who stocks an affordable selection of 18th- and 19th-century tapestries and textiles, and decorative objects.

While you are in Camden Passage, do visit the Pierrepoint Row Arcade. **Art Nouveau Originals** (5) offers affordable Arts and Crafts as well as Art Nouveau pieces from around 1900. **Judith Lasalle** (7) stocks books, prints, games, toys and rocking horses and caters for all budgets. Just off Camden Passage is **The Tadema Gallery** (10 Charlton Place), which has a good selection of 20th-century art as well as jewellery ranging from Art Nouveau pieces to striking 1960s designs. It is open on Wednesdays and Saturdays or by appointment (Tel: (020) 7359 1055).

A short walk away is **Patric Capon** (350 Upper Street), an absolute must for collectors of timekeepers. The stock includes unusual carriage clocks, marine chronometers and barometers from the 18th and 19th centuries. The shop is open Wednesdays and Saturdays or by appointment (Tel: (020) 7354 0487). Almost 30 dealers are housed under one roof nearby at **The Mall Antiques Arcade**. Look out for **Andrew Lineham**'s shop with its fine selection of European glass and porcelain, which includes a wide range of

20TH-CENTURY COLLECTABLES

New production techniques and materials resulted in an explosion of fun objects in the 1950s and 1960s, from moulded plastic chairs to "space age" lighting. These items are very kitsch, but definitely collectable and there is a growing demand for them. New colours and patterns were found on ceramics: flying ducks are highly sought after, and cats and dogs were a favourite decorative motif. Poodles appeared on everything from handbags to teacups, reflecting a contemporary fascination for all things French and a yearning for frivolity after the austerity of the war years. Names to look out for include Terence Conran for household items and Jacqmar printed scarves, and all rock and pop memorabilia.

If the era's naive jollity appeals to you, then head for Alfie's (see page 21) or the antiques market in Bermondsey (see page 27). You'll also find 1950s and '60s items on stalls in the Portobello Road (see page 19) and Camden Lock (see opposite).

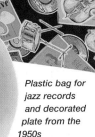

Plastic bag for jazz records and decorated plate from the 1950s

Colourful canalware at Camden Lock market

French and Bohemian opaline glass. Just around the corner is **Yesterday's Child** (Angel Arcade, 118 Islington High St) selling dolls dating from 1800 to 1925. Again, the shop is only open on Wednesdays and Saturdays.

CULTURAL CAMDEN AND HAMPSTEAD
Camden is packed with museums with unusual specialist collections, historic houses and contemporary art galleries, as well as being home to the magnificent **British Library** with its collection of original manuscripts from the Magna Carta, to Shakespeare to Jane Austen, to Handel to the Beatles.

If you like antique toys you'll love **Pollock's Toy Museum**, an intriguing collection housed in a maze of rooms crammed with all sorts of playthings from the past: teddy bears, dolls, tin toys and the unique miniature theatres that Pollock made famous during the Victorian era.

Pre-World War II Dinky trucks and box

Just a short walk from Camden Town tube station is **The Jewish Museum**, which explains the history of the Jewish community in Britain and has one of the world's finest collections of Jewish ceremonial art.

When **Sigmund Freud** fled Nazi Austria in 1938, he settled in London and his home, containing his extraordinary personal collection of antiquities and books, is now a museum. You can even see the famous carpet-covered couch where the analyst listened to his patients' "free association".

If you want to go further out, to Hampstead, there is **Keats House**, a delightful Regency house where the 19th-century poet John Keats wrote many of his best-loved poems. The rooms he occupied have been kept as they were, with his writing desk and bookcase filled with his books. This is where he met his fiancée Fanny Brawne, and visitors can see the engagement ring he gave her which she wore until her death. Keats left England for the sake of his health and died, at the age of 26, in Rome where there is also a museum dedicated to him (see page 239).

Kenwood House, standing on the edge of Hampstead Heath, is a stunning Neo-classical villa built by Robert Adam. It houses an outstanding collection of paintings, including works by Botticelli, Gainsborough and Reynolds. The Great Room is considered by many to be one of the architect's finest interiors. The museum also has a collection of 17th-century Dutch and Flemish art.

● **British Library**, 96 Euston Rd, NW1. Tel: (020) 7412 7332.
● **Pollock's Toy Museum**, 1 Scala St, W1. Tel: (020) 7636 3452.
● **The Jewish Museum**, 129–131 Albert St, NW1. Tel: (020) 7284 1997.
● **The Sigmund Freud Museum**, 20 Maresfield Gardens, NW3. Tel: (020) 7435 5167.
● **Keats House**, Keats Grove, NW3. Tel: (020) 7435 2062.
● **Kenwood House**, Hampstead Lane, NW3. Tel: (020) 8348 1286.

CAMDEN LOCK MARKET
If you fancy something a little more lively (and enjoy crowds), **Camden Lock Market** in the heart of Camden Town is a colourful, offbeat place with around 350 shops, stalls and workshops set in yards, stables and covered halls around the picturesque 1820s Regents Canal. The market draws over 150,000 visitors a week (making it one of London's top tourist attractions) and sells everything from handmade clothing and jewellery to contemporary art to antiques and collectables. It's a bit of a free-for-all, but great fun, and you can often turn up an interesting find. When you need a break there are plenty of good restaurants, cafés and pubs nearby.

DON'T MISS
The London Canal Museum, housed in an 1860s ice warehouse on the Regents Canal, tells the story of London's inland waterways and provides a fascinating insight into the lives of the people who lived and worked on them. Exhibits include a wonderful old canal boat and collections of Measham pottery and canal art. 12–14 New Wharf Rd, N1. Tel: (020) 7718 0836. Closed Mon., except Bank Hols.

Keats House in Hampstead

BLOOMSBURY

The focal point of the Bloomsbury Group of artists and intellectuals a century ago (look out for the blue plaques that mark where luminaries such as Bertrand Russell and Virginia Woolf once lived), Bloomsbury is now the area to come to find silver and Chinese art.

COLLECTING MANIA

Most people visiting Bloomsbury will head straight for the British Museum, but the area is also home to a number of much smaller collections that antiques lovers won't want to miss. Anyone interested in Chinese art should visit the **Percival David Foundation of Chinese Art**, situated in a 19th-century townhouse just round the corner from the British Museum. Here is the finest collection of Chinese ceramics outside China, with hundreds of pieces from the Song, Yuan, Ming and Qing dynasties. Sir Percival David, a pioneering scholar of Chinese art, assembled the collection and donated it to the University of London. A short walk away is the wonderfully eccentric **Sir John Soane's Museum**. Soane, an architect, was a compulsive collector and built the museum as a home for himself and his treasures. It is a curious mix of elegant simplicity and overwhelming clutter, full of paintings, drawings, statuary and architectural fragments. He bequeathed his collection to the nation on condition that nothing was changed.

- **Percival David Foundation of Chinese Art**, 53 Gordon Square, WC1.
Tel: (020) 7387 3909.
- **Sir John Soane's Museum**, 13 Lincoln's Inn Fields, WC2.
Tel: (020) 7405 2107.

Interior of the Sir John Soane's Museum

BRITISH SILVER

London is a great source of British silver, although you may find pieces vary in quality. Check for appropriate wear and match the surface, style and decoration with information from hallmarks. For the best quality silver, check out the **London Silver Vaults**. Dozens of dealers offer a wide range of antique and modern silver, jewellery, plate, clocks, watches and a myriad *objets d'art* and collectables.

- **London Silver Vaults**, 53–64 Chancery Lane, WC2.
Tel: (020) 7242 3844.

George I sugar castor, crafted in silver, English; George II silver-handled basket

---

COVENT GARDEN

COVENT GARDEN SHOPPING

This is one of London's most popular attractions as there is always something going on, including street theatre acts. It was a fruit and vegetable market from the 1670s until the early 1970s when traders were moved to Battersea. Jubilee Market, on the south side of the piazza, has an antiques market on Monday mornings which attracts dozens of traders and hundreds of tourists. Despite the crowds you can often pick up a bargain. There are also art, craft and souvenir stalls throughout the week and a whole range of high-quality designer clothing shops.

Covered market in the heart of Covent Garden

CITY & EAST LONDON

The City is where London began – its streets and wharves teemed with traders when the West End was still green fields. This is where the museums that best recreate London's past are found.

Ceramic jug, with old nursery rhyme, 1950s

THE CITY

The Romans first established a stronghold here in the 1st century AD, but it was when Edward the Confessor moved his court to Westminster in 1060 that London really began to develop. The City and its people have been devastated three times: first by the Great Plague of 1665, followed a year later by the Great Fire and then by German bombers during World War II.

Today it is very much a working centre. Few people live here, so although it is busy on weekdays, it is deserted at weekends – even the pubs and restaurants close. Most of the ancient remains now lie beneath office blocks, but you will still come across coats of arms and street names that give clues to the past.

As well as obvious attractions such as the Tower of London and St Paul's Cathedral, there is plenty more to interest those keen on the past. **The Museum of London** is one of the best-kept secrets of the capital. It overlooks part of the Roman and medieval city wall, with two levels of galleries that trace the chronology of London.

In the East End is **Dennis Sever's House**, a Georgian house of 1724. This recreation of the past is meticulous – as if the inhabitants have just left.

The Geffrye Museum perfectly recreates domestic English interiors from Elizabethan to 1950s Utility and modern-day loft apartments. It is the only museum in the country to exhibit a specialist collection of English furniture and decorative arts arranged as a chronological series.

English Victorian brooch, with diamonds set in gold

BOW PORCELAIN

Founded in 1744, Bow is arguably the earliest of the English porcelain factories. For over 30 years Bow produced huge quantities of Oriental-style blue and white porcelain, coloured wares that were inspired by Japanese Kakiemon porcelain and a range of Meissen–type figures from its factory in the East End. Bow's extensive output means that there are plenty of items still available. Various incised marks were used, the most common mark on figures being a red anchor and dagger. But wares were often unmarked. Pieces with handles usually feature a heart-shaped terminal unique to the factory, and later Bow figures have tall, raised Rococo scroll bases and extensive bocage (leafy encrustations).

Early Bow figure, c.1744–76, one of a series with heads that depict classical Muses

Treen horse head snuff box, c.1840

- **The Museum of London**, London Wall, EC2.
  Tel: (020) 7600 0807.
- **The Geffrye Museum**, Kingsland Rd, E2.
  Tel: (020) 7739 9893.
- **Dennis Sever's House**, 18 Folgate St, E1.
  Tel: (020) 7247 4013.

SHOPPING

For 19th- and 20th-century jewellery, visit **Joseph and Pearce** (63–66 Hatton Garden, EC1. Tel: (020) 7405 4604), which is open by appointment, and **A.R.Ullmann** (10 Hatton Garden). **LASSCO** is housed in an old church (St Michael's, Mark St, EC2) and specializes in architectural antiques from chimney pieces to garden ornaments to stained glass. **Ash Rare Books** (153 Fenchurch St, EC3) sells old books, maps and prints and also offers a picture-framing service. **Halcyon Days** (4 Royal Exchange, EC3) stocks 18th- to early 19th-century enamels, Georgian and Victorian scent bottles, objects of vertu and treen (see page 46) and smaller pieces of Georgian furniture.

Panelled dining room of Dennis Sever's house in London's East End

SOUTH OF THE RIVER

Until recently, many visitors never bothered to cross the Thames, but attitudes have changed. As well as a host of new attractions on the South Bank, antiques shoppers are lured by the bargains that can be found further south.

Festival of Britain scarf, 1951

Ceramics and silver in Bermondsey Friday market

WHAT TO SEE ON THE SOUTH BANK

The **London Eye**, the highest observation wheel in the world, offers unparalleled views over the city. Close by is the **South Bank Complex** of concert halls and galleries surrounding the Festival Hall, built to mark the 1951 Festival of Britain.

The wharfs and warehouses further east are a reminder of the time when this stretch of the Thames incorporated the world's largest port. The area declined along with the city docks, but recent investment has brought it back to life, and it is now home to some of the most exciting developments in the capital.

The newly renovated Art Deco **Oxo Tower** is the centrepiece of an area filled with cafés and artists' workshops.

Butler's Wharf is a complex of both listed warehouses and modern buildings with shops,

Copper and brass coffee pot, ebonized wooden handle, by Christopher Dresser, c.1885

Cigarette cards from the 1930s and '40s

restaurants and galleries. Here you will also find the exquisite **Bramah Tea and Coffee Museum**, which has a wonderful collection of more than 1,000 teapots, spanning four centuries. The museum tells the fascinating story of how tea was first brought to Europe.

Hay's Galleria, on the site of London's oldest wharf, is another area where shops mix with restaurants and galleries. It also has street theatre and a good craft market.

Further east, the **Imperial War Museum** gives visitors an idea of what it was like to live through past wars, with exhibits of weapons, poetry, art, photography and film.

The **St Thomas's Old Operating Theatre, Museum and Herb Garret** is an unusual place to visit, with the only operating theatre to survive from pre-anaesthetic days. The Old Hospital is believed to date from 1106, though it moved to its present site in 1862. The herb garret was used to store medicinal herbs.

- **The London Eye**, Jubilee Gardens, SE1. Tel: (0870) 500 0600.
- **South Bank Complex**, SE1. Tel: (020) 7928 3144.
- **Oxo Tower Wharf**, Bargehouse Street, South Bank, SE1. Tel: (020) 7401 2255.
- **Bramah Tea and Coffee Museum**, The Clove Building, Maguire St, SE1. Tel: (020) 7378 0222.
- **The Imperial War Museum**, Lambeth Road, SE1. Tel: (020) 7416 5000.
- **St Thomas's Old Operating Theatre**, 9A St Thomas Street, SE1. Tel: (020) 7955 4791.

SOUTH-EAST LONDON

For antiques hunters with the time to venture off the beaten track, south-east London has plenty to offer and is home to many historic buildings, as well as some fascinating smaller museums and galleries.

Eltham Palace was once a sprawling, moated Tudor palace but today the only surviving part of the medieval building is the great hall, built by Edward IV in the 1470s. In 1933, Stephen Courtauld, millionaire and patron of the arts, bought the site and built and furnished a magnificent Art Deco house, incorporating the 15th-century hall. The house and garden have recently been restored by English Heritage and are now open to the public.

The **Dulwich Picture Gallery** was the first purpose-built art gallery in England. Designed by the architect Sir John Soane (see page 24) and situated in the delightful 18th-century Dulwich Village, it boasts an outstanding collection of Old Masters. It is also worth taking a stroll around the village itself as it has a number of interesting antiques shops.

Not far from Dulwich is the small but outstanding **Horniman Museum**. Exhibits include Asian, American and African art and artifacts and an important collection of musical instruments from around the world.

● **Eltham Palace**, Court Yard, SE9. Tel: (020) 829 2548.

● **Dulwich Picture Gallery**, Gallery Rd, SE21. Tel: (020) 8693 5254.

● **Horniman Museum**, 100 London Road, SE23. Tel: (020) 8699 1872.

SHOPPING

Walk down almost any high street in southeast London and you will find at least a couple of antiques shops. It is also a great place to go for architectural salvage. The biggest antiques market in the area is **Bermondsey**, which stands on the site of Bermondsey Abbey. Little now remains of the original building except one side of a medieval gatehouse and the carved capitals in the vestibule of St Mary Magdelene Church in Bermondsey Street. Alongside the outdoor market are indoor ones along Tower Bridge Road and in Bermondsey Street and Long Lane. The market is open from 5am until 2pm on Fridays.

Portable gramophone from the Peter Pan factory, early 1900s

The loggia of the Queen's House

HISTORIC GREENWICH

Just 13km (8 miles) downstream from central London lies Greenwich, home of the **Old Royal Observatory**, where World Time is set and where East meets West at the Greenwich Meridian, (0° longtitude). Visitors can actually stand with one foot in each hemisphere. In Greenwich Park fascinating relics of Britain's seafaring past are in the **National Maritime Museum** with globes, maps and royal barges. Also in the park is England's first Classical building, the **Queen's House**, designed by Inigo Jones and completed in 1635. The Great Hall is decorated with paintings of the Muses, the Virtues and the Liberal Arts. The wonderful painted hall and chapel of the **Royal Naval College** was designed by Sir Christopher Wren in the late 1600s and is well worth a visit. Nearby is the famous **Cutty Sark**, an original tall-masted tea clipper, now a museum, and just next door is a splendid Victorian market, with a range of handcrafted items. There is also a big antiques market every weekend, which has masses of bric-a-brac, books and good vintage clothing.

● **Old Royal Observatory, National Maritime Museum and Queen's House**, Greenwich, SE10. Tel: (020) 8858 4422.

● **Old Royal Naval College**. Tel: (020) 8269 4747.

● **Cutty Sark**. Tel: (020) 8858 3445.

Royal Greenwich Observatory, founded 1675

The old operating theatre at St Thomas's, with an original 19th-century operating table

---

SHOPPER'S TIP

Antiques hunters looking beyond central London should visit Wimbledon. Drop in on **Adams Room Antiques** (18–20 Ridgeway) for 18th- and 19th-century English and French furniture. In Barnes, SW13, visit **Christine Bridge** (78 Castelnau), who has 18th- and 19th-century glass decorative items. The shop is open by appointment only (Tel: (020) 8741 5501). Look out here, too, for **Tobias and the Angel** (68 White Hart Lane), which has a huge stock of textiles, furniture and decorative objects.

WHERE TO EAT AND DRINK

Quality Chop House
94 Farringdon Rd, EC1
Tel: (020) 7837 5093
Famed for its large portions of good quality, no-nonsense food, the Chop House (above) dates back to 1869. Karl Marx is known to have been a customer here.

The Criterion
224 Piccadilly, W1
Tel: (020) 7930 0488
Designed in 1873 by Thomas Verity, the Criterion is London's only Neo-Byzantine restaurant. Its grand entrance evokes the Arabian Nights, and the food is equally glamorous.

L'Escargot
48 Greek St, W1
Tel: (020) 7437 2679
Set in a Georgian town house, L'Escargot has a brasserie and a more formal restaurant upstairs.

Rules
35 Maiden Lane, WC2
Tel: (020) 7836 5314
Over 200 years old with stunning Regency decor, Rules was popular with everyone from Charles Dickens and Lillie Langtry (Edward VII's mistress) to Charles Chaplin.

OXO Tower Brasserie and Restaurant
Barge House St, SE1
Tel: (020) 7803 3888
Set on the eighth floor of the Art Deco tower, the OXO Tower has wonderful views over London and up and down the Thames.

The Ritz
150 Piccadilly, W1
Tel: (020) 7493 8181
The wonderfully Rococo Palm Court is *the* place for afternoon tea, offering silver pots, tiered cake stands, dainty sandwiches and a harpist.

The dining room of the Ritz

WHERE TO STAY

The Gore
189 Queen's Gate, SW7
Tel: (020) 7584 6601
Located between Harrods and Kensington Palace, this charming hotel, established 1892, is full of character. There are walls covered with paintings, Oriental rugs on the floors and the bedrooms are furnished with antiques.

The Cadogan
75 Sloane St, SW1
Tel: (020) 7235 7141; Fax: (020) 7245 0994
Lillie Langtry's house forms part of this imposing late Victorian building. Oscar Wilde was arrested in room 118, an event immortalized in a poem by the late Poet Laureate John Betjeman.

Hazlitts
6 Frith St, W1
Tel: (020) 7434 1771
Fax: (020) 7439 1524
In the centre of Theatreland, this hotel occupies three historic houses and is furnished with antiques. It offers all modern amenities while still retaining its old-fashioned atmosphere.

Bedroom at Hazlitts

The Rookery
Peter's Lane, Cowcross St, EC1
Tel: (020) 7336 0931; Fax: (020) 7336 0932
Get a feeling of Georgian London in this hotel, located a short distance from St Paul's Cathedral. The Rookery is the only remaining early house in Peter's Lane. A cosy, welcoming atmosphere pervades, with open fires, mellow wood panelling and period furniture.

The Portobello
22 Stanley Gardens, W11
Tel: (020) 7727 2777; Fax: (020) 7792 9641
A stylish Notting Hill hotel with eclectic Victorian furnishings where all the rooms are different; some have four poster beds, others feature Victorian bathing machines – one even boasts a Japanese water garden.

Dorset Square Hotel,
39–40 Dorset Sq, NW1
Tel: (020) 7724 3328;
Fax: (020) 7723 7874
The rooms of this small hotel in a pair of Regency town houses near Baker St are decorated in lovely rich colours and are full of antiques.

The drawing room, Dukes Hotel

Dukes Hotel
St James Pl, SW1
Tel: (020) 7491 4840; Fax: (020) 7493 1264
Set in its own flower-filled, gas-lit courtyard, this discreet, comfortable Edwardian hideaway is decorated in English country house style. It has a recently opened health spa.

Thistle Bloomsbury
Bloomsbury Way, WC1
Tel: (020) 7242 5881; Fax: (020) 7831 0225
A fine Edwardian hotel with old-world charm and a comfortable, relaxed atmosphere. Turret rooms have curved, six-window walls.

IN THE AREA

English papier mâché snuff box, c. 1740

Less than an hour west of London is **Windsor** with its famous castle – the only royal residence to have been in royal occupation without a break since the days of William the Conqueror. Edward III (r.1327–77) was responsible for the greater part of the building, but it was George IV (r.1820–1830) who turned the medieval castle into a truly royal palace. A fire in 1992 caused extensive damage, but the rooms have been restored to their former glory. Highlights include the State Apartments, even grander than those of Buckingham Palace, and the Queen's art collection. Don't miss Queen Mary's Dolls' House, designed by Sir Edwin Lutyens in the 1920s. It is equipped with electricity and running water and the books in the library were specially commissioned miniatures by leading authors of the day.

Facing Windsor across the Thames is the lovely old village of **Eton** and its College, the country's oldest public school. At the **Eton Antiques Centre** (17 High Street) you will find 19th- to early 20th-century furniture, china and glass and collectables. Further along, at No 93, is **Mostly Boxes**, which specializes in antique wooden, mother-of pearl and tortoiseshell boxes.

About 80km (50 miles) south-west of London is **Petworth**, a pretty town and a haven for collectors, with over 25 shops selling high-quality antiques. Start in the High Street with **Lesley Bragg Antiques** which has 18th- and 19th-century furniture, silver, porcelain, textiles, and even garden furniture. Close by is **Granville Antiques**, which stocks pre-1840 furniture, accessories and pictures. In New Street, **Antiquated** has 18th- and 19th-century painted

Petworth's White and Gold Room, with its marble chimneypiece (1775) and Rococo mirror

furniture and 19th-century rocking horses. Nearby, **Red Lion Antiques** stocks 17th- to 19th-century country house furniture.

In the Market Square you'll find **Ronald G. Chambers Fine Antiques**, which sells 18th- and 19th-century furniture and objets d'art, and **Richard Gardner Antiques**, which has a good stock pf English and continental porcelain.

In East Street there is **William Hockley Antiques**, which stocks decorative items and early English pottery, and the **Petworth Antique Market**, with 36 dealers stocking everything from books and furniture to brass, copper, pictures and textiles. A good selection of barometers, clocks, and other instruments can be found at **Baskerville Antiques** in Saddlers Row.

The Sussex chair, an Arts and Crafts design that first appeared c.1865

View of Eton High Street

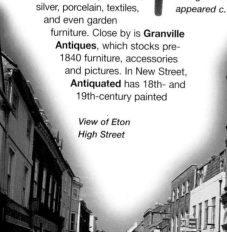

BRIGHTON

A curious but appealing mixture of raffishness and refinement pervades Brighton. Behind the brash excitement of its beachfront lie hushed Regency squares and ancient alleys that are a magnet for collectors.

Sign at the entrance to The Lanes, Brighton's ancient alleyways

THERE WAS A TIME WHEN BRIGHTHELMSTONE was just a small fishing village – in the early 17th century its total extent was the few streets that make up The Lanes today (see page 32).

At that time the seaside held no pleasurable connotations for the well-to-do and high society, but then, around the middle of the 18th century, came a new outlook on health, hygiene and the sea. Dr Richard Russell's *A Dissertation on the Use of Sea Water in Diseases of the Glands* laid the foundations for an attraction to the sea and beach life that has never waned.

The Victorians popularized the pleasure pier, and the Sea Life Centre on the seafront is still housed in the vaulted arcades constructed for a marine menagerie in 1872. In the 1960s Brighton was a favourite rendezvous for rival gangs of Mods and Rockers on their scooters and motorbikes, and "a dirty weekend in Brighton" spoke volumes about illicit affairs...

Conferred city status by the Queen in 2000, Brighton has survived, and thrived, on its many-faceted reputation, and its young, cosmopolitan inhabitants give it a liveliness and edge lacking in some staider coastal towns. I enjoy the mix of tiny alleyways and grand Regency architecture, sun and fun at the seaside and the sense of travelling back into a more glamorous past. The Lanes are always busy, but there are antiques shops all over Brighton as well as in Hove, just along the coast.

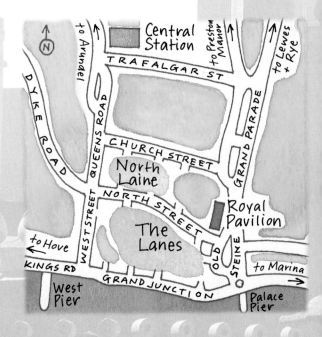

REGENCY EXTRAVAGANZA

In the 1780s the future George IV was a young man in his twenties, dedicated to drinking, gambling and sensationalism. His love affair with a young widow, Maria Fitzherbert, was mostly conducted in Brighton and in 1785 he secretly married her without the King's permission.

They set up home in a farmhouse close to the sea which was transformed into a grand "marine pavilion" for the Prince. With his father's increasing bouts of insanity, Prince George was declared Regent in 1811, and his ever more lavish lifestyle demanded an ever more extravagant setting. In 1815 John Nash, the Prince's favoured architect (creator of London's Regent St and Regent's Park), began work on the exotic **Royal Pavilion**.

Chinoiserie was in vogue and in Nash's eastern fantasy mandarins nod in the Long Gallery, dragons curl around lights and pillars, and the resplendent scarlet and gold Music Room is lit by lotus lanterns. Even the kitchen's pillars are fashioned into lofty palm trees. Not everyone was entranced by Nash's creation – the wit Sydney Smith said scornfully: "It's as if St Paul's had come down to the sea and pupped" – but it is a splendid monument to a dissolute but romantic figure.

Regency Brighton survives in more restrained mode in many other parts of the town. **The Theatre Royal** in New Rd opened its doors in 1807 and in **The Lanes** (see next page) you can still spot shopfronts from the period. Squares such as **Regency Sq** and **Brunswick Sq** in neighbouring Hove have retained the pleasing symmetry of Neo-classical Regency architecture.

● **Royal Pavilion**, Old Steine. Tel: (01273) 290900.

● **Regency Town House**, 13 Brunswick Sq, Hove. Tel: (01273) 206306.

The King's apartment at the Royal Pavilion

PLACES TO VISIT

Brighton's central Palace Pier (built 1896) has evolved into a modern pleasure palace, complete with funfair and amusement arcades, but the **West Pier**, left to rot since

The West Pier, undergoing restoration

World War II, is being restored to its turn-of-the-century splendour. Work will not be complete until 2003, but special tours (hard hat and life-jacket supplied!) explain the pier's history and the problems of restoring a 130-year-old structure in such demanding conditions. A riveting and probably unique experience, if not a little eerie as you imagine holidaying Edwardians strolling along its

wooden promenade to breathe in the invigorating sea air and perhaps enjoy an end-of-the-pier show in the 1903 theatre. Rather like walking on the *Titanic* ...

At **Preston Manor** you enter the world of the Edwardian gentry. Over 20 rooms are open, including bedrooms and the nursery upstairs and the butler's pantry and servants' quarters below stairs in the basement, and all are furnished with memorabilia, silver and family portraits to complete a picture of family life in the opening years of the 20th century.

● **West Pier Trust tours**. Tel: (01273) 207610 for information.

● **Preston Manor**, Preston Park, off London Rd. Tel: (01273) 290900.

IF YOU HAVE TIME ...

The **Museum and Art Gallery** housed in the Pavilion's grandiose former stables, has a good collection of paintings, musical instruments and period costume.

Lovers of Victoriana should seek out the **Booth Museum of Natural History** (194 Dyke Rd).

At Portslade, near Hove, is **Foredown Tower**, one of the very few camera obscura in the country, housed in a 1909 water tower.

SHOPPING

A cornucopia of bric-a-brac and collectables

THE LANES

This is usually the first place collectors of antiques and collectables head for, and there is immense appeal in the area's narrow, twisting streets and covered passages (no cars could pass through here even if they were allowed to). The range of shops has expanded over the years to include art and craft galleries, New Age therapies, fashion boutiques, perfumers and pavement cafés, but The Lanes are still particularly good for jewellery, silver and small collectables. Be alert, though, for the occasional unscrupulous dealer.

Look out for:
Sue Pearson's shop (131/2 Prince Albert St) is crammed with dolls, teddy bears and doll's house furniture – somewhere to indulge in a little nostalgia and where I regret washing my 1950s Merrythought teddy!
You'll find English and Continental furniture and decorative antiques at **Tapsell Antiques** (59 Middle St and 10 Ship St), and also at **Dermot and Jill Palmer Antiques** (7–8 Union St), which is good for textiles as well.

Finely cut cranberry drinking glass, c.1880

NORTH LAINE

Not Lane but Laine, a reminder that this was once an agricultural area and the laine was an old measure of land. Like The Lanes, this is a maze-like network of alleys, with everything from beads to pottery and bric-a-brac to period clothing for sale among its 300-plus shops. On Saturdays there's also a lively street market for collectables.

Look out for:
Snooper's Paradise (7–8 Kensington Gdns) is two floors crammed with antiques and bric-a-brac where you can never tell what you might find.
In addition to furniture

Emerald and diamond bee brooch, 1880

and lighting at **Oasis Antiques** (39 Kensington Gdns) you will find an eclectic mix of gramophones and radios, lace and linen and collectable modern pieces.

OTHER HUNTING GROUNDS

Art Deco Etc (73 Upper Gloucester Rd) is only open Sunday afternoons unless you make an appointment on (01273) 329268, but it is well worth a visit especially for its Poole pottery. If you are looking for something special ask for the owner, John Clark.
Brighton Flea Market is a large covered market open daily at Upper St James's St, Kemptown – you will find everything here from toys and dolls to collectables and ceramics. **The House of Antiques** (39 Upper North St) holds an excellent and varied stock of jewellery and silver.
In Hove, **Michael Norman Antiques** (82 Western Rd) specializes in English furniture, as does **Yellow Lantern Antiques** (34 Holland Rd, Hove), where you will also find French and English clocks.

Regency dining chair, c.1810, with typical overstuffed seat and lyre back

LEWES

Up on the downs, less than half an hour's drive away, is the old county town of Lewes, once a Saxon stronghold. The 14th-century barbican is an imposing remnant of an even older Norman castle. **Anne of Cleves House,** *c.* 1480, is a local history museum, although the fourth of Henry VIII's wives (and the only one to outlive him by more than a year) never actually lived here. The High Street is a picturesque medley of architectural styles and home to many antiques shops. A visit to the **Fifteenth Century Bookshop** at 99 High St is a trip back into childhood, or even into grandmother's childhood, as you seek out old favourites, especially children's books.

At **Lewes Antiques Centre** (20 Cliffe High St) nearly 60 stallholders deal in china and glass, metalware and furniture, and some architectural salvage.

A busy stall in Upper Gardener Street, Brighton

Ashcombe Coach House, just outside Lewes on the A27, stocks furniture and objects dating mainly from the 17th and 18th centuries. It's open by appointment only, so phone (01273) 474794.

AUCTION HOUSES

Wallis and Wallis, West St Auction Galleries, Lewes. Tel: (01273) 480208.
Gorringe's, 15 North St, Lewes. Tel: (01273) 472503. Terminus Rd, Bexhill-on-Sea. Tel: (01424) 212994.

WHERE TO EAT

A stroll down Preston Street or along the seafront will give you an idea of the huge range of eating places in Brighton, from a floating Chinese restaurant to traditional pubs. But, since we are beside the sea, I'll recommend two brilliant fish restaurants.

English's
29–31 East St
Tel: (01273) 327980 or 325661
The Oyster Bar, with its original marble counter, is just one of the things that draws me to this seafood heaven. Once a little row of fishermen's cottages, this restaurant in the Lanes has evolved into a series of comfortable dining rooms decorated with murals that recall Edwardian scenes – look out for Oscar Wilde watching a performance of his own play, *The Importance of Being Ernest,* in the Minton Room.

Wheeler's
16–17 Market St, The Lanes
Tel: (01273) 325135
Wheeler's is practically an institution, and is an offshoot of the London restaurant, Wheeler's of St James, established in 1856. Behind its distinctive green façade it offers everything from skate to potted shrimps, and from lobster to sea bass. In hot weather the front opens up onto the market square.

WHERE TO STAY

As Brighton is a seaside resort it is endowed with a great many hotels, guest houses and B&Bs; the tourist office has a comprehensive list (see Useful Addresses at the end of the book). These are just two that are particularly appealing in character.

The Old Ship
King's Road
Tel: (01273) 329001; Fax (01273) 820718
This 16th-century hotel was bought by Nicholas Tettersells with the money given to him by Charles II as a reward for taking the king to safety in France. It is now a popular hotel offering modern facilities with an old world charm, oak-panelled bar and Regency ballroom.

Topps
17 Regency Sq
Tel: (01273) 729334; Fax: (01273) 203679
This is a wonderful hotel. It consists of two Regency town houses that have been beautifully furnished with antiques. Most of the 15 bedrooms have gas-coal fires and large bathrooms.

IN THE AREA

Both east and west of Brighton the coast and downs of Sussex are full of treasures for the antique lover. I could spend (and have spent) days in Arundel, and love the very different houses of **Parham, Uppark** and **Charleston.**

In **Rye** the 11th-century Mermaid Inn is little changed since it was a smugglers' hangout in the 18th century, and you can still imagine wagons of contraband ("brandy for the parson, baccy for the clerk ...") being wheeled through the ancient cobbled streets at the start of their run up to London. The quays (some way from the sea due to silting) nowadays stock more legitimate but no less fascinating wares.

YORK

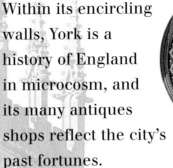

Within its encircling walls, York is a history of England in microcosm, and its many antiques shops reflect the city's past fortunes.

The glorious Rose Window of the Minster

YORK GREW UP WHERE THE RIVER FOSS flows into the larger Ouse and it dominates the Plain of York. No modern buildings have been allowed near the Minster (begun in 1220, completed 1470), and walking round the city on walls that were built in medieval times provides timeless views across rooftops and gardens.

Tourism is now the city's leading industry, and York is likely to be on many visitors' "must see" lists. Over the years, residents have fought hard to maintain its distinctive features: the glorious York Minster, along with 18 other medieval churches, three miles of medieval city walls, a wealth of extensive Roman, Saxon and Viking ruins, handsome Georgian and Jacobean architecture and a selection of fascinating museums. Other treasures include the 11th-century St Olave's Church, the Mansion House with its magnificent silver collection and behind that the Guildhall, which was built in 1448, largely destroyed in World War II and restored in 1960.

The York Civic Trust led the battle to protect the city's old buildings and champions careful renovation and adaptation to new uses. But it is a living, working city, and one which has steadfastly refused to accommodate the car, so that its narrow streets and alleyways and compact layout make it ideal to explore on foot. Streets that recall past trades – Coppergate, Stonegate, the Shambles – are now full of antiques and bric-a-brac shops.

For a different perspective on the city, take a leisurely boat trip from Lendal Bridge or Kings Staith downstream to Bishopthorpe Palace, which has been the residence of the archbishops of York since the 13th century.

Monk Bar, one of the city's gates

A 19th-century street recreated in the Castle Museum

LAYERS OF HISTORY

Down the centuries battles have raged around York's walls and each invader has left a legacy. Generations of historic buildings shape today's city. It began as provincial Roman Eboracum, then became a centre of Anglo-Saxon Christian learning. It was sacked by the Vikings, then by the Normans, who destroyed and then rebuilt the city, giving it a castle and the walls that still stand. Medieval York was England's second city, growing rich on the wool trade. In the 19th century it embraced the railway, and boasted the world's largest railway station.

Anglo-Saxon helmet

The glory of York is, of course, its great **Minster**, the largest Gothic church in Britain. Do not miss the Great West Window (one of 128 stained glass windows), known as the "heart of Yorkshire" because of the shapes in the tracery work. The Great East Window is the largest medieval glass window in existence. Visit the foundations to see the smaller Norman church which stood on the spot, and below that the Roman excavations. Also make sure you see the crypt's 12th-century Romanesque treasures.

Jorvik Viking Centre is a recreation of a Viking community, based on a five-year excavation project. You can travel back in time to the sights, sounds and smells of a Viking street.

The **Castle Museum** is housed in two converted 18th-century prison buildings (you can visit highwayman Dick Turpin's cell). Walk along a cobbled Victorian street complete with recreated craft shops, or visit a chocolate exhibition (York's other industry) or the exhibit which shows the evolution of vacuum cleaners, toilets, bicycles and other appliances.

Opposite the museum stands Clifford's Tower, built in the 13th century to mark the hanging of Roger de Clifford following his capture at the Battle of Boroughbridge. In 1190 a castle on this site was subjected to anti-Jewish riots. Given the option of death or baptism, they chose mass suicide, burning the tower to the ground. The **Merchant Adventurers' Hall** was built and owned by one of the richest medieval guilds. It took 11 years to build, from 1357, and contains the largest timber-framed hall in York.

- **York Minster**, Deangate. Tel: (01904) 557200
- **Jorvik Viking Centre**, Coppergate. Tel: (01904) 643211/543403 (for advance bookings).
- **Castle Museum**, Tower St. Tel: (01904) 653611 for information.
- **Merchant Adventurers' Hall**, Fossgate. Tel: (01904) 654818.

The **Archaeological Resource Centre** is Britain's first hands-on archaeology centre that encourages visitors to touch and examine the artifacts. Open to the public in school holidays, but check access beforehand.
- **Archaeological Resource Centre**, St Saviourgate. Tel: (01904) 543402.

The timber-framed Merchant Adventurers' Hall

WHERE TO EAT

19 Grape Lane
19 Grape Lane
Tel: (01904) 636366
Set in a 16th-century, Grade II listed building, this restaurant is one of the best in York, with a relaxed atmosphere and very good food.

Little Bettys
46 Stonegate
Tel: (01904) 622865
With home-made cakes served in a medieval building, where better to spend an afternoon taking high tea? They also serve light lunches reflecting their Yorkshire and Swiss specialities.

Black Swan
Peaseholme Green
Tel: (01904) 686911
For a traditional pub with good bar food, try the oak-panelled Black Swan. This has been an inn since the 18th century, but the building was then already old. Records show it was built for the Bowes family (from which Queen Elizabeth the Queen Mother is descended) in the 14th century.

WHERE TO STAY

Middlethorpe Hall
Bishopthorpe Road
Tel: (01904) 641241; Fax: (01904) 620176
This wonderful William III house is a part of the Historic House Hotels group (see Useful Addresses), with many modern features such as a pool and a gym. Although it is expensive, the atmosphere is well worth the price.

The Grange
1 Clifton
Tel: (01904) 644744; Fax: (01904) 612453
Set in a Regency town house conveniently close to the city centre, the bedrooms in this lovely 200-year-old hotel are individually decorated with period charm.

Abbots Mews
Marygate
Tel: (01904) 634866. Fax: (01904) 612848
This small hotel was once a coachman's cottage and coach house. It is not far from the Yorkshire Museum Gardens and makes an attractive alternative to the big, expensive hotels.

The Shambles, with its medieval jettied buildings

SHOPPING

At the heart of the city is King's Square, where street entertainers are a particular feature in summertime. In one corner of the square is the beginning of the Shambles, one of the best-preserved medieval streets in Europe. It was originally called Fleshammels – meaning "the street of butchers" – and the broad window sills were used to display the meat. The butchers have long gone, but in their place is a fine selection of craft and gift shops. Close by is Fossgate, with furniture, book and antiques shops.

Stonegate is also a good area to explore. It gets its name from the fact that the huge stones used in the building of York Minster were dragged along here after being floated up the river by barge. Two narrow passages lead into Stone-gate Arcade, the city's most attractive covered street. Planners resisted knocking down old properties to give the arcade a more hidden feel. In addition there is Gillygate, which was for years threatened with demolition. When this was lifted many smaller traders who could not afford the high city centre rents moved in, to provide an interesting mix of arts and crafts shops, antiques and bric-a-brac shops.

Look out for:

The York Antiques Centre at 2 Lendal, offers antique and collectable items from the 18th, 19th and 20th centuries, while at **Ruth Ford Antiques** (39 Fossgate) you will find 18th- and 19th-century furniture, treen and collectables.

Bishopsgate Antiques (23–4 Bishopsgate St) has a general stock of antiques and, as a bonus, is open Sunday mornings.

Barbara Cattle (45 Stonegate) offers a wide range of jewellery and silver from the Georgian period to the present day.

Minster Gate Bookshop (8 Minster Gate) has old maps, prints, antiquarian books; and also does valuations and restorations. Near the Minster is **The Red House Antiques Centre** (Duncombe Place), which is a branch of Harrogate's The Ginnel (see page 39).

Robert Morrison and Son (131 The Mount) is a mile from the city centre; here you can find fine English furniture from 1700–1900, as well as porcelain and clocks.

Tomlinson Antiques, at Moorside in Tockwith, is a warehouse of furniture from many periods.

AUCTION HOUSES
Stephensons,
10 Colliergate.
Tel: (01904) 625533.

English oak chest, c.1650

PLACES TO SEE

Dessert course at Fairfax House, c.1763

a collection of old engines, it demonstrates 150 years of British railway history and is probably the biggest and best in the world. A giant turntable is regularly activated so that exhibits have access to the present-day railway system and occasionally go out on runs. Among the vast array of cars and engines is Queen Victoria's lavish royal car and the first stagecoaches on wheels. Indeed, even though I am not a railway enthusiast, I find there is something here for everyone.

Collecting domestic and agricultural implements from bygone days is increasingly popular. The **Yorkshire Museum of Farming** on the outskirts of the city has displays of 19th- and 20th-century machinery and tools, as well as a reconstruction of a rural village from the Dark Ages and a Roman fort.

In the 1750s Charles Gregory, the last Viscount Fairfax, acquired **Fairfax House** and had John Carr remodel it for his daughter Anne. The exquisite plasterwork and panelling you see today is the result of painstaking restoration carried out by craftsworkers in the late 1980s after years of neglect (the building has been both a cinema and a dance hall in its time), and gives a real feel for how the house must have looked in the 18th century. Many of the items used to furnish the house were bequeathed by the great-grandson of the founder of Terry's, the York chocolate house.

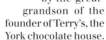

Victorian Valentine cards

The house is regularly used for imaginative exhibitions and entertainments.

Quite different, but no less fascinating, is the **National Railway Museum**, housed beside the modern station. Much more than

● **Fairfax House**, Castlegate. Tel: (01904) 655543. Tours on Fridays. Opening times vary (closed Jan/Feb.)
● **National Railway Museum**, Leeman Rd. Tel: (01904) 621261.
● **Yorkshire Museum of Farming**, on A166 (eastern outskirts of city). Tel: (01904) 489966.

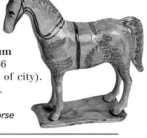

A Yorkshire pottery horse

SHOPPER'S TIP

For a little peace and quiet try the Yorkshire Museum Gardens, laid out in the early 19th century by the Yorkshire Philosophical Society in the grounds of St Mary's Abbey. This is the site where every three years the **York Mystery Plays** – traditional renditions of biblical stories aimed originally to bring Bible teaching to the illiterate masses – are performed. The next will be held in 2003.

IN THE AREA

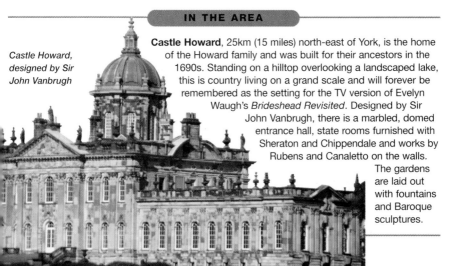

Castle Howard, designed by Sir John Vanbrugh

Castle Howard, 25km (15 miles) north-east of York, is the home of the Howard family and was built for their ancestors in the 1690s. Standing on a hilltop overlooking a landscaped lake, this is country living on a grand scale and will forever be remembered as the setting for the TV version of Evelyn Waugh's *Brideshead Revisited*. Designed by Sir John Vanbrugh, there is a marbled, domed entrance hall, state rooms furnished with Sheraton and Chippendale and works by Rubens and Canaletto on the walls. The gardens are laid out with fountains and Baroque sculptures.

HARROGATE

Harrogate's multitude of antiques shops reflect the status held by this fashionable spa town a hundred years ago.

ORIGINALLY, HARROGATE was the perfect stopping-off point for aristocrats en route from a tiring London season to grouse-shooting in Scotland. From the late 1800s until World War I, it was the north's leading spa town, its medicinal springs the fashionable destination for a health cure. Today's visitors may not "take the waters" with quite the same dedication, but Harrogate still retains its air of gentility with fine architecture and elegant public gardens. It is ideal as a base from which to explore North Yorkshire and the Dales. And for those weary from a long day's antiques-hunting, there is the perfect antidote: a Turkish bath in one of the country's most attractive and exclusive steam rooms.

The town is also known for its colourful common, The Stray, and for the Northern Horticultural Society's ornamental Harlow Car Gardens. Each year in July and August, Harrogate celebrates an International Festival of Music and Arts.

HISTORY REVISITED

TAKING THE WATERS

The town developed as a spa after the discovery of Tewit Well in 1571. It became particularly popular in the 19th century, when there were more than 80 springs (sulphurous, saline and chalybeate). They were used for drinking and bathing and were believed to be beneficial for those suffering from rheumatic, skin, heart and other complaints. Of particular interest are the **Royal Baths and Assembly Rooms** and the **Royal Pump Room**, which now houses a museum of local history. There is a fine collection of 19th-century china and jewellery, as well as an example of an 1874 penny farthing bicycle.

● **Royal Pump Room Museum**, Crown Pl. Tel: 01423 503340.
● **Harlow Car Gardens** (see above), Crag Lane. Tel: 01423 565418.

Local commemorative biscuit tin

SHOPPING

The Ginnel (in the Corn Exchange Building) is the place for both serious collectors and browsers. It has 50 units full of antiques. Every item has been dated and verified by a vetting board of three independent experts.

Elaine Phillips Antiques (1–2 Royal Parade) specializes in oak and country furniture from 1600 to 1850, while **Sutcliffe Galleries**, at No 5, is an ideal place to pick up 19th-century paintings and **David Love** (No 10) carries a large range of English and Continental antiques.

A number of dealers are based in Montpellier Gardens. **Thorntons**, at No 1, has 17th- to 19th-century furniture, porcelain, arms and armour and scientific instruments. **Charles Lumb and Sons** (next door) sells furniture from the 17th to the early 19th century, as well as period accessories, and **Walker Galleries** (No 6) stock oil paintings, watercolours and 18th-century furniture. **Armstrong** (10–11 Montpellier Parade) has a wide range of fine English furniture, glass and works of art (mainly 18th century).

You'll find a large stock of jewellery and English silver plate at **Ogdens** (38 James St), and **Paul M. Peters Antiques** at 15a Bower Rd (bottom of Station Parade) carries a broad stock, including some unusual items.

Chris Wilde Antiques, in The Courtyard, Mowbray Sq., has furniture and longcase clocks of between 1730 and 1920. **Haworth Antiques** (26 Cold Bath Road) also have clocks, which they restore, as well as Georgian and Victorian furniture.

Alexander Adamson (Flat 1, 19 Park View. Tel: 01423 528924 for an appointment) stocks 17th- to 19th-century furniture and Chinese, Continental and English porcelain.

AUCTION HOUSES

Morphets, 6 Albert St. Tel: 01423 530030. For occasional sales of antiques and works of art, as well as house clearance sales. **Tennants** in Leyburn. Tel: 01969 623780.

Montpellier Parade

WHERE TO EAT AND DRINK

Betty's
1 Parliament Street
Tel: (01423) 502746
This famous cake shop has been run by the same family since 1919, and is famed for its cakes and pastries, although you can also have breakfast, lunch and dinner.

Drum and Monkey
5 Montpellier Gardens
Tel: (01423) 502650
The restaurant in this pub is very popular so it is advisable to book. The menu is restricted to seafood or fish.

WHERE TO STAY

White House
10 Park Parade
Tel: (01423) 501388; Fax: (01423) 527973
An ornate Victorian exterior hides a house with a very graceful interior.

The Boar's Head Hotel
Ripley Castle Estate
Tel: (01423) 771888
This old coaching inn is part of the Ripley estate (see below) and is elegantly furnished with many antiques from the castle.

IN THE AREA

One of my favourite trips is to nearby **Ripley**. Inglebys have lived at Ripley Castle since the 1320s and it is now in the custody of the 28th generation. A 19th-century Ingleby, enamoured of Alsace Lorraine, gave the village a French Gothic-style face-lift. The cobbled market square and pretty houses and shops provide a delightful excursion.

The town of **Knaresborough** is mentioned in the Domesday Book and its streets are lined with fine 18th-century houses. On its outskirts is England's oldest tourist attraction, opened to the public in 1630, Mother Shipton's Cave. It was the birthplace of Ursula Sontheill, a local prophetess. But its real curiosity is a natural wonder: leave an item such as a glove or a child's toy on the smooth, dripping surface of the cave and within a few weeks it will be preserved in limestone.

● **Ripley Castle**. Tel: 01423 864600.

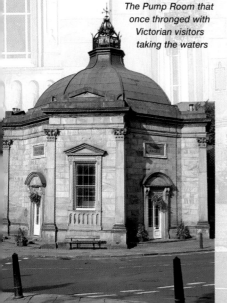

The Pump Room that once thronged with Victorian visitors taking the waters

MANCHESTER

Manchester's enviable legacy of art and rare books comes from the riches of Victorian trade.

A museum model of the textile machinery on which Manchester built its wealth

MANCHESTER DATES BACK TO ROMAN TIMES, but came into its own with Richard Arkwright's steam-powered spinning machine and the subsequent Industrial Revolution of the late 18th century. You just need to stand in Albert Square and look up at the Gothic Town Hall, or enter the Free Trade Hall, home of the Halle Orchestra, to realize that the city's Victorian fathers had money and knew how to spend it.

Mancunians have known the best and worst of being a great trading city. Industrialization brought worker exploitation and slum conditions, but this in turn inspired radical free thinkers, including women's suffrage campaigner Emmeline Pankhurst (her house in nearby Chorlton is now a museum). Another result was the foundation, in 1821, of the *Manchester Guardian* (now *The Guardian*) national newspaper.

HISTORY REVISITED

KING COTTON

Once, 80 per cent of the world's cotton passed through Manchester. Flemish weavers brought their craft here in the 14th century, but it was when the Bridgewater Canal opened in 1761 that the great leap forward in technology occurred, as coal brought into the city cheaply by barge could generate steam to run the mills. In 1819 factory workers rioted against oppressive laws; mounted troops panicked and charged the crowd, killing 11 people in what became known as the Peterloo Massacre (after the Battle of Waterloo four years earlier). However, the tragedy heralded reforms such as the Factory Act. By 1830, the world's first railway linked Manchester to Liverpool's docks 36 miles away and put the city at the heart of the Industrial Revolution.

PLACES TO VISIT

Manchester Town Hall has been described as the best single monument to high Victorian taste in Britain. It was designed by Alfred Waterhouse and you can take guided tours of the historic staterooms and council chambers.

Behind Manchester's Cathedral (which has the best medieval woodwork in the north of England) is the best-kept secret of the city, **Chetham's Library and School of Music**. Once religious quarters, the buildings date from 1421; the public library, the oldest in the country, dates from 1655. On Wednesdays, during term time, there is a free tour of the buildings, with a concert in the music school.

Another gem is the late Victorian Gothic **John Ryland's Library**, which houses a great collection of manuscripts and printed works, including the oldest fragment of the New Testament, a Gutenberg Bible, and a first edition of Shakespeare's sonnets.

● **Town Hall**. Tel: (0161) 234 5000.
● **Chetham's Library**. Tel: (0161) 834 9644.
● **John Ryland's Library**. Tel: (0161) 834 5343.

SHOPPING

Audrey Sternshine's **A.S. Antique Galleries** (26 Broad St, Salford) is probably Britain's best outside London for Art Nouveau and Art Deco. **Boodle & Dunthorne** (1 King St) is good for 18th- and 19th-century silver, clocks and Victorian jewellery. **The Ginnell Gallery Antique Centre** (18–22 Lloyd St), opposite the Town Hall, is a treat for antiquarian books; it also has Art Deco, Art Nouveau and 1950s pottery. **In-Situ Architectural Antiques** (Worsley St) stocks items such as fireplaces, doors, radiators and gardenware.

AUCTION HOUSES

Capes Dunn & Co, 38 Charles St. Tel: (0161) 273 1911. Fortnightly sales on Tuesdays. **Acorn Philatelic Auctions**, Salford. Tel: (0161) 877 8818. Tuesday, every five weeks.

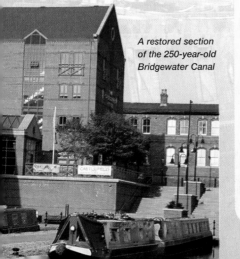

An Art Deco Amazon in silvered bronze, c.1925

A restored section of the 250-year-old Bridgewater Canal

The Japanese Garden at Tatton Park

Greater Manchester has many great country houses: the half-timbered 16th-century manor of Wythenshawe Hall; 18th-century Platt Hall, where (for free) you can see one of the country's best collections of English costume. **Tatton Park** is an early 19th-century house designed by James Wyatt. It sits amid a land-scaped deer park, providing a fine setting for the Egerton family's collections of pictures, books, glass, silver and specially commissioned Gillow furniture. It is also the venue for annual antiques fairs. The grandeur of the house extends to the gardens with a fernery, orangery and Japanese gardens.

● **Tatton Park**, Knutsford. Tel: (01625) 534400; Infoline: (01625) 534435.

WHERE TO EAT AND DRINK

The Lincoln
1 Lincoln Square, City Centre
Tel: (0161) 834 9000
This popular contemporary restaurant provides a welcoming atmosphere and serves traditional food in a modern way.

Simply Heathcotes
Jacksons Row, off Deansgate
Tel: (0161) 835 3536
This was the city's original oak-panelled register office. Apart from the restaurant, there is a cookery school and a wine bar featuring live jazz.

WHERE TO STAY

Some of the most interesting hotels in Manchester were once warehouses for goods that sailed up the Manchester Ship Canal.

The Victoria and Albert Hotel
Water Street
Tel: (0161) 832 1188; Fax: (0161) 834 2484
This converted mid-19th-century waterside warehouse has an award-winning restaurant.

The Crown Plaza Manchester – The Midland
Peter Street
Tel: (0161) 236 3333; Fax: (0161) 932 4100
This is probably the best known of Manchester's hotels, right in the city centre, big and bustling, but still full of Victorian character – it is where Mr Rolls met Mr Royce in 1904.

BATH

The town that grew around the thermal springs of Aquae Sulis is still famed for its handsome Georgian architecture and its fine shopping.

Rococo mirror, c.1770

LONG BEFORE THE ARRIVAL OF THE ROMANS in the first century AD, Bath was already known for its thermal springs. The Romans built baths around the springs and a temple, as well as the town which they called Aquae Sulis. Through Saxon times, the town prospered and the huge church which stood on the site of the present abbey was considered the religious capital of Britain. In AD973 England's first King, Edgar, was crowned here. The town slowly declined until the 1600s when Queen Mary, desperate for an heir, decided to bathe there. Within ten months she gave birth to a son and a new age dawned for Bath. In the 18th century, it was fashionable to "take the waters" which flowed from the ground at the rate of half a million gallons a day and at a constant steaming 116°F. Together with his son John, the architect John Wood the elder, inspired by the Italian architect Palladio, created a harmonious vision from the mellow local stone, to build "a new Rome". The terraces and crescents were lined with wide parades, enabling ladies in their stylish dresses to spread their voluminous trains.

That most fashion-conscious of dandies, Beau Nash, organized the daily routine of the aristocratic visitors and improved security on the streets with better lighting and the banning of swords. Under his patronage, Bath became a city of balls and concerts, as well as gambling and shopping. It was the place to be seen during the season – Jane Austen and Samuel Pepys were among its famous visitors. Given its reputation, it is perhaps surprising that Bath's Georgian heyday lasted for only about 60 years from the 1720s.

Gorgon's head in the Roman Baths

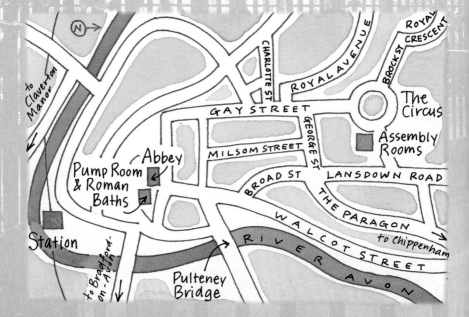

HISTORY REVISITED

LEGACY OF THE ROMAN BATHS

It was the Celtic King Bladud who, it is said, first discovered the medicinal properties of the springs in Bath 860BC. A leper and an outcast, he cured himself by rolling in the warm mud.

The Romans, who first set up camp in the area in AD44, used the hot springs for their baths, with hot, warm and cold areas, as well as places for saunas and massages. The baths were also used for entertainment and worship. After the departure of the Romans the town suffered from Anglo-Saxon raids and it was not until the early 1700s that a temple dedicated to the goddess Sulis Minerva was excavated.The collection of Roman votive offerings found there is the best in England. These can be seen by visitors to the **Roman Baths Museum**, together with the sheets of pewter carrying pleas for divine intervention that were thrown into the Sacred Spring. The Great Bath, decorated with statues of Roman emperors, was not discovered until the 1870s. This is the original swimming pool and it was opened to the sky by the Victorians.

The Museum and nearby **Pump Room** are the first stop on everybody's itinerary. Built in 1791 and opened by Beau Nash, it was a medicinal and social centre. A statue of Nash – who arrived in Bath in 1704 and was appointed Master of Ceremonies – still stands in the Pump Room today. Visitors can enjoy a musical accompaniment as they sip the spring water – usually only a sip because it smells of bad eggs.

The spa water had always been regarded as a cure for venereal diseases. There were complaints of "people of both sexes bathing by day and night naked; and dogs, cats, pigs and even human creatures hurl'd over the rails into the water". Beau Nash introduced formal codes of dress and behaviour; he also regulated the charges made by sedan chair attendants. Despite competition from Harrogate (see page 38) and Cheltenham (see page 54), with which it is often compared due to their similar architecture, Bath very quickly became *the* spa to visit.

- **Roman Baths Museum**, Stall St. Tel: (01225) 477784. Open daily – varies according to season.
- **Pump Room**, Stall St. Tel: (01225) 477738. Open daily at 9am, but closing times vary.

The Roman Baths in the shadow of the Abbey

PLACES TO VISIT

Near the Pump Room is **Bath Abbey**. Founded in 1499 it is an example of late Perpendicular Gothic style; the fan vaulting and stained glass windows are particularly fine. Within the abbey are the Heritage Vaults, telling the story of Christianity in Bath since Roman times. There are memorial tablets to Beau Nash and to Dr Oliver, of Bath Oliver biscuit fame.

Built by John Wood the younger, the **Assembly Rooms** were a fashionable meeting place where the elite gathered for glittering balls. Jane Austen depicts the atmosphere of gossip and flirtation in some of her novels, notably

Episcopal tomb in Bath Abbey

in *Northanger Abbey*. The Assembly Rooms now house the **Museum of Costume**, which displays 400 years of fashion – from Nell Gwyn to Twiggy.

Visit the **Building of Bath Museum** for a comprehensive account of how the city has developed over the centuries. The **Pulteney Bridge**, designed by Robert Adam in the 1770s, is lined on either side with shops and connects the town centre to Great Pulteney Street, the grandest thoroughfare in Bath.

- **Bath Abbey**, Abbey Churchyard. Tel: (01225) 422462. Open daily except if special service being held.
- **Assembly Rooms and Museum of Costume**, Bennett Street. Tel: (01225) 477000. Open daily.
- **Building of Bath Museum**, The Paragon. Tel: (01225) 333895. Closed Mon (except public hols) & Dec to mid-Feb.

ANTIQUES IN CONTEXT

Bath is a World Heritage Site and is full of architectural masterpieces and curiosities. From the grand sweeps of the crescents of Camden and Lansdown to quaint cobbled alleyways full of antiques shops, visitors can wander through the centuries.

Interior of No 1 Royal Crescent

GEORGIAN AND REGENCY BATH
Bath inspired the works of many artists, writers and musicians, including Charles Dickens, Thomas Hardy, Sir Walter Scott and George Handel, but it is Jane Austen with whom the city is most closely associated. From 1801 to 1804, she lived at 4 Sydney Place and readers of her work can tour the Bath she describes – the Pump Room, the Assembly Rooms and the Crescent. The 1995 film of her novel *Persuasion* was shot in the city.

To see the best of Georgian Bath, begin at the north side of Queen's Square; John Wood the elder, Bath's foremost architect, lived at No 24. Close by is The Circus, three curved terraces that form a perfect circle. The style of columns follows a classical order followed in the 18th-century: Doric on the ground floor, then Ionic and then finally Corinthian.

Just around the corner is the **Royal Crescent** (1767–74), 30 terraced houses which must be among the most famous in the world. Many well-known people have lived here: William Pitt the elder, prime minister during the late 1700s, lived at No 7, the African explorer David Livingstone at No 13 and the painter Thomas Gainsborough at No 17. The first house, No 1, is open to the public; the Bath Preservation Trust has beautifully restored and furnished it in the style of the late 18th century. It gives you a taste of the 18th-century aristocratic lifestyle, including that of the Duke of York who lived here. The house furnishings include details such as a dog-powered spit used to roast meat in front of the fire in the kitchens.

● **1 Royal Crescent**. Tel: (01225) 428126.

GEORGIAN SILVER
By the second half of the 18th century, silversmiths were incorporating Neo-classical style into their elegant and intricate designs for tableware. One innovation was covers for sauce and soup tureens. New ideas included trays with handles, entrée dishes for either hot or cold food, dish warmers, salt cellars and oval-shaped latticework baskets. In earlier times guests brought their own cutlery for meals, but by the 1700s a host provided individual sets of knives, spoons, forks, and serving utensils, each carrying a design unique to the set.

Coffeepot in the pear shape popular in the 1760s

A Pembroke table, c.1790 (left). The grand sweep of the Royal Crescent (below)

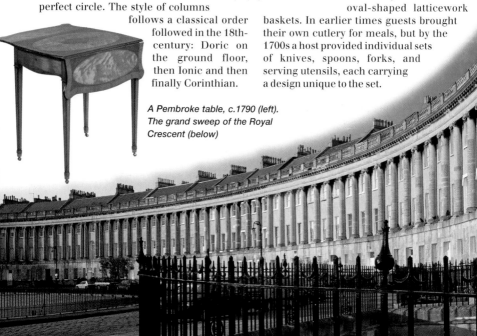

SHOPPING

The size of Bath makes shopping both accessible and comfortable. This is one of Britain's most important centres for antiques, and Bath's Antique Dealers' Association (see Useful Addresses at the end of the book) has over 70 members, who are very helpful and knowledgeable. Look out for furniture, ceramics and small decorative pieces.

The area around Abbey Green and York Street is one of the oldest in Bath and here you will find a wealth of interesting shops, selling everything from Russian crafts to antique lace and lacquerware. One of the city's most picturesque sights is 18th-century Pulteney Bridge, designed by Robert Adam and based on the Ponte Vecchio in Florence (see page 246), one of the few bridges in the world with shops built into its structure. At the western end of the bridge you'll find the Victoria Art Gallery, while on the city side

A covetable English bureau bookcase, c.1750

are some of the best jewellers, as well as numerous art and bookshops.

Look out for:
Assembly Antiques Centre (5–8 Saville Row) is a charming spot where you can pick up 18th- and 19th-century furniture and Art Deco items, tea caddies and pictures, lighting and decorative effects.

Cameo glass, c1880. The overlaid white glass has been cut away to create the decoration.

At **Geoffrey Breeze** (6 George St) you can buy furniture from the last three centuries, and **Mary Cruz** (5 Broad St) has an extensive stock of furniture, decorative items, paintings and sculptures from the 18th to 20th centuries. (Tel: 01225 334174 for a Sunday appointment.)

Andrew Dando (4 Wood St, Queen Sq) runs one of my favourite antiques shops. It's great for both English and Continental pottery and porcelain from the 17th- to mid-19th century and many interesting topographical prints.

D & B Dickinson (22 New Bond St) specializes in jewellery, silver and Sheffield plate from the 18th and 19th centuries, and **E.P. Malory and Son** (1–4 Bridge St and 5 Old Bond St) stocks period silver, Sheffield plate and objets of vertu.

Pennard House Antiques (3–4 Piccadilly, London Rd) has an eclectic selection of the unusual: pine and French provincial furniture from the 17th to 19th centuries and 19th-century decorative items.

Quiet Street Antiques (3 Quiet St and 14–15 John St) offers a splendid collection of furniture (English mahogany, 1750–1870), Royal Worcester porcelain and lots of clocks.

Sheila Smith Antiques (Stand 16, Bartlett St) offers a variety of fans, needlework tools and accessories and **Bartlett St Antiques Centre** carries a broad range of general antiques.

In Walcot Street, **Walcot Reclamation** (No 108) has a nationwide reputation for its architectural salvage items, and at **Source** (Nos 93–95) church and bar fittings, industrial lighting, medical cabinets and metalware are assembled in stables that used to belong to houses in the Paragon. **The China Doll**, in the same street, provides the most comprehensive collection of doll's house furniture and accessories imaginable, even fragile miniature wine glasses.

FAIRS AND MARKET

Bath Antiques Market (Guinea Lane, off Lansdown Rd) open Wednesdays only and offers a variety of antiques and collectables.

AUCTION HOUSES

Aldridges of Bath, Newark House, 26–45 Cheltenham St. Tel: (01225) 462830.
Gardiner Houlgate, 9 Leafield Way, Corsham, nr Bath. Tel: (01225) 812912.
Phillips, 1 Old King St. Tel: (01225) 310609.

Shop-lined Pulteney Bridge over the River Avon

Take a break at **Sally Lunn's House** in North Parade Passage. It is said to be the oldest house in Bath and dates from 1482. Sally Lunn, a French Huguenot, came to Bath in 1680 and established herself as a baker to fashionable society. With a recipe said to be handed down through the generations, you can discover the taste of a Sally Lunn cake for yourself in the coffee room, before visiting the small basement museum and shop.

The oldest house in Bath: Sally Lunn's House

COLLECTING TREEN

A particular favourite of mine is treen – small artifacts turned from a single piece of wood. Some rare examples date from the late 17th century, with the greatest quantity, if not quality, from the 19th century. The choice is extensive: drinking vessels, salt cellars and spice and snuff boxes.

Initially sycamore, walnut, yew and fruitwoods were used. Then it was imported pine, boxwood and maple, and finally exotic timbers such as lignum vitae, ebony, teak and mahogany. The finest pieces were produced from 1720 to the end of the century when the quality of the work was spectacular. You used to be able to find treen quite easily, but anything dating from before the 19th century is now very rare.

A late 18th-century fruitwood snuffbox

WHERE TO EAT AND DRINK

Popjoy's Restaurant
Sawclose
Tel: (01225) 460494
Beau Nash entertained the cream of 18th-century society here and Popjoy's retains its air of elegance. You can dine downstairs, or upstairs in a lovely Georgian drawing room.

Pump Room
Abbey Churchyard
Tel: (01225) 444477
In addition to the famous morning coffee, lunches and afternoon tea (often accompanied by a string trio), there is the Terrace restaurant in the Victorian extension with views over Bath. It is open for evening meals during the Bath Festival and in August and December.

Number Five
Argyle Street
Tel: (01225) 444499
Just off Pulteney Bridge, this candle-lit bistro offers tasty home-made soups as well as more elaborate fare such as roast quail on wild rice.

WHERE TO STAY

The Royal Crescent
16 Royal Crescent
Tel: (01225) 823333; Fax: (01225) 339401
Set in the centre of the wonderful Georgian Royal Crescent, this must surely be one of the best hotels in Great Britain. It offers the very best service in a quiet and luxurious setting. The town house is expensive, but with 45 antique-filled bedrooms and a grand atmosphere this might be the place to treat yourself.

Bath Lodge Hotel
Warminster Road, Norton St Philip
Tel: (01225) 723040; Fax: (01225) 723737
This small hotel lies 7 miles south of Bath, but if you have a car it is well worth the journey. Built in 1806, it has open fires in the winter and exposed beams. All eight rooms are ensuite on a B&B basis, with evening meals at the weekend.

Bath Priory
Weston Road
Tel: (01225) 331922; Fax: (01225) 448276
A 19th-century stone building set in large gardens, the priory is within walking distance of the city centre. The restaurant is highly recommended.

Queensberry
Russel Street
Tel: (01225) 447928; Fax: (01225) 446065
This elegant 18th-century hotel occupies three town houses, close to the Royal Crescent. It boasts a fine interior and courtyard garden. The hotel's Olive Tree Restaurant is renowned.

Claverton Manor, just outside Bath, is home to the **American Museum**. This unexpected gem takes a fascinating look at early American and Colonial lifestyles. There are 18 fully furnished rooms recreating different eras and guides will tell you all about the religious sects, Shaker furniture, Native American art and quilts.

Bradford on Avon, about 8 miles south-east of Bath, was once at the heart of the textile industry. It is particularly noted for its picturesque 13th-century bridge with a domed structure that was once a chapel and then became a lock-up in the 17th century. Shop for antiques here in Woolley St and Market St.

Bristol's pre-eminence as a port since the 17th century means that goods and ideas from all over the world have passed through and influenced this busy city.

King Brennus depicted on St John's Gate

BRISTOL

BRISTOL IS A CITY OF CONSTANT VARIETY. Ancient buildings are set against imaginative modern civic development – the new Broad Quay water feature, for example, recalls Bristol's former seafaring history (it is from here that, in 1497, John Cabot set sail for North America). Great ships no longer unload their cargoes here, but the waterfront is being revitalized. Clifton, once a village but now a suburb, became a highly desirable address in the late 18th century when wealthy Bristolians built houses on Clifton Down. Grand terraces overlook the dramatic Avon Gorge and Clifton Suspension Bridge built by the Victorian railway engineer Isambard Kingdom Brunel.

HISTORY REVISITED

TRADE AND THE SEA

Built near the mouth of the River Avon, Bristol was the main British port for trade with the American colonies. In the 17th and 18th centuries cargoes included cotton, corn and tobacco – and slaves. A wealthy merchant of the late 18th century is likely to have lived in a residence similar to **The Georgian House**.

The city also pioneered the era of the ocean-going steam liner with the *SS Great Britain*. Launched in 1843, the ship was beached in the Falkland Islands in 1886. It was towed back in 1970 and now stands in its original dry dock next to the **Maritime Heritage Centre**.

- **The Georgian House**, 7 Great George St. Tel: (0117) 921 1362.
- *SS Great Britain* and **Maritime Heritage Centre**, Gas Ferry Rd. Tel: (0117) 926 0680.

ANTIQUES IN CONTEXT

BRISTOL GLASS

Cobalt imported to the city influenced the distinctive colour used in the production of "Bristol blue" glass from about 1760 to 1825. Only a few blue pieces were actually made in Bristol, and "Bristol" glass includes most blue, green and amethyst glassware made throughout Britain at this time. You may find decanters with their distinctive gilt labels, finger bowls, drinking glasses and scent bottles.

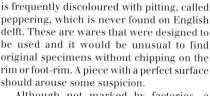

Bristol blue decanter, c.1785

ENGLISH DELFT

Bristol was one of the main sources in the 17th and 18th centuries for English delft pottery. English potters recognized a market among the newly created middle classes for an agreeable alternative to the prized but expensive porcelain from China. Centres for the production of delft were established in several cities, including Bristol. Dutch Delft (see page 136) was decorated in much the same style as imported Ming porcelain, but the decoration of English delft tended to be more fluid and rather naively drawn. The English also favoured bold flower or oak-leaf patterns and portraits of monarchs such as Charles II or William and Mary.

English delft tends to be coarse and hard and more thickly potted than Dutch Delft, where the thick white glaze

is frequently discoloured with pitting, called peppering, which is never found on English delft. These are wares that were designed to be used and it would be unusual to find original specimens without chipping on the rim or foot-rim. A piece with a perfect surface should arouse some suspicion.

Although not marked by factories, a considerable amount of 18th-century delft is dated, which may be another helpful clue to identification. Rare examples of early English delft are highly desirable and can fetch good money. However, it is possible to find good, albeit damaged, pieces of early delft at very reasonable prices.

English delft plate, c. 1750–60

PLACES TO VISIT

Because of its docks and factories, Bristol was a prime target for bombing in World War II. Consequently, its centre has been largely rebuilt. The best part of the old city is the Broad St, King St and Corn St area. Here you can find an interesting covered market, part of which is to be found in the Corn Exchange, designed by John Wood the elder in 1743. Outside this building are the four bronze Bristol Nails, actually pedestals dating from the 17th century; the city's merchants used them as tables when they were buying and selling, hence the expression "to pay on the nail".

At the head of Broad St is St John's Gate with its colourful medieval statues of Bristol's two mythical founders, the Kings Brennus and Benilus. Nearby, between Lewin's Mead and Colston St, is Christmas Steps, a steep lane lined with superb shops.

The perpendicular church of **St Mary Redcliffe** is one of the largest in the country, and is far more spectacular than the cathedral across the water. It is considered a very fine church indeed, and Elizabeth I described it as "the fairest in England". Its tall spire was hit by lightning in the 15th century

Brunel's SS Great Britain, the largest ship of her time

Hotwell with views of Clifton Suspension Bridge in the background

and was not rebuilt until 400 or so years later. At the **City Museum and Art Gallery** you will find a collection of Chinese glass (the largest outside China), a wide variety of Roman tableware, as well as Bristol glass, and paintings that include works by Bellini and Renoir.

Christening bowl (1837) painted by William Fifield

● **St Mary Redcliffe**, Redcliffe Way. Tel: (0117) 929 1541.
● **City Museum and Art Gallery**, Queen's Road. Tel (0117) 922 3571.

SHOPPING

Bristol's antiques shops are the perfect place for searching out an extensive range of antiques – everything from books to church pews.

Look out for:
Arcadia Antiques (Clifton Arcade, Boyces Avenue, Clifton) sells general antiques, including sofas and chairs, paintings and jewellery. **Robert Mills Architectural Antiques** (Narroways, Eastville) carries a huge stock of salvaged architectural items, from stained glass and panelling rescued from churches to entire shop interiors. His stock ranges from 1750 to the 1920s.

Silver-topped perfume bottle, c.1860

FAIRS AND MARKETS
Bristol Antiques Market, Broad Plain, off Temple Way. Tel: (0117) 929 7739. Open daily. The broad range of stock includes jewellery, toys, furniture and collectables.

AUCTION HOUSES
I always pay a visit to **Bristol Auction Rooms**. They operate from a converted church on the corner of Apsley Rd and Whiteladies Rd and hold regular auctions. Tel: (0117) 973 7201.

WHERE TO EAT AND DRINK
Harveys
12 Denmark Street
Tel: (0117) 927 5034
The cuisine is a contemporary French affair, and the wine list is impressive. The building was once a medieval wine cellar, used for sherry bottling.

Highbury Vaults
St Michael's Hill, Cotham
Tel: (0117) 973 3203
In early Georgian times the site was a gaol, but it is now a bustling friendly pub. Be sure to try the local beers; the pub food is very good.

WHERE TO STAY
Hotel du Vin
The Sugar House, Narrow Lewins Mead
Tel: (0117) 925 5577; Fax: (0117) 925 1199
An imaginative conversion of a series of warehouses, Mr Reed's Sugar House was built in 1728 when the River Frome flowed past its windows. The hotel is serious about its wine list, and its menus are equally impressive.

Berkely Square Hotel
15 Berkely Square, Clifton
Tel: (0117) 925 4000; Fax: (0117) 925 2970
This elegant Georgian hotel is set in a peaceful square, the decoration is tasteful and the restaurants are good. After a day in the city you can relax in the stylish basement cocktail bar.

Henbury Lodge
Station Road, Henbury
Tel: (0117) 950 2615; Fax: (0117) 950 9532
This ex-stable block, dating from 1760, has been beautifully converted with individually styled bedrooms. The garden is a delight in summer.

IN THE AREA

Take a day out to **Wotton-under-Edge**, about 30km (20 miles) north-east of Bristol. Like many small towns in the area its prosperity was based on wool, and you can visit the heritage centre (in what was the fire station) which explores Wotton's past. The **Wotton Auction Rooms** (Tel: 01453 844733) do fantastic house clearances. Just outside Wotton is **Newark Park**, where classical Adam-style panelled rooms heavily disguise its hunting lodge origins. Here you are on the edge of the Cotswolds (see page 50), a popular and picturesque hunting ground for antiques lovers.

COTSWOLDS

Between Bath and Stratford-upon-Avon stretches a world of honey-coloured cottages, impossibly pretty waterside villages and a treasury of antiques: the Cotswolds. For many this area is the essence of Englishness.

The distinctive face of Long St clock, Tetbury

Dollar St, in the Cotswolds market town of Cirencester

LIKE SO MANY VISITORS WHO COME BACK TIME AFTER TIME, I find the small villages and rugged landscape of the Cotswolds beautiful and romantic. An accident of geology has provided the region with a building material – the oolitic Cotswold limestone – that gives an attractive mellow feel and sense of unity to the whole area, from Hidcote and Chipping Campden in the north to Wotton in the south.

The Cotswolds are wonderful to explore, and for antiques hunters there is a wealth of shops and galleries. I would particularly recommend Stow-on-the-Wold, Burford, Broadway and Tetbury, but most of the towns and villages are close together and several can be covered in a day without feeling rushed. I just love to jump in the car to see where the road leads. Cirencester, sometimes called the Capital of the Cotswolds, and Cheltenham are gracious Regency towns, yet not far away lies the secluded Slad valley about which the poet and novelist Laurie Lee wrote so lyrically.

In 1996 the Cotswolds were declared an Area of Outstanding Natural Beauty. There are reasons for visiting at any time of year – in order to appreciate the gorgeous gardens and picturesque high streets, and there are obvious advantages to visiting out of season. In spite of the relatively small area, however, you will find the Cotswolds home to many towns and villages with thriving antiques centres. Among the narrow streets and busy fairs, you can buy everything from fine furniture and paintings to lace and toys.

WEALTH FROM WOOL

A long-woolled, shaggy sheep introduced to the Cotswolds by the Romans became known as the Cotswold Lion; its wool formed the raw material for an industry that thrived until the 19th century. The steep, narrow valleys with their racing streams provided the power to run the area's woollen mills. From the Middle Ages villages and towns such as **Stroud**, **Wotton-under-Edge**, **Chipping Campden**, **Chalford** and **Painswick** all prospered from dyeing and fulling, spinning and weaving – the streams, it is said, would run red with Stroudwater Scarlet dye. The medieval market halls that still stand in many of the pretty town squares supplied weavers and cloth merchants from all over Europe; many of the treasured Flemish tapestries you can see in Brussels and Bruges (see pp.124–133) were worked in fine-spun Cotswold wool.

Reminders of the source of the region's wealth are everywhere, from pubs called The Clothiers Arms to Tetbury's annual woolsack race. On the parish church at **Cranham**, just north-east of Painswick, there are sheep shears carved among the gargoyles, and wool merchants lying at rest in **Northleach** church have their feet on sheep's backs or woolsacks. At **Uley**, once famed for its blue cloth produced for the Navy, you can see the rows of weavers' cottages, with the grander houses of the mill owners around the green. The old mills, some very imposing, are now usually put to

A Cotswold Lion sheep

other purposes – Stroud's District Council sits in what was **Ebley Mill**, for example, and **Egypt Mills**, in neighbouring Nailsworth, is now a restaurant. A very few, such as some around **Chalford**, are still working, and at **Cotswold Woollen Weavers** you can still see Victorian looms at work as a commercial concern run on traditional lines.

Ebley Mill, now Stroud's council offices

● **Cotswold Woollen Weavers**, Filkins (south of Burford). Tel: (01367) 860491.
● **Tetbury Woolsack Race**, Spring Bank Holiday (1st Monday in May).
● See Cotswold Lion sheep saved from near-extinction at **Cotswold Wildlife Park**, nr Burford. Tel: (01993) 823006.

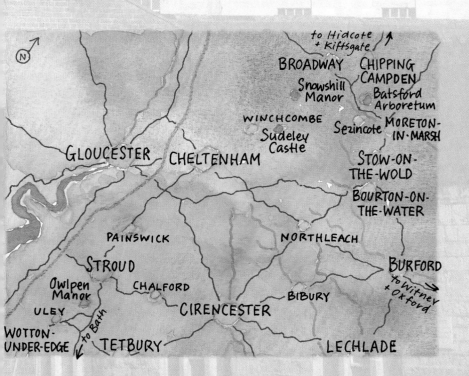

AROUND THE COTSWOLDS

This beautiful area is famous for its excellent antiques shops, arts and crafts, restaurants, picturesque pubs and tempting tearooms.

Antiques shops in Burford High Street

CIRENCESTER

Along with St Albans (Verulamium) and York (Eboracum), Cirencester (Corinium) was one of the largest towns in Roman Britain after London. Even today, any building project in the area must be preceded by a formal archeological investigation. Modern-day Cirencester is a busy market town with an excellent reputation for crafts. Among the many treasures in its magnificent parish church is a rare survival of Tudor silver – a cup made for Henry

Durham House in Stow-on-the-Wold

VIII's second wife, Anne Boleyn, in 1535. **Thomas St, Dollar St** and **Coxwell St** all have fine houses built by prosperous wool merchants in the 17th and 18th centuries. **William H. Stockes** in **The Cloisters**, Dollar St concentrates on antiques from the 16th and 17th centuries and has a good range of early furniture and accoutrements such as brass chandeliers. **Brewery Yard** is a craft-lover's delight.

STOW-ON-THE-WOLD

One of the larger Cotswold towns, the final battle of the Civil War was fought here in 1646. In old English, it means "meeting place on the hill". The Square is a good place to start. Here you'll find, among others, **Antony Preston Antiques**, with its collection of period lighting and 19th-century furniture. On one

Early 19th-century enamel wine label

corner of The Square is **Baggott's of Church St** which, along with its sister establishment, **Duncan J. Baggott** in Sheep St, stocks furniture from the 17th up to the 19th centuries, as well as smaller domestic items such as pottery, treen (see page 46) and ironware. Sheep St has many more shops of interest, including the large **Durham House Antiques Centre**, where dealers' specialities range from antiquities to fine linen and lace. **Christopher Clarke Antiques**, on the corner of Sheep St and The Fosseway, always has an exciting and interesting stock of 18th-, 19th- and early 20th-century furniture, as well as animal artifacts in many media – paintings, prints, carvings, bronzes, sculpture and toys. In Brewery Yard, off Sheep St, **Samarkand Galleries** is an exotic emporium selling kilims and Oriental rugs.

Huntington Antiques, at The Old Forge in Church St, has an extensive selection of early country furniture, with metalware, treen and tapestries.

A 17th-century oak gateleg table with barley twist legs and stretchers

I have long admired the Arts and Crafts Movement and the work it inspired, ever since living in a late 19th-century house in Kent. **Ruskin Decorative Arts** (at 5 Talbot Court) specializes in decorative, expertly made objects from this period, as well as pottery and glass from 1860 to 1940.

BOURTON-ON-THE-WATER

A classical "water village" on the Windrush, Bourton's best known attraction is its **Model Village**. Seek out the 18th-century water mill for the **Village Life Exhibition**, an appealing jumble of artifacts and household equipment from a century and more ago. There is a blacksmith's forge, a recreated kitchen, and other reminders of how dramatically life has changed in the past hundred years.

Sampler by Catherine Anne Crump dated 20 October 1834

The **Cotswold Motoring Museum** in Sherbourne St re-opened in the summer of 2000 and is described as an Aladdin's cave for collectors of automobilia. The major exhibits are complemented by items that make this museum so special – newspapers and magazines, picnic hampers, games and jigsaws, elaborate pins to secure motoring ladies' millinery – anything with a motoring theme. Tel: (01451) 821255.

BURFORD

It may be a surprise to some of you, but growing up in the Scottish Borders I learned to hit a mean drive with a 3-wood. While many of my friends headed for sunny climes, most of my holidays were spent at St. Andrews, the home of golf. So I have a soft spot for all the sporting memorabilia in **Manfred Schotten Antiques** at 109 High St.

Between Burford and Cheltenham lies the charming village of Northleach. The **Doll's House** in Market Place is a mecca for all lovers of doll's houses and their furniture and furnishings. Phone ahead to check up on their opening hours. Tel: (01451) 860431.

MORETON-IN-MARSH

Berry Antiques, at 3 High St, has furniture, Victorian paintings and porcelain. And further along the High St is **Astley House**, which as a large stock of 19th and 20th-century paintings; they usually also have a good selection of charming botanical prints.

If you fish, make an appointment to visit **Simon Brett's** collection of antique rods and fishing paraphernalia in the High St. Tel: (01608) 650751.

CHIPPING CAMPDEN

Great pains have been taken to preserve the old-world appeal of this town. The **Guild of Handicrafts**, formed in 1902, was inspired by William Morris, a pioneer of skilled craftsmanship over mass production.There are craft shops in the renovated **Silk Mill**.

SHOPPER'S TIP

About halfway between Burford and Oxford is the blanket-making town of Witney. At 96–100 Corn St is **Witney Antiques**, which I love for its fabulous selection of samplers and its once yearly sampler exhibition. They also have a good stock of 17th- and 18th-century furniture, clocks and metalware.

GLOUCESTERSHIRE GARDENS

Kiftsgate Court gardens

There are more private gardens open to the public here than in any other English county, and of every size and style, from the Tudor knot garden at **Sudeley**

Castle to the National Trust's experimental organic garden at **Snowshill** or the Japanese teahouse with bronze deer at **Batsford**. My weakness is for the quintessentially English garden: lush herbaceous borders, bowers half-hidden by blowsy summer roses, lavender on the air. All of this sums up **Hidcote Manor** which even has a lavender named after it. An American, Major Lawrence Johnston, began its garden in 1908 and his work continued for over 40 years. His vision was of a garden of themed "rooms", each contained within its own hedge or wall. Just down the road is **Kiftsgate**, home of the original Kiftsgate rose, now over 20m (60ft) high and a stunning sight in early summer. Not all gardens are typically English, however. **Sezincote**, just outside Moreton-in-Marsh, is a Moghul-style house, with Regency-style manor gardens. Sezincote was the inspiration behind the Brighton Pavilion (see page 31).

The Lawrence Johnston rose

The charming village of Broadway, once known as "The Painted Lady of the Cotswolds"

BROADWAY

One of the most scenic villages in the region, this is recommended in spite of the many visitors in summer. The art galleries in Broadway are very good and you can pick up fine furniture from the workshops of the late Gordon Russell. The Norman church outside the village takes you back in time and should not be missed.

BUYING FURNITURE

Here are a few furniture dealers I can recommend: **Jacqueline Hall Antiques**, 29 Suffolk Parade, Cheltenham. Tel: (01242) 224182 for opening hours. **Paul Nash Antiques**, Cherington, near Tetbury. By appointment only. Tel: (01285) 841215.
Robin Shield Antiques, 15 Michaels Mead, Cirencester. By appointment only. Tel: (01860) 520391.
Geoffrey Stead, Wyatts Farm, Todenham, Moreton-in-Marsh. By appointment only. Tel (01608) 6650997.
Keith Hockin Antiques, The Square, Stow-on-the-Wold. Tel: (01451) 831058.

Early 19th-century Windsor chair

BUYER'S TIP

Single chairs are still very underpriced, so creating a harlequin set is much cheaper than buying a matching one. When you see a chair you like, preferably a standard 18th- or 19th-century style, buy it and take a photo. Then you have a reference as you keep an eye out for others of the same or similar style. Or, much more daring, choose an era and build up a set from the same period but of different styles.

CHELTENHAM

Mineral springs were discovered in 1716 and a pump room constructed, but Cheltenham did not become a fashionable spa town until 1788 when George III spent several weeks there taking the waters. High society then adopted the town as a summer resort and rows of Regency houses were built near the Pittville Pump Room.

To rediscover Regency Cheltenham, start at the Promenade, laid out in 1817, then stroll up to the Imperial Gardens and into Montpellier Walk to admire the classical façades and the wrought-iron balconies. In the town centre the **Cheltenham Art Gallery and Museum** has many exhibits on the town's history, and a comprehensive display of furniture made by members of the Cotswolds branch of the Arts and Crafts movement.

The **Holst Birthplace Museum** is the modest house where Gustav Holst spent his early life and it tells much about the composer's life at the turn of the 19th century.

Cheltenham is famous for its festivals: the music festival in July and a literature festival in October. It also has a racecourse, which in March is a mecca for racing enthusiasts, when the prestigious Cheltenham Gold Cup and the Champion Hurdle are run.

A little way to the west of the town is **Sudeley Castle**, the last home of Catherine

Gordon Russell dressing table

Parr, Henry VIII's sixth wife. She died here in 1548 and is buried in the castle's chapel.

- **Cheltenham Art Gallery and Museum**, Clarence Street. Tel: (01242) 237431.
- **Holst Birthplace Museum**, Clarence Road. Tel: (01242) 524846.
- **Sudeley Castle**, Winchcombe. Tel: (01242) 604357.

Trelliswork Worcester basket, c.1770

Cheltenham is still the fashionable shopping centre it has been for over 200 years. **Cheltenham Antiques Centre**, 50 Suffolk Rd, houses numerous shops selling Georgian silver, Victorian clocks and 20th-century memorabilia. **Montpellier Clocks**, at 13 Rotunda Terrace, specializes in clocks of all sorts, and at the top of the Promenade is **H. W. Keil**, where you will find interesting early lighting as well as 17th- and 18th-century furniture.

TETBURY

Just another pretty Cotswold town until Prince Charles moved to nearby Highgrove, Tetbury now attracts royal watchers. But the real pleasure lies in strolling by the 17th- and 18th-century buildings housing antiques dealers. **Long St**, the main street, is full of antiques shops, many situated in fine old Georgian townhouses. At No 45, enjoy browsing for objects that vary from prints to small decorative pieces and 18th- and 19th-century furniture at **Ball and Claw Antiques. The Antiques Emporium**, in an old chapel, includes 40 dealers offering fine and country furniture and domestic collectables. At **Artique**, 18 Church St, George Bristow has a fabulous stock of textiles, carpets, furniture, ceramics, metalware and *objets d'art*.

The Antiques Emporium, Long St, Tetbury

WHERE TO EAT AND DRINK

Lower Slaughter Manor
Lower Slaughter (off A429)
Tel: (01451) 820456
If you are in the area, and even if you are not, make every effort to eat at this beautiful mid-17th century Cotswolds manor. The menu, based on French classics, is renowned. It is not to be missed.

Lygon Arms
Broadway
Tel: (01386) 854424
One of the best restaurants in the area, it is the country cousin of London's Savoy – need I say more. It also has some elegant bedrooms.

Colesbourne Inn
Colesbourne, nr Cheltenham
Tel: (01242) 870376
Built in 1825 for the coach trade from London, the Colesbourne has retained all the trappings of a traditional coaching inn, including a welcoming open fire in winter. The menu, by contrast, is modern and inventive. If you're staying overnight, ask for a four-poster bed.

WHERE TO STAY

Calcot Manor
Tetbury
Tel: (01666) 890391; Fax: (01666) 890394
Parts of this property date back to the 14th and 15th centuries. It is an excellent place to take children, with a great family room and a playroom supervised by a nanny. The renovated stable house also has a very good menu served in the conservatory (definitely for the summer only as it can get very cold in other seasons).

Cotswold House
Chipping Campden
Tel: (01386) 840330; Fax: (01386) 840310
Set in a 17th-century house, this hotel is smart and stylish, with fine service and some of the best bedrooms in the area, all individually decorated.

Wyck Hill House
Burford Road, Stow-on-theWold
Tel: (01451) 831936; Fax: (01451) 832243
The hotel is situated in an 18th-century manor house with great views over the Windrush Valley. The restaurant is also very good, although the formal setting is not always what you need after a day of hard shopping.

Collin House
Collin Lane, Broadway
Tel: (01386) 858354; Fax: (01386) 858697
The 17th-century features of this hotel are being carefully restored. The inglenook fireplace holds a log fire for cold winter nights. The bedrooms are in a traditional style. There is also a fine restaurant.

Bibury Court Hotel
Bibury, nr Cirencester
Tel: (01285) 740337; Fax: (01285) 740665
A comfortable yet elegant country manor house that has been standing here since the 16th century, the Bibury Court is full of character and has an excellent restaurant.

The Cotswolds are a hugely popular tourist destination, so it would be as well to book somewhere. The Cotswold Visitor Information Centre produces accommodation leaflets, and the local tourist offices can also help with bookings (see Useful Addresses at the end of the book).

EDINBURGH

Edinburgh is regarded as one of Europe's most handsome capitals, famous for its its annual arts festival. Shopping in the Old Town and along the historic Royal Mile is always rewarding.

Greyfriars Bobby, a canine hero

EDINBURGH HAS ALWAYS BEEN A CITY OF TWO HALVES. Once divided by a lake, it is now split into old and new. The Old Town, with its crowded tenements and bloody past, straddles the ridge between the castle and the 16th-century Palace of Holyroodhouse. The New Town to the north evolved after 1767 when wealthy merchants expanded it in an orderly grid. Almost every street has a view – of the Firth of Forth, the castle, the Pentland Hills, Calton Hill or of Arthur's Seat. This is Edinburgh's most important landmark: a rocky peak, originally volcanic, in the open grounds of Holyrood Park.

The entrancing Museum of Childhood

Confined by the city wall, the Old Town grew upwards. Everything – from the Scotch Whisky Centre, Parliament House, St Giles Cathedral and the Museum of Childhood – is here. Finds in antiques shops here reflect the full gamut of Edinburgh's history, from ancient maps to such Scottish curiosities as Mauchlinware and tartanware. While exploring, seek out Greyfriars Church. Near the gateway is Greyfriars Bobby, a unique statue to a little terrier who guarded his master's grave for 14 years; he was even granted citizenship, so he'd not be destroyed as a stray.

Every year in late summer Edinburgh overflows with international artists and performers as it plays host to one of the world's most important arts events: The Edinburgh Festival.

Edinburgh Castle, seen from Grassmarket

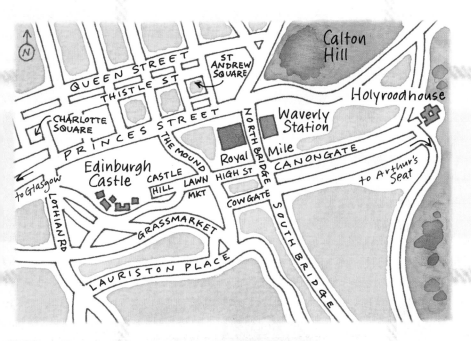

SCOTLAND'S CAPITAL

Castle Rock dominates the city centre. Early signs of habitation here date back to 850BC. Then it was captured by the Angles in the sixth century. They rebuilt the fortress here and were unbeaten for the next 300 years. The castle was first used for royalty by Malcolm II in 1018, and it was from this time that the city began to grow, with the first effective town wall built c.1450. Despite attacks from the English during the following 200 years, the castle continued to be a royal residence until James VI moved to London in 1604, following his succession to both the English and the Scottish Crowns. The 1707 Act of Union reduced Edinburgh's importance, although cultural and intellectual life continued to flourish.

Model of the religious leader, John Knox, in his house

The best place to start looking at Edinburgh is the Royal Mile, made up of four ancient streets that linked the castle to Holyroodhouse in medieval times. The castle has been a royal residence since the 11th century. Here are St Margaret's Chapel, the Crown Room containing the Scottish crown jewels and the Royal Apartments, where Mary, Queen of Scots gave birth to James VI.

One of the most striking buildings is **St Giles Cathedral**, the most important

Preston Pans ewer (date unknown), depicting Robert Burns

church in Scotland. The building was completed in 1465, although there has been a church on this site since the 9th century. One of the most interesting corners of the cathedral is the Thistle Chapel, built in 1909 for the Knights of the Most Ancient and Most Noble Order of the Thistle.

The extraordinary **John Knox's House** on the Royal Mile dates from c.1490 and has original gables, beams and religious carvings. A leading figure of the Reformation, John Knox was responsible for the Reformed Church of Scotland, and for the change to Protestantism in 1599. **Canongate Tolbooth** with its picturesque turrets and clock is an interesting example of 16th-century architecture and now houses **The People's Story**, a fascinating museum telling the story of the life, work and pastimes of ordinary Edinburgh people from the 18th century to the present day.

Holyroodhouse, the official residence of the Queen in Scotland, is at the bottom of the Royal Mile. Access is restricted, although the Throne Room and Royal Dining Room are open and so are the grounds and abbey ruins. Mary, Queen of Scots, lived here from 1561 to 1567.

- **Edinburgh Castle**. Tel: (0131) 225 9846.
- **St Giles Cathedral**, High St. Tel: (0131) 225 9442.
- **John Knox's House**, High St. Tel: (0131) 556 2647.
- **Canongate Tolbooth/The People's Story**, Canongate. Tel: (0131) 529 4057.
- **Holyroodhouse**. Tel: (0131) 556 1096.

ANTIQUES IN CONTEXT

With its dramatic setting and striking architecture ranging from medieval to Georgian, Edinburgh (once described as "the Athens of the North") is renowned for superb museums and art galleries.

An elegant drawing room in the Georgian House

Mauchlinware bellows, intended as a souvenir, not for use

ART IN EDINBURGH

The **National Gallery of Scotland** has a wonderful collection of European and British paintings from the 15th to the 19th century. The **National Gallery of Modern Art**, set in sizeable grounds, displays most of the European and American giants of the 20th century, from Pablo Picasso to Roy Lichtenstein, and sculpture by Henry Moore and Eduardo Paolozzi. There is a superb exhibition at the **Scottish National Portrait Gallery** on the fascinating history of Scottish monarchs from Robert the Bruce to Queen Anne. The **Royal Museum of Scotland** tells the story of Scotland. Medieval chessmen from the Isle of Lewis, Scotland's earliest crown jewels, the Ellesmere railway locomotive and icons of the 20th century are among the key exhibits.

- **National Gallery of Scotland**, The Mound. Tel: (0131) 624 6200.
- **National Gallery of Modern Art**, Belford Rd. Tel: (0131) 556 8921.
- **Scottish National Portrait Gallery**, Queen St. Tel: (0131) 624 6200.
- **Royal Museum of Scotland**, Chambers St. Tel: (0131) 225 7534.

PLACES TO VISIT

The beautifully restored **Georgian House** has been refurnished to show how Edinburgh's elite lived in the 1700s. At the **Museum of Childhood**, the world's first such museum, are over 10,000 items used or made by children around the world. The **Writer's Museum**, in the 17th-century **Lady Stairs House**, contains manuscripts of three famous Scottish authors: Robert Burns, Sir Walter Scott and Robert Louis Stevenson. Along the street is **Gladstone's Land**, a six-storey building dating from the 1550s and furnished in the style of a 1620s merchant house.

- **Georgian House**, 7 Charlotte Sq. Tel: (0131) 225 2160. Closed Nov–Feb.
- **Museum of Childhood**, High St. Tel: (0131) 529 4142.
- **Writer's Museum**, Lawnmarket. Tel: (0131) 529 4901.
- **Gladstone's Land**, Lawnmarket. Tel: (0131) 226 5856. Closed Nov–Mar.

SHOPPING

In the Old Town, the Royal Mile is a superb shopping area offering tartans, tweeds, whiskies and crafts. You will also find specialist kilt-makers. In Victoria Street is a great flea market.

Look out for:
W.M. Armstrong and Sons in Grassmarket is a treasure trove of second-hand retro garments with some real gems for sale. **Joseph Bonner** (72 Thistle St) is exquisite, boasting the largest stock of antique jewellery in Scotland. **Just Junk** (87 Broughton St) has anything from a vintage slot machine to a Sixties' dining set; also a good selection of antiquarian books.

Behind Princes Street is Rose Street with lots of speciality craft shops. Stockbridge, north-west of New Town, has boutiques and

---

TRY NOT TO MISS ...

The **Museum of Scotland** which opened on St Andrew's Day 1998. This striking building beside the Royal Museum houses more than 10,000 of the nation's rarest and most precious treasures, showing Scotland's geological development and archeology, then 600 years of Scotland as an independent nation, through to the last three centuries as part of the United Kingdom.

THE TRUTH ABOUT TARTAN

Tartans were worn by Highlanders in patterns (or setts) to identify members of the same clan. After the 1745 rebellion, wearing tartan was forbidden, and the law vigorously enforced, so over time the weaving patterns were lost. George IV, however, liked tartan, and his visit to Scotland in 1822 brought a new enthusiasm for it and inspired families to research their clan tartans.

antiques shops, including **Mon Tresor** (St Stephen St).

Laurance Black (60 Thistle St) has Scottish furniture, decorative items, glass, pottery, tartanware and treen. The **Carlton Gallery** (10 Royal Terrace) carries paintings, particularly Scottish marine and watercolour prints, all from the 19th and 20th centuries.

If it's good quality furniture from a wide range of periods you're after, then look no further than **Georgian Antiques** (10 Pattison St, Leith Links). At 173 Canongate, the **Carson Clark Gallery** specializes in antique maps.

MAUCHLINWARE AND TARTANWARE

As Scotland became a fashionable Victorian holiday destination, two types of souvenir ware became popular. Mauchlinwares (from Mauchlin, Ayrshire) are domestic items made usually from sycamore and decorated with a typical scene or view. J.J. Smith was the main producer of these items from the 1820s. He also made Tartanware, again small wooden domestic items, this time decorated with a distinctive tartan pattern.

AUCTION HOUSES

Phillips, 65 George St. Tel: (0131) 225 2266.
Lyon and Turnball, 33 Broughton Pl. Tel: (0131) 557 8844.
Bonhams, 24 Melville St. Tel: (0131 226 3204).

Tartanware ink blotter, popular in the 19th century

WHERE TO EAT AND DRINK

The Witchery
322 Castlehill
Tel: (0131) 225 5613
Dating back to the 15th century and located at the top of the Royal Mile, this is one of Edinburgh's best restaurants. You can eat either in the converted schoolyard ("the secret garden") or the more traditional main dining room. The Scottish-influenced menu always lives up to its reputation.

Café Royal
19 West Register Street
Tel: (0131) 556 1884
An historic city centre bar, this looks as though it has barely changed in 100 years. It has amazing stained-glass windows, superb Victorian tiled walls and murals depicting famous inventors from William Caxton to James Watt. The oyster bar here is one of several dotted all over Edinburgh. They are casual places where you can eat and drink from lunchtime until late. Menus usually include beef and chicken dishes too.

Bennet's Theatre Bar
Leven Street
Tel: (0131) 229 5143
Art Deco elegance, with good food and an eclectic variety of beers.

The Cask and Barrel
Broughton Street
Tel: (0131) 556 3132
A traditional unpretentious pub with high booths and a wide selection of beers.

WHERE TO STAY

The Caledonian
Princes Street
Tel: (0131) 459 9988; Fax: (0131) 225 6632
A dominant red sandstone building from the turn of the last century, this hotel was originally built as a station house. The rooms have been furnished in immaculate Edwardian style.

Royal Terrace Hotel
Royal Terrace
Tel: (0131) 557 3222; Fax: (0131) 557 5334
One of Edinburgh's best hotels, this mid-19th-century building is full of fine furnishings and most rooms include a spa bath.

Roxburghe Hotel
6 Charlotte Square
Tel: (0131) 225 3921; Fax: (0131) 240 5555
This is a grand, traditional, mid-19th-century hotel stands in a tree-lined square in one of Edinburgh's most prestigious city-centre locations. It has two good restaurants.

IN THE AREA

Cross the Firth of Forth (look out for the wonderful railway bridge as you do) and go a little upstream to **Culross**, a small, perfectly preserved town from the late 16th century. In the palace, Culross's largest house, you can see how a well-to-do merchant of the 17th century would have lived – admire the wooden barrel-vaulted ceiling painted with allegorical scenes. From the stone tolbooth of 1626 (in Scotland a tolbooth served as a town's courthouse and jail), you can wander up cobbled streets lined with whitewashed cottages to the ruins of the Cistercian Abbey and stunning views across the Firth.

GLASGOW

Glasgow's legacy of fine Victorian buildings, museums and galleries recalls the prosperity of its industrial past. Now one of Britain's liveliest cities, antiques hunting here often turns up the unexpected.

GLASGOW (ITS CELTIC NAME, GLAS CU, means "dear green place") grew up around its cathedral built in 1156 on the site of a 6th-century church founded by St Mungo. The only mainland Scottish cathedral to have survived the religous reforms that swept through Scotland, Glasgow Cathedral is a shining example of pre-Reformation Gothic architecture. The most interesting part is the lower church, with many pillars topped by exquisitely carved rib-vaulting overlooking the tomb of St Mungo. In the cathedral's precinct in Castle Street is the St Mungo Museum of Religious Life and Art, the world's first museum devoted solely to this theme, containing superb artifacts from many countries; outside is the surprise of a Zen garden. A Victorian cemetery filled with fascinating crumbling monuments to the dead of Glasgow's merchant families is behind the cathedral.

In 1451, the city became the site of the University of Glasgow, Scotland's second university, sadly swept away during the Industrial Revolution. In its place, trading, shipping and factory magnates built magnificent mansions and warehouses, monuments to the city's mercantile wealth. There was a decline from the mid-20th century, but Glasgow reinvented itself and by the 1990s was enjoying a new prosperity. When shopping, look out especially for items that would have been manufactured here or come through the port in its earlier heyday: Chinese porcelain, tribal art, the locally made Clutha glass and Victorian lighting.

Above: a late 17th-century engraved silver quaich or drinking vessel and, top, a skean dhu and sheath, silver with a bog oak handle (c.1890)

Interior of the Tenement House, an early 20th-century time warp

THE MERCHANT CITY

Glasgow's diverse and dynamic Old Town, created c.1750 on a grid system, is known as the Merchant City. The Royal Exchange, now Stirling's Library, is here, and so are the City Chambers. Built in 1880 by William Young, this is one of the finest public buildings of 19th-century Britain with, grand marble and granite interiors in Italian Renaissance style.

In the 1700s most of the tobacco trade between America and Europe came through Glasgow, but even after the trade declined in the 1800s, the city prospered from textiles, shipbuilding, coal and steel. Labour was in demand and people poured in from the Highlands and Ireland to swell the workforce. But outward prosperity masked appalling work conditions.

The city's wealthy citizens spent vast fortunes building up the large art collections which now form the basis of the city's superb galleries. The **Art Gallery and Museum**, Scotland's most popular gallery, is best known for its 17th-century Dutch and 19th-century French paintings. Scottish painters of luminous landscapes and still lifes are well represented by Arthur Melville, Sir William McTaggart, Francis Campbell Cadell and, among the moderns, Bruce McLean, David Hockney and Jasper Johns. The **Hunterian Art Gallery** opened in 1807. It has work by Charles Rennie Mackintosh (see next page), the largest print collection in Scotland and, most famously, the art of American painter James McNeill Whistler.

A fascinating record of how Glasgow's poor lived during

The opulent Victorian City Chambers

the early 1900s has been preserved in **Tenement House**, with the original fixtures and fittings of a family who lived there for 50 years.

● **Art Gallery and Museum**, Argyle St, Kelvingrove. Tel: (0141) 287 2699.
● **Hunterian Art Gallery**, Hillhead St. Tel: (0141) 330 5431.
● **Tenement House**, Buccleuch St. Tel: (0141) 333 0183. Open pm Mar–Oct only,

Novelty ceramic chess set (mid-20th century); main pieces depicted historical figures and were once filled with whisky

ANTIQUES IN CONTEXT

Glasgow is best known for its elegant architecture and the extensive collections of artworks in its many fine museums and galleries.

The main entrance to the Burrell Collection, bequeathed to the city in 1944

PLACES TO VISIT

The **Burrell Collection** is a must-see, one of my very favourite places and Glasgow's star attraction. Scottish shipping magnate Sir William Burrell built up an amazing collection of art from around the world – ancient civilizatons, medieval Europe and the Orient are all represented in a building specially constructed in 1983 in Pollok Country Park. You will find anything from Chinese porcelain and medieval furniture to paintings by Renoir and Cézanne. The floors are carpeted so that the visitor can view the beautifully displayed treasures in silence. Some galleries are reconstructed rooms from Hutton Castle, Burrell's residence.

A short walk away is **Pollok House**, the best historic house from 18th-century Glasgow. It has a wonderful collection of Spanish, British and Dutch paintings. At the **Glasgow School of Art**, Mackintosh's masterpiece

Clutha glass

built between 1897 and 1909, you will find striking contrasts in each room such as grille-covered windows on one side with elaborate wrought-iron decoration facing them.

- **The Burrell Collection**, 2060 Pollokshaws Road. Tel: (0141) 287 2550.
- **Pollok House**, 2060 Pollokshaws Road. Tel: (0141) 616 6410.
- **Glasgow School of Art**, 167 Renfrew St. Tel: (0141) 353 4500.

CLUTHA GLASS

In the early 19th century, William Haden Richardson II was operating a business manufacturing gas tubes and fittings when his interest in glass led to an offer from James Couper and Sons to join them at the City Glass Works in Glasgow. In 1853, at the age of 28, he took over management of the works and became sole proprietor in 1900. Under his direction the company employed Christopher Dresser, a leading pro-industrial designer to make the Clutha range based on ancient examples such as Roman, Persian and Middle Eastern. The most common colour was a bubbly green made in shapes which were inspired originally by Roman glass but can rarely be matched to known Roman shapes. As more Clutha pieces have been identified, the range of colours and designs known to have been made by the factory to Dresser's designs include pink, white, green, red and blue glass applied in random swirling lines on assymetric shapes, as well as more formal striped effects. Other designs came from the Glasgow architect George Walton whose work was similar to Dresser's.

CHARLES RENNIE MACKINTOSH

The work of this leading Scottish designer (1868--1928) is distinguished by its elegant lines and surprising modernity. His unique style was based on decorative elements from ancient Celtic and Oriental art, as well as the Pre-Raphaelites and the Arts and Crafts Movement. Mackintosh wanted his pieces to be complementary, be it a building's architecture or the textiles, furniture or flatware inside it. His best-known examples are the Glasgow School of Art, which he designed in 1896, and the Willow Tea Room of 1904 (see opposite).

Rennie Mackintosh chair and Glasgow School of Art plaque, by Talwyn Morris (c. 1898–1900)

SHOPPING

Victorian Village Antiques (93 West Regent St) has shops on three floors. If hunting for lace or other textiles, or costume jewellery, look out for **Saratoga Trunk**. **Tim Wright Antiques**, at 147 Bath St, has a range of ceramics, mirrors and furniture.

Commemorative Wemyss ware goblet, 1980

In King's St you'll find a row of stalls in **King's Court Antiques and Collectables Market**, and a traditional street market (Paddy's) opposite. For something a little different, try **The Barrows**, a flea market held on Gallowgate every weekend. There are almost 1,000 stalls – though it's notorious for designer frauds. Further afield in the Clyde Valley are countless craft and antiques shops, part of the charm of the area's small towns.

The Barrows (pronounced "barras") flea market

MARKETS AND FAIRS

First held in 2000, **Antiques for Everyone** is set to become a regular date in late August: more than 200 antiques dealers offer fine art and high-quality antiques, vetted by experts.

AUCTION HOUSES

Christie's, 164–166 Bath St. Tel: (0141) 332 8134.
McTear's, Clydeway Business Centre, 8 Elliot Pl. Tel: (0141) 221 4456.
Phillips, 207 Bath St. Tel: (0141) 223 8866.

WHERE TO EAT AND DRINK

Nairns
13 Woodside Crescent
Tel: (0141) 353 0707
Owned by the Nairns brothers, this elegant 19th-century terraced town house has four individually designed bedrooms. One of my favourites.

The Rogano
11 Exchange Place
Tel: (0141) 248 4055
The Art Deco furnishings here date from 1935. The menu features fresh seafood and an imaginative wine list.

Horseshoe Bar
17 Drury Street
Tel: (0141) 229 5711
Glasgow's most famous bar has remained almost unchanged since 1884. Fame stems from its bar – the longest in the United Kingdom. Full of Glaswegian character.

Willow Tea Rooms
217 Sauchiehall Street
Tel: (0141) 332 0521
Lovely place to stop for afternoon tea, this is a reconstruction of Mackintosh's original (see left).

The Buttery
652 Argyle Street
Tel: (0141) 221 8188
Delightful setting for haute cuisine, dating back to 1869. Downstairs is the Belfry, a superb wine bar serving food.

WHERE TO STAY

One Devonshire Gardens
Devonshire Gardens
Tel: (0141) 339 2001; Fax: (0141) 337 1663
Sumptuously decorated and occupying three classic terrace houses, it seems like a luxurious country house. An excellent restaurant here, too.

Town House Hotel
21 Royal Crescent
Tel: (0141) 332 9009
Lovely B&B in a traditional Edwardian town house with smart modern furnishings.

The New Lanark Mill Hotel
Lanark
Tel: (01555) 667200; Fax: (01555) 667222
Unlike any other hotel in Scotland. Rooms in this imaginatively restored, 18th-century cotton mill (see below) retain original features such as Georgian windows and barrel-vaulted ceilings.

IN THE AREA

The award-winning World Heritage Village of **New Lanark** was built as a model community in the early 19th century. Founded in 1785 as a completely new kind of industrial settlement, based on cotton-spinning mills powered by water from the River Clyde. The workforce was provided with tenement-style housing and profits from the business financed a series of social and educational reforms to improve the workers' quality of life. It has been restored as a museum, designed to bring history alive.

BELFAST

Despite having had more than its fair share of negative publicity over recent years, you would be hard pressed to find a more genuinely friendly city than Belfast.

Walter Crane calendar, c.1897, made for the Royal Ulster Works

THE SITE OF "BÉAL FEIRSTE"(Mouth of the Farset) has been occupied from the earliest times; however, the modern city really only dates from the 17th century. Linen and shipbuilding industries – both still important today – developed and thrived, and it became one of the powerhouses of the Industrial Revolution. As seat of government in Northern Ireland after Partition in 1920, Belfast's importance continued to grow.

Although years of economic decline and conflict have left their mark, an industrial and cultural renaissance is now in full swing and, with its fascinating history waiting to be explored, Belfast proves to be a surprisingly engaging city.

HISTORY REVISITED

BIRTHPLACE OF THE *TITANIC*

Two of the world's largest cranes, "Samson" and "Goliath", dominate Belfast's eastern skyline, marking the shipbuilding yard of Harland and Wolff. The yard is best known for building some of the biggest passenger ships ever to take to the seas: the *Olympic*, the *Britannic* and, most famously, the *Titanic*. *Titanic* memorabilia is becoming increasingly collectable, from photographs of the ship under construction to survivors' letters, and the ill-fated liner has become part of the mythology of the city. Plans for a museum of the yard's history have been proposed, and there is an exhibition relating to the *Titanic* at the Ulster Transport Museum (see In the Area) and a memorial to the *Titanic*'s casualties near the City Hall.

Ticket for the launch of the Titanic in 1911

PLACES TO VISIT

The history of Ulster is well served in Belfast. For the broadest scope, visit the **Ulster Museum**, set in the verdant surroundings of the **Botanic Gardens**, where you can see Celtic jewellery, and the fine silver, tapestries and furnishings that once filled the province's great houses, as well as treasures recovered from Spanish Armada ships that foundered off the coast. **Belfast Castle**, built in 1870, has wonderful views over the city as well as a heritage centre and an antiques shop.

- **Ulster Museum and Botanic Gardens**. Tel: (028) 9038 3001. Museum open pm only at weekends; gardens open daily.
- **Belfast Castle**, Antrim Rd. Tel: (028) 9077 6925/9037 0133.

SHOPPING

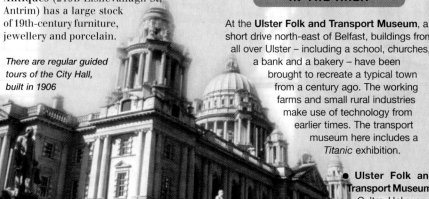

For a range of antiques shops, head for Donegall Pass, which runs west from Shaftesbury Square. Along here you will find shops such as **The Wake Table, Alexander the Grate and Carroll's**, all of them offering everything from traditional Irish furniture to fine glass and old musical instruments.

Early 20th-century pieces from Ulster's Belleek Porcelain Factory

T.H. Kearney & Sons at Treasure House, 123 University St, deals mostly in smaller items, while **The Bell Gallery** (13 Adelaide Park) specializes in 19th- and 20th-century British and Irish art and will undertake valuations and restoration work.

Just north of Belfast, **MacHenry Antiques** (Caragh Lodge, Glen Road, Jordanstown, Newtown Abbey) deals in Georgian and Victorian furniture and objects (open 2–7pm or by appointment. Tel: (028) 9086 2036). **Emerald Isle Books** (539 Antrim Rd) stocks travel, Ireland and theology books. **Country Antiques** (219B Lisnevanagh St, Antrim) has a large stock of 19th-century furniture, jewellery and porcelain.

There are regular guided tours of the City Hall, built in 1906

Entrance to one of the city's oldest passageways

WHERE TO EAT AND DRINK

Belfast has a wealth of historic pubs, and they are still very much the centre of social activity. **The Crown Liquor Saloon** in Great Victoria St belongs to the National Trust and is the best-preserved Victorian pub in Northern Ireland. Also good fun are the **Duke of York** in Commercial Court, one of Belfast's oldest streets, and **McHugh's Bar** in Pottinger's Entry, with a history going back more than three centuries.

WHERE TO STAY

Culloden Hotel
142 Bangor Road, Holywood, Co. Down
Tel: (028) 9042 5223; Fax: (028) 904 26777
A 19th-century hotel overlooking the Lough, this has period furnishings and every luxury.

McCausland Hotel
38 Victoria Street
Tel: (028) 9022 0200; Fax: (028) 9022 0220
This luxury boutique hotel has individually decorated rooms and an excellent restaurant.

Outside Belfast but within easy reach are:
Bushmills Inn
9 Dunluce Road, Bushmills, Co. Antrim
Tel: (028) 2073 2339; Fax: (028) 2073 2048
Set beside the world's oldest whiskey distillery, this coaching inn features antique furniture and open fires, and the restaurant specializes in locally caught salmon.

Galgorm Manor
136 Fenaghy Road, Ballymena, Co. Antrim
Tel: (028) 2588 1001; Fax: (028) 2588 0080
Set in a wooded estate, this historic residence has welcoming open fires, Waterford crystal chandeliers and an old bar with a cobbled floor.

IN THE AREA

At the **Ulster Folk and Transport Museum**, a short drive north-east of Belfast, buildings from all over Ulster – including a school, churches, a bank and a bakery – have been brought to recreate a typical town from a century ago. The working farms and small rural industries make use of technology from earlier times. The transport museum here includes a *Titanic* exhibition.

- **Ulster Folk and Transport Museum**, Cultra, Holywood. Tel: (028) 9042 8428.

DUBLIN

Dublin's turbulent history stretches from Celtic times to the struggle for independence in the last century, but today the city's past can be rediscovered in its streets and antiques shops.

Typical Georgian doorway with a segmented fanlight

DUBLIN IS OFTEN REFERRED TO AS A GEORGIAN CITY and, architecturally speaking, the 18th century was truly Dublin's golden period. The middle classes and aristocracy (often English absentee landowners) built wonderful town houses, and you can still enjoy the classical proportions and elegance of the work of Georgian architects such as Richard Castle and James Gandon as you stroll through the city's streets and squares. Dublin was one of the first cities to have planned development, and the Royal Dublin Society, established to promote arts, crafts and agriculture, was founded in 1731.

Dublin's museums and historical sites are full of memories of the Celts and Vikings whose stories and legends are part and parcel of the fabric of Ireland.

Historical and architectural attractions and myriad craft and antiques shops may seem reason enough to visit, but the city's appeal lies in the friendliness of the Dubliners. Enjoy the *craic*, the fast and witty talk that fills the bars and cafés. Any time I am in Dublin I head for the Horseshoe Bar in the Shelbourne Hotel and never fail to meet a friend. As the satirist Brendan Behan once remarked: "Dublin is very adjacent."

Dublin is compact and driving can be a nightmare – so forget about a car and explore this vibrant and "villagey" city on foot.

Irish George III dining chair in mahogany

EARLY DUBLIN

There is evidence to suggest that the site of Dublin was inhabited as early as 7500BC. Celts first settled in the area in the 7th century BC, and following invasion in the 9th century AD the area became a Viking stronghold. At **Dublin's Viking Adventure** you can take a boat and travel back in time to a Viking village where you can talk to locals and see their daily work, with all its smells and sounds. This interactive experience is one of the best ways to learn about the tumultuous history of the town of "Dyflin" in the 9th and 10th centuries. The display of Viking artifacts discovered on the site is considered to be one of the most extensive outside Scandinavia.

Christ Church Cathedral is Dublin's oldest building. Originally a wooden construction, it was built in 1038 for Dunan, the city's first bishop, by Sitric, the king of the Dublin Norsemen; it was subsequently rebuilt in stone. Much of the cathedral was reworked in the 1870s, but the imposing doorway in the south transept is a fine example of 12th-century Irish stonecarving. The large crypt, dating from 1172, houses some fascinating relics.

The region had been fervently Christian since the arrival of St Patrick in 432. A church has existed on the site of **St Patrick's Cathedral** since 450, making it the oldest Christian site in Dublin. It is said that St Patrick baptized his converts in the church's well. In 1191 the old wooden building was replaced by the stone edifice that still stands today and which is Ireland's largest church.

Of all Ireland's religious memorabilia, the most precious and renowned must surely be the exquisite Book of Kells. This is a medieval illuminated manuscript of the four gospels, in Latin and in a Celtic script, believed to date from 800. Its origins are uncertain, but it is probably the work of monks from the Scottish island of Iona, who, fleeing their original home to escape marauding Vikings, arrived at Kells Monastery in County Meath.

This breathtaking work of art was given to **Trinity College** in the 17th century. The book is now the focus of a marvellous exhibition that uses the latest technology to explain the

Detail of an illumination in the Book of Kells

lavishly decorated pages. Mechanical aids have been used to turn several pages in sequence so that visitors can see the quality and variety of the handwritten text and illumination.

Once the home of British viceroys in Ireland, **Dublin Castle** is a complex of 18th- and 19th-century buildings, which also incorporates the Record Tower. This is the only remaining portion of the original Anglo-Norman fortress, dating from 1258. Within the castle are the State Apartments, government offices, galleries and courtyards, a Gothic revival church, and the Undercroft where a Viking fortress once stood.

- **Dublin's Viking Adventure**, Essex Street West, off Fishamble St, Temple Bar. Tel: (01) 679 6040.
- **Christ Church Cathedral**, Christ Church Pl. Tel: (01) 403 9472 for info.
- **St Patrick's Cathedral**, Patrick Cl. Tel: (01) 475 4817.
- **Trinity College**. Tel: (01) 608 2320.
- **Dublin Castle**, Dame St. Tel: (01) 677 7129.

Dublin Castle showing Bedford Tower of 1760

ANTIQUES IN CONTEXT

An integral part of Dublin's appeal for antiques lovers is its history,
in particular the shaping of the city in Georgian times. Its museums
and galleries give a real insight into the city's past.

GEORGIAN DUBLIN

Dublin's largest square, the green and serene **Merrion Square**, was laid out in 1762 and is surrounded by elegant Georgian town houses whose coloured front doors and classical pediments epitomize Georgian Dublin. The playwright Oscar Wilde, whose statue can be seen in the square, and the poet W.B. Yeats are among those who once lived here. Overlooking the square from the west is the National Gallery (see opposite).

The rear drawing room of Number 29

For a taste of life in a middle-class Georgian home, visit **Number 29**. This is 29 Lower Fitzwilliam Street, which was built in 1794 for a Mrs Elizabeth Beattie. The house is maintained in the style that she would have known at the end of the eighteenth century. After an explanatory slide show, you can walk through the museum and imagine what living in Dublin would have been like at that time. Items from the National Museum have been used to furnish the house, and the exquisite pieces of furniture in several rooms demonstrate the high quality of Irish cabinet-making in the 18th century.

In **Newman House**, which faces St Stephen's Green, you can see some of the most perfectly conserved Georgian rooms in the city. Dublin's Catholic University was founded here by Cardinal Newman and, fittingly, the houses are now owned by University College, Dublin. A tour includes an explanation of the painstaking restoration work and a chance to see some fine 18th-century interiors, including a classroom which shows the kind of room that the writer James Joyce might have used when he was a student here at the end of the 19th century.

Scallop-edged Irish saltcellar, c.1800

● **Number 29**, 29 Lower Fitzwilliam St.
Tel: (01) 702 6165.
● **Newman House**, 85–86 St Stephen's Green.
Tel: (01) 706 7422. Open June–Aug only.

IRISH GLASS AND DELFTWARE

Glass development in England was hampered by the the 1745 Excise Act. The direct result of this was the production of thinner glass, which was cheaper but unsuitable for cutting. As a result the cut glass industry became established in Ireland, where the Excise Act did not apply, making it easier to produce quality cut glass. Both English and Irish craftsmen were employed in the industry and the style of glass that developed became known as Anglo-Irish.

The popularity of the distinctive blue and white tin-glazed earthenware emerging from Holland, especially Delft (see page 142) led to the establishment of a number of new centres producing their own, similar pieces. Dublin was one of these. The prime name in Dublin delftware was Henry Delamain, who bought the delft factory in Dublin in 1752 and devoted himself to building up the works. The quality was extremely high, and the factory continued for nearly 20 years after his death in 1757.

Keep an eye out for puzzle jugs, bleeding bowls, apothecaries' pill slabs and other unusual items. The extemely rare earlier designs are admired for their delicacy and simple forms, and prices can often be higher than for Dutch Delft.

Irish inlaid Georgian marble fireplace, c.1790, by Peter Bossi

PLACES TO VISIT

For all aspects of the decorative arts, visit the **National Museum of Ireland, Collins Barracks**. The Barracks, begun in 1700, are the oldest military barracks in Europe and now house an eclectic collection which ranges from fine Irish silver to the gauntlets worn by William III at the Battle of the Boyne, from an exhibition of ceramics to a lifebelt salvaged from the *Lusitania*, and from 18th-century chairs to early scientific instruments.

Dublin's original **National Museum**, on Kildare Street, is home to the Ór – "Ireland's Gold" – one of the best collections of Bronze Age jewellery in western Europe. The exhibition includes the Tara Brooch – a large disc of white bronze, chased with an intricate Celtic design, and which dates from the 8th century. There are also exhibitions on Viking and prehistoric Ireland and the Road to Independence.

The Tara Brooch, part of Ireland's Ór

Every major European school of painting is represented in the **National Gallery**, but it is worth visiting in particular for its collection of works by Irish artists. An entire room is devoted to the paintings of Jack Yeats (1871–1957), brother of the poet W.B. Yeats.

At **The Chester Beatty Library** are rare books, priceless manuscripts and paintings from Middle and Far Eastern cultures.

At **Temple Bar** you will find the National Photographic Archive, the Irish Film Centre and Irish Film Archive, The Ark, which is a cultural centre for children, and other attractions which include various concerts and screenings.

● **National Museum, Collins Barracks**, Benburb St, and original **National Museum**, Kildare St. Tel: (01) 677 7444.
● **National Gallery**: Merrion Square West. Tel: (01) 661 5133. Guided weekend tours.
● **Chester Beatty Library**, Dublin Castle. Tel: (01) 407 0750. Closed Mon Oct–Apr.
● **Temple Bar**, Meeting House Square. Tel: (01) 671 5717 for Temple Bar Culture Line.

National Museum of Ireland, Collins Barracks

LITERARY DUBLIN

Dublin has connection with many notable literary figures, although some deserted their native city. The political playwright George Bernard Shaw, famous for rejecting the Nobel Prize for Literature in 1925, was born in Dublin in 1856 but left at the age of 20, and Samuel Beckett, winner of the Nobel Prize for Literature in 1969, forsook Ireland for France in the 1930s. Oscar Wilde also ended his days in France, but in Merrion Square you can see where he lived as a child. Also in the square are the former homes of other literary residents such as the poet and dramatist who co-founded Dublin's Abbey Theatre, W.B. Yeats, and horror-storyteller Joseph Le Fanu. The creator of Dracula, Bram Stoker, was also born in Dublin.

James Joyce spent little of his adult life in Dublin but drew on the city of his birth for his books, especially for Ulysses, peopled with real-life Dubliners. Jonathan Swift, author of *Gulliver's Travels*, spent his childhood in Dublin. In 1713 he became dean of St Patrick's Cathedral, where he is buried.

● **James Joyce Cultural Centre**, 35 North Great George's St. Tel: (01) 878 8547. Organizes walking tours of Joyce's Dublin.
● **Dublin Writers Museum**, 18–19 Parnell Square North. Tel: (01) 872 2077.

Irish playwright Oscar Wilde (1854–1900)

DUBLIN SILVER

In 1807 Dublin was made one of the assay centres for silver which, until then, had to be sent to London for assaying – a time-consuming and expensive undertaking. The Dublin hallmark is the Irish harp surmounted by the English crown. You can see gold and silversmiths at work at the Powerscourt Townhouse.

SHOPPING

Edward Butler's antiques shop

From the early 1700s the landed gentry built beautiful country houses and furnished them in a grand style. In Dublin you will find a sophisticated selection of the very best in Irish antiques.

FRANCIS STREET

Running from just west of St Patrick's Cathedral north towards the Liffey River, Francis Street and the alleys that run off it are great places for antiques hunting.

Look out for:
Fleury Antiques (57 Francis St) stocks 18th- and 19th-century furniture, decorative objects, sculptures, paintings, silver and porcelain. **Kevin Jones Antiques**, just up the road at Nos 65–66, has paintings, *objets d'art*, and 18th- and 19th-century furniture in stock. You'll also find **Roxane Moorhead Antiques** here, with chandeliers a speciality.

At Nos 43–44 **O'Sullivan Antiques** sells 18th- and 19th-century furniture, paintings, mirrors and mantelpieces.

Odeon (69–71 Francis St) is the only one of its kind in Dublin: a great Art Deco shop.

Mid 19th-century Irish marquetry davenport in cedar and Killarney yew

Zoetrope (c.1872)

AROUND GRAFTON STREET

The many small streets around pedestrian Grafton Street are full of antiques dealers and interesting small shops.

Look out for:
Powerscourt Townhouse Centre (entrance off South William St or Johnson Court Alley) is in the late 18th-century town house of the eminent Viscount Powerscourt. Among its myriad small craft and antiques shops is **The Silver Shop**, which has a wide-ranging collection of both antique and modern silver. You will also find fine quality antique jewellery, silver, paintings and decorative items at **Courtville Antiques. Anthony Antiques** (7, 8 & 9 Molesworth St) offers decorative antique furniture, mirrors, brass, chandeliers and paintings.

H. Danker (10 South Anne St) has high-quality silver, jewellery, *objets d'art* and paintings. **J.W. Weldon** (55 Clarendon St) stocks jewellery, as well as antique and provincial Irish silver.

OTHER HUNTING GROUNDS

Edward Butler's shop (at 14 Bachelor's Walk, near O'Connell Bridge) sells 18th- and 19th-century furniture, paintings and clocks, as well as a variety of nautical and other scientific instruments. **Timepiece Antiques** (57–58 Patrick St) specializes in Irish and French clocks from the early 18th to the early 20th century.

At **Architechtural Classics** (5a South Gloucester St), you will find a diverse stock including garden ornaments, fireplaces, ironwork and brass fixtures and fittings.

TEMPLE BAR

From the riverside of the Liffey, the narrow Merchants' Arch opposite Ha'penny Bridge will bring you out into the bustling Temple Bar area, with its array of bars and galleries. In the 1960s artists settled in this area just south of the Liffey, drawn to the area by cheap

---

SHOPPER'S TIP
When you cannot walk another step, head for St Stephen's Green, just south of the National Museum. With its expanses of lawn and large lake, this is a great place to relax while you admire the Georgian and Victorian buildings that surround you. It was one of the ancient commons and was enclosed in 1664. Lunchtime open-air concerts are held here during the summer.

No trip to Dublin would be complete without a taste of Guinness. Where better to learn its history (and have a pint) than the place where it all started? At the **Guinness Experience** in the St James Gate Brewery, which Arthur Guinness bought in 1759, you can discover how Ireland's distinctive beer is made.

If he can say as you can
Guinness is good for you
How grand to be a Toucan
Just think what Toucan do

● **Guinness Experience**, Market St. Tel: (01) 408 4800.

The Odeon, specializing in Art Deco

rents and short-term leases. Today the streets are pedestrianized and Temple Bar has a wonderful bohemian atmosphere. Shops and stalls spill out over the cobbled streets, and its galleries and craft shops offer a huge range of individual arts.

Meeting House Square is a great place to sit outside in the summer and listen to classical concerts and watch a free film or two (just collect a ticket from the Information Centre).
● **Temple Bar Information Centre**, 18 Eustace St. (Tel: (01) 671 5717).

FAIRS AND MARKETS
For five days at the end of September each year, the Royal Dublin Society in Ballsbridge hosts the **Irish Antique Dealers' Fair**; all participants belong to the Irish Antique Dealers' Assocation. Tel: (01) 285 9294 for more information.

AUCTION HOUSES
James Adam, 26 St Stephen's Green. Tel: (01) 676 0261.
Whyte's, 30 Marlborough Street. Tel : (01) 874 6161.

WHERE TO EAT AND DRINK
Le Coq Hardi
35 Pembroke Road, Ballsbridge
Tel: (01) 668 9070
Situated in a Georgian house, this restaurant is famous for John Howard's Coq Hardi chicken; reservations are essential.

Beaufield Mews Restaurant
Woodlands Aven, Stillorgan
Tel: (01) 288 0375
A great combination of restaurant and antiques shop that really works.

No visit to Dublin would be complete without a trip around some of the best pubs, which include:

The Brazen Head, Bridge St Lower
O'Donoghue's, Merrion Row
O'Neill's, Suffolk St
Oliver St John Gogarty, Fleet St
Slattery's, Capel St
The Stag's Head, Dame Ct
Toners, Baggot St

WHERE TO STAY
Shelbourne Hotel
27 St Stephen's Green
Tel:(01) 676 6471; Fax: (01) 661 6006
One of the grandest hotels in Dublin, with an old-fashioned elegant charm. The Edwardian tea rooms serve proper tea in the afternoons.

Ariel Guest House
52 Lansdown Road, Ballsbridge
Tel: (01) 668 5512; Fax: (01) 668 5845
Ask for a room in the main Victorian house for an antiques-filled, comfortable place to rest your head. Michael O'Brian serves a good Irish breakfast. Lansdown Road station is nearby.

Merrion Hotel
Upper Merrion Street
Tel: (01) 603 0600; Fax: (01) 603 0700
A luxury hotel with pool, gym, steam and beauty treatment rooms, as well as two wonderful restaurants, within a terrace of four restored Georgian houses.

Entrance to the Shelbourne Hotel

On the coast just north-east of the city sits **Malahide Castle**, looking much more like a traditional castle than Dublin's own. It was home to the Talbot family for nearly 800 years and contains a huge collection of Irish portraits. In the magnificent grounds is the Fry Model Railway, one of the largest in the world.

Not far away is **Newbridge** (you can buy joint tickets for the two houses), a demesne or manor house in the finest tradition of Irish Georgian architecture. Built in 1737, it has been beautifully preserved, from the exquisite interior plasterwork to the blacksmith's forge and the dairy in the restored courtyard.

FRANCE

THE ANTIQUES
LANDSCAPE

I don't need antiques-hunting as an excuse to visit France — the food and wine, the countryside and the châteaux are reason enough. Yet these attractions are intimately tied to what fills the shop windows of antiquaires and the stalls of brocante fairs all over the country; with such an appreciation of the table the French have also produced wonderful porcelain and glassware to set it off. French monarchs and the aristocracy share a history of being great patrons of the arts and, Louis XIV, Louis XV and Louis XVI in particular took a very personal interest in the porcelain factories in Vincennes and Sèvres, and also at Saint-Cloud, Chantilly and Limoges. Faience pottery factories produced highly individual provincial styles, from the rustic Rococo of Quimper to Strasbourg's bright enamel colours and the delicate florals of Marseille.

Opaline glass was an appropriate material for delicate pieces such as this egg, made c.1860, suspended in an ormolu mount.

Pottery and porcelain, along with other tableware, silver, linens and household goods, are all found in such quantity partly because of the French laws of inheritance. In France all children inherit equally so, over the generations, large houses and their contents proliferated, each needing to be supplied with everything from batteries de cuisine to beds. Some of these may be the work of famous manufacturers — a commode by François Linke, a Jacob Petit teapot, a Clichy paperweight — while the appeal of other items may be in their evocation of the past.

In the late 19th century French clockmakers began mass production on a large scale and in markets you can still come across 100-year-old carriage- and mantel-clocks at very reasonable prices. Many of the cheap movements no longer work and would probably not be worth restoring, but if you like the look of a particular clock and it is inexpensive, there's no reason why you shouldn't buy it for its ornamental value rather than for its time-keeping is there?

I have a special weakness for antique fabrics, and France has a rich legacy of textile manufacturing – just think of Gobelins tapestries, Aubusson rugs, Lyon silk and toile de Jouy. I once bought, for a song, a very pretty piece of 18th-century toile that I had noticed being used as a table cover in a bric-a-brac shop in La Gironde. Passementerie, the braiding and tassles that finish off upholstery and curtains, is also a good find, as are 18th- and 19th-century dresses and waistcoats, lace and accessories such as parasols and beaded bags. Retro clothing – la fripe – is big business in Paris, particularly around the Passy district, and designer labels crop up surprisingly often among second-hand clothing. The same is true of costume jewellery, even by such well-known names as Coco Chanel and Christian Dior.

The puces (flea markets) that ring Paris, particularly Les Puces de St-Ouen, and the array of dealers in Provence's L'isle sur la Sorgue are hugely popular. Large antiques markets are a feature of many other French towns. Lille, Amiens and Strasbourg are all famous for theirs, and Orléans and La Rochelle on the Atlantic coast are great hunting grounds. Wherever you are, a newsagent will be able to sell you a brochure or booklet on local markets and antiques fairs – foires à brocantes. This is how I have come across unexpected finds from Cherbourg in the far north to Bages, near Perpignan, in the lee of the Pyrenees.

This French wooden cherub with finely modelled wings and hair and naturalistic facial features dates from the late 17th century.

PARIS

Paris is a mix of distinctive districts. With lively markets as well as wonderful shops, there's always something to find.

Chinnard's La République, *Musée Carnavalet*

PARIS IS A VOGUISH CITY, AND HAS SET many important trends. Its style has been hugely influential, from Louis XIV's Versailles and Napoleon III's Second Empire to Art Nouveau and the Avant-Garde. It is home to Lalique, Baccarat, Sèvres and Gobelins, world famous names in glass, porcelain and tapestry.

Every area of Paris is distinct, and has its own particular character – from the glittering showrooms in rue de Rivoli and the Palais-Royale to the antiquarian bookshops of the Left Bank and the charming little boutiques of the Marais. The street markets, too, are always exciting, and there are many to choose from. Best of all, of course, is St-Ouen flea market in the north of Paris, at Porte de Clignancourt. This is the biggest antiques market in France, where collectors from far and wide come in the certain knowledge that they will find something to interest them among the millions of items on offer.

There are an infinite number of sights to see while staying in Paris, and it would be impossible to cover them all. Top of any list should be a trip to Versailles, an afternoon in Jardin du Luxembourg or a coffee in the Café de Flore. Beyond that you will have to decide what you most want to see. For a good introduction to Paris, head for the Musée Carnavalet (see page 82), which is devoted to the city's history.

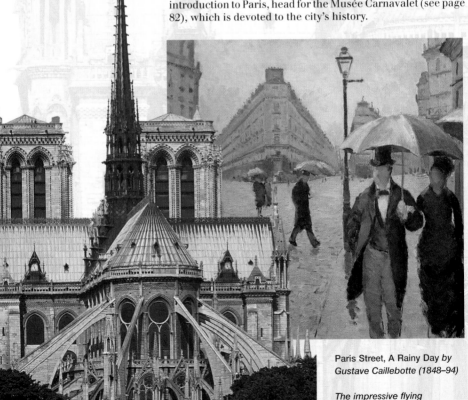

Paris Street, A Rainy Day *by Gustave Caillebotte (1848–94)*

The impressive flying buttresses of Notre-Dame, built between 1163 and 1250

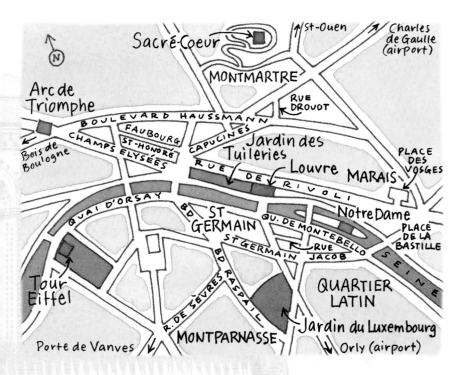

QUICK GUIDE TO ANTIQUES

● **Louvre and Opéra** The royal Right Bank in the 1st *arrondissement* has the best antiques shops in Paris. Head for the streets around the Louvre and Palais-Royal. The major auction houses are here, too, around rue Drouot.

● **St-Germain and the Left Bank** The 5th and 6th *arrondissements* have everything from exclusive art galleries to bric-a-brac. The best places can be found around La Carré Rive Gauche, boulevard St-Germain, rue St-Paul and in the Village Suisse.

● **Le Marais** The 4th *arrondissement* is one of the most pleasant places to shop, with lovely boutiques and specialist shops. Wander along rue des Francs-Bourgeois, and look into the little courtyards of Village St-Paul.

● **Montmartre** Visit the 18th *arrondissement* to get to the heart of the arts in the city.

● **La Bastille and the north-east** The 11th, 12th and 13th *arrondissements* have a number of places to visit, including the arches of the Viaduc des Arts.

Souvenir scarf from the 1950s, showing details of the telephone exchange

AUCTION HOUSES

La Gazette de l'Hôtel Drouot is a weekly magazine which gives details of auctions not just in Paris, but in all France.

Hôtel de Drouot, 9 rue du Drouot. Tel: (01) 48 00 20 20. Paris's premier auctioneers.

Christie's, 9 avenue Matigon. Tel: (01) 40 76 85 85.

Sotheby's, 76 rue de Faubourg-St-Honoré. Tel: (01) 53 05 53 05.

Crédit Municipal, 55 rue des Francs-Bourgeois. Tel: (01) 44 61 64 00.

Head of cherub carved from wood and painted, 1680

ANTIQUES FAIRS

Biennale des Antiquaires: September antiques extravaganza around the Carrousel du Louvre.

Les Quatre Jours de Quartier Drouot: Open days, around rue Drouot, in October.

Foire Internationale à la Brocante et de Jambons: Bric-a-brac and ham fair, Ile de Chatou, in March and the autumn.

Le Salon des Antiquaires: Monthly shows organized in various venues around Paris. For more details contact Pro-Evénements at 78 rue d'Auteuil. Tel: (01) 40 71 90 22.

LOUVRE & OPERA

The Right Bank, *Rive Droite*, is the centre of royal and administrative Paris, where the palaces of the Louvre and Tuileries set the pace for elegant shopping. It is also home to some of the best restaurants in town.

Simple and stylish design for a 1920s Lalique perfume bottle

Antiques shop in Quartier Drouot, home to France's major auction houses

The Right Bank is royal Paris, typified by the Palais-Royal and the Tuileries gardens, as well as the **Musée du Louvre**, where the kings of France lived for some 400 years. A museum since 1793, the Louvre houses the royal art collection started by François I (1515–47) with Leonardo da Vinci's *Mona Lisa* and other Italian works, and later augmented by Napoleon's plunder in various cities of Europe. You can pick up a floorplan on arrival in the reception area beneath the 1989 glass pyramid in place du Carrousel.

I often head for the *objets d'art* galleries in the Richelieu and Sully Wings, where there is a rich collection of Limoges enamels, silver, jewellery, glassware, early clocks and French furniture from the 16th to the 19th century.

On the same side as the Richelieu Wing are three other museums: the **Musée des Arts Décoratifs** (due for completion in 2002), **Musée de la Publicité** and **Musée des**

Arts de la Mode et du Textile, which have been undergoing fundamental rearrangement as part of the Grand Louvre project. The decorative arts museum is magnificent, by far the best place to go to see French styles of furniture and decoration, from Louis XIV, XV and XVI through Empire to Art Nouveau and Art Deco periods. The fashion museum has both historic and international collections, and the publicity museum has advertising posters from 1700 to 1945.

One of the city's most radiant museums is the **Musée de l'Orangerie**. Naturally lit, it has 20th-century paintings by Pierre Auguste Renoir, Pablo Picasso, Henri Matisse and Amedeo Modigliani. Pride of place goes to Claude Monet's waterlily series, painted specially for the Orangerie's oval rooms.

The **Musée Jacquemart-André** is the former home of an officer of the Imperial Guards, Edouard André, and his wife Nélie Jacquemart, who lived here at the end of the 19th century. Now owned by the Institut de France, the museum still houses the couple's unique art collection which includes works from the Italian Renaissance and the French 18th-century school, as well as fine tapestries, furniture and manuscripts.

At the recently renovated **Musée Guimet** you can see an outstanding collection of Oriental and Asian art with fine examples of statuary (particularly figures of Buddha) from Japan, Indonesia and Vietnam.

● **Musée du Louvre**
Tel:(01) 40 20 51 51.

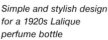

Galerie Colbert, covered passages named after Louis XIV's minister

TRY NOT TO MISS...

Lalique and Baccarat are famous for the glass and crystalware they have produced for decades. They are still in business: **Lalique**, a top name in Art Nouveau and Art Deco, is at 11 rue Royale, and **Baccarat**, the largest French producer of cut-glass tableware, is at 11 place de la Madeleine. It also has a museum (see page 85).

● **Musée des Arts Décoratifs, Musée de la Publicité / Musée des Arts de la Mode et du Textile**, Palais du Louvre. Tel: (01) 44 55 57 50. Closed Mon.
● **Musée de l'Orangerie**, Jardin des Tuileries, pl. de la Concorde. Tel: (01) 42 97 48 16.
● **Musée Jacquemart-Andre**, 158 bd Haussman. Tel: (01) 42 89 04 91.
● **Musée Guimet**, pl. d'Iéna. Tel: (01) 47 23 61 65. Closed Tues.

Illumination from The Hours of Maréchal *by Jean de Boucicant in Musée Jacquemart-André*

SHOPPING

From the Palais-Royal to the rue de Drouot, you should be able to find just about everything, from a Baccarat *presse papier* (paperweight) or a Christofle silver salver to a Romanesque Limoges crucifix or a Louix XV commode.

The area around the Louvre and Palais-Royal is the place to look for quality antiques. An old department store (2 place du Palais-Royal) is now **Louvre des Antiquaires**, with 250 upmarket antiques shops. Here you will find Art Nouveau and Art Deco items as well as watches, jewellery, *objets d'art* and Napoleon III furniture.

Rue Faubourg-St-Honoré is a shopping centre, with glass-roofed arcades such as Galerie Royale and Passage Royale. Here you will find fashion houses and jewellers. Big names include Pierre Cardin (No 59) and Christian Lacroix (No 73).

Antiques shops in arcades around the Palais-Royale specialize in stamps but there are also musical boxes, walking sticks and period clothes.

North from place de la Madeleine is boulevard Malesherbes – rich in antiques – and boulevard Haussmann, which runs east past the Opéra Garnier along to boulevard Montmartre and has shops such as **Soustiel**, specializing in Islamic and Oriental art.

Just north of here, between rue de Faubourg Montmartre and rue la Fayette, is rue Drouot, where you can find France's leading auctioneers, **Hôtel de Drouot**. They have been here since 1858, although the current aluminium-and-marble building dates from the 1980s. Its 16 sale rooms can turn up the most surprising items.

Ceramics and porcelain can be found at **Rieunier and Bailly-Pommery** (25 rue Peletier). For fine art, head to **Calmels Chambre Cohen** (12 rue Rossini). Good sources of Art Deco are **J. M. Le Mouel** (22 rue Chauchat) and **Millon** (18 rue de la Grange-Batalière).

Several antiques shops line three passages that lead off the rue de la Grange-Batalier, including **Ciné Doc**'s cinema finds.

Sèvres butter dish, cover and stand painted with flower sprays c.1760

THE LOUIS STYLES

LOUIS XIV, XV, XVI

The three most important eras of furniture-making fell under the 14th, 15th and 16th Bourbon kings named Louis. **Louis Quatorze** (1643–1715), the Sun King and builder of Versailles, used furniture and decorative arts to glorify his reign. Much of the furniture was the work of André-Charles Boulle, who was appointed royal cabinet-maker in 1672. Typical pieces reflect his passion for exotic woods and a widely acclaimed skill in marquetry. **Louis Quinze** (1715–74) and his mistress Madame de Pompadour triumphed French Rococo. Chairs became more comfortable and more elegant, with twisting carved foliage and serpentine curves characteristic of the style. **Louis Seize** (1774–92), beheaded during the French Revolution, was less frivolous, and looked more to classical roots. Table and chair legs were straightened, and a high point in cabinet-making was reached, thanks in part to German craftsmen. All three styles were revived during the 19th century.

Louis XIV ormolu-mounted commode, attributed to André-Charles Boulle

Louis XVI-style beech painted chair, c.1780

ST GERMAIN AND THE LEFT BANK

The intellectual Latin Quarter of Paris lies on the left bank of the River Seine. Around the famous cafés of boulevard St Germain are scores of antiques shops, galleries and antiquarian dens.

Musée d'Orsay, Paris's great art museum, is housed in a Belle Epoque railway terminus

This traditional arty quarter of Paris is not the avant-garde, bohemian place it once was but continues to be a firm favourite. First-time visitors to the city, having visited the Louvre

and the cathedral of Notre-Dame on the Ile de La Cité, are bound to head over a bridge to boulevards Saint-Michel and Saint-Germain. This is where 20th-century intellectuals such as Albert Camus and Jean-Paul Sartre grappled with theories of existentialism at Les Deux Magots and the Art Deco Café de Flore (Nos 170 and 172), while the world's literati gathered at Shakespeare and Co. (37 rue de la Bûcherie), a wonderful old bookshop that still attracts visitors from far corners of the world.

Locket pendant, c.1890. Pearl and enamel decoration on gold

PLACES TO VISIT

Most of what is best about the Latin Quarter is out on the streets, in the boulevards and in the cafés and bars. There are, however, two outstanding museums in this part of the city: the **Musée d'Orsay** and the **Musée National du Moyen-Age**.

The Musée d'Orsay was built as a railway terminus in 1900 and converted into a museum in the 1980s. If you visit only one art gallery in Paris, this should be it, because it captures the essence of the city's artistic endeavour between 1848 and 1914, with works by Edouard

---

ART NOUVEAU PIECES

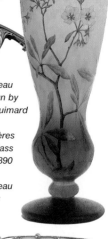

THE NEW ART OF THE BELLE EPOQUE

Although Art Nouveau was a Europe-wide movement of the late 1800s and early 1900s, especially in Brussels (see page 127), and influenced Tiffany in the US, it is associated in people's minds with France, because of the many famous designers who worked in this style. Art Nouveau coincided with France's own Belle Epoque. In Paris it lives on in the 86 Metro entrances designed by **Hector Guimard** (1867–1942). Some great exponents made high-priced furniture, jewellery and curios. There were also the glass-makers **René Lalique** (1860–1945) and **Emile Gallé** (1846–1904). The finest Art Nouveau façade in the city is at 29 avenue Rapp, near the Champ de Mars, where **Jules Lavirotte** went into flights of erotic fantasy in 1901. Prime examples of French Art Nouveau are at the Musée des Arts Décoratifs (see page 78) and the Musée d'Orsay (above).

Art Nouveau Metro sign by Hector Guimard

Daum Frères cameo glass vase, c.1890

Art Nouveau dragonfly brooch, 1905

Manet, Edgar Degas and Vincent Van Gogh among its collection. There are also paintings by Delacroix, whose nearby house and studio have become the **Musée Eugène Delacroix**. He lived here from 1857 until his death in 1863, and there is a permanent exhibition dedicated to both his life and work.

The Musée National du Moyen-Age is reputedly the best medieval museum in Europe, with a collection that includes sculptures, illuminated manuscripts, Limoges enamels and ivories. It is housed in a building designed in 1500 as the city residence for the Abbots of Cluny, who were originally from Burgundy. The gardens are a delight and, if you see nothing else here, visit the room with the wonderful tapestries of the Lady with the Unicorn. An apogee of *millefleurs* style, it is one of the most impressive artworks from the Renaissance.

This area stretches west to take in the Village Suisse near **La Tour Eiffel**, the city's best known landmark, where on a clear day you can see for 70km (45 miles) from the viewing gallery 274m (840ft) high.

- **Musée d'Orsay**, 1 rue de Bellechasse. Tel: (01) 40 49 48 14. Closed Mon.
- **Musée National du Moyen-Age – Thermes de Cluny**, 6 pl. Paul-Painlevé. Tel: (01) 53 73 78 00. Closed Tues.
- **Musée Eugène-Delacroix**, 6 rue de Furstenberg. Tel: (01) 44 41 86 50. Closed Tues.
- **La Tour Eiffel**, Champ de Mars. Tel (01) 44 11 23 45.

SHOPPING

Antiques shops cluster around the Left Bank. Le **Carré Rive Gauche** is an area of galleries, shops and dealers and spreads from the river down to rue de l'Université.

A starting point might be Quai Voltaire. There are around 30 dealers here, including the primitive art and Middle Ages specialists **Guy Ladrière** (No 11) and **Bresset et Fils** (No 5), who deal in works from the Middle Ages, Renaissance and the 17th century, and many

Baccarat "flaconde chemise", c.1840 (top); Lalique Pour Homme perfume bottle (limited Millennium edition); Gallé wheel-engraved cameo vase, c.1920 (bottom)

more in the surrounding streets leading down to rue de la Université and rue Jacob. **Sylvain Lévy-Alban** (No 14 rue de Beaune) has a wide choice of 18th-century furniture. There are almost as many dealers in rue de Bac, including the famous modern art gallery, **Galerie Maeght** (No 42). **Boîte à Musique** (No 96) is the place to go for old musical instruments. You should also take a stroll down rue de Lille, running beside the Musée d'Orsay, and rue de Verneuil, as they are also well endowed with antiques and bric-a-brac shops.

Saint-Germain, the magnificent boulevard of the Left Bank, lies just to the south. There are more than 20 antiques shops in this chic road and a number of streets leading off it also make fruitful hunting grounds. Rue de Seine, rue Bonaparte and, running between them, rue des Beaux-Arts, have a clutch of galleries. On the south side are antique and antiquarian book shops in rue Tournon and boulevard Raspail, such as **Librairie Gallimard** (15 boulevard Raspail) and **Librairie Janus les Enfants Terribles** (220 boulevard Raspail). In rue des Saints-Pères, there's a concentration of some 30 dealers. Many share the same premises, such as **Michel Lalay** (No 2), who specializes in furniture from the 1930s to the 1950s. He shares a unit with **Cabinet d'Amateur**.

Rue des Saints-Pères leads you into rue Sèvres, where you can find **La Galerie des Antiquaires du Bon Marché**, at No 38, a two-storey building that houses 38 antiques dealers. They are open Monday to Saturday, from 9.30am to 7pm.

One of the greatest areas for antiques shops on the Left Bank is in avenue de Suffren, running parallel to the Parc de Champ de Mars, which has La Tour Eiffel at one end and l'Ecole Militaire at the other. On the corner by the Military Academy is the **Village Suisse** (No 78). Around 150 antiques specialists are open from Thursday to Monday, 11am to 7pm. **Maxime Fustier** (76–76 bis Grand Place) specializes in Empire furniture, **Maud et Réné Garcia** (Galerie 66) sell primitive art and **A. Bozon** (57 place de Lucerne) has a selection of 19th-century prints.

SHOPPER'S TIP

A lively time to visit Left Bank antiques shops is when the dealers in Carré Rive Gauche put on **Les Cinq Jours de l'Objet Extraordinaire**. During these five days in May they take a particular theme to show special items. The shops are open on the Sunday, and a variety of events are organized in the evenings.

19th-century silver Neo-classical dish and liner, marked Bointaburet à Paris

LE MARAIS

Le Marais, one of the most popular areas for shopping in Paris, is rich in grand houses and quaint with small streets of smart shops and cafés. For antiques, the courtyards and streets of Village Saint-Paul are among the most evocative in the city.

Place des Vosges, the regal square at the centre of Le Marais, built for Henri IV in 1605

This is the part of Paris that I like the most. Lying between the Hôtel du Ville (the city hall) and the place de la Bastille, Le Marais is a wonderful mix of pretty, small streets bustling with little boutiques, galleries, cafés and *hôtels particuliers* – grand mansions that, in pre-revolutionary France, were home to the aristocracy. Today Le Marais is also the centre of a thriving Jewish community, around rue des Ecouffes and rue des Rosiers, where Le Loir Dans la Théière is just one of the *salons du thé* which give Le Marais its unique atmosphere.

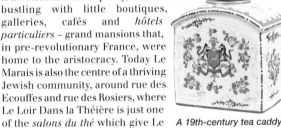

A 19th-century tea caddy, decorated with a coat of arms, by Samson of Paris

Marais means "marsh", and that is just about all that was here until 1605 when Henri IV began building the place des Vosges, a symmetrical colonnaded square that remains at the heart of the district. The celebrated hostess and writer Madame de Sévigné was born here in 1626, and from 1832 to 1848 Victor Hugo lived at No 6, where he wrote *Les Misérables*. The aristocratic houses, which were built soon afterwards, survive mostly to the west of this square.

PLACES TO VISIT

The **Musée Carnavalet** traces the history of Paris, and has wonderful interiors and furnishings from all over the city. The Hôtel Carnavalet was built in 1564 by Nicolas Dupuis and the adjoining Hôtel le Peletier de St-Fargeau was built a century later. Mirrors, panelling and ceilings have been transported here from other town mansions to re-create, among others, the 1761 reception room of the Montmartre Hôtel d'Uzès, the Blue Room of Louis XV, and an entire Art Nouveau shop – the Fouquet Jewellery Boutique from Royale – by Alphonse Mucha.

The **Musée Cognacq-Jay** is a small but superb collection of 18th-century furniture and decor in the Hôtel de Donon, dating from 1575.

Hôtel Libéral Bruand was designed by its eponymous resident, also the architect of Les Invalides, and it now houses **Musée Bricard**, a wonderful collection of door furniture from all ages.

Last, though not least, is the **Musée Picasso** in the 1656 Hôtel de Salé, once owned by a salt tax collector. Along with the Museu Picasso in Barcelona (see page 216), this is one of the world's best museums dedicated to Pablo Picasso's work and has paintings, ceramics and sculpture from his long life.

Small provincial Louis XV fruitwood secrétaire, c.1760

TRY NOT TO MISS...

The oldest surviving houses in Paris are in Le Marais. Hôtel de Sens, a turreted, Gothic fantasy at 1 rue de Figuier, is one of the few medieval buildings in Paris but the north side of the district, off the rue de Temple and once the fief of the Knights Templar, has buildings that claim to be older. At 3 rue Volta the Anahi restaurant is in a building that dates from the 16th century, and at 51 rue de Montmorency is the Auberge Nicolas Flamel, which was built in 1407 and is now a bistro.

• **Musée Carnavalet** and **Hôtel le Peletier de St-Fargeau**, 23 rue de Sévigné.
Tel: (01) 44 59 58 58.
• **Musée Cognacq-Jay**, 8 rue Elzévir.
Tel: (01) 40 27 07 21.
• **Musée Bricard**, 1 rue de la Perle.
Tel: (01) 42 77 79 62.
• **Musée Picasso**, 5 rue de Thorigny.
Tel: (01) 42 71 25 21.

SHOPPING

Le Marais is a great place to browse and shop, with fashionable boutiques and specialist shops selling novel and interesting items for the home. The main street of Le Marais, leading into place des Vosges, is rue des Francs-Bourgeois. For smaller antique items, head to **Objet** (No 9) and, for silver pieces go to **Argenterie des Francs** (No 17). Place des Vosges itself has a handful of antiques shops nestling among its arcades.

Bisecting rue des Francs-Bourgeois is rue de Sévigné where there are a couple of antiques shops, including **Licorne** (No 38), a treasure trove of sparkling costume jewellery. Rue Vieille de Temple also cuts across rue des Francs-Bourgeois, and here you will find a dozen galleries and antiques shops in which to browse.

The rue des Rosiers (so called after the rosebushes within the old city wall), lies at the heart of the colourful Jewish quarter. Recharge yourself with a delicious snack from one of the bakeries or delicatessens in the area.

The biggest antiques attraction in Le Marais is between place des Vosges and the river, in rue Saint-Paul where the **Village Saint-Paul** (No 17) is home to more than 40 shops and galleries, open from Thursday to Monday. The "village" takes in small side streets and

A shop in the Jewish quarter, one of the most distinctive parts of Le Marais

Vincennes bleu celeste seau à liqueur, 1754

courtyards of the pleasant residential area lying between rue Saint-Paul and rue Charlemagne, to the west.

At cours St-Paul, don't miss **Claude et Lina Sélect** if you are a fan of Japanese antiques. Here you will also find **Stéphane Olivier**, who has a selection of gardening tools and outdoor ornaments, and **Romaric et les Souvenirs de Gabriel**, which stocks beautiful 19th-century puppets. **Nicole Mallet** is the place to go for wooden sculpture and furniture from the 18th century. On rue St-Paul, **Jacqueline Forlarni** (No 7) specializes in 17th- and 18th-century furniture and **Marlie Antiquités** (No 27) sells a wide range of ceramics and *objets d'art*.

CLOCKS

UNE TRADITION HOROLOGIQUE

France has a long tradition of clock-making, and many timepieces from the past 200 years are still in circulation. The mass production of clocks was pioneered in France by the company Japy Frères (founded in 1772, and in operation until the early 20th century). This was one of the largest French clock-making firms, specializing in decorative carriage clocks, an area of clock-making in which France excelled. Richly decorated, the most desirable carriage clocks today have enamel or porcelain panels, with *grande sonnerie* striking. French carriage clocks usually have a mark, as well as a serial number. Most French carriage clocks originally came in a leather carrying case.

Swiss-born Abraham-Louis Breguet (1747–1823) was one of the greatest watchmakers of all time, credited with having designed the first carriage clock. He founded his company in Paris, and it continued to make clocks and watches well into the 20th century.

A French ormolu mantel clock, c.1875, by Japy Frères, pioneers of mass production clocks

THE HILL OF MONTMARTRE

The high point of the city used to be a small village of windmills. Discovered by turn-of-the-century artists, the area became a cultural centre and remains a popular tourist attraction today.

A poster of the Moulin Rouge, early 1900s

The city's famous art district on La Butte, a hill on the north side of town and topped by the white 19th-century church of Sacré Coeur, may have lost its reputation as being at the cutting edge of artistic expression, but it maintains a village atmosphere. The pleasure here is in the lanes and small squares, such as place des Abbesses and the touristy place du Tertre, the highest square in the city which is lined with cafés and dates back to the end of the 18th century.

Montmartre's tradition for the risqué continues in place Pigalle and at the Moulin Rouge, which opened as a dance hall in 1900, giving Henri de Toulouse-Lautrec endless subjects to paint. The can-can is still performed nightly, although feathers, sequins and rhinestones are now the chorus girls' minimal requirements. Another dance hall is Moulin de la Galette, where Auguste Renoir and Vincent Van Gogh had rooms. Now a restaurant, it is one of two remaining windmills out of more than 30 that once turned on La Butte.

Hand blown green glass flacon with gold decoration, c.1860

Bateau-Lavoir, in place Emile Goudeau, is the famous residence and workshop of artists such as Pablo Picasso, Juan Gris and Amedeo Modigliani. It burned down in 1971, but a replica has replaced it, and it still has studio space to let.

The dominant dome of Sacré Coeur

PLACES TO VISIT

For a flavour of this colourful area, visit **Musée de Montmartre**, housed in a 17th-century mansion. Maurice Utrillo, Raoul Dufy and Pierre-Auguste Renoir had studios here. Original Toulouse-Lautrec posters and Modigliani paintings and Clignancourt porcelain are on display. **Espace Montmartre-Salvador-Dalí** has a small collection of bronzes and later works by the Spanish surrealist artist.

- **Musée de Montmartre,** 12 rue Cortot. Tel: (01) 46 06 61 11.
- **Espace Montmartre-Salvador-Dalí,** 11 rue Poulbot. Tel (01) 42 64 44 80.

SHOPPING

Some not-too-serious shopping is to be had in Montmartre. Around Sacré Coeur are **Brakha Dorra (**55 rue du Mont Cenis), which sells bric-a-brac, and **Passa Tempo** (54 rue Lamarck), and in rue des Abbesses are **Briard-Ebene** (No 1) and **Belle Abbesse** (No 11). **Alain Atlan** (56 rue Caulaincourt) specializes in Directoire, Empire and 19th-century items. There are several bric-a-brac shops in rue Caulaincourt.

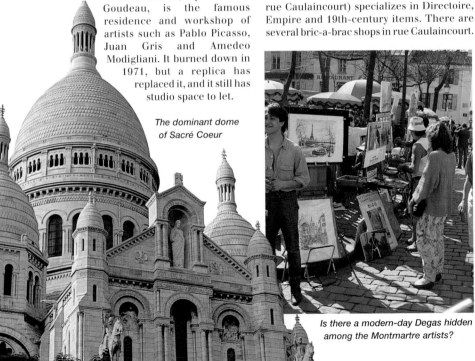

Is there a modern-day Degas hidden among the Montmartre artists?

PLACE DE LA BASTILLE AND THE NORTH EAST

The lights don't burn quite so brightly beyond Le Marais, but these districts are becoming more popular. Shops and markets are cheaper, and the galleries and workshops in the railway arches near the Opéra de Paris Bastille are attracting people in search of something different.

The lighted arch windows of the Viaduc des Arts, housing art galleries and artists' workshops

Beyond Le Marais and place de la Bastille, the 10th, 11th and 12th *arrondissements* arc round from Montmartre in the north to the city's famous cemetery, Cimetière Père Lachaise, in the east, and down to the River Seine at Bercy. Two of the city's main stations are here, the Gare du Nord and the Gard de l'Est, and just east runs the Canal St-Martin with shady walks beside old warehouses. Rue de Belleville runs north-east into the working-class Belleville district where dance halls were popular in the 1930s and 1940s. Edith Piaf is said to have been born at No 72, in 1915.

A 1940s chair, beech stained to look like fruitwood

PLACES TO VISIT
Parisian nostalgia is at its best at the **Musée Edith Piaf**, where memorabilia has been collected by devoted fans and is on display in two rooms.

Founded as the Saint-Anne glass-works in 1764 in Lorraine, and moved to rue du Paradis in 1832, the Baccarat company has set up the **Musée du Crystal Baccarat** next to its showrooms. Some 1,200 pieces are on show, including glassware created for royalty, exhibitions and fairs. Some of the paperweights produced by Baccarat have fetched record prices in recent years.
- **Musée Edith Piaf**, 5 rue Crespin-du-Gast. Tel: (01) 43 55 52 72. Viewing by appointment only.
- **Musée du Crystal Baccarat**, 30 bis, rue du Paradis. Tel: (01) 47 70 64 30.

SHOPPING
Just behind the great glass modern Opéra de Paris Bastille you will find the rue de Charonne. I have picked up some good 1960s items among the half dozen or so antiques and bric-a-brac shops here, which include **Lavigne-Bastille**, **Verreglass** and **L'Art du Temps**. Just a few blocks further south you will find **Marché d'Aligre**, a lively market where some three dozen stalls are set up each morning (but not on Mondays) with small household items and other bric-a-brac.

A couple of streets away in the avenue Deaumesnil there is **Le Viaduc des Arts**, a series of bright new workshops under old railway arches. You can watch craftsmen at work as they restore musical instruments and furniture. There are plenty of crafts to buy too. Artists, furniture-makers, milliners, jewellers and lighting specialists, are all busy here, creating the antiques of tomorrow.

A restored rocking horse, complete with gleaming leather and brass tack

---

SHOPPER'S TIP
Porte de Montreuil on the Périphérique ring road beyond Bastille holds the smallest of the city's flea markets – **Puces de Montreuil**. Started in the 19th century by rag-and-bone men in the town of Maubert, the market is best for linen and clothes, but little else. Open Saturday to Monday from 9am to 7pm, and worth a visit if you are in the area.

LES PUCES DE ST-OUEN

Absolutely every kind of collectable and curiosity you can imagine (and plenty you can't) turns up at Clignancourt, the largest antiques and bric-a-brac market in France. From erotica to rock and roll, Louis Quatorze to Lalique, this is antiques hunting at its most entertaining.

Stringed instruments and exquisite rugs for sale in the flea market at Clignancourt

More than 120,000 people visit Saint-Ouen each weekend, making it one of France's top attractions. This is Paris's flea market *par excellence*, or rather flea markets, for Saint-Ouen is a dozen different markets fused into an enormous site north of the city just beyond the Périphérique at Porte de Clignancourt.

Flea markets (*puces*) date back several hundred years, when rag-and-bone men, *les chiffoniers* (from *chiffon*, meaning rag*)*, went through the city's rubbish at night. In the 19th century they took their wares to what was waste ground beyond the new city walls – and beyond the city's taxmen – to sort through them. Before long curious Parisians came at weekends to see if there were any bargains to be had, particularly after the Metro arrived in 1908. Today, there are 16km (9 miles) of aisles with about 2,500 stalls.

To get to the market from the Metro, you have to walk through **Marché Malik**, a covered market selling cheap clothes to young people. Saint-Ouen's markets are open on Saturday and Sunday, and part-open on Monday. They start around 9am

and close by about 7pm. Dealers descend on the markets on Friday night; get there early on Saturday for the best of the days' finds. Credit cards are accepted at larger stalls, though you may get a better price for cash.

● **Market Tours** lasting half a day give inside information of stalls and stallholders past and present. Contact the Seine-Saint-Denis Tourist Board, 21 avenue Karl Marx, Bobigny. Tel: (01) 41 60 06 03.

MARCHÉ VERNAISON

Beside avenue Michelet, this is the oldest, largest and brightest corner of Saint-Ouen, and its nine narrow *allées* brim with goodies. This is the place for furnishing fabrics, linen and clothes, and there are also a number of glass and jewellery dealers. I always love having a rummage through the Art Nouveau clothes on **Françoise**'s stall, and the embroidered silks and damasks at other stalls (Allée 1).

Janine Giovannoni and **Francine** (both Allée 7) are also good places to find lace and fabrics, while **Maïte Poupées** (Allée 10) has

French bronze statue, 1870s

lovely dolls from the late 19th and early 20th centuries. Collectables range from key rings at **Françoise Chappuy** (Allée 5) to **Béatrice Cuvelier**'s stall of erotica (Allée 8).

Chez Loisette (136 avenue Michelet), is one of half a dozen cafés and restaurants in Clignancourt. Edith Piaf is said to have begun her singing career in this open-air café; other hopefuls try to follow in her wake.

MARCHÉ BIRON

This is the more expensive end of the market, although only small items of furniture tend to be sold here because there is little space. The stalls line the two aisles selling decanters,

A variety of 19th-century chairs can be found in Marché Biron

desks, *armoires* and Louis XIV chairs. Art Nouveau specialists are **Alexia Say** and **Jean Doutrepont** (both Allée 1) and there is plenty of Lalique at **E. Boland** (also Allée 1).

MARCHÉ MALASSIS
This can be found opposite Marché Vernaison in rue des Rosiers. It is housed in a modern, two-storey building, although the Malissis market has occupied the site for more than a century. On the ground floor, provincial kitchenalia fills **Nicole Aker**'s stall, and leather armchairs are a speciality of **Le Club**. Gentlemen may also furnish their libraries from the first floor, where **L'Homme de Plume** sell desks and writing accessories, bookcases and library steps.

MARCHÉ DAUPHINE
Opened in 1991, this two-storey market is well worth a visit. Furniture dating from as early as the 17th century may be found here, as well as original Chanel outfits. Specialists on the ground floor include **Présents Passés**, for old work tools and implements, **Thierry Amblard** for luggage and **Diamantina** for jewellery and Cartier watches. Upstairs you should look out for enamel kitchenware, books and marine memorabilia. Northern European furniture fills the large premises of **Mammoth Antiek**, part of the large Dutch chain.

MARCHÉ SERPETTE
This is the best equipped of the various markets and is the place to head for if it starts to rain. On the corner of rue des Rosiers and rue Paul Bert, the building is a converted coach-builders and has six aisles. Everything here tends to be in very good condition, so dealers from around France come here to buy. For something different there are Art Deco cocktail bars from **Jean-Paul Costey** and top-quality 20th-century jewellery from **Olwen Forest** (both Allée 3). If it's spectacular mirrors or chandeliers you're after, then **Marie-Eve Rosenthal** (Allée 4) has a wide selection.

MARCHÉ PAUL BERT
This open-air market with seven aisles runs around two sides of Marché Serpette. Although less expensive than the indoor markets, it's worth browsing among the wrought iron and country *objets*. **Bachelier Antiquités** (Allée 1), for example, usually has a good deal of rural domestic ware, while **Marc Maison** (Allée 6) has large-scale items for the home and garden. More modern pieces can be found at **Vingtième Siècle** (Allée 6), which specializes in furniture and fittings from the 1950s to the 1970s.

RUE DES ROSIERS
Around 50 dealers operate in the central rue des Rosiers where large, old commercial properties have been converted into an antiques emporia. In rue des Roses look for **Mem Antiqués**, **Marché Cambo**, and **Marché Dauphine**, as well as ceramics specialists **Aijolate Antiquités** and **Marché Antica**. On the Périphérique side, in rue Lécuyer, **Marché Lécuyer-Vallès** and **Marché Hall de la Brocante** are good places to browse.

A typical flea market stall, with an eclectic and entertaining mix of items for sale

---

1930S AND 40S FURNITURE

THE AGE OF ART DECO
The Exposition des Arts Décoratifs in 1925 marked the gradual transition from Art Nouveau to Art Deco. The latter was a much more controlled, angular form of expression, which acknowledged both Cubism and jazz as its roots. The strong geometric lines and hard glossy surfaces continued up until the war. At its most lavish, Art Deco design included the use of bronze and silver, shagreen, ivory and mother of pearl inlay, and metallic threads in velvets and chiffons. Espace Landopwski, in the Boulogne-Billancour suburb, has a museum dedicated to the 1930s.

● **Musée des Années 30**, 28 avenue André-Morizet. Tel (01) 55 18 46 45.

Armchair with the distinctive angularity of the era

MONTPARNASSE & PORTE DE VANVES

South of the *Rive Gauche* lie the Jardin du Luxembourg, the old literary haunts of Montparnasse and, further still, the colourful flea market at Porte de Vanves.

Books from the covered Marché du Livre Ancien

The open-air flea market in Porte de Vanves

PORTE DE VANVES

This flea market is just four stops from Montparnasse on the Metro, where Porte de Vanves marks a gate on the south side of the old city walls. Before the market was set up here in 1965, rag-and-bone men traded in Vanves, which is now a city suburb a little further south. Today, the **Puces de Vanves** goes on all day on Saturday and Sunday. It is a temporary outdoor market and nothing like Clignancourt, although that does not mean it is not worth seeking out, especially for small items for the kitchen and bedroom.

Goods arrive in cars and vans which are unpacked onto tarpaulins and makeshift stalls along avenues Marc Sangnier and George Lafenestre. An identity permit set out on the stall is often the only way of knowing which stall belongs to whom. Look out for antique lace from **Daniel Sanz** and eclectic glassware from **Claire Lavoine**. A number of stallholders specialize in household linen, and the **Antoines** have a good selection of rural kitchenware. Elsewhere there are postcards, posters, period designer clothes, textiles, jewellery, flatware, faience and engravings.

Near the flea market is the **Marché du Livre Ancien**, a second-hand and antiquarian book market, which is held every weekend in a couple of old iron-framed covered markets.

More than 50 dealers set up their stalls here from 8.30am to 6.30pm on Saturday and Sunday. The large range of articles on offer includes newspapers and magazines. There is a permanent letter-box to post requests for titles or to use to find somebody who might want to buy from you.

MONTPARNASSE

Pablo Picasso and other painters moved here from Montmartre when rents there started to soar around 1900. The literati gathered too. Jazz clubs took off, and most creative talent in Paris in the first half of the 20th century spent time in the area. Now it is dominated by the city's tallest building. Tour Montparnasse is 230m (690ft) tall, and has a bar and restaurant on the 26th floor. For something more nostalgic head to La Closerie des Lilas, in boulevard Montparnasse, an 1840s dance hall where fashionable Parisians now dine.

Streets to look out for in terms of antiques are boulevard de Vaugirard, which runs past the main-line station from the tower and has more than a dozen antiques shops, and boulevard Raspail. There is also a good concentration of shops in rue de Sèvres where **La Galerie des Antiquaires du Bon Marché**, set up in 1975, is home to some 15 dealers.

There is also a lively morning street market in boulevard Edgar Quinet every Wednesday and Saturday.

Period poster, a typically Parisian souvenir

GOBELINS TAPESTRIES

The Gobelin district of Paris, south-east of Montparnasse, takes its name from the tapestry factory started here, around 1450, by Jean Gobelin, a dyer. Under Louis XIV the workshops joined with those in Maincy, south of the city, to form the Royal Manufactory.

La Manufacture Nationale des Gobelins is still in business and continues to produce tapestries according to over 500 years of tradition, working only in daylight and using 14,000 different colours.

Uncommon view of La Coupole, which is usually crowded with people, noisy and very Parisian

WHERE TO EAT AND DRINK

La Coupole
102 boulevard Montparnasse, 14th Arr.
Tel: (01) 43 20 14 20
The 1927 Latin Quarter restaurant and dance hall attracted writers and artists for decades. Today they still come here at times. Marc Chagall's daubs remain on the pillars.

Grand Véfour
17 rue de Beaujolais, 1st Arr.
Tel: (01) 42 96 56 27
Established in 1784, this restaurant has period features throughout. Napoleon dined here, as did Victor Hugo and Colette, and probably everyone who was anyone in the past 250 years. The decor is unbeatable, and the food is great too.

Le Dôme de Marais
53 rue des Francs-Bourgeois, 4th Arr.
Tel: (01) 42 74 54 17
From 1920 to 1930, this pre-Revolutionary building served as the auction house for the state pawnbrokers. Today the sumptuous octagonal dining-room, furnished with gilt and cherubs, serves excellent food.

Le Procope
13 rue de l'Ancienne Comédie, 6th Arr.
Tel: (01) 40 46 79 00
Stop for a coffee in what claims to be the world's first coffee house. It was founded in 1686 and was recently revamped in 18th-century style.

Le 59 Poincaré
59 avenue Raymond-Poincaré, 16th Arr.
Tel: (01) 47 27 59 59
Celebrated chef Alain Ducasse has three Michelin stars for this restaurant, situated in a Belle Epoque mansion, so you can expect wonderful food. Closed Sat and Sun, and mid-July to mid-August.

The elegant interior and avenue view of the star-rated Le 59 Poincaré

WHERE TO STAY

Paris is full of charming small hotels, some with only half a dozen rooms. For more information, see Useful Addresses section at the end of the book.

Le Relais de Louvre
19 rue de Prêtres St-Germain l'Auxerrois, 1st Arr.
Tel: (01) 40 41 96 42; Fax: (01) 40 41 96 44
Beside St-Germain church and behind the Louvre, this 18th-century building is a mid-priced hotel with a long history and filled with tasteful antiques.

Hôtel de Crillon
10 place de la Concorde, 8th Arr.
Tel: (01) 44 71 15 00. Fax: (01) 44 71 15 02
This dazzling Neo-classical fantasy is for those with no money worries. Catch sight of the rich and famous in its gilded mirrors and dine at the glorious Ambassadors restaurant.

Duc de St Simon
14 rue de St Simon, 7th Arr.
Tel: (01) 44 39 20 20; Fax: (01) 45 48 68 25
Furnished with lovely antiques, the hotel has a lounge and bar converted from an old stone cellar. Ask for a room with a roof terrace.

De l'Odéon
13 rue St-Sulpice, 6th Arr.
Tel: (01) 43 25 70 11; Fax: (01) 43 29 97 34
Oozing with character and a maze of narrow corridors and stairs, this building dates from the 16th century. Brass bedsteads and four-posters are part of the wonderful decor. Not cheap.

Hôtel Esmeralda
4 St-Julien-le-Pauvre, 5th Arr.
Tel: (01) 43 54 19 20; Fax: (01) 40 51 00 68
This inexpensive hotel overlooks the Seine and Notre-Dame. Few floors are straight in this 1640 building, which is suitably furnished with antiques.

Hôtel du Jeu de Paume
54 rue St Louis-en-L'ille, 4th Arr.
Tel: (01) 43 26 14 18; Fax: (01) 40 46 02 76

Lobby of the Hotel du Jeu de Paume

This unique 17th-century hotel was once the royal "real" tennis court, commissioned by Louis XIII.

Quai Voltaire
19 quai Voltaire, 6th Arr.
Tel: (01) 42 61 50 91; Fax: (01) 42 61 62 26
In the Carré Rive Gauche antiques area, most of its rooms overlook the river. This mid-priced 1850s hotel has seen Wilde and Wagner.

Hôtel de la Place des Vosges
12 rue de Birague, 1st Arr.
Tel: (01) 42 72 60 46; Fax: (01) 42 72 02 64
The layout of this 17th-century house is as it was when a mule hirer lived here. Very small rooms; from the attic you can see the Bastille column.

St James Paris
43 avenue Bugeaud, 16th Arr.
Tel: (01) 44 05 81 81; Fax: (01) 44 05 81 82
Formerly known as the St James Club, this 1890 château is at the end of a driveway in a quiet residential quarter. Impeccable service.

Château de Vaux le Vicomte, which inspired Louix XIV to commission the Palace of Versailles

The problem with making trips out of Paris is that you are spoilt for choice, with countless museums and châteaux within easy reach.

Versailles was built for Louix XIV in 1668 and is the most sumptuous palace in Europe. It lies 18km (12 miles) south-west of the city, and you will need a day to make the most of its ornate salons with their fabulous furnishings and paintings, the glittering hall of mirrors, the marble courtyard, the Chapelle Royale, the numerous fountains and the vast gardens, designed by France's great landscape gardener, André Le Nôtre, with the magnificent Grand Canal and the Petit and Grand Trianons. A bonus for antiques hunters are **Les Antiquaires de Versailles**, where 40 dealers sell, among other things, 16th–19th-century faience and porcelain, 18th- and 19th-century furniture, ceramics and *objets d'art*.

The Baroque masterpiece of the **Château de Vaux-Le-Vicomte**, 48km (30 miles) south of Paris, was the inspiration behind Versailles and remains one of the grandest châteaux in France. Its rooms are decorated in Louis XIII style, and Charles LeBrun's frescoes are a delight. The gardens, with fountains and ornamental lakes, were the first major work by André Le Nôtre.

The **Musée de la Toile de Jouy**, 15km (10 miles) south-west of Paris, is dedicated to the printed cotton and linen fabrics made famous by the factory at Jouy-en-Josas, founded in 1760 by Franco-German Christophe-Philippe Oberkampf. The original technique had been invented by Irishman Francis Nixon and was stolen by Oberkampf, who used company spies to copy the designs onto cloth with invisible ink. The Jouy factory became so important that Louis XVI gave it royal supplier status in 1783.

The **Sèvres** porcelain factory moved to Sèvres (Metro, Pont de Sèvre) from Vincennes in 1756

Early 19th-century French toile

Sèvres bulb pot, c.1757, with rose de Pompadour ground and landscapes in cartouches

and began to produce tableware and *objets d'art* for Louis XV and Madame de Pompadour at the palace of Versailles. As a result of this royal patronage, the popularity of Sèvres porcelain grew among Europe's aristocracy. Its output included groups of lovers and children – favourite Rococo themes – as well as tableware and ornamental pieces decorated with bouquets and sprigs of flowers. The full range of Sèvres ware over the centuries can be seen at the city's ceramic museum.

● **Le Château de Versailles**, Versailles. Tel: (01) 30 83 78 00. Closed Mon.
● **Les Antiquaires de Versailles**, 10 rue André-Chénier, Versailles. Tel: (01) 39 50 70 09.
● **Château de Vaux-le-Vicomte**, Maincy, Seine-et-Marne. Tel: (01) 64 14 41 90. Open Easter to mid-November.
● **Musée de la Toile de Jouy**, 54 rue Charles de Gaulle, Jouy-en-Josas. Tel: (01) 39 56 48 64.
● **Musée National de la Céramique**, pl. de la Manufacture, Sèvres. Tel: (01) 41 14 04 20.

Just as white Caen stone was used to build Normandy's abbeys and churches, so its orchards and clay have provided the materials for fruitwood furniture and local earthenware.

The iron Gros-Horloge in Rouen was forged in 1389

NORMANDY

MUCH OF NORMANDY'S APPEAL stems from rural tradition. Typical of the region's architecture are the robust timber-framed manors and town houses, picturesque dovecots and châteaux. The cuisine is rich in produce from the land – specialities include cheese and excellent butter, and cider made from the fruit of the orchards that dominate much of the landscape. Even the fruitwood furniture has a characteristic sturdiness to it.

For the antiques hunter there is a vast wealth of pewter pots and copper pans, butter churns and cider jugs. There are Dieppe ivory carvings and Bresle glass. Textiles can be found too, dating from the 17th century when, under the patronage of Louis XIV, royal lacemakers were set up at Alençon and carpet- and tapestry-makers at Beauvais.

Above all, Normandy is a must for pottery lovers. Caen and Bayeux each had fine pottery styles, and Rouen perhaps the finest. It was in Rouen that faience reached a peak of perfection between 1650 and 1800. Some rare examples can be seen at the city's Musée de la Céramique, and include Oriental-style pieces typical of the late 18th century.

Panel from the Bayeux Tapestry: Harold's audience at Rouen Palace

HISTORY REVISITED

WILLIAM THE CONQUEROR

The Normans were Vikings who, in AD911, settled around the Seine under Rollo, a man so large it was said that no horse in Norway could carry him. Less than 100 years later the Norsemen were on the move again. The Hautevilles from Coutances went south, becoming princes in southern Italy and Syria and kings of Sicily, while Rollo's descendant, William the Bastard, Duke of Normandy (born to a tanner's daughter in Falaise), crossed the channel in 1066 to become the Conqueror of England. A tapestry commissioned by William's half-brother Odo, Bishop of Bayeux, is one of the great artworks of the Middle Ages telling, in 58 scenes, the story of William's conquest.

● The tapestry can be seen at: **Centre Guillaume le Conquérant**, rue de Nesmond, Bayeux. Tel: (02) 31 51 25 50.

AROUND NORMANDY

Upper (*Haute*) Normandy has its capital at Rouen, a half-timbered town of booksellers and faience. Lower (*Basse*) Normandy takes in Caen and Bayeux, where lace is still made, and Honfleur, the little port that inspired the Impressionists.

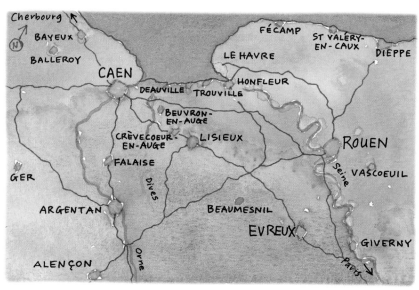

ROUEN

Despite bomb damage during World War II, Rouen remains a picturesque city with its half-timbered houses and breathtaking Gothic cathedral. Much of the city centre is traffic-free – just as well as some streets are hardly wide enough for two people to walk down. The most photographed is the rue du Gros Horloge, overlooked by the **Gros Horloge**, a Renaissance tower with a striking clock faced in gilded lead. A single hand tells the time, day of the week and moon phase. This street leads to place du Vieux Marché, a lively square of timber-framed cafés where mussels and fries (*moules frites*) are a

Rue du Gros Horloge

speciality. Here a market is held from Tuesday to Sunday morning. Joan of Arc was burnt by the English in this square in 1431. The Cathédral Notre-Dame, painted many times by Monet, is beautifully lit up at night. The cours des Librairies next to the cloisters was once filled with booksellers' stalls, while the Booksellers' Staircase of 1480 is so delicate it is amazing that it is still intact. Monet's

series of paintings of the cathedral are a highlight of the **Musée des Beaux-Arts**, one of France's finest galleries, with Spanish, Italian and Flemish works, as well as French. Rouen also has one of the world's largest collections of wrought-iron in the **Musée Le Secq des Tournelles**.

● **Musée des Beaux-Arts de Rouen**, 1 place Rostout, rue Thiers. Tel: (02) 35 71 28 40.

● **Musée Le Secq des Tournelles**, rue Jacques-Villon. Tel (02) 35 71 28 40.

FAIENCE

For centuries Rouen's speciality has been faience, beautiful ceramics made of local clays and finished with highly colourful designs. By the end of the 17th century, when Edmé Poterat held the monopoly for manufacture, the city had become France's main centre for these ceramics. Made of red clay and solidly potted, they developed their

Rouen faience pieces from the 1920s

own look, such as the *style rayonnant* of blue and white, or red and black circles. Highly decorative, sometimes with written homilies, they echoed patterns found in silverware and lace. This was in part due to the fact that Louis XIV sought to boost revenues by melting down large numbers of silver ornaments. Bare tables were then laid with the best ceramics, designed to look like the missing silver.

Exhibits in the Musée de la Céramique, Rouen

● **Musée de la Céramique**, 1 rue Faucon. Tel: (02) 35 07 31 74.

SHOPPING

There are about 40 antiques shops in Rouen and the city's antiques quarter is one of the best in northern France. It lies between the cathedral and the church of St-Ouen, around the **Aître St-Maclou**, a charnel house where skeletal carvings mark a former plague cemetery. English is usually well understood, although you may get a better deal if you can speak French, and there are several British and American dealers here. The *quartier* begins in rue St Roman, where two houses (Nos 52 and 54) date from the 14th century,

Low 1930s table: Normandy's forests have kept furniture makers in wood

and place Barthélémy. **Max Tetelin**'s shop (No 10) is ideal for regional antiques, from *armoires* to Bayeux faience. There are a number of book and print shops here, such as **Librairie Metais** (2 place Barthélémy). Look out for early editions of *Madame Bovary* by Gustave Flaubert who was born and lived in Rouen. The lane moves round to the left, down rue Damiette, where you can find **Nicole Labiche** (No 10), who sells solid Normandy farm tables, walnut *armoires* and furniture from the Vendée.

FAIRS AND MARKETS

There is an antiques market all day Tuesday in **place des Emmurées** and a Sunday morning market can be found at **place Saint Marc**. Antiques fairs are held at the **Parc des Expositions de Rouen** during January, June and October.

Interior view of Monet's house at Giverny

The Impressionist art movement began in Normandy. The Impressionists' aim was to capture, in a realistic way, the light, colour and spirit of the outdoors, rather than reproduce a landscape in a studio. Several paintings depict views of Normandy's spectacular coastline as the River Seine widens towards the sea.

The inspiration for this innovative mode of painting – thought outlandish by many of their contemporaries – was begun by the artist Eugène Boudin, who was born in 1824 in the picturesque port of Honfleur at the mouth of the Seine. He painted seaside holidaymakers at Trouville and Deauville in their bustling dresses and jaunty suits. Boudin became mentor to a young caricaturist, Claude Monet from Le Havre, and showed him how to paint in this new style. One misty spring morning in 1872 Monet painted a picture of his home port, and called it *Impression: Soleil Levant*, which caused a derisive critic in Paris to call Monet and his colleagues "Impressionistes". Monet's beautiful garden at Giverny, between Rouen and Paris, is now one of the most popular tourist stops in France and is worth a visit for the house as much as for the famous garden. He lived here from 1883 until his death in 1926. The interior, in blues and yellows, shows the influence of Japanese ware that had just become popular in Europe.

● **Musée Claude Monet**, Giverny, near Vernon. Tel: (01) 32 51 28 21. Open daily April–October.
● **Musée Eugène Boudin**, place Erik-Satie, Honfleur. Tel: (02) 31 89 54 00.

The Entrance to Trouville Harbour, Eugène Boudin

The Vieux Bassin and St Etienne church, Honfleur

HONFLEUR

The romantic port of Honfleur at the mouth of the Seine was a favourite haunt of the Impressionists. Its hub is the 17th-century Vieux Bassin, where slate-roofed houses jostle for space on the quayside. The seafaring heritage is clear in the wooden church of Ste Catherine, built by ships' carpenters and roofed with chestnut shingles. St Etienne, on the quayside, houses the **Musée de la Marine**, with model boats and seafaring memorabilia. The highlight of the **Musée d'Ethnographie et d'Art Populaire** in the 17th-century prison is a reassemblage of rooms from a 16th-century town house from Lisieux.

Art galleries outnumber antiques shops by about four to one. **Boscus** (26 rue de la Chaussée) specializes in Art Deco. **Antiquité Alais** (53 rue de Puits) sells French furniture from the 17th century onwards. **La Brocanterie** (11 cours de Fossé) has a fine art gallery as well as antiques. **St Léonard**, a Norman church, hosts an antiques market on the second Sunday of every month.

● **Musée de la Marine**, quai St-Etienne. Tel: (02) 31 89 14 12.
● **Musée d'Ethnographie et d'Art Populaire**, rue de la Prison. Tel: (02) 31 89 14 12.
Both museums closed end Dec. to mid-Feb.

An 18th-century Normandy fruitwood armoire on cabriole feet

TRY NOT TO MISS ...
The **Château du Champ de Bataille** near Neubourg for a flavour of the region's glorious past. Known as the "Norman Versailles", this splendid late 17th-century building has been restored and beautifully furnished in Louis XVI Neo-classical style. Its extensive garden was designed by André Le Nôtre. Daily guided visits.
Tel: (02) 32 34 84 34.

CAEN

After D-Day in 1944, the battle for Caen lasted two months, and there are many reminders in and around the town of this tragic time. But the capital of Basse Normandie has fully recovered and much restoration work has been done. The **Musée des Beaux-Arts**, in the imposing castle ruins, has collections of French, German and Oriental porcelain, goldwork, furniture and paintings. The castle also contains the **Musée de Normandie**, which is devoted to life in the region and has displays of lace, cheese and copper items.

There are at least half a dozen antiquarian bookshops in the town and Caen's antiques trade is concentrated near the Hôtel de Ville on rue Ecuyère, known locally as rue d'Antiquitaires. Specialists here include **Marthe Goday** (No 25) for splendid Bayeux porcelain, **Jean Louis Antiquités** (No 16) for 19th-century mirrors and glass and **Victoria** (No 48) for English Victorian furniture and silver.

Belle Epoque (266-8 rue St-Jean) has an assortment of French furniture, bronzes and faience from the turn of the 20th century. You may even come across a piece of Caen porcelain. This tableware was made by d'Aigmont-Desmares and Decheval from 1793 to 1806, and typical designs are of landscapes in black within square panels suspended from green and gold wreaths.

The **Salon de Brocante** holds a three-day antiques fair the first weekend of December.
● **Musée des Beaux-Arts**, Château de Caen. Tel: (02) 31 30 47 70.
● **Musée de Normandie**, Château de Caen. Tel: (02) 31 30 47 50.

BAYEUX

People who come to Bayeux to see its world-famous tapestry (see page 91) are delighted to find a strong tradition of crafts. Lacemaking, which in the late 19th century employed 18,000 people, is an art still practised at the **Conservatoire de Dentelle** in the 18th-century Hôtel de Doyen. This non-profit-making concern was set up in 1901 to keep alive Normandy tradition and craftsmanship, and it runs workshops for both tapestry and lacemaking.

Bayeux is also known for a particular style of colourful faience. The local factory only closed in 1951, but the best pieces are from the 19th century. Look out particularly for those by the early 19th-century potter, Joachim Langlois. Examples can be seen in the **Musée Baron Gérard**, along with an eclectic collection of archeology, porcelain, lace, furniture and fine art.

Exquisite antique lace can be found among the many antiques shops around the 11th-century cathedral, notably at **Naphtaline** (16 parvis Notre-Dame), which also specializes in tapestries and porcelain. **Troc Saint Martin** (6 bis, rue Saint-Martin) has a wide selection of furniture and *objets*, and has a large showroom to the east of the town.

Conservatoire de Dentelle, 6 rue Lambert Leforestier. Tel: (02) 31 92 73 80.
● **Musée Baron Gérard**, place de la Liberté. Tel: (02) 31 92 73 80.

A Rouen faience dish c.1760–70

ANCIENT CRAFTS

Beauvais, famed in the 18th and 19th centuries for its carpets, was also a centre for tapestries from the 17th century onwards, following the founding of the city's factory by Flemish weavers, Louis Hinart and Phillipe Behagle, in 1664.

Point d'Alençon lace takes its name from the town of its origin, and has a distinctive geometric pattern.

For more than 300 years the copperware capital of Normandy has been Villedieu-les-Poêles (*poêle* is a copper pan). You will find antique and traditionally made copperware all over the region.

Copper and brassware, a feature of Normandy

WHERE TO EAT AND DRINK

Normandy is renowned for its laden tables and the quality of its farm produce. Try the local cider and Tripe à la mode de Caen (don't be put off by the thought of eating tripe).

La Couronne
31 place du Vieux Marché, Rouen
Tel: (02) 35 71 40 90
The "oldest restaurant in France" (it claims to date back to 1345) is something of an institution, with elegant furniture.

Auberge de la Butte, Rouen

Auberge de la Butte
69 route de Paris, Rouen
Tel: (02) 35 80 43 11
A staging post since 1850 with period furniture and pictures of old Rouen. Traditional Norman dishes.

La Marmite
3 rue de Florence, Rouen
Tel: (02) 35 71 75 55
The candle-lit dining rooms of this 18th-century building have wonderful atmosphere.

WHERE TO STAY

Hôtel de Bordeaux
9 place de la République, Rouen
Tel: (02) 35 71 93 58; Fax: (02) 35 71 92 15
This 150-year-old hotel is reasonably priced, with views of either the cathedral or the Seine.

Hôtel de la Cathédrale
12 rue St-Romain, Rouen
Tel: (02) 35 71 57 95; Fax: (02) 35 70 15 54
This attractive 17th-century town house with a courtyard is close to the cathedral and very reasonably priced (it serves breakfast, but has no restaurant).

La Ferme St-Siméon
Route A, Marais, Honfleur
Tel: (02) 31 881 78 00; Fax: (02) 31 89 48 48
Beautiful, but expensive, this 18th-century farmhouse set above the town once belonged to a Mère Toutin. The Impressionists – Claude Monet, Camille Pissarro, Paul Cézanne – would gather here in the company of contemporaries such as Erik Satie (who apparently enjoyed the cider).

L'Absinthe
10 quai de la Quarantaine, Honfleur
Tel: (02) 31 89 23 23; Fax: (02) 31 89 53 60
A former 16th-century presbytery, set right in the heart of the old town. Seven very comfortable guestrooms in a setting full of Norman character.

Hôtel Saint Etienne
2 rue de l'Academie, Caen
Tel: (02) 31 86 35 82; Fax: (02) 31 85 57 69
Centrally located near the Hôtel de Ville, this delightful 18th-century townhouse gives a real feel of old Normandy.

BORDEAUX

The riverside warehouses of France's third largest port were once filled with wine and other goods. Now some of them have been converted into cavernous showrooms for antiques dealers.

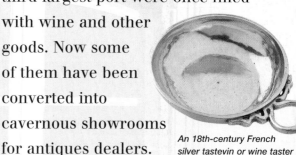

An 18th-century French silver tastevin or wine taster

BORDEAUX MEANS WINE. There's no getting away from it. Why should anyone try? For centuries its great wines were shipped from the eight kilometres of quays lining the crescent-shaped bend of the River Gironde, which gave ancient Aquitaine's capital the nickname of "moon port". In their heyday, the cool custom-built warehouses that ran back in narrow strips from the quai des Chartrons were so long that workers would get from one end to the other by bicycle. Today far less wine is exported by sea and antiques emporia have found these warehouses ideal homes. Among things to look out for when browsing the shops, or the lively place Saint-Michel market are little *tastevins*, often made of silver, used for wine tasting.

Bordeaux has a long history and an elegant dignity. The old town, Vieux Bordeaux, has 5,000 preserved period buildings, mostly from the 18th century, and the waterfront has a classical grandeur, especially around place de la Bourse and esplanade de Quinconces. Its claim to be Europe's largest square makes the esplanade a spacious setting for seasonal antiques fairs.

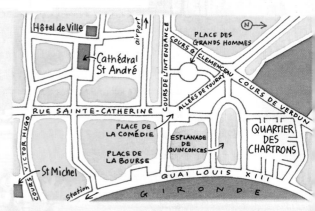

HISTORY REVISITED

WINE-TASTING IN BORDEAUX

Clairet has been popular ever since it was served at the coronation of England's Henry II and his wife Eleanor of Aquitaine in 1154. The word "claret" is still used to describe Bordeaux wines that have been produced here since Roman times. **Maison du Vin**, in an 18th-century building shaped like a ship's bow, is the headquarters of the Bordeaux Wine Council and provides information on wines and châteaux to visit. **Vinorama**, north of the town centre, explains the history and manufacturing process of wine, and the entrance fee includes tastings.

● **Maison du Vin**, 1 cours du 30 juillet. Tel (05) 56 00 22 88.
● **Vinorama**, 12 cours Médoc. Tel: (05) 56 39 39 20.

Detail of a façade in quai des Chartrons

PLACES TO VISIT

A glimpse of the furniture, art and household items from the region's past can be seen at the **Musée d'Aquitaine** and at the **Musée des Arts Décoratifs**, which has everything from fancy door knockers to ornate clocks. The **Musée des Beaux-Arts** has a good mix of paintings from the Renaissance onwards, including masterpieces by Rubens and Renoir, while the **Musée des Douanes** has entertaining explanations of the city's maritime past, and gives an excuse to visit the inside of the 18th-century Bourse, or Stock Exchange.

● **Musée d'Aquitaine**, 20 cours Pasteur. Tel: (05) 56 01 51 00.
● **Musée des Arts Décoratifs**, 39 rue Bouffard. Tel: (05) 56 00 72 50. Closed Tues.

Bordeaux platter, c.1780. Bordeaux pottery is very similar in style to Moustiers (see page 118).

have showrooms on three floors, selling regional furniture, which usually includes some beautiful inlaid pieces, and Art Deco items.

FAIRS AND MARKETS

There is a lively market in **place Saint-Michel** every day except Saturday. There are regular *brocante* (bric-a-brac) fairs at **Hippodrome du Buscat** and antiques and *brocante* fairs four times a year in the airy esplanade of Quinconces. Each January the **Salon des Antiquités de Bordeaux-port** holds a fair in quai des Chartrons, and the Parc des Expositions de Bordeaux-Lac holds the **Salon des Antiquaires du Sud-Ouest**.

Bric-a-brac stalls in place St-Michel

● **Musée des Beaux-Arts**, 20 cours d'Albert. Tel: (05) 56 10 25 16. Closed Tues.
● **Musée des Douanes**, place de la Bourse. Tel: (05) 56 52 45 47.

SHOPPING

The main shopping area radiates out from place de la Comédie outside the Grand Théâtre, built in 1780 by architect Victor Louis and Bordeaux's pride and joy. Rue Ste-Catherine heads off from here, as do cours de l'Intendance and allée de Tournai.

There are three main antiques areas of the old town: rue Notre-Dame lies just north of the church of Notre-Dame in the Quartier des Chartrons. Among the many shops here is the **Village Notre-Dame**, with 30 antiques dealers and items from the 18th century to the 1930s. **Rue Bouffard** has several dozen shops, many specializing in furniture and *objets* from the 18th and 19th centuries.

Le Passage Saint-Michel, one of the most popular shopping streets, occupies a former banana warehouse where 45 dealers

An 18th-century dining room in the Musée des Arts Décoratifs

WHERE TO EAT AND DRINK

Le Relais de Compostelle
759 route de Bayonne, Pessac
Tel: (05) 56 84 10 91
On the outskirts of Bordeaux, this 17th-century restaurant is a gastronome's delight. Dine on seafood and regional dishes. Prestigious wines.

Le Clavel St Jean
44 rue Charles-Domecq
Tel: (05) 56 92 63 07
This modern bistro is far from historic, but there are only a few places in the city to try Bordeaux wine by the glass and this is one of them.

WHERE TO STAY

Grand Hôtel Français
12 rue du Temple
Tel: (05) 56 48 10 35; Fax: (05) 56 81 76 18
An elegant 18th-century mansion, with modern comforts, close to the cathedral, museums and wine centre (but with no restaurant).

Hôtel de l'Opéra
35 rue Esprit-des-Louis
Tel: (05) 56 81 41 27; Fax: (05) 56 51 78 80
By the Grand Théâtre, and from the same late-18th-century period, though it has been much modernized. L'Opéra is a friendly establishment offering good value.

IN THE AREA

St-Emilion, about 30km (20 miles) east of Bordeaux, is one of the most delightful wine villages, and worth a stopover for a meal, if not the night. Its steep little streets and squares tumble over with vines, and a locust tree shades the pretty main square. Explore the exciting subterranean Eglise Monolithe, hewn out of solid rock by Benedictine monks, and browse the little town's two antiques shops: Carrefour des Temps in rue La Grande Fontaine and Les Métiers du Vin in rue La Petite Fontaine.

BIARRITZ

The antiques shops in fashionable Biarritz stock wonderful pieces that once graced the many wealthy family homes in the area.

Opaline glass egg in ormolu mount, c.1860

SILVER TEA SERVICES, TABLE DECORATIONS, jewellery and furnishings from the Second Empire – items on sale in any French antique shop could well have started life in Biarritz. Eugénie, empress of the Second Empire, started the ball rolling, and this city by the sea was a favourite of the British playboy king, Edward VII, and of Leopold III of the Belgians. In the 1930s, trendsetters such as Coco Chanel vied to build glamorous villas, then in the 1950s American film stars brought the surfing craze. The Hôtel du Palais remains one of the best in Europe, the clink of fine china still comes from the *salons du thé*, and the casinos' wheels spin as decadently as ever. Overlooking a great sweep of Atlantic beaches, Biarritz hasn't lost its charm.

French silver coffeepot, c.1880

HISTORY REVISITED

A ROYAL RESORT

Biarritz is Empress Eugénie's town. A Spanish countess who married Napoleon III, she had visited the little Basque whaling port as a child, and in 1854 she had a villa built overlooking the Grand Plage. The railways arrived in 1855, and the *beau monde* followed. The imperial court resided here every summer, with boat trips and regattas, horse racing on the beach, fireworks and musical *soirées*. So many crowned heads stayed that it became known as the "Beach of Kings". After their exile in 1870, Villa Eugénie was turned into a hotel and casino. It was demolished following a fire in 1903 and the Hôtel du Palais was built in its place.

Hôtel du Palais, on the site of Villa Eugénie

PLACES TO VISIT

Much of the delight in exploring Biarritz comes from looking at the Art Deco buildings. It is no surprise to find among them museums dedicated to the decadent and exotic, such as chocolate and oriental antiquities. More traditionally, the **Musée Historique de Biarritz** has costumes and jewellery from the rich and royal days of the town, while the **Musée de la Mer**, in a 1930s' Art Deco building, records the town's whaling past. Something not to miss is the Romano-Byzantine-Moorish exuberance of the **Chapelle Impériale**, built for Eugénie.

● **Musée Historique de Biarritz**, rue Broquedis. Tel: (05) 59 24 86 28. Closed Thurs & Sun.
● **Musée de la Mer**, esplanade du Rocher de la Vierge. Tel: (05) 59 22 37 00.
● **Chapelle Impériale**, rue Pellot. Tel: (05) 59 22 37 10.

Cherrywood armchair, a 1940s' reinterpretation of Directoire style

SHOPPING

About 40 antique shops are scattered around Biarritz. **Passage Gambetta**, selling furniture and *objets* at 40 rue Gambetta, is one of several antiques shops in this street that runs beside Les Halles, the daily indoor market. It's worth browsing place Georges Clemenceau, with furniture at **Damais**, and **Emé Pariente**'s gallery where she sells paintings and old prints ("just things that I like," she says). **Antic Jewels** (10 place Bellevue) sells Second Empire jewellery. **St Charles Antiquaires** in place St Charles has items from the 1920s to the 1970s, including Italian and Lalique glass.

FAIRS AND MARKETS

There is no regular market in Biarritz, but on the first Sunday of the month antiques hunters head for the market at the inland village of **Ahetzi**, 10km (6 miles) south.

Twice a year, in April and August, a **Salon des Antiquaires de la Côte Basque** is held in Bellevue, the seafront venue in the centre of Biarritz.

WHERE TO EAT AND DRINK

Café de Paris
5 place Bellevue
Tel: (05) 59 24 19 53
This Art Deco restaurant near the seafront has an adjoining Bistrot Bellevue for fish dishes.

Ramona
5 rue Centre
Tel: (05) 59 24 34 66
A Belle Epoque brasserie with a good, reasonably priced menu.

WHERE TO STAY

Hôtel du Palais
avenue de l'Impératrice
Tel: (05) 59 41 64 00; Fax: (05) 59 41 67 99
Share rooms with ghosts of bygone crowned heads of Europe. Fantastically elegant but not stuffy, the Palais has a magnificent view over the Grand Plage. Its Biarritz restaurant serves the best of Basque food.

Maison Garnier
29 rue Gambetta
Tel: (05) 59 01 60 70; Fax: (05) 59 01 60 80
There are only seven rooms in this 19th-century hotel, but they have each been beautifully restored, with period furniture.

Château de Claire de Lune
48 avenue Alan-Seegar
Tel: (05) 59 41 53 20; Fax: (05) 59 41 53 29
An elegant *fin-de-siècle* family house in a quiet park on the south side of the town, with welcoming hosts.

IN THE AREA

Biarritz is in the fascinating Basque country, a place of customs and outlook allied to the Basques of Spain and quite different from the rest of France. For a glimpse of Basque life, visit the region's capital, **Bayonne**, where a museum of local life reopened in June 2001 after a long period of renovation. Even before the restoration it was seen as one the best of its kind in France. While in the town, check out the Bonnat art gallery, which has works by Leonardo da Vinci, Nicolas Poussin and Jean Ingres. In the market place by the cathedral there's a flea market on the first Friday and Sunday of each month, and some Biarritz antiques dealers also have shops in Bayonne.

DORDOGNE & LOT ET GARONNE

Antiques hunting in this beautiful region may turn up anything from silverware that has graced a château table to a carved pipe in which locally grown tobacco was once smoked.

Statue of Cyrano de Bergerac

THIS REGION OF SOUTHWESTERN FRANCE between the volcanic hills of the Auvergne and the coastal lowlands that border the Atlantic is one of the earliest cradles of human habitation. The limestone caves of Lascaux, near Montignac, boast some of the world's most spectacular Paleolithic cave paintings, discovered by four local schoolboys in 1940.

The seven rivers of the Dordogne were once the region's highways – Bergerac wine was transported by cargo boats to the sea and watermills made paper and ground walnuts for oil.

There are around 1,500 great houses in the region, from châteaux to *manoirs* and *gentilhommières* (homes of the gentry), and nowhere else in France can you find such a density of medieval and Renaissance buildings and such a wealth of fascinating architectural detail. Although many of the furnishings were brought down from Paris, wealthy households looked to nearby Limoges for porcelain and exquisite enamelware, and Aubusson for the finest carpets and tapestries.

Over the years, mansions and farms have been lost through laws of inheritance which spilt up property among children and grandchildren until the estates were gone, sending on to the market furniture, linen, clocks, silver and bric-a-brac. But don't expect anything too fashionable. Everything arrives late in the Dordogne: Gothic architecture, Protestantism and fashions in furniture all turned up long after they had been well established elsewhere in France.

BATTLES AND BELIEFS

Throughout its long history the region has witnessed more than its fair share of religious and political turbulence.

The most disruptive moment, which left its mark on the shape of the towns and style of its architecture, was the Hundred Years War with England. It continued, one way and another, from 1337 to 1453, but trouble with England had been brewing for some time.

The region was allied to neighbouring Aquitaine. In 1152 Eleanor of Aquitaine, divorced from Louis VII of France, married French-born Henry Plantagenet, Duke of Normandy and Count of Anjou, who became Henry II of England. He laid claim to further French lands and his successor, Richard the Lionheart, died while fighting for these lands at the battle of Chalus, north of Périgueux. At the same time, Simon de Montfort, an Anglo-Norman noble and opportunist, had been savagely suppressing Cathar heretics in the south on behalf of the Pope. His campaign brought him north, and towns and fortresses fell to him all the way to the Périgord. Bitter encounters took place at Castelnaud where the château is now the **Musée de la Guerre au Moyen Age**, which records the story of medieval warfare. The English hold over the region was strengthened by the creation of *bastides* (see page 103), which were fortified by both the English and the French.

The Hundred Years War began when Richard the Lionheart's descendant, Edward III, assumed the title of king of France, but there was no sustained military campaign, just a succession of skirmishes, sieges and battles in which both brigands and nobles took

Autoire, a village with many manoirs, typical of the Quercy region in the upper Dordogne

part. In the course of these upheavals, fortresses along the Dordogne changed hands half a dozen times. The people suffered enormously, and their woes were increased when bubonic plague swept through the area.

In the end, the English were driven out, and for a short time there was peace. This was broken in 1562 by the French themselves in a series of wars of religion between Catholics and the Protestant Huguenots. The 1598 Edict of Nantes provided a brief respite from persecution, but it was revoked by Louis XIV in 1685, and within a few years over 400,000 Huguenots had fled to other parts of Europe and America.

Religious wars were followed by civil revolt, caused by the high levels of taxation imposed on the peasants and the bourgeoisie. The French Revolution of 1789 brought a redistribution of land and estates but 19th-century prosperity, with new farming methods, was shortlived. By the beginning of the 20th century the rural population had fallen by a quarter, as farms and smallholdings were abandoned in favour of the promise of a richer life in towns that were becoming increasingly industrialized.

A pair of 19th-century French opaline glass vases

● **Musée de la Guerre au Moyen Age**, Château de Castelnaud, Castelnaud-la-Chapelle. Tel: (05) 53 31 30 00.
● **Musée Militaire du Périgord**, 26 rue Farges, Périgueux. Tel: (05) 53 53 47 36.

Château de Castelnaud, one of the best preserved fortresses in the region

AROUND THE DORDOGNE

Many of the towns in the region have remained unchanged for hundreds of years, and part of the pleasure of shopping here is that the antiques are contemporary with their surroundings.

Place des Oies in Sarlat, one of the best preserved Renaissance towns in France

SARLAT-LA-CANEDA

Don't be surprised to see film crews in Sarlat. Historical dramas can be enacted here without changing a thing, because the town has the finest collection of medieval and Renaissance buildings in France, and the atmosphere of many of its streets is little changed since the 16th century. It's also a thriving, bustling town and a good base for antiques hunting.

The Chapelle des Pénitents Bleus beside the 17th-century cathedral, is all that remains of the 12th-century Benedictine monastery from which the town grew. The half-timbered houses beside the chapel in the lovely cour des Chanonines are 15th century, and the theatre next to the cathedral used to be the bishop's palace. Its Italianate loggia was built for Niccolò Gaddi, a bishop of Sarlat who came from Florence. Among the houses to look out for are the Maison de la Boétie, a highly ornamented building dating from 1530, the 14th-century Hôtel Plamon in place des Oies (still reserved

Silver Limoges snuff box with enamelled lid, c.1875

for the goose market) and the medieval houses and courtyards around passage de Segogne. Rue Salamandre is named after the salamander emblem

Dainty faience bowl with floral decoration, 1920

of Francis I, and this device can be seen on a number of houses in the town. The main square, place de la Liberté, is overlooked by the 17th-century town hall. The famous Saturday market here is full of regional produce and locally crafted pieces. Sarlat has half a dozen antiques shops. For furniture and local *objets*, try **Atelier** in place de la Cathédrale or **Bennati** on route de la Canéda. There is also a **Brocante d'Automne** fair held on the third Sunday of October.

PERIGUEUX

The capital of the Périgord region is full of architectural riches, from Roman ruins to Renaissance town houses. The Romans built the town of Vesunna on the banks of the River Isle. The Tour de Vésone in the lower Quartier de la Cité marks the site of the temple, and at the nearby Porte Normande you can see the Roman wall. The **Musée du Périgord** near the cathedral has an impressive collection of ancient Roman mosaics, pottery and glass and gives an account of the long prehistory of the region.

The cathedral area around **Saint-Front** is the heart of the medieval city. The cathedral square holds Perigord's best markets on Wednesdays and Saturdays: foie gras and walnut oil are specialities of the region. The architecture is wonderful: stroll down rue Aubergerie and rue de la Constitution and look out for the corkscrew staircase in **Maison Estignard** in rue Limogeanne, which also has two of the town's dozen or so antiques shops, including **Suzanne Bonnelie** and **Galerie Medicis**. Antiques fairs are held regularly at the **Salon des Antiquaires de Périgueux-Ouest**.
● **Musée du Périgord**, 22 cours Tourny. Tel: (05) 53 53 10 63.

BERGERAC

The town that has adopted the large-nosed romantic hero Cyrano de Bergerac (Edmond Rostand's famous fictional character actually came from Bergerac near Paris), grew up as a commercial centre for salt and wine. The Cloître des Récollets is a former monastery with extensive cellars, which houses the **Maison du Vin**, where you can find out about the region's famous wines. The 19th-century church of Notre Dame in place Gambetta has a large Aubusson tapestry of the town's coat of arms on display. The square and the surrounding streets are packed with market stalls on Wednesdays and Saturdays. Head for rue de Fontaine to find antiques shops, such as **Pomme de Pin** and **Vieux Bergerac**. There is also a flea market held here on the first Sunday morning of each month.

● **Maison du Vin**, place de la Myrpe. Tel: (05) 53 63 57 55.

COLLECTING PIPES AND SNUFF BOXES

Tobacco growing was introduced to this part of France in the 19th century, and you can still see drying sheds on local farms. Bergerac is the centre of the industry and the Institut du Tabac is open weekdays during the summer. The town also has France's only **Musée du Tabac,** with three floors of smokers' paraphernalia. The antique pipes on sale in local shops generally date from 1880 to 1920. Amber was often used for mouthpieces to cool the smoke, and the most elaborate have silver mounts and are embellished with

Silver snuff box with vacant cartouche for initials, c.1875

jewels. Pipe tampers, tobacco jars and pocket-sized "pebbles" are all highly collectable, as are snuff boxes. The museum has a shoe-shaped snuff box, and some are painted with elegant nudes.

● **Musée du Tabac**, Maison Peyrarade, Bergerac. Tel: (05) 53 63 04 13.

EYMET

To the south of Bergerac on the River Dropt is the small market town and *bastide* of Eymet, founded in 1270. A ruined 14th-century château lies within its walls and the pretty central square is surrounded by picturesque stone and half-timbered houses. A small local museum exhibits regional crafts and describes local customs.

● **Musée Municipal**. Tel: (05) 53 23 74 95. Open am only Mon–Fri, and Sat pm.

Bric-a-brac stalls in the arcaded market square of a bastide

BASTIDE TOWNS

A unique feature of this part of France are the *bastides*. These towns were built in the 13th and 14th centuries at a time when the rural population was scattered and difficult to administer. Streets were laid out in a rigid grid pattern around a central square and plots were designed to maximize space for tax revenue. A *bayle* was employed to persuade people to come and live in the *bastides*, and each citizen was given enough land outside the town to support a family. During the Hundred Years War armies began to fortify the towns with ramparts pierced by a town gate, and *bastides* became military bases for both the English and the French. Churches were founded and the original, cheaply built properties were replaced. The characteric overhanging balconies were a clever ploy by some home owners to increase the size of their property without incurring extra tax. In the main squares, the only place where commercial activity was permitted, arcades were erected by shopkeepers to keep customers dry. Among the best examples of *bastides* are **Domme**, **Monpazier** and **Monflanquin**, which has a *bastide* museum.

● **Musée des Bastides**, Monflanquin. Tel: (05) 53 36 40 19.

Monpazier, a bastide which has barely changed since the Middle Ages

DOMME

One of the most spectacular views of the Dordogne is from this perfect fortified *bastide*, on a lofty bluff high above the river. Another major attraction is the 17th-century covered market in La Place de la Halle. **James Antiquité** is in the square here. There is also a grand covered market in the exemplary *bastide* of **Monpazier** (see page 103), south of Domme. Rebuilt in the 16th century, the market retains some of the original containers for measuring goods. South of Monpazier is **Biron**, domain of the premier barony in Périgord and a spectacular castle.

● **Château de Biron**, 25 rue du Président Wilson, Biron. Tel: (05) 53 63 13 39. Closed Jan.

ALONG THE DORDOGNE

The small towns along the River Dordogne are some of my favourite places. There is so much to look at, so many buildings bursting with history. I've bought original French painted furniture from **Au Vieux Lalinde** in the village of Lalinde between Domme and Bergerac. One of my favourite purchases is a *semainière*, a uniquely French piece of furniture. It has seven drawers, one for each day of the week. More elaborate examples than mine have a desktop that folds down from the top three drawers.

South of Lalinde is the medieval village of **Issigeac** where I have found some good Strasbourg faience and beautiful opaline glass. Between Lalinde and Domme are many other places to stop and browse, including **Le Buge**, **St Cyprien** and **Beynac**.

Above Domme is **Rocamadour**, set high on a cliff above the Alzou valley. It has been a place of pilgrimage since the discovery in

Provincial rush chair, c.1870, and 18th-century ormolu-mounted semainière

the 12th century of the remains of St Amadour, a supposed servant of the Virgin Mary who became a hermit here. The town is as full of souvenir sellers today as it was in the Middle Ages. It is built on three levels, and pilgrims used to enter on their knees to climb the 261 steps of the Grand Stairway. Of particular interest to collectors of toys is Rocamadour's **Musée du Jouet Ancien**, where you can see dolls, early games and ingenious automata.

Autoire, above Rocamadour, is perhaps the prettiest of all the towns along the Dordogne. Its many *manoirs* have ivy-covered turrets and towers typical of the architecture of the Quercy, a region of pigeon lofts (*pigeonniers*) and stone huts called *caselles*.

● **Musée du Jouet Ancien**, place Ventadour, Rocamadour. Tel: (05) 56 33 60 75.

CAHORS

Caught in a loop on the River Lot, the capital of Upper Quercy is a bright and busy town. As Roman Divona, it was famous for its linen cloth. It has a fantastic 14th-century fortified bridge, Pont Valentré, still open to traffic. Its main avenue, Boulevard Gambetta, is named after the town's favourite son, Léon Michel Gambetta, the 19th-century Republican leader. The Cathédrale St-Etienne is typical of the domed churches of the Quercy region, and to the south of it is a popular covered market. Book and bric-a-brac shops can be found in the nearby streets of the old town, where surviving Renaissance houses are richly carved. Look out for local antiques in **Pierre Fraissinet**, 99 rue du Roi, one of several antiques shops in the town.

AGEN

In surveys of the state of people's happiness in France, the people of Agen have been found to be the most content. Perhaps it's an effect of the prunes they famously produce!

There is a good Musée Municipal in the town centre, housed in four buildings including a prison, where iron rings are still fixed on top of the walls. It has on show works by Francisco de Goya and Giovanni Tiepolo, Impressionist paintings by Eugène Boudin and Gustave Courbet, and a Greek statue of the Venus du Mas, found in a nearby Roman villa

The old town of Bergerac has many picturesque corners such as this attractive small square and fountain

The charming old fortified village of Loubressac, with great views to the Auvergne and Dordogne

There are around a dozen antiques shops in Agen and several antiquarian bookshops. Visit **Colette Milliard** at 22 Richard Coeur de Lion, **Bareyre Antiquités**, 12 rue Garonne or **Bon Vieux Temps** (12 rue des Cornières) for a flavour of what's to be found in the region. There's a bric-a-brac market every Saturday and on the first Sunday in October in rue Les Rameaux, and five Monday *brocante* fairs during the year.

● **Musée Municipal des Beaux-Arts**, place du Docteur Esquirol. Tel: (05) 53 69 47 23.

CORDES

In the 13th and 14th centuries, this *bastide* precipitously perched overlooking the River Cérou, grew rich on linen and leather. Much money was spent on building splendid Gothic *manoirs*; the **Maison du Grand Venneur** and **Maison du Grand Fauconnier** along rue Grand are particularly outstanding. It's also a sign of the town's wealth that stone, and not timber, was used for the pillars of the covered market. After falling into disrepair, the town was restored after World War II thanks to the enthusiastic efforts of the artist Yves Brayer, and many artists are still attracted to the pretty town.

Cameo glass vase signed Barg, c.1920

Antiquités Lamazière, in avenue du 8 Mai 1945, and **Joel Berthelot**, at 4 rue de la Gaudane, are two antiques shops among many galleries and souvenir sellers.

SHOPPER'S TIP

One of the surprises of the area is the amount of costume jewellery on sale. Among trays of cheap brooches and imitation pearls I've more than once come across vintage pieces from the 1920s, '30s and '50s. Look for a name or a recognizable symbol. Many of France's leading names in fashion also designed jewellery and their pieces are keenly collected.

WHERE TO EAT AND DRINK

Hercule Poirot
2 rue de la Nation, Périgueux
Tel: (05) 53 08 90 76
This restaurant may be named after a 20th-century Belgian detective, but you will enjoy the best Périgord cuisine beneath vaulted ceilings over 400 years old.

L'Esplanade
Domme
Tel: (05) 53 28 31 41
This is the restaurant with a view, in the town with a view. Come to this lovely stone building at sunset and sample regional specialities in the beamed dining room.

Hôtel de Château
1 rue de la Tour, Lalinde
Tel: (05) 53 61 01 82
This little château by the river is part of the Logis chain. There is a terrace overlooking the water, and sound local cooking.

WHERE TO STAY

Many of the châteaux and large hotels often close in winter, usually Nov–Easter.

Château de Puy Robert
1 route de Valojoulx, Montignac-Lascaux
Tel: (05) 53 51 92 13; Fax: (05) 53 51 80 11
This neo-Renaissance château is ideally placed for visiting the area. Book well ahead and ask to stay in the boudoir, which is hidden way up in a turret overlooking the park – it's a romantic idyll.

Le Moulin de l'Abbaye
1 route Bourdeilles, Brântome-en-Périgord
Tel: (05) 53 05 80 22; Fax: (05) 53 05 75 27
A picture-postcard, flower-covered building on the River Donne, this was home to the Seigneur de Brântome (1530–1614), who wrote about the scandalous lives of the Valois court. Delightfully furnished with antiques, the restaurant serves local specialities on the terrace in summer. Closed in winter.

Manoir d'Hautegente
Coly, Dordogne
Tel: (05) 53 51 68 03; Fax: (05) 53 50 38 52
This lovely mansion just to the north of Sarlat used to be the mill and forge of an abbey. It is now a peaceful hotel with a fine library, private fishing and a swimming pool.

Château de Mercuès
Mercuès, Lot
Tel: (05) 65 20 00 01; Fax: (05) 65 20 05 72
Parts of this former summer home of the bishops of Cahors are more than 1,200 years old. Bedrooms overlook the château's vineyards; ask the owner, Georges Vigouroux, to show you round his impressive cellar of vintage Cahors wine.

Château de Roumégouse
Route de Rocamador, Rignac, Gramat
Tel: (05) 65 33 63 81; Fax: (05) 65 33 71 18
The château used to welcome travellers on the pilgrim route to Santiago de Compostela. Today guests stay in bedrooms which have been decorated by owners Luce and Jean-Louis Lainé in different period styles from throughout the house's history, ranging from Louis XIV to Napoleon III.

LYON

The talent of the region's craftsmen, especially its weavers, brought fame to Lyon, and in France's second city today you can find some of the best antiques in the country.

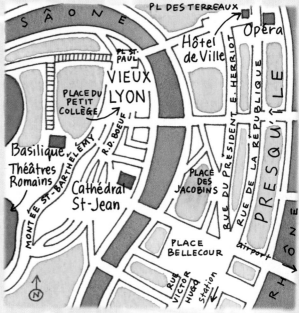

An écuelle (Meissen, c.1740), a soup ensemble popular in France in the 18th century

SITTING ASTRIDE THE GREAT WATERWAYS of the Rhône and Sâone, Lyon is a halfway house between north and south, and many people, many ideas and many different goods have come from this area. Arriving from Paris, you get your first indication of the character and climate of southern France here, and 500 years ago wealthy Italian merchants and bankers would make Lyon a staging post on their way to Paris.

Lyon is also an industrious town, and walking through the lanes of Vieux Lyon, you realize what talented craftsmen have lived here. Some of France's great cabinet-makers (*ébénistes*)

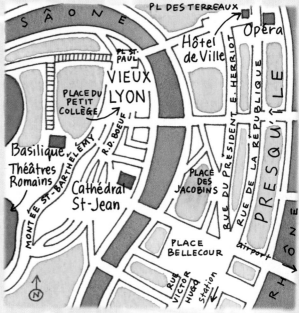

had their *ateliers* here, musical instrument makers, too. Their patrons had grown rich on the craft industries of printing and textile manufacture in the centuries before the Industrial Revolution. In Vieux Lyon, the wonderfully atmospheric old quarter of the town, the narrow cobbled streets are lined with the salmon pink Renaissance houses that were once occupied by *canuts*, the city's silk weavers who contributed so much to the reputation of Lyon as a textile centre.

Lyon is an elegant town today, and I always look forward to browsing in the rue Auguste Comte, one of the best antiques shopping streets in France. Lyon is also renowned for its restaurants, and with a thousand to choose from with menus ranging from simple fare to extravagant feasts, there is never any chance of getting tired of its food.

PLACES TO VISIT

Being a natural crossing point, just where the Saône and Rhône meet, the site of Lyon was settled early, and both the Greeks and Romans built cities here. To get your bearings, take a cable car from near the tourist office in Vieux Lyon up to the Colline de Fourvière. On the hill's southern slope is the underground **Musée de la Civilisation Gallo-Romaine**, and through windows you can look out on to two nearby amphitheatres, which are still used for performances. The **Grand Théâtre**, built in 56BC, is the oldest in France. At the top of the hill sits the **Basilique Notre-Dame de Fourvière**, an unmissable late-19th-century fit of enthusiasm which the Lyonnais have come to love. From the basilica, the chemin de la Rosarie is a meandering path leading back down to the old town. Cross any of the bridges onto the **Presqu'île**, the last wedge of land between the rivers before they meet.

The **Musée des Beaux-Arts** has France's second most important fine art collection after the Louvre. It is housed in a former convent, and the galleries are grouped around the cloister gardens. The collections cover every era from ancient Greece to the present day, and from local pottery to Byzantine ivory carvings. Artists of the 19th and 20th centuries are especially strong here, and look out, too,

The basilica of Notre-Dame de Fourvière, set high up above the Sâone

for the Lyonnais "troubadour" artist Fleury Richard (1777–1852) whose work was much admired by the Empress Josephine.

● **Musée de la Civilisation Gallo-Romaine**, 17 rue Cléberg. Tel: (04) 72 38 81 90.
● **Musée des Beaux Arts**, Palais Saint-Pierre, 20 place des Terreaux. Tel: (04) 72 10 17 40.

HISTORY REVISITED

THE SILK INDUSTRY

From the 14th century until the Industrial Revolution thousands of small workshops produced coloured silks in Lyon. Initially, weavers worked at home, *en famille*, but at the beginning of the 19th century Joseph Marie Jacquard (1752–1834) invented the jacquard loom. His new machines stood almost 4m (12ft) high, which meant that the silk workers, the *canuts,* were no longer able to work at home. So they installed themselves on the hill of Croix Rouge, where they built workshops that would take the tall machines. You can still see the *traboules*, covered passages between the houses through which workers could scurry back and forth with their precious fabrics, keeping them out of the rain. The whole district reverberated to *bristanclaque* – a word invented to imitate the sound of the machines. Working

up to 18 hours a day, however, the *canuts* famously revolted on several occasions, and their struggle made them as well known as the textiles they produced.

You can see demonstrations on different types of looms at **La Maison des Canuts**. Most spectacular is the weaving of Genoa velvet, for which 800 bobbins form loops which are cut line by line to give a deep pattern in three-colour relief.

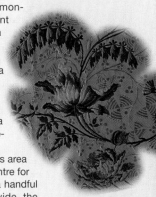

Fragment of silk in the Musée des Tissus

The Rhône-Alpes area remains a world centre for silk-weaving, and a handful of craftsmen provide the museums and palaces of Europe with the brocades of a bygone era.

Research is carried on at the **Musée des Tissus**, the textile museum housed in the 18th-century Hôtel de Villeroy. This is also where you can follow the story of the silk makers, from the Renaissance up until today, with hundreds of examples of tapestries and costumes, from Lyon and all over the world.

● **La Maison des Canuts** 10–12 rue d'Ivry. Tel (04) 78 28 62 04. Closed Mon in Aug.
● **Musée des Tissus** 34 rue de la Charité. Tel (04) 78 38 42 00.

Hangings and lengths of antique fabric on display in the fascinating Musée des Tissus

ANTIQUES IN CONTEXT

To appreciate the craftsmanship of previous centuries, step into a Renaissance house in Vieux Lyon, and you will be taken back to a time of *ébénistes*, glassblowers and puppeteers. The finely crafted goods they produced can still be found in Lyon's antiques shops.

Lyon is a great place to put antiques into perspective: just walking round the old town and looking at the wonderful old town houses in streets such as rue St Jacques gives a sense of the city's past. In these houses the wealthy would employ craftsmen to enrich the fabric of their lives with beautiful furniture, luxurious drapes and exquisite fine art.

One of the most beautiful is the Hôtel de Gadagne, built in 1527 and shortly afterwards the property of the Gadagne Florentine banking family. Fully restored, today it is home to the **Musée Historique de Lyon** and the **Musée de la Marionnette**. Evoking Lyon from the middle ages to the 19th century, the history museum gives an idea of the crafts in the town.

Scent bottles in an opaline coffret (c.1850) in vert feuille or leaf green, which "fires" to emerald

The marionnettes are a tradition that was begun in 1808 by Laurent Mourguet who created a puppet family of *canut* silk workers named Guignol, Madelon and Gnafron, and the museum now has a collection of puppets from all over the world.

In the 18th and 19th centuries Lyon had scores of small furniture workshops and some notable *ébénistes*, or cabinet-makers, such as Pierre Nogaret, a *maître ébéniste* whose furniture is in the city's museums, and Claude Montagnut, whose ingenious mechanical devices included a self-folding *prie-dieu*, made around 1855.

A traditional marionette shop in Vieux Lyon

The **Musée des Arts Décoratifs**, alongside the Musée des Tissus (see page 107), has spacious rooms with displays of furniture made by Lyonnais cabinet-makers and 18th-century harpsichords made by the Lyonnais company of P. Donzelague. It also has the best collection of Italian Renaissance maiolica in France.

● **Musée Historique de Lyon** and **Musée de la Marionnette**, Hôtel de Gadagne, place du Petit Collège. Tel: (04) 78 42 03 61.

● **Musée des Arts Décoratifs**, rue de la Charité. Tel: (04) 78 38 42 00

OPALINE GLASS

In the 19th century French glassmakers began to manufacture a translucent, coloured glass which had a slightly milky or opal-like appearance. They called it *en couleurs opales* or simply *opale*, but today this highly collectable glassware is called opaline. It has a particular "fire" – a dramatic change of colour – when held to the light, notably in the pink *gorge de pigeon* (pigeon's throat) which shows blood red in the light. This was achieved by adding bone ash (calcium phosphate) or tin oxide to the mix. The most renowned French makers of opaline were Baccarat, Choissy-le-Roi and Saint Louis.

SHOPPING

There are more than 100 shops in Lyon, but the showcase antiques street is undoubtedly **rue d'Auguste Comte**, running between place Bellecour and place Carnot. Along here, and in the surrounding streets, you can find the most fascinating antiques showrooms and, for a price, pick up some top-quality pieces.

Look out for:
Charles Balaÿ (No 8) has furniture and painting mainly from the 18th century, while **Gallerie Yves Chalvin** at No 25 has 19th- and 20th-century furniture and paintings.

Late 19th-century walnut canapé in Louis XV style

Arachaïa (No 10) deals in archeological finds and primitive art. **Gallery Michel Descours** at Nos 31 and 44 specializes in antique jewellery and trinkets; and **La Pharmacopée Antiquités** at No 56 sells, among other things, furniture from the 1930s to the 1950s.

VILLEURBANNE

Lyon's other great antiques hunters' ground is on the east bank of the Rhône, beside the Parc de la Tour. In a two-storey modern building at 117 boulevard Stalingrad, is **La Cité des Antiquaires** (open Thurs, Sat, Sun 9.30am–12.30pm and 2.30–7pm; closed Sun pm June–Aug). Around 150 shops fill the building and what they have to sell is in the main less expensive than in Auguste-Comte, but you should purchase with caution, as fakes are not uncommon.

The restaurant-lined rue du Boeuf

Look out for:
Monique Cattin (1.1) specializes in Lyon and Beaujolais furniture. **Nicole Dentelle** (1.5) has antique textiles and household linen from the 19th century, as well as *objets d'art* and jewellery. **Jean-Marie Maire** (1.8) has furniture from the 1920s to the 1940s, especially chairs, and **Galerie Hadrien** (2.34) has a range of Art Deco pieces. **Daniel Brillat** specializes in faience apothecary jars.

FAIRS AND MARKETS

Each autumn a large antiques fair is held at **Villefranche-sur-Saône**, just north of Lyon. Tel: (04) 78 98 02 02, for information.

WHERE TO EAT AND DRINK

Lyon claims to have the greatest concentration of Michelin-starred restaurants in France. The city's *bouchons*, traditional bistros with their picturesque interiors, are always tempting.

Brassserie Georges 1836
30 cours de Verdun, Perrache
Tel: (04) 72 56 54 54
This is one of the oldest brasseries in Europe and dates from 1836. Although the seating arrangements resemble a railway restaurant car, the Art Deco interior is wonderful.

Le Bouchon aux Vins
62 rue Mercère
Tel: (04) 78 38 47 40
A *bouchons* that's very typical, and very popular with the locals. It serves sturdy food including *pot au feu* and has good Rhône wines.

La Meunière
11 rue Neuve
Tel: (04) 78 28 62 91
An inexpensive place for a cheerful meal in original 1920s surroundings. Drink wine in the thick glass pots that are a Lyon speciality.

WHERE TO STAY
La Tour Rose
22 rue du Boeuf
Tel: (04) 78 37 25 90; Fax: (04) 78 42 26 02
This small, luxury hotel only has 12 rooms, but they are decorated to show the history of silk and each room reflects a different period. The restaurant is highly recommended.

Hôtel Carlton
4 rue Jussieu
Tel: (04) 78 42 56 51; Fax: (04) 78 42 10 71
The Belle Epoque era is recalled in this hotel, but the rooms have plenty of modern comforts.

Cour de Loges
6 rue du Boeuf
Tel: (04) 72 77 44 44; Fax: (04) 72 40 93 61
In the middle of Vieux Lyon, this luxury hotel comprises four adjoining Renaissance mansions.

IN THE AREA

About 35km (20 miles) north-east of Lyon is **Pérouges**, a picturesque medieval town consisting almost entirely of 15th- and 16th-century houses, with stone-paved streets and narrrow alleys. You can browse the galleries and shops selling traditional crafts of the Bresse area, such as distinctive blue Meillonas earthenware. You can stop for a meal at the town's ancient hotel, Ostellerie de Vieux Pérouge, which dates back to the 13th century. **Vienne**, 25km (15 miles) south of Lyon, has superb Roman ruins (two temples, an amphitheatre and a "pyramid"), a 12th-century cathedral and two early Christian churches.

MARSEILLE

France's oldest port has been trading with Africa and the East since the 6th century BC. Its *soukh*-like market streets still give the town an African flavour.

Pierced bouquetière in Marseille faience, c.1760

LA CANABIÈRE IS MARSEILLE'S LIVELY MAIN STREET, a broad avenue that descends to the Vieux Port (old port), used since the days of the Greeks, where fishing boats bob and restaurants serve steaming bowls of *bouillabaisse*. In La Canabière is France's oldest stock exchange with a collection of items from *outre mer* – the land beyond the sea. The port's exotic, African flavour spills into the streets leading from La Canabière, groaning with stalls and pavement-sellers with their wares on flattened cardboard boxes. Many antiques shops are in this area too, and if you want to take a step back into Marseilles' past, the city has a number of mansions with reconstructed rooms from the 18th and 19th centuries.

HISTORY REVISITED

THE AFRICAN CONNECTION

Marseille, founded by the Greeks as Massalia in AD600, has always been a major port and a window on the other countries of the Mediterranean. Its fortunes flagged when the Americas were discovered and the Atlantic trade opened up, but they revived in 1830 when the French colonized Algeria. When the Suez Canal opened in 1869 liners as well as cargo ships would make this a port of call heading east. The bombing of the entire dock area in World War II led to the discovery of the old Roman docks, which can now be visited (closed Mondays).

● **Musée des Docks Romains**, 28 pl. Vivaux. Tel: (04) 91 91 24 62.

Silver, enamel and coral anklet typical of the North African jewellery traded in Marseille for centuries

PLACES TO VISIT

Some of Marseille's museums also offer the chance to see into some fine old houses. A small collection of Egyptian artifacts is held in **Vieille Charité** (built 1671) and in the 16th-century Maison Diamantée is the **Musée de Vieux Marseille**, with its 18th-century Provençal furniture. The grand house built in 1873 for a merchant, **Alexandre Labadié**, contains tapestries, furnishings and musical instruments. Visit the **Musée des Arts et Traditions Populaires** for an insight into life from the 17th to 19th centuries.

● **Vieille Charité**, 2 rue de la Vieille Charité. Tel: (04) 91 14 58 80.
● **Musée de Vieux Marseille**, 2 rue de la Prison. Tel: (04) 91 55 28 68.
● **Musée Grobet-Labadié**, 140 boulevard Longchamp. Tel: (04) 91 62 21 82.
● **Musée des Arts et Traditions Populaires**, 5 place de Héroes. Tel: (04) 91 68 14 38. Closed Tues.

SHOPPING

Around **Cours Julien** there are many antiques shops and, on the second Sunday of every month, a flea market. A Sunday flea market is also held in rue Frédérique-Sauvage, and boulevard Fifi de Turin has a **Village des Antiquaires**. Worth exploring, too, is **Espace Madrigue** in chemin de la Madrigue-Ville. Parc Chanot has *brocante* (bric-a-brac) fairs and a **Salon d'Antiquaires** in October.

Hopeful hunters among Marseille bric-a-brac

Look out for:
Atelier Carbonel (rue Neuve Ste-Catherine 47) is a famous *santon* seller, with a museum. Provençal furniture is a speciality at **Provence Antiquité** (18 rue des Trois Frères Barthélémy) and at Edouard and Hélène Balestra's **Au Carrosse d'Or** (254 ch. de l'Armée d'Afrique). You'll find local paintings at **Galerie David Pluskwa** (304 rue de Paradis). **Soldats** (33 rue St Jacques) has been turning out model soldiers since Napoleonic times. For north African products, try **Néapolis** (19 bd Baille).

Notre-Dame-de-la-Garde rising up beyond the Vieux Port

MARSEILLE FAIENCE

The green floral plate below (c.1760) is relatively rare; Marseille faience more usually resembles the blue Moustiers plate, top, of the same era (see page 118). A feature of Marseille is *petit-feu* enamelling, a method of firing at low temperature which allowed subtle pastel colours. It reached a peak under Veuve Perrin and others in the late 18th century.

● **Musée de la Faïence**, Château Pastré. Tel: (04) 91 72 43 47.

WHERE TO EAT AND DRINK

Café de la Mode
11 La Canabière
Tel: (04) 91 91 21 36
Inside the fashionable Musée de la Mode, make this a day-time stop to look at 20th-century costume and whatever is the current exhibition.

Miramar
12 quai du Port
Tel: (04) 91 91 10 40
Great, traditional *bouillabaisse* at a price, this is one of the Vieux Port's best known restaurants and a Marseille institution. Closed most of Aug.

WHERE TO STAY

Mercure Beauvau Vieux Port
4 rue Beauvau
Tel: (04) 91 54 91 00; Fax: (04) 91 54 15 76
The Beauvau opened its doors in 1816 and has entertained celebrities from George Sand and Chopin to Jean Cocteau. Rooms are furnished with Louis XIII and Empire antiques.

Abbaye de Sainte-Croix
route du Val de Cuech, Salon-de-Provence
Tel: (04) 90 56 24 55; Fax: (04) 90 56 31 12
Converted monks' cells with rustic furniture, a 12th-century cloister and surrounded by lavender fields: it's worth the 35-km (20-mile) journey.

IN THE AREA

Cassis, 20km (12 miles) east of Marseille, is a truly relaxing haven and still the charming fishing port that artists such as the Fauvist André Derain used to paint a century ago. Winston Churchill painted here, too. There's an 18th-century town hall to see, and a restored 14th-century castle. But I suggest sitting in a waterside café, eating seafood, drinking dry white Cassis wine and watching the world go by. If you want to stay, try the tiny **Le Clos des Arômes**, 10 rue Paul Mouton. Tel: (04) 42 01 71 84; Fax: (04) 42 01 31 76.

PROVENCE

Colourful textiles and decorated furniture are lasting souvenirs of one of the most pleasurable antiques hunting grounds.

Examples of mid-18th-century Provençal faience

PROVENCE HAS BOTH SOPHISTICATED TOWNS SUCH AS NICE and hilltop villages that seem caught in the Middle Ages. Parts of the coast are magnets for international socialites, but the waterlands of the Camargue at sunrise are magically peaceful.

For me, what makes the region particularly exciting is that the past never seems far away. The *tuiles romaines* that cover low-pitched roofs are a legacy of the Romans who enjoyed the good life here, and a *mas*, a typical farmhouse with cool, tiled floors and a large kitchen leading from a courtyard, is little changed since Julius Caesar's day. Provençal homes were always furnished in an individual style. Made almost exclusively of mahogany, with some cherry, the furniture is often colourfully decorated with flowers and other motifs, and perhaps the initials of the original owner. Few chairs have survived, but there are

A 19th-century Provençal fabric, with typical Oriental-inspired motifs

plenty of wardrobes to be found, as well as kitchen items such as dough bowls (*pétrins*), fancifully carved and decorated store cupboards (*panetières*) and ironwork (*ferronerie*) from the hearth and stove. The sun ensures long days out of doors: garden furniture, statuary and decorated sundials all find their way into antiques shops. This is a land of scents, so look out, too, for pretty glass perfume bottles and other small items such as snuff boxes made of orange-scented bergamot, a citrus tree with a flower that is used in perfumes and tea as well as in snuff. The hillsides that smell so delicious also produced medicinal herbs, which in turn fuelled a demand for apothecaries' jars. Moustiers-Sainte-Marie provided them. The town is still famous for its faience, which at one time was the sole preserve of counts and kings.

Provence is different in so many ways: it has all you expect, and yet is still full of surprises, from the château of the Marquis de Sade in Sénanques to the quirky little museum devoted to corkscrews in the Lubéron village of Menerbes.

Map showing Provence region with locations including Lyon, Orange, Sorgues, Forcalquier, Roussillon, Apt, Céreste, Moustiers Ste-Marie, Digne-les-Bains, Alpes Maritimes, Monaco, Nice, Antibes, Gordes, Parc du Lubéron, Grasse, Cannes, Avignon, Arles, Nîmes, Camargue, Aix-en-Provence, Marseille, Toulon, Rhône, Durance.

PROVINCIA ROMANA

Provence has some of the finest Roman remains in Europe. The Romans arrived in the south-east corner of ancient Gaul in the second century BC and called it simply Provincia Romana – a Roman province. Local Gallic tribes were not easily subdued but, when they were, the Romans wanted to show who was in command. The names of the vanquished tribes, sometimes depicted as captives, naked and in chains, were picked out on their monuments and triumphal arches, from La Turbie, above Monaco, to Glanum, Carpentras and Orange.

The building work the Romans undertook, with theatres, baths and aqueducts, was remarkable, and many major towns of the region have evidence of their Roman past in their fabric. Reused stones can be seen in buildings everywhere. In the first century AD, the emperor Augustus built the Aurelian Way, a highway from Rome to Arles, and amphitheatres were constructed in Arles, Nîmes, Nice, Fréjus, Orange and Vaison-La-Romaine.

Fréjus became the second largest port after Marseille. It was the first Roman town to be founded in Gaul, by Julius Caesar in 49BC, but Romans under Caius Sextus had settled in 121BC at Aix-en-Provence, which for a while was capital of Roman Gaul, though there is little to see of it today.

At first allies of the Greeks in Massalia (Marseille), the Romans later took over the town and it remained the most important port on the coast. They also enlarged the town that the Massalia Greeks had built at Glanum, just outside Arles, making it a main stopping point and a crossroads on the road west to Spain, and north to Lyon.

Among the many Roman sites in Provence, three are outstanding. **Les Arènes** in Arles is an enormous and wonderfully preserved arena. It seats 20,000 and is now used for festivals and bullfights. The **Théâtre Antique d'Orange** has the most complete Roman theatre, seating 10,000. An annual music festival, the Chorégies d'Orange, has been held here since 1849. Outside Arles, near St-Rémy, where Van Gogh lived, is **Glanum**, one of the most extensive Roman sites, which, because it was abandoned, was never built over.

● **Les Arènes**, Arles. Tel: (04) 90 96 03 70.
● **Théâtre d'Orange**, Orange. Tel: (04) 90 51 17 60.
● **Site Archéologique de Glanum**, St-Rémy-de-Provence. Tel: (04) 90 92 23 79.

Roman triumphal arch at Glanum,
the oldest in France

AROUND PROVENCE

Hunting for antiques is just one way of enjoying Arles, Avignon, Aix-en-Provence and the lovely villages of the south. If you find an antiques shop closed on Monday, it's probably because the owner is in L'isle sur la Sorgue, the biggest centre for antiques outside Paris.

ARLES

The most traditional town of the south is also one of the most characterful. This was where Vincent Van Gogh came in 1888, and you can see his bright colours in the traditional costumes and textiles, known as *indiennes*, produced here since the 17th century. (A local chain of shops, **Souleido**, sells quality Provençal-patterned tableware and linen.) Van Gogh spent his last, productive years nearby, in **Maison de Santé St-Paul**, a peaceful Romanesque building that was once a monastery. Visitors are given a tour and you can recognize scenes he painted. Arles is noted for its Roman remains (see page 113), but most important for antiques lovers is the Museon Arlaten (see right).

Paintings by Monique Giardini in the Museon Arlaten

Browse antiques and *brocante* shops near the Arènes and Musée Reattu. An antiques market is held on boulevard de Lice on the south side of the old town on Wednesday and Sunday mornings. There are a dozen antique shops in Arles, where the queen bee is Elisabeth Maurant at **Maurant** (4 rue de Grille). She has four shops and specializes in Provençal furniture, particularly 17th- and 18th-century *armoires* (Arles produced a distinctive, florid style of furniture), as well as Second Empire longcase and bracket

Antiques shop in a quaint side street in Arles

clocks. Mme Maurant also organizes the town's **Salon des Antiquités et de la Brocante** at the Palais de Congrès every September.
● **Maison de Santé St-Paul**, av Van Gogh, St-Paul-de-Mausole. Tel: (04) 90 92 77 00.

TRADITIONAL PROVENCE

The **Museon Arlaten** in Arles was set up by the great champion of the way of life in the region, Frédéric Mistral, with money he received from the Nobel Prize for literature in 1904. His intention was to record the rich traditions of local life, and domestic interiors have been reconstructed in a 16th-century *hôtel*. Exhibits ranging from kitchenware to amulets and musical instruments all give an excellent idea of the kind of fascinating local antiques that may turn up in the area.
● **Museon Arlaten**, Hôtel Laval-Castallane, rue de la République. Tel: (04) 90 93 58 11.

AVIGNON

From 1309 to 1377, Popes ruled Christendom from Avignon, challenging the supremacy of Rome. Although the **Palais des Papes** is magnificent, nothing remains of its furnishings, but two modest museums in the town have examples: **Musée Calvert** has ceramics, sculptures and paintings, including the Avignon school, and **Musée Louis Vouland** has 18th-century furniture, ceramics and Gobelins tapestries.

Avignon has over 40 antiques shops, where *bois doré* (gilded wood) and polished surfaces dazzle. Try **Midi Antique** in rue Grand Fustière for furniture, and **Hervée Baume** in Petite Fustière for local antiques from garden furniture to Art Deco. You'll find 19th-century Provençal paintings at **Art Gallery** (2 rue Joseph Vernet), old prints at **Galerie Gérard Guerre** (1 Plan de Lunel) and faience at **Dervieux** (11 rue Félix-Gras). On Sunday mornings a flea market fills place des Carmes.
● **Palais des Papes**, place du Palais. Tel (04) 90 27 50 74.
● **Musée Calvert**, 65 rue Joseph Vernet. Tel (04) 90 86 33 84.
● **Musée Louis Vouland**, 17 rue Victor Hugo. Tel (04) 90 86 03 79.

Pont St-Bénézet, Avignon, built in the 12th century and left stranded by floods and war

Browsing in l'Isle-sur-la-Sorgue

L'ISLE SUR LA SORGUE

This pretty town near Avignon is set among a network of canals dotted with moss-covered waterwheels, with delightful, shady streets and pleasant cafés. The five branches of the River Sorgue that run through the town once turned the wheels that powered the medieval cloth industry here. Many houses date from the 16th and 17th centuries when silk workers made the town rich, and the finest buildings can be seen in place de la Liberté and place de l'Eglise, where the *fin-de-siècle* **Café de Paris** is the best place to soak up local colour. Ask at the tourist office (see Useful Addresses at the end of the book) about guided historical tours of the town.

SHOPPING

Today everyone in France knows La Sorgue for one thing: its antiques. This is the largest antiques centre in France outside Paris and between 2,000 and 3,000 people descend on it every weekend. The shops and antiques "villages" are open on Saturday, Sunday and Monday from 10am to 7pm, but the best time to visit is Sunday morning, when other stalls are set up and a food market spices the air with fruit, garlic, peppers and herbs.

The range of shops and stalls is amazing. There are bargain stalls alongside high-priced shops. Many antiques dealers in the region have premises here, working in their own home towns during the week and then opening their shops in La Sorgue only at the weekends.

Provençal faience plate, c.1765, by Veuve Perrin

Among the antiques shops and stalls you can find kitchenalia, enamels and fabulous textiles and linens of all kinds. It is also a good place to pick up English porcelain.

Look out for:

Rives de Sorgues, avenue de la Libération, is a small gallery of 20 dealers, specializing in a variety of antiques from Art Deco to textiles and regional furniture.

L'île aux Brocantes, 7 avenue des 4 Otages, has 40 dealers, many of whom specialize in Provençal and "bistro" furniture from the 17th century to the 1950s. It has a pleasant riverside café, Chez Nane, with a shady terrace. **Les Boutiques de l'Orée** is in a modern building at place de l'Orée de l'isle. Here 20 dealers sell Provençal paintings, silverware, 18th- and 19th-century *objets* and wallpaper. **Hôtel Dongier** in place Gambetta has ten showrooms, many of them large, such as that of **Marie-Claire Reynaud** who has items for each room and the garden, from 17th–19th-century Provence. **Le Village des Antiquaires**, in avenue de l'Egalité, has 100 dealers, a restaurant and a *salon de thé* in a 19th-century spinning mill, Les Tapis d'Avignon, beneath which flows a branch of the Sorgue. Dealers here pride themselves on restoration work, offering items from enamelled teapots to Provençal furniture with coats of arms. There are 30 or so dealers in **Le Quai de la Gare**, an old warehouse in avenue Julien Guigne. Other smaller sites are **La Rendez-Vous des Marchands** (89–91 avenue de la Libération), **La Cour de François** in an old quay in rue Rose Gaudard and **le Carré de l'isle** in avenue des 4 Otages.

TRY NOT TO MISS...

L'isle-sur-la-Sorgue's four-day **Foires Antiquités et Brocantes**. They are held at Easter and in August and are extremely popular. Stalls spread out down cours René Char (named after the poet who was born here in 1907) and Parc Gauthier, and the town's population swells by some 50,000 as antiques hunters from all over France hope to *chiner* – to stumble across something unexpectedly. There can be few more serendipitous places for browsers to spend a day out.

Gordes, typical of the villages perchés found in the hills of Provence

GORDES

This picture-book hilltop town is one of the most desirable addresses in Provence. Its medieval streets and lanes are wonderful to wander around at any time of year. The excellent shops include one or two selling antiques. The town is dominated by the 16th-century **Château de Gordes**, built on the site of a 12th-century fortress. This is where the Hungarian Op artist Victor Vasarely lived until his death in 1997.

● **Château de Gordes**, place du Château. Tel: (04) 90 72 02 75.

ROUSSILLON

Golden yellows, glowing reds and soft browns – Roussillon's buildings have the warmest colours of any Provençal town and many artists have been inspired here. These are truly the colours of the earth, for they have been extracted from Roussillon's extraordinary quarries at the **Chaussée des Géants** (the Giant's Causeway), which produced 17 distinct colours of ochre for export. The quarries were closed in 1958, when their excavations threatened to undermine the town. Also take a look at the **Val des Fées** (Valley of the Fairies) with its breathtaking Cliffs of Blood.

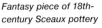

Fantasy piece of 18th-century Sceaux pottery

Roussillon's narrow streets are full of galleries and artisan shops. Look out for enamel and glassware as you head for the pretty central square where the russet and terracotta of the buildings are offset with green and blue paintwork.

APT

Ochre is still mined and refined at Apt, which has been a centre for pottery-making since the early 18th century. The first faience and earthenware factory here was Le Castelet, founded in 1728 by César Moulin, which remained in the hands of the family until 1852. Le Castelet's English-style wares included

Painted wooden doorway in Roussillon

agate and yellow-and-brown marbled ware in shapes often inspired by silverware. Today the best-known potteries are **Elzéar Bennet** and **La Veuve Arnoux**.

There are a handful of antiques shops in the town, and some just out of town, such as **L'Air du Temps**, a marvellous warehouse on the N100 towards Avignon. A Saturday market around rue des Marchands has a carnival atmosphere with musicians, comedians and sundry characters mingling among stalls selling all kinds of produce.

A **Foire Expo Brocante** is held on Mondays in the place Saint-Pierre in the centre of town, and the **Salon des Antiquitaires** on the last weekend of July is a major event, attracting buyers from all over Europe.

Apt is also France's confectionery capital, specializing in crystallized fruit. **La Bonbonnière**, 13 rue de la Sous-Préfecture, is the place for sweets, chocolates and all local confectionery.

AIX-EN-PROVENCE

Aix-en-Provence was once the home of Provence's most respected monarch, Good King René (1409–80), but don't be surprised to hear American accents nowadays in the streets of this bustling town of tree-lined avenues and elegant fountains; several popular international schools are based here. The town's grandest street is cours Maribeau,

Ebulliently decorated 16th-century fireplace in the Great Hall of the Château de Gordes

SANTONS

It is impossible to travel in Provence without noticing the figures called *santons* (from *santouns*, meaning small saints). *Crêches* – tableaux of the nativity – were introduced from Italy in the 17th century, and the *crêches*'s articulated wooden dolls became ever more ornate until, in the 18th century, fully animated marionnettes were performing in church. During the French Revolution (1789) churches were closed and people were not able to enjoy this traditional aspect of their Christmas, so an enterprising statue-maker from Marseille, Jean-Louis Lagnel, began to make small, inexpensive figures for people to set up cribs in their own homes. The brightly painted pottery figures proved popular, and the range grew to take in such characters as hunters, knife-grinders and milkmaids. **Aubagne**, which had a tradition of *terre rouge* earthenware, became a centre for *santon*-making. Historic figures populate the **Musée du Vieil Aix** in Aix-en-Provence, and Marseille's **Foire aux Santons** runs from the last Sunday in November until 6 January.

Paul Cézanne's studio, as he left it almost 100 years ago, at his home at Aix-en-Provence

with cafés on one side (try **Les Deux Garçons** at No 35, a splendid gilt and mirror *fin-de-siècle* parlour where the arty crowd go) and elegant 17th- and 18th-century mansions on the other.

The **Musée Granet**, next to St-Jean-de-Malte, where the counts of Provence lie buried, is in a 17th-century priory, and its collection of paintings includes Avignon Primitives and eight minor works by Paul Cézanne (1839–1906). The painter's home is on the outskirts of the old town. His studio looks as if he has just left it for a day out to paint his favourite scene, the nearby Montagne Ste-Victoire.

The **Musée Paul Arbaud** near the Fontaine des Quatre Dauphins has one of the best collections of Moustiers faience in Provence (see page 118), including

Early 19th-century "hobnail-cut" glass powder box

a delightful piece made in 1982 to mark the bicentenary of the Montgolfier brothers' first hot-air balloon flight. The **Musée de Tapisseries** also has theatrical costumes alongside its examples of Beauvais tapestries (see page 95).

● **Musée Granet**, 13 rue Cardinale. Tel: (04) 42 38 14 70.
● **Atelier de Cézanne**, 9 ave Paul. Tel: (04) 42 21 06 53.
● **Musée Paul Arbaud**, 2a rue du 4 Septembre. Tel: (04)42 38 38 95.
● **Musée des Tapisseries**, 28 place de l'Ancien Archevêché. Tel: (04) 42 23 09 91.

SHOPPING IN AIX

With around 60 antiques shops and regular markets, Aix is a great place for antiques hunters, although you can expect its popularity to be reflected in the prices.

Look out for:

For Provençal furniture and *objets* from the 17th to 19th centuries try **Jean Isabelle et Thierry**, at 19 rue Emeric David, behind the Palais du Justice; for faience and mirrors, look in on the **Marchés aux Palais** at 1 rue Chastel.

In the old Quartier Mazarin south of cours Mirabau there are a number of interesting shops, particularly along rue Cardinale, where **Librairie des Livres** is just one of a number of antiquarian bookshops in this scholarly town.

The markets of **Aix-en-Provence** are among the best in the area. There are antiques and *brocante* (bric-a-brac) stalls every Tuesday, Thursday and Saturday morning near the Palais de Justice. On the last Monday of every month there is a much bigger *brocante* market in place Jean d'Arc, where a five-day antiques extravaganza takes place in December.

Picturesque Moustiers-Sainte-Marie

FORCALQUIER

The town takes its name from its ancient lime kilns (*furnus calcarius*). Its golden age was the 12th century, when the local counts embellished their castle and minted their own coins. A ruined tower is all that is left of the castle, but other buildings in the old town survive, some with their doorways sculpted with plaques and scrolls. There was a Jewish quarter around the synagogue in rue des Cordeliers and there are guided tours to Couvent de Cordeliers, built in the 12th to 14th centuries.

There are half a dozen antiques shops in the old town, and a good place to start is place Saint-Michel, where **Jean Leinart** has a superb shop filled with antiquarian books and general antiques.

Faience candlestick, 1765, made in Marseille

Forcalquier comes alive on Monday, market day, when stalls in place du Bourguet and the surrounding lanes are laden with local produce and above-average *objets artisanaux*. This is a social as well as a business occasion, and people come to chat and relax in the cafés. On Sundays in July and August there's a flea market, and in the first two weeks of August the **Festival de Haute Provence** brings arts and crafts from the region.

Mane, 4km (2 miles) south of Forcalquier, has two antiques shops: **Patrick Holvoet** in La Placette and **Lefort** in avenue Burlière. It's a good place to buy textiles, sheets and kitchen towels. On the outskirts of the town, on the road to Apt, stands **Notre-Dame de Salagon**, a large 12th-century church with a 15th-century monastic residence and 17th-century farm buildings. Now a conservation centre, it has a museum showing traditional rural items such as farm implements, kitchen utensils and children's toys. Also along this road is the

Château de Sauvan, a classic 18th-century château with lawns and a lake. There are guided tours of its furnished interior.
● **Notre-Dame de Salagon**, 3km (2 miles) from Forcalquier, on N100 out of Mane). Tel: (04) 92 75 19 93.
● **Château de Sauvan**, near Mane on N100. Tel: (04) 92 75 05 64.

MOUSTIERS-SAINTE-MARIE

Moustiers is spectacularly set at the entrance to the Verdon Canyon, beneath a huge pendant star hung on a chain between two cliffs. The little town is a centre for arts and crafts and can become very crowded in holiday time, especially in August. Its name is synonymous with the pretty faience that spills out of shops into the narrow streets. You can buy lovely antique faience at **Marie-Moustiers** in rue de la Bourgade. Current makers of faience include **Soleil**, which has a sale room in the town's former olive oil mill, and the high-quality house of **Atelier de Segriès**.

An 18th-century faience pharmacy pot marked B. Clerissy

PROVENÇAL FAIENCE

The secrets of faience were brought to Moustiers-Sainte-Marie, so the story goes, by a monk from Faenza in Italy, where maiolica was made. He passed the formula for tin-glazed earthenware to Antoine Clérissy, a local potter, who founded the family firm that made Moustiers faience famous. Clérissy's blue-and-white style of decoration can be divided into two distinct periods. The first, (1680–1710), shows the influence of Florentine engraver Antonio Tempesta. The second, (1710–40), took

Painted provincial commode in beech and cane, c.1760

its inspiration from the great decorator and designer, Jean Bérain (1640–1711), and brought Moustiers ware to the height of its fame. Bérain master-minded entertainments for Louis XIV at Versailles, and there is a theatrical quality to many of the larger pieces *à la Bérain*, which are adorned with architectural motifs and arabesques. Another key *faïencier* was Joseph Olerys, who began working in 1738 and introduced purples, greens and oranges to the palette.

● **Musée de la Faïence**, placette du Prieuré. Tel (04) 92 74 67 84.

DIGNES-LES-BAINS

Capital of Alpes-de-Haute-Provence, Dignes is the last stop on the leisurely Train des Pignes, a local railway line that runs down to Nice. Ornaments made of *étoiles des Alpes*, fossilized starfish found in the black shale of the region, were once a local speciality. The **Musée Municipal** in the old town hospice

houses an impressive collection of 19th-century Provençal paintings.

● **Musée Municipal**, 64 boulevard Gassendi. Tel (04) 92 31 45 29.

Near the museum is **Betty Gleise**, one of two antiques shops in the town. Digne has a spectacular lavender festival every summer and two **weekly markets**, held on Wednesday and Saturday.

Pretty gold and coloured glass nécessaire, mid-18th century

SHOPPER'S TIP

The main buyers of Provençal furniture are the people of Provence themselves, who take a great pride in traditional crafts-manship. One piece of furniture unique to the area is the *radassié*, a settle with a wicker base, to seat from two to six people, which was tucked into the chimney recess for intimate moments or gossip. To possess one was a sign of social position.

WHERE TO EAT AND DRINK

Every town in Provence has a central square with a café and this is usually the best place to sit and watch the world go by over a coffee or a glass of wine. Hotels often have excellent restaurants.

La Bastide de Moustiers
chemin de Queinson, Moustiers-Sainte-Marie
Tel: (04) 92 70 47 47
Treat yourself to a wonderful meal in this 17th-century *bastide* outside Moustiers. It boasts a kitchen garden, extensive grounds and one of France's top chefs, Alain Ducasse.

Le Vaccarès
place du Forum, Arles
Tel: (04) 90 52 09 40
With a terrace overlooking the forum, this is one of Arles' most atmospheric restaurants. It serves great local food, such as marinated beef cooked with anchovies, and is not too expensive.

La Fontaine
5 rue Fontaine d'Argent, Aix-en-Provence
Tel: (04) 42 27 53 35
You won't have any trouble finding a restaurant in Aix, but in the city of fountains why not eat at a restaurant that has its own? Good Provençal food.

La Cuisine de Reine
rue Joseph Vernet, Avignon
Tel: (04) 90 85 99 04
This restaurant and *salon de thé* overlook an 18th-century Cloître des Arts. The imaginative menu includes *pique-nique à la maison*.

Oustau de Baumanière
Oustau de Baumanière, Les Baux
Tel: (04) 90 54 33 07
At the foot of the extraordinary medieval town of Les Baux, famous for its troubadours, this beautiful 18th-century olive mill is a culinary high spot. Closed Jan–Feb.

WHERE TO STAY

Some of the most charming places to stay are farmhouses and traditional *mas*: look for signposts, or enquire at local tourist offices (see Useful Addresses at the end of the book). It's best to book in July/August when the French are *en vacance*.

Hôtel d'Arlaten
26 rue de Sauvage, Arles
Tel: (04) 90 93 66; Fax: (04) 90 49 68 45
This is the beautifully restored 16th-century home of the Counts of Arlaten. Its Roman foundations can be seen through the *salon*'s glass-panelled floor, and its walled garden is delightful for leisurely summer breakfasts.

Le Manoir
8 rue d'Entrecasteaux, Aix-en-Provence
Tel: (04) 42 26 27 20; Fax (04) 42 27 17 97
Old-style hotel in a quiet street of Vieil Aix, with a 16th-century cloister in which to enjoy breakfast.

Le Ferme Jamet
chemin de Rhodes, Avignon
Tel: (04) 90 86 16 74; Fax: (04) 90 86 17 72
Popular with performers during the July Avignon Festival, this 16th-century farmhouse just outside the town is decorated in Provençal style.

Château l'Arc
chemin Maurel-Fuveau, Arc
Tel: (04) 42 29 80 80. Fax: (04) 42 29 80 85
Twelve suites are done out in period style in this 17th-century Provençal *bastide*. There are views of Paul Cezanne's much painted Montagne Ste-Victoire, as well as golf and a swimming pool.

Château d'Allemagne-en-Provence
Allemagne-en-Provence, near Forcalquier
Tel: (04) 92 77 46 78; Fax: (04) 92 77 73 84
This historic château dates from the 12th century and has three sumptuously decorated rooms. Open to the public in the summer.

BELGIUM & THE NETHERLANDS

THE ANTIQUES LANDSCAPE

In their chequered history the Low Countries have been ruled by Spain, France and Austria, and their reputation for tolerance meant that refugees fleeing religious persecution also settled here, bringing their crafts and customs with them, so that antiques have accumulated here from all over Europe.

After the revocation of the Edict of Nantes in 1685, religious freedom in France was once more curtailed, and countries to which the French protestant Huguenots fled benefited from their contributions to art and architecture and to crafts such as furniture-making and silversmithing. The interior of the Dutch palace of Het Loo was largely fashioned by Daniel Marot, a refugee from Paris who came under the wing of William II of Orange.

In the wake of tulipmania, tulipières such as this 17th-century Delft example were in great demand.

The art of tin-glazed earthenware was brought here by Italian immigrants at the very beginning of the 16th century – there is a record of a Guido Andries at work in Antwerp by 1508. Centres such as Haarlem, Rotterdam and Amsterdam became major producers of pottery, each developing their individual style, from Brussels faience to, most famous of all, Delft (see page 142).

Attend an auction in, say, Amsterdam or Brussels, and the ceramics alone reflect this rich cultural history: colourful regional pottery, 18th-century porcelain from Tournai and Weesp, decorative Art Deco pieces by Keramis (more highly prized outside their native Belgium), innovative art pottery by Rozenburg and N.S.A. Brantjes & Co. The most headline-grabbing sales, though, are those of Far Eastern porcelain salvaged from shipwrecks (see page 135). For every ship that foundered, however, many more arrived safely and their enormous cargoes – a ship easily carried over 100,000 items – entered Dutch *households and, in due course, antiques shops and stalls. If you know what you are looking for you may find underpriced 18th- and early 19th-century wares among later pieces.*

The Dutch acquired territories from Surinam to parts of Ceylon and, most importantly, the spice-rich lands of southeast Asia. Vereenigde Oost-Indische Compagnie, the Dutch East India Company, looked after Dutch interests in Malacca and Indonesia and traded with India, China and Japan. The town houses of prosperous burghers back home swelled with Oriental ceramics and silks, lacquered fans, jade and ivory carvings and exotic hardwood furniture. In the 1920s Antwerp was still the massive import centre it had been since the 16th century, and the amount of ivory that came in through this one port influenced the trend in the use of ivory in Art Deco figures.

Despite their long shared history, the items that fill the antiques shops of the Netherlands and Belgium can be very different. Of course, you will find Delftware in Ghent and Flemish lace in The Hague (make sure you can tell the difference between hand-made and machine-made lace), but only Belgium took Art Nouveau to its heart (see page 127). In Brussels, in particular, but also in the smart shops of Ghent and Antwerp, you will find vases, figurines and lamps, door furniture, glass panels and textiles with the fluid forms that make the style instantly recognizable.

Advertisement for an Art Nouveau exhibition. Original posters such as this are highly sought after and there are many copies around.

BRUSSELS

Hunting for antiques in Brussels is always exciting, whether you're interested in old Flemish lace or the organic forms of Art Nouveau.

Godfroy du Bouillon, leader of the first Crusade

DESPITE THE MODERN GLASS AND STEEL office buildings that now exist in the capital of the European Union, Brussels remains at heart a provincial city, and echoes of its past are never far away. Little is left of the old city ramparts, but the innermost ring road, enclosing the Pentagon, roughly follows their line, and cobbled streets remain around the splendid Grand-Place.

Over the centuries, Brussels has been shaped by the different cultures of the foreign powers that have ruled it. It was from here that Godfroy de Bouillon instigated the first Crusade against the Holy Land in 1096, and artists and artisans flourished under the patronage of the Burgundian dukes who held sway over medieval Flanders. For most of the 18th century the region was part of the Austrian Empire, but in 1830 Belgium finally won her struggle for independence. Brussels became the capital and Leopold of Saxe-Coburg (uncle to Queen Victoria), the new country's first king.

One of the liveliest cities in Europe at the end of the 19th century, with modish cafés and Art Nouveau architecture, Brussels suffered terribly during two world wars, but with the World's Fair in 1958 and the birth of the EU, it has regained its zest for life.

The old guild flags that fly on festival days around the Grand-Place

LA GRAND-PLACE

Described by Victor Hugo as "the most beautiful place on earth" and by Jean Cocteau as "the richest theatre in the world", the Grand-Place is a mix of Renaissance, Flemish Baroque and Gothic.

In 1695, in a bid to defeat the English and Dutch, Louis XIV ordered the bombardment

Carving on La Maison du Renard, guildhouse of the haberdashers

of Brussels and 4,000 houses were destroyed. But within four years, the spectacular Grand-Place emerged from the ruins.

The façades of the Grand-Place are breathtaking, each full of historical detail. Many are guildhouses, such as **La Maison du Renard**, the haberdashers' guild house with its academic sculptures. **La Louve**, with its bas-relief of the wolf suckling Romulus and Remus, is the house of the guild of archers, and **La Brouette**, house of the wax chandlers, has two wheelbarrows framing the doorway. **Le Cornet**, the house of the boatmen, has a gable in the form of the stern of a ship. On the south side there is the **Maison des Ducs de Brabant**, shared by six guilds with 19 busts of dukes and duchesses, decorated with pilasters in 18 carat gold leaf.

At the southwestern end the **Hôtel de Ville**, with its 300-foot high tower, is a Gothic masterpiece. Visitors can wander through reception rooms, salons and galleries, all hung with paintings and exhibiting busts, Gothic panelling and magnificent tapestries. Facing it across the square stands **La Maison du Roi**. Originally a bread market – no king ever lived here – the building has served as home to the Duc de Brabant, tax collector's office, law courts and prison. It has been rebuilt twice and today

is a great example of Neo-gothic architecture complete with flying buttresses, loggia and a balcony. It houses the **Musée de la Ville**, which presents every aspect of the history of Brussels. Its many treasures include precious tapestries and the collection of costumes from all over the world sent to the little statue known as the **Mannekin-Pis** (you can see him on the corner of nearby Rue du Chêne).

The Grand-Place looks particularly dramatic in the early evening, with gables and the spire of the Hôtel de Ville lit against the darkening sky, and comes to life with the daily flower market and the Sunday morning bird market.

● **Hôtel de Ville**. Tel: (02) 279 4365.
● **Maison du Roi/Musée de la Ville**. Tel: (02) 279 4358. Check opening times for both.

Spectacular flower market in the Grand-Place

ANTIQUES IN CONTEXT

A rich heritage of artists and artisans that began with its pre-eminence in the production of textiles and tapestries in the Middle Ages, makes Brussels a repository of treasures from Old Masters to Art Nouveau.

A 1920s ceramic vase by Boch Frères, typical of their work

Brussels tapestry, one of a series depicting Roman triumphs (mid-16th century)

BRUSSELS FAIENCE

This became well-known when Corneille Mombaers and Thierry Witsenburg founded their factory in 1705. From 1724 onwards, tureens and other vessels were produced. The glaze often ran, giving a streaked or marbled effect. Brussels faience shares similarities with contemporary Delft and northern French pottery. Most of the major factories had closed by the end of the 19th century.

PLACES TO VISIT

The **Musées d'Art Ancien** and **d'Art Moderne**, which are next to each other, cover the fine arts. To the east of the town are the Museums of the Parc de Cinquantenaire, including the 140-room **Musées Royaux d'Art et d'Histoire**. In the park is the Pavillon des Passions Humaines, Victor Horta's first work, open only on request. The **Musée du Jouet** is a toy museum housed in a family mansion. The **Musée Charlier** is a mansion decorated by Horta, by now a leading Art Nouveau architect. It contains 18th-century furniture and has a wonderful collection of paintings and Belgian sculptures. The **Musée Van Buuren** is another stately home turned into a museum. It has a fine display of 16th- to 20th-century paintings in lovely Art Deco settings. The **Théâtre de Toone**, dating back to 1830, is a puppet theatre, where you can relax and relish the performance.

BRUSSELS TAPESTRY

In 1515, Pieter Coecke van Aelst was commissioned by Pope Leo X to produce The Acts of the Apostles, a series of tapestries based on Raphael's cartoons (preparatory drawings). They boosted Brussels' reputation for providing the best tapestries in the world.

It became customary to commemorate the deeds of rulers in tapestries and these are memorable for their boldly foreshortened figures and their naturalistic animals.

In the early 17th century, Rubens added to the tapestry industry by supplying weavers with numerous cartoons. Their base, the Gobelins factory, was nationalized in 1662 and used specifically to produce furnishings for the Crown, so the main centre of tapestry production moved to Paris. Brussels continued to flourish as a centre for tapestry until the 18th century when the last workshop closed. Good places to see tapestries include the Hôtel de Ville and the museums in the Parc du Cinquantenaire.

Performance of Pitje La Mort at the Théâtre de Toone

● **Musées d'Art Ancien and d'Art Moderne**, rue de la Régence. Tel: (02) 508 3211.
● **Musées Royaux d'Art et d'Histoire, Parc du Cinquantenaire**. Tel: (02) 741 7331.
● **Musée du Jouet**, 24 rue de l'Association. Tel: (02) 219 6168.
● **Musée Charlier**, 16 avenue des Arts. Tel: (02) 218 5382.
● **Musée Van Buuren**, 41 avenue Leo-Errera. Tel: (02) 343 4851.
● **Théâtre de Toone**, 6 impasse Schuddeveld. Tel: (02) 511 7137.

LACE

Unlike many other arts or crafts there are no famous names in lace-making, no fragments signed by the Rembrandt of the lace world. This was a cottage industry, with most work being carried out, unrecorded, in private homes. Many styles of lace, from needlepoint to pillow lace, have been made here since the early 16th century and Brussels lace is among the best in the world. Needlepoint lace, or *point de gaze*, is very delicate, made with patterns and ground-worked at the same time. Cardonnet is stitched round the main elements of the pattern. Pillow lace includes lace called *point plat* and *point d'Angleterre*. Brussels lace was unrivalled in the 18th century when it was fashionable to wear lace displaying shaded flowers and fruit and detailed raised work. Later work has simpler scattered floral motifs on a plaited or *vrai droschel* ground.

Machine-made net was first produced in Brussels in 1768 and from the early 19th century was often used as a ground on which to apply motifs of either needlepoint or pillow

Finely worked lace panel of, appropriately, a lace-worker

lace. This was known as Brussels appliqué. Sadly it is now difficult to find true Brussels lace; much comes from sweat shops in the Far East. It is often cheaper to buy antique lace in London. The **Musée du Costume et de la Dentelle** specializes in the art of lace and has some extraordinary pieces.

● **Musée du Costume et de la Dentelle**, rue de la Violette. Tel. (02) 279 4350.

Many bobbins are required for a complex pattern

ART NOUVEAU

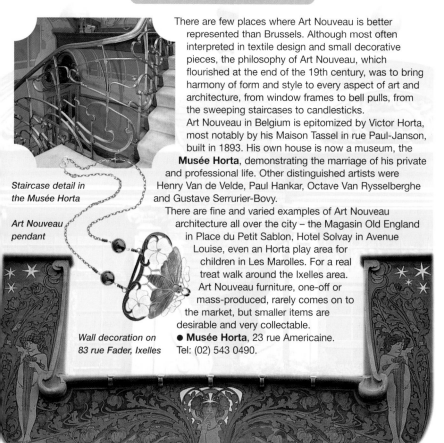

Staircase detail in the Musée Horta

Art Nouveau pendant

Wall decoration on 83 rue Fader, Ixelles

There are few places where Art Nouveau is better represented than Brussels. Although most often interpreted in textile design and small decorative pieces, the philosophy of Art Nouveau, which flourished at the end of the 19th century, was to bring harmony of form and style to every aspect of art and architecture, from window frames to bell pulls, from the sweeping staircases to candlesticks.

Art Nouveau in Belgium is epitomized by Victor Horta, most notably by his Maison Tassel in rue Paul-Janson, built in 1893. His own house is now a museum, the **Musée Horta**, demonstrating the marriage of his private and professional life. Other distinguished artists were Henry Van de Velde, Paul Hankar, Octave Van Rysselberghe and Gustave Serrurier-Bovy.

There are fine and varied examples of Art Nouveau architecture all over the city – the Magasin Old England in Place du Petit Sablon, Hotel Solvay in Avenue Louise, even an Horta play area for children in Les Marolles. For a real treat walk around the Ixelles area. Art Nouveau furniture, one-off or mass-produced, rarely comes on to the market, but smaller items are desirable and very collectable.

● **Musée Horta**, 23 rue Americaine. Tel: (02) 543 0490.

SHOPPING

Tailors' dummies among the varied items for sale in rue des Renards

When shopping for antiques in Brussels the principal shopping area is around the Place du Petit Sablon, its big sister the Place du Grand Sablon and from there along the streets of Rue Haute and Rue Blaes, which run beside each other into the heart of the district of Les Marolles.

SABLONS
In the Place du Grand Sablon, there is a smart antiques market each Saturday and Sunday morning as well as the permanent antique shops.

Brass chandelier typical of the Flanders style

Look out for:
Around Place du Grand Sablon, **Costerman** at No 5 is a shop carrying a varied selection of good antiques. No 8, **Antiquités**, is a small

gallery of shops selling all sorts of things, but look out for maps, prints and silver.

Rue de Rollebeek is a lovely street and worth a visit even if you do not want to shop. But look out for No 39, **Chintz Shop**, which specializes in floral fabric, furniture and quilts. **Daniel Traube**, at No 33, is a shop that deals in antique and old walking sticks. There is also No 19, **La Feuillée d'Armoise**, which houses just about a little of everything – a great shop in which to spend time browsing. No 13, **Marie Storms**, specializes in semi-precious jewellery and even boasts the Belgian royal family among its clients.

LES MAROLLES
Until the 15th century, the district known as Les Marolles was outside the city walls because of the unpleasant smells that were produced by the work of local tanners. Although Les Marolles has a colourful and artistic history (the painter Breugel the Elder lived at rue Haute 132) it has never been a smart area and has suffered waves of urban planning. Alongside the great shops, some unexpected delights survive. In rue des Visitandines (off rue du Miroir) is the striped Eglise des Brigittines, a perfect little Baroque Belgian church that is now run as a theatre. In the rue des Tanneurs is the Palais du Vin, very dilapidated now, but you can still make out the different wine areas of Europe painted on the façade. And keep an eye open for some of Brussels' famous comic-strip murals in rue Haute, rue du Chevreuil and rue des Renards, where there are also several interesting antique shops.

Look out for:
Rue Blaes is fast being renovated and new shops are moving in to provide an interesting mix. **La Manufacture** at No 52 stocks bookcases and beautiful decorative pieces. At No 50, **Apostrophe** is a shop with a difference –

SHOPPER'S TIP
If you're not buying chocolate or some of the wonderful varieties of beer or gazing at the sensational lace, keep an eye open for brassware, Old Master sketches, glass and Oriental ceramics. You can often pick up early Oriental ceramics that can go unnoticed among the 19th-century pieces – but make sure you've done your reserach before you buy.

Advertisement for an Art Nouveau exhibition. Such posters are very collectable

WHEN IN BRUSSELS...

...experience beer with a difference. You will find bars and cellars that pride themselves on the quality and variety of their beers, from the local gueuze and seasonal lambic to brews flavoured with fruits including raspberry, cherry and apple. Le Falstaff, 17-23 rue Henri Maus, has one of the finest examples of Art Nouveau woodwork in the city. Other places with the old Brussels spirit are: A la Becasse, Au Bon Vieux Temps and A la Mort Subite.

Art Nouveau interior of Le Falstaff, c1903

it specializes in Fifties and Sixties memorabilia and has lots of famous old brand-named items. **Passage 125 Blaes,** with over two dozen stalls on three floors, is full of all sorts of antiques. It is a veritable treasury of delights.

At **51 rue Haute** there is another Aladdin's cave but run by a single dealer. You'll find candle holders alongside old baths and furniture of all kinds.

FAIRS AND MARKETS

A flea market has been held in **Place du Jeu de Balle** since 1873. It runs every day, though the best day is Sunday. Expect a car boot sale atmosphere.

AUCTION HOUSES

Among the city's many auction houses are: **Horta,** 70–74 avenue de Roodebeek. Tel: (02) 741 60 60. **Béguinage,** rue de Rouleau 10. Tel: (02) 218 17 42. **Hotel des Ventes Flagey,** rue de Nid 4. Tel: (02) 644 97 67.

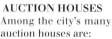

Cretonne fabric by designer Paul Iribe, 1911

WHERE TO EAT AND DRINK

La Tour d'y Voir
8 Place du Grand-Sablon. Tel: (02) 511 4043
Sited in a 14th-century chapel, this restaurant is truly original: the chef improvises from ingredients on that day's "mystery menu".

Les Salons de L'Atalaïde
89 Chaussée de Charleroi
Tel: (02) 537 2154
Once an auction house, this Moroccan-inspired restaurant now serves French cuisine.

'T Kelderke
15Grand-Place. Tel: (02) 513 7344
This 17th-century vaulted cellar in the Grand-Place serves traditional Flemish dishes.

Dozens more restaurants and cafés, including the popular Chaloupe d'Or, spill out into the Grand-Place; just stroll around the perimeter until you find one you like.

WHERE TO STAY

Hotel Amigo
Rue de L'Amigo
Tel: (02) 547 4747

This atmospheric hotel , incorporating an old paved street, has impressive 18th-century tapestries, and regularly hosts a range of eminent guests. The name is an ironic reminder of the Spanish prison that stood here when the Spain ruled the region.

La Chaloupe d'Or

Le Dix-Septième
25 Rue de Madeleine
Tel: (02) 502 5744 Fax: (02) 50 6424
Once the residence of the Spanish ambassador, this elegant, 17th-century hotel is luxurious and quiet, with fine antique furnishings.

Stalls in the Place du Jeu de Balle

IN THE AREA

Where Brussels is cosmopolitan, **Antwerp** is pure Flanders, the city of Rubens, Van Dyck and diamonds. It is also rich in antiques shops. Venture in any direction from the medieval Grote Markt and you'll find streets lined with antiques and collectables. Try Hoogstraat, off the south-west corner of the square, then wander down Kloosterstraat and eastwards to Leopoldstraat. Or take Schutterhofstraat on your way to the Wapper, to visit the Baroque house in which Rubens lived and worked. As well as his studio and garden, several of his masterpieces are hung here, including his portrait of the young Anthony Van Dyck.

BRUGES

Bruges is one of Europe's best-preserved medieval cities. Visitors flock here for the art and architecture, to eat well and to visit its antiques markets.

BEGIJNHOF

Carved figure of a béguine at a window in the Begijnhof

BRUGES IS A PLACE OF CANALS AND BRIDGES, in fact its name in Flemish – Brugge (pronounced Bruhg-guh) – means "bridge". During the 13th century, its merchants exported Flemish cloth and imported goods from across Europe. Bruges became Europe's financial focus: the site of the world's first stock exchange and the centre of the diamond and lace trades. At the end of the 1400s the waterway that linked the city to the North Sea began to silt up and the merchants and traders left. It was not until the Belgian elite discovered Georges Rodenbach's late 19th-century novel, *Bruges-la-Morte* (set in Bruges's abandoned streets), that the city began to reawaken. Fortunately, the developers never got their hands on Bruges – it is quite possible to walk for hours without running out of cobbled streets or wonderful buildings to view. In 2002 Bruges will be European City of Culture.

Visitors remark on the contrast between beauty and darkness: the beauty of its canals meandering between gabled houses; the darkness in the work of the city's artists: court painter Van Eyck and Flemish Primitives such as Hieronymus Bosch whose renowned paintings are filled with scenes of horror and despair. But there is another side to the city in its basement jazz clubs, design shops and organic restaurants. Bruges is compact, so it's easy to get around, either by boat or on foot.

17th-century Flemish candlestick

A WALK AROUND OLD BRUGES

To get an immediate flavour of Bruges, start from the **Markt** early in the morning as the cobbles are being cleaned and the street vendors are setting up their stalls. The Markt (pictured above) is dominated by its Gothic city hall – the Halles – and the best place to view the city is from its 13th-century belfry, the nearest thing in Bruges to a skyscraper.

Just minutes away is the **Burg**, a square in the centre of medieval Bruges in which you can see nine centuries of different architectural styles. There is the **Stadhuis**, a fine Gothic building, with its 48 statues of Flemish nobles – recent editions have replaced the 14th-century originals. The **Heilig Bloed Basiliek**, also in the Burg, is an odd-looking building: it consists of a 12th-century Romanesque church with a Gothic one constructed on top and linked by a flight of Renaissance steps. From here it is just a stroll to the banks of the Dijver canal with antiques and flea markets crowding the banks and a cluster of art galleries.

Wander down to the **Minnewater** ("Lake of Love"), a man-made lake created in the 13th century that could take up to 100 ships. This area used to be the city's docks when Bruges was a thriving port. Close by is the **Arentshuis Garden**, where there is a lovely series of bronze statues by Rik Poot, representing the Four Horsemen of the Apocalypse.

Getting around

There are plenty of sight-seeing tours and, unlike Venice or Amsterdam, the canals of Bruges are not used commercially, so a boat trip is relaxing and there is a great amount to see. A horse-drawn tram or horse-drawn carriage is another relaxing way to get around.

The Begijnhof: one house is set up as a museum

If you are feeling really energetic then try a guided tour by bicycle around the villages surrounding Bruges.

The Begijnhof

Begijnhofs – *béguinages* in French-speaking Belgium – are residences dating from the 13th to 15th centuries and can be found throughout the Low Countries. Their original purpose was to provide shelter for a community of lay sisters (*béguines*) who lived and dressed as nuns, but did not take vows. They engaged in good works for the community and church, but at the same time took part in conventional family life. Today, the begijnhofs offer very tranquil settings, rather reminiscent of almshouses, and have become popular tourist sights.

The Begijnhof in Bruges was founded in 1245 to house women whose husbands had died during the Crusades.

● **Begijnhof**. Tel (050) 338560. Open Dec–Feb: Wed, Thurs, pm only.

Exquisite lace butterfly worked in linen thread, c.1890

PLACES TO VISIT

The **Groeningemuseum** has a wonderful collection of early Flemish masters such as Hans Memling and Jan van Eyck, works by Hieronymus Bosch and surrealists René Magritte and Paul Delvaux, and a display of antique lace.

The **Brangwynmuseum** is named after the architect and artist Frank Brangwyn, whose Welsh parents lived in Bruges in the 1800s. His legacy, a vast collection of his work, is housed here along with an exhibition of lace, pottery, pewterware and porcelain.

Furnished as a wealthy burgher's house of the 15th century, the **Gruuthusemuseum** has a large collection of furniture, weapons, coins, stunning tapestries, musical instruments and, for those of a more bloodthirsty nature, instruments of torture and a real guillotine.

For a complete change of scene, try the **Straffe Hendrik** brewery, where you can join a tour of the works. See the cooper's workshop and visit their 1900s' tavern with the chance to taste the wonderful white beer, so called because of its light colour.

At the **Kantcentrum** displays of exquisite antique lace show the high quality of this ancient craft. There are afternoon demonstations at the centre.

Canal view of the commanding belfry of Bruges

- **Groeningemuseum**, Dijver 12. Tel: (050) 448711.
- **Brangwynmuseum**, Dijver 16. Tel: (050) 448711. Both museums closed Tues.
- **Gruuthuse-museum**, Dijver 17. Tel: (050) 448711.
- **Straffe Hendrik Brouwerij De Halve Maan**, Walplein 26. Tel: (050) 332697.
- **Kantcentrum**, Peperstraat 3a. Tel: (050) 330072.

SHOPPING

Bruges has about 30 antiques shops in and around the **Markt**. The Bruges Tourist Office has a free guide listing members of the town's arts and antiques association (see Useful Addresses at the end of the book). There is

Copper pans so typical of Belgian bric-a-brac shops

plenty of choice for both the antiques connoisseur and the casual browser in Bruges's tangle of cobbled streets.

Look out for:
Marc Michot at Groene Rei 3. Since 1970, this shop has special-ized in Chinese works of art dating from "earliest times" to the 1900s. The collection includes ceramics, jade and ivory. **Antiek Meire** (Sint-Salvatorskerhof 9) has a wide range of 17th- and 18th-century Belgian and Dutch furniture, medieval sculpture, bronze, copper and tinware, and items of Delft. **Papyrus** (Walplein 41) features 18th-century English furniture, European and American silver, Chinese works on paper, Japanese wood cuts and, unusually, antique harps and harpsichords.

Jean Moust (Mariastraat 15) specializes in 17th-century Flemish and Dutch Old Master

Antiques shop in Bruges showing local finds

WHEN IN BRUGES...

... time your visit to coincide with the annual **Kunst & Antiekbeurs**. This international fine art and antiques fair is held the first week of November at the superb medieval belfry in the Grote Markt. Over 50 international renowned art and antique dealers display European paintings and furniture, Asian art, archeological items, sculpture, ethnic art, glass, jewellery, silver, clocks, engravings and tapestries. Each object is checked for authenticity. Tel: (050) 354007; Fax: (050) 370587; e-mail: msa@publigil.be

paintings and decorative objects from the 16th to 19th centuries.

Vincent Lebbe has owned the charming **Het Witte Huis** at Gistelsesteenweg 30 for over 20 years. His speciality is 17th–19th century oak, mahogany and walnut furniture from France, Holland, Belgium and

An 18th-century Dutch desk with parquetry patterning

England; he also sells paintings, engravings and many decorative objects.

Among the specialities of the merged businesses of **Kasimirs' Antique Studio** (Rozenhoedkaai 3) and **De Grote Markt** (Markt 7) are mahogany furniture from England, France and Holland, 19th-century Gustavian furniture, antique silver and glass and other decorative objects.

Bruges lace is a popular souvenir and there are boutiques selling lace both old and new everywhere. Some of the lacemakers even sit outside their shops so that you can watch them at work. Several places sell less expensive, but still pretty, examples of machine-made lace and embroidered cotton.

For curiosities on the theme of day and night drop into **Dag & Zone** (Langestraat 3), and if you have an interest in antique posters

and packaging, then don't miss out on **Oud Tegelhuis** (Peerdenstraat 2).

FAIRS AND MARKETS

Every Saturday and Sunday afternoon there is a flea market in **Vismarkt** (during the week it sells fresh fish). During the summer, there are antiques stalls all along the **Dijver canal**. Throughout the year there is a traditional Saturday market – the largest in Bruges – at **'t Zand**, which then becomes a busy flea market during July, August and September.

Browsing in one of Bruges's many flea markets

WHERE TO EAT AND DRINK

Bruges is endowed with so many excellent restaurants (a huge number of which have Michelin stars and other accolades) that you need never worry about eating well – and portions are usually generous too.

The elegant period dining room of the De Snippe Hotel

Den Gouden Harynk
Groeninge 25
Tel: (050) 337637
Chef Philippe Serruys creates truly inspired dishes for this small dining room filled with antiques.

De Karmeliet
Langestraat 19
Tel: (050) 338259
Exquisite food and wines can be found in this delightful 18th-century house with its English-style garden.

't Bourgoensche Cruyce
Wollestraat 41
Tel: (050) 337926
Built at the turn of the last century, this elegant dining room has a beautiful setting overlooking a canal. Customers feast on fish, poultry or crepes.

Hof van Cleeve
Kruishoutem
Tel: (093) 835848
Pieter Goossens has turned this small country house 20km (12 miles) from Bruges, into one of the best restaurants around. Local produce is used extensively, with mushroom specialities in season.

WHERE TO STAY

Hotels in Bruges are often fully booked, so consider staying in nearby Ghent. Too long over-looked, it is a charming town in its own right.

De Snippe Hotel
Nieuwe Gentweg 53
Tel: (050) 337070; Fax (050) 337662
De Snippe was once the mayoral residence and is renowned for its cuisine. The 18th-century building has been restored around a lovely winter garden.

Hotel Sofitel
Boeveriestraat 2
Tel: (050) 449711; Fax: (050) 449799
Within the shell of a 17th-century monastery, the Sofitel has large rooms and a good restaurant.

Oud Huis Amsterdam
Spiegelrei 3
Tel: (050) 341810; Fax: (050) 338891
Situated along a charming canal and housed in original 16th-century buildings, this is a restful oasis in the heart of the city.

St Georges
Botermarkt 2, 9000 Ghent
Tel: (09) 224 2424; Fax: (09) 224 2640
A hostelry since 1228, this lays claim to being one of the world's oldest hotels. Charles V stayed here, as did Napoleon, and its banqueting hall has witnessed many historic moments.

Hostellerie Shamrock
Muziekbos, B-9680 Maarkedal
Tel: (055) 215529; Fax: (055) 215683
This English-style manor house a short distance from both Bruges and Ghent is small and welcoming, with antiques in the bedrooms.

AMSTERDAM

The past and the present sit comfortably side by side along Amsterdam's picturesque canals, and connoisseurs rate this cosmopolitan and dynamic city as one of the great antiques centres of Europe.

The landmark clocktower of the Westertoren

WITH ITS WORLD-RENOWNED MUSEUMS, masterpieces by Rembrandt, Franz Hals, Johannes Vermeer and other Dutch Old Masters and its wealth of diverse architecture, the so-called "Venice of the North" provides a cultural feast for all the senses. Church bells, organ grinders and street musicians contribute to the unique ambience of this city, and

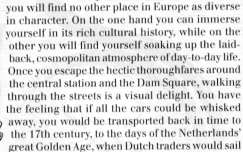

you will find no other place in Europe as diverse in character. On the one hand you can immerse yourself in its rich cultural history, while on the other you will find yourself soaking up the laid-back, cosmopolitan atmosphere of day-to-day life. Once you escape the hectic thoroughfares around the central station and the Dam Square, walking through the streets is a visual delight. You have the feeling that if all the cars could be whisked away, you would be transported back in time to the 17th century, to the days of the Netherlands' great Golden Age, when Dutch traders would sail home with porcelain from China and Japan and exotic spices from the East Indies.

Within the spider's web of canals and narrow streets that make up the city centre, nowhere is far from the attractions of the Spiegelkwartier, Amsterdam's pretty antiques area.

THE DUTCH IN THE ORIENT

During the late 16th and early 17th centuries, Chinese porcelain became a sought-after commodity throughout Europe.

Portuguese merchants had already established the "kraak porcelain" trade, so-called because of the carrack ships they used – and were importing late Ming dynasty porcelain to Europe from the Far East. In 1602, two of their vessels, the *San Jago* and the *Santa Catarina*, were captured by the Dutch, yielding thousands of items, and the repercussions were two-fold. First, by selling the porcelain for high prices at auction, the Dutch created a demand that led

Chinese vegetable tureen made for export, c.1817, recovered from a shipwreck

During the second half of the last century, several shipwrecks were discovered, having been left undisturbed for 200–300 years. One such find was the *Geldermalsen*, a massive vessel from the VOC fleet that sank in 1752. The 100,000 pieces of Chinese porcelain she had on board attracted huge interest when they were auctioned.

You can discover Holland's glorious past as a seafaring nation in the **Nederlands Scheepvaartmuseum**, former arsenal of the 300-year-old Amsterdam Admiralty. There are ship's models, old maps and paintings, as well as the Royal golden sloop, and a reconstruction of the ill-fated Dutch East Indiaman sailing ship.

● **Nederlands Scheepvaartmuseum**, Kattenburgerplein 1. Tel: (020) 523 2222. Closed Mon except public holidays.

Nederlands Scheepvaartmuseum

to local manufacturers in places such as Delft making their own versions of the popular blue and white porcelain (see page 142). Imports from the Far East continued well into the 17th century, until civil war in China brought an end to the Ming dynasty and disrupted trading. Secondly, it prompted the establishment of the Vereenigde Oost-Indische Compagnie – VOC (Dutch East India Company), one of several European companies set up to protect trading interests with the Orient.

BROWN CAFES

Dutch social life has always revolved around cafés, which have as much cultural value as a museum with their interesting cast of characters and diverse characteristics. Traditional brown cafés are identified by their picturesque dark wooden interiors and cosy lanterns and tables, which are often covered with incongruous Persian rugs. The name is derived from the fact that the walls and ceilings have turned brown from age and cigarette smoke. **Papaneiland** (Prinsengracht 2) is one of Amsterdam's oldest (1641), its Delft tiles and leaded glass windows still reflecting the ambience of days gone by.

ANTIQUES IN CONTEXT

When exploring the historic inner city and the streets that link the concentric canals, a great way to learn about Dutch antiques is to visit some of the canal-house museums. These 17th-century residences with their ornate gables are part of every image of Amsterdam.

The magnificent Amsterdam Historisch Museum

DOMESTIC INTERIORS

Despite the lively trade in treasures from the Orient, the Netherlands were not without treasures of their own. Marble fireplaces would be surrounded by Delft tiles, and many an embossed cabinet contained a small Delft collection. Engraved chests from Zeeland, ornate panelled Frisian wardrobes and Frisian clocks with heavy brass fittings were also common. In the early 1800s, house interiors followed the sober Biedermeier and Empire styles, with dark colours, heavy furniture and wooden panelling. In the late 1800s, tastes shifted and it was fashionable to emulate a Louis XVI style, with glittering chandeliers and gilded furniture upholstered in blue, yellow and purple damask.

An Arita gallipot, c.1680, made in Japan for the Dutch East India Company

Two fine examples of grand 17th-century canal houses are the **Van Loon** and **Willet-Holthuysen Museums**; they are beautifully maintained and provide a fascinating glimpse into Amsterdam's past. The **Amsterdam Historisch Museum**, in a former orphanage, traces the city's rich history from the 13th to the 18th century.

The **Koninklijk Paleis** is a former town hall, built in the mid-17th century but turned into a royal palace by Louis Napoleon in 1808. The monumental Empire-style furnishings

symbolize his powerful position in Europe at the time. The **Beurs van Berlage** (the former stock exchange), built in 1903, is the city's first building in the Dutch Modernist style and is the architect Hendrikus Petrus Berlage's masterpiece. It is worth a visit, whether to attend a concert by the resident Netherlands Philharmonic Orchestra, a book fair, or one of the many exhibitions on architecture and design. Inside the spacious main hall, you can admire the ironwork and Romanesque and Neo-Renaissance motifs.

- **Museum van Loon**, Keizersgracht 672. Tel: (020) 624 5255.
- **Museum Willet-Holthuysen**, Herengracht 605. Tel: (020) 523 1822.
- **Amersterdam Historisch Museum**, Kalverstraat 92. Tel: (020) 523 1822.
- **Koninklijk Paleis**, Dam Square. Tel: (020) 620 4060. Open Easter, summer and autumn school holidays, pm daily; at other times Tues, Wed, Thurs 1–4pm. Tel to confirm hours in case of royal events (020) 623 3819.
- **Beurs van Berlage**, Damrak 213–277. Tel: (020) 530 4141.

UNUSUAL COLLECTIONS

In addition to the special "museum houses" along the canals, there are several museums that hold unusual collections. Two such examples are the **Bijbels Museum Amsterdam** (Biblical Museum) and the **Theater Instituut Nederland** (Theatre Museum). Set in two adjacent canal houses (*c.*1662), the interior of the splendidly

Exterior of Willet-Holthuysen Museum

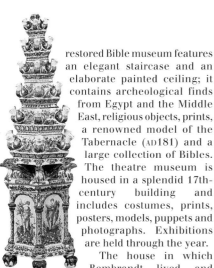

restored Bible museum features an elegant staircase and an elaborate painted ceiling; it contains archeological finds from Egypt and the Middle East, religious objects, prints, a renowned model of the Tabernacle (AD181) and a large collection of Bibles. The theatre museum is housed in a splendid 17th-century building and includes costumes, prints, posters, models, puppets and photographs. Exhibitions are held through the year.

Late 17th-century tulipière

The house in which Rembrandt lived and worked, **Museum het Rembrandthuis**, has been recently renovated and, in the future, will be furnished more completely in the manner in which one of Holland's most famous artists lived. If your favourite is Vincent Van Gogh, then you will find 200 paintings and 500 drawings of the artist at the **Van Gogh Museum**.

The stately **Rijksmuseum** is over 200 years old and one of the world's leading museums. This "cathedral of culture" is the Netherlands' largest museum and receives over a million visitors each year. It was designed by architect Petrus Josephus Cuypers in a blend of Gothic and Renaissance styles. Over the years the original design has had many alterations, including the addition of several new wings. This magnificent museum continues to evolve, and houses the world's largest collection of paintings by the Dutch Old Masters, from Rembrandt to Vermeer.

● **Bijbels Museum Amsterdam**, Herengracht 368. Tel: (020) 624 2436.

● **Theater Instituut**, Herengracht 168. Tel: (020) 551 3300. Closed Mon.
● **Museum het Rembrandthuis**, Jodenbreestraat 4–6. Tel: (020) 624 9486.
● **Van Gogh Museum**, Paulus Potterstraat 7. Tel: (020) 570 5200.
● **Rijksmuseum**, Stadhouderskade 42. Tel: (020) 673 2121.

TULIPMANIA

During the 16th century a curious flower was brought to Europe from Asia. Its name was "tulipan" and its cultivation became a passion. By the 1630s tulipmania was a widespread craze in Holland, and bulbs, imported from Turkey and traded on the exchange, were considered more exotic than emeralds, Arab stallions and Ming vases. Aristocrats snapped up flowers in rare colours, but even ordinary burghers traded in red or yellow tulips. This widespread preference for flowers over jewels is seen as part of the essential bourgeois nature of Dutch culture.

A Dutch cabinet in simulated rosewood, with pastoral scene painted on the doors; late 17th-century

OLD MASTERS

The Jewish Bride (c.1666), by Rembrandt, on display in the Rijksmuseum

DEPICTING LIFE AT HOME

There is a great diversity in the individual work of Dutch Old Masters, yet they all employed a deceptively natural and realistic style in their painting techniques.

Rembrandt (1606–69) is rightly most admired for the striking depth of character captured in his portraits, but he also painted some of the finest domestic scenes of the 17th century. Domestic interiors and pastoral scenes were popular subjects of the time, and the work of Rembrandt and many of his contemporaries give an insight into Dutch everyday life at the time. **Jan Steen**, also associated with the genre, is considered the finest after Rembrandt and Frans Hals. **Gerrit Dou** began with portraits and progressed later on to domestic scenes. Later still, he painted a series of night scenes, lit only by a candle. There is a symbolism which sets a moral tone in both the pastoral landscapes of **Jacob van Ruisdael**, and the tranquil scenes of **Johannes Vermeer**, who showed a remarkable ability to portray the subtleties of light on different shapes and surfaces with great accuracy.

SHOPPING

Furry collectables in the Spiegelkwarter

SPIEGELKWARTER

With over 80 shops and galleries, Amsterdam's Spiegelkwarter offers something for every predilection and every budget. This charming area around the Spiegelgracht and the Nieuwe Spiegelstraat is near the city's main canals and close to the Rijksmuseum. The museum served as a catalyst for developing the quarter when it opened its doors in 1885. Since then it has made many purchases from dealers within the quarter, and in the 1990s presented an exhibition which featured local acquisitions.

The Spiegelkwarter has been described as a "permanent antiques fair" with its wealth of Golden Age paintings, tapestries, furniture, sculpture, textiles, jewellery, ceramics, porcelain, glass, medical instruments, dolls and toys, clocks, silver, bronze and pewter and other decorative objects of various eras from all over the world. Despite its renown, the neighbourhood remains a village, with a fishmonger, bookshop and local cafés. The dealers take pride in the quality of their goods, whether they are selling an antique tile for a *tientje* (10 florins) or a jade snuff bottle worth thousands.

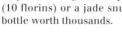

An antique of the future: a Gerrit Rietveld occasional table

Look out for:
Aronson Antiquairs (Nieuwe Spiegelstraat 39) is a family operation established in 1881 which offers a range of classic and colourful Delft as well as silver and furniture.

Also in Nieuwe Spiegelstraat, at No 49, **Beekhuizen Antiques** specializes in pewter from Western Europe dating from the 15th to the 19th centuries, and the stock here includes

A Dutch floral marquetry and walnut display cabinet

anything from goblets and lidded tankards to candleholders.

Family-run **Frides Laméris Antiques**, at Nieuwe Spiegelstraat 55, carries stock of elegantly etched 18th-century glass.

If you're looking for furniture and decorative art between 1880 and about 1940, **Kunsthandel Frans Leidelmeijer** (Nieuwe Spiegelstraat 58) features traditional Dutch design with a diverse inventory of works including Hendrik Petrus Berlage and Gerrit Rietveld.

Although regarded as an expert on Indo-Javanese art from 500 to 1500, Jaap Polak's diverse inventory at **Kunsthandel J. Polak** (Spiegelgracht 3) includes Gothic sculptures, Chinese tomb figures, Romanesque ivory and Indian miniature paintings.

Kunsthandel Inez Stodel (Nieuwe Spiegelstraat 65) is a jewel box of a little shop. It specializes in 16th- to 19th-century jewellery and is noted for its fantastic window displays.

OTHER HUNTING GROUNDS

The sixth-generation family business of **Gebroeders Douwes Fine Art** (Stadhouderskade 40) first carried out restoration work, then developed their expertise to become dealers of paintings from the Dutch and Flemish Old Masters, 19th-century Dutch Romantic and French paintings and Russian Social Realism.

The unusual speciality of **Thom and Leni Nellis** (Keizersgracht 541) is the tools of the trades from 18th- and 19th- century medical experts such as physicians, dentists and pharmacists.

ANTIQUES FAIRS

The week-long **Pan Amsterdam** is presented at the RAI Parkhal at the end of November each year. More than 110 dealers from all over the Netherlands and Belgium are represented, and they always offer a diverse range of fine art and sculpture, jewellery, furniture, glass and *objets d'art*.

TEFAF Maastricht, the European Fine Art Fair, is held each March in Maastricht, 270km (170 miles) away in the south of the country. It is considered the world's leading art and antiques fair with more than 200 leading dealers from all over Europe, USA and Canada. It has earned its reputation not only for the quality and variety of the exhibits but also for the participation guidelines.

For catalogues and more information on both fairs, contact: infopan@tefaf.com.

*Amstel porcelain
plate, c.1800*

FLEA MARKETS

Antiekmarkt de Looier in Elandsgracht (open daily except Friday) is fun, although it is not renowned for great prices and unique finds. Still, it has a changing stock, with all sorts of curiosities.

The **Nieuwmarkt Antiekmarkt**, held Sundays from May to September, carries an assortment of books, furniture and *objets de curiosité*.

The dealers at the busy **Noordermarkt** market on Monday mornings include a woman who sells interesting china and table settings. The scene seems from another era.

Waterlooplein market has lost some of its its allure, but it is still worth a quick browse.

AUCTION HOUSES

Eland de Zon en Loth De Gijselman,
Elandsgracht 68. Tel: (020) 623 0343.
Christie's, Cornelis Schuytstaat 57. Tel: (020) 575 5255.
Sotheby's, De Boelelaan 30. Tel: 550 2200.

The Nieuwmarkt Antiekmarkt

SHOPPER'S TIP

Amsterdam has a wealth of second-hand shops and is a haven for authentic vintage clothing. **Lady Day** (Hartenstraat 9) has a good selection of very well-made fashion clothes, sportswear classics and period footwear. For clothes from the 1940s and '50s head for **Laura Dolls** (Wolvenstraat 7), and for '60s and '70s outfits, visit the **Bebop Shop** (Nieuwendijk 164).

WHERE TO EAT AND DRINK

Dorrius
Nieuwezijds Voorburgwal 5
Tel: (020) 420 2224
With its original furnishings from the 17th century, Dorrius is an institution when it comes to authentic Dutch cooking. There is a good range of soups on the menu and you can enjoy them with duck, deer or even lamb sausages. In October, sauerkraut is featured in many varieties.

The beamed dining room of Dorrius

The Pancake Bakery
Prinsengracht 191
Tel: (020) 625 1333
Huge savoury or sweet pancakes, ever-popular in the Netherlands, are served in a cosy atmosphere of a 17th-century warehouse cellar.

Poentjak Pas
Nassaukade 366
Tel: (020) 618 0906
Dutch colonials brought back the concept of the *rijstaffel* – a seemingly endless banquet of spicy little dishes – from the East Indies.

WHERE TO STAY

Seven One Seven
Prinsengracht 717
Tel: (020) 427 0717; Fax: (020) 423 0717
This classical 19th-century guesthouse is an exclusive canalside landmark. There are eight rooms, each filled with modern or classical art.

Ambassade Hotel
Herengracht 341
Tel: (020) 555 0222; Fax: (020) 555 0277
An elegant 18th-century hotel on a picturesque canal. It has 59 beautifully furnished rooms.

Amstel Inter-Continental
1 Professor Tulpplein
Tel: (020) 622 6060; Fax: (020) 622 5808
Lavishly furnished 19th-century hotel on the River Amstel, this is popular with visiting celebrities and royalty.

Canal House
148 Keizersgracht
Tel: (020) 622 5182 Fax: (020) 624 1317
This family-owned hotel has been expertly converted from canalside merchant houses. Lots of antiques and a charming breakfast room.

Toro
Koningslaan 64
Tel: 673 7223 ; Fax: 675 0031
There are views of the Vondelpark form this grand 19th-century antiques-filled hotel.

THE HAGUE

The Hague is aristo-
cratic yet intimate, a
city of royal palaces
and great museums
that never feels over-
bearing or grand.

*Dish from 1780s
depicting William V of
Orange (1748–1806)*

ONCE A SIMPLE HAMLET near a count's castle (it's official name,
's-Gravenhage, means "the Count's hedge"), The Hague has
been the seat of the House of Orange since 1815. Huis ten Bosch,
the royal residence of Queen Beatrix and Prince Claus, is here,
and many other palaces, such as Lange Voorhout, Kneuterdijk,
and Noordeinde, bear witness to its long royal heritage. The
stately Binnenhof, home of the Dutch parliament, has stood at
the centre of political life in the Netherlands for centuries.

The Hague (Den Haag in Dutch) is also known as the "widow
of Indonesia", due to the many Dutch and Indonesians who fled
the former colony to take up residence here. This aristocratic-
exotic mix has influenced the essential domesticity of The
Hague and is reflected in the quality of museums, galleries and
restaurants, and in the various antiques and contemporary
shops in a city of contrasts where old and new are interwoven.

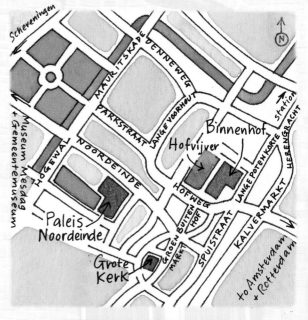

HISTORY REVISITED

MESDAG AND HIS PANORAMA

Hendrik Willem Mesdag (1831–1915) was a painter and collector of
the Hague School whose memorable contribution to Dutch art is the
Mesdag Panorama. This enormous cylinder-shaped painting is of
the nearby fishing village of Scheveningen in 1881 and is a monument
of cultural and historical importance. The **Museum H.W. Mesdag**,
once the Mesdags' home, houses works by artists of the Hague
and Barbizon schools, such as Anton Mauve, Camille Corot, Jean-
François Millet, Charles-François Daubigny and Théodore Rousseau.
Museum H.W. Mesdag, Laan van Meerdervoort 7f. Tel: (070) 362
1434. **Panorama Mesdag**, Zeestraat 65. Tel: (070) 310 6665.

PLACES TO VISIT

The **Gemeentemuseum** reopened its doors in 1998 after major renovation and special attention is given to the Art Nouveau period. The museum also has a Fashion Gallery and impressive displays of glass, Hague silver and porcelain from The Hague and Delft.

Formerly the residence of a bibliophile and collector, the **Museum Meermanno-Westreenianum** now houses an extensive collection devoted to the art of the book and the history of printing.

Interior of the Gemeentemuseum

Dutch chest of the typically bulbous shape of the late 18th century

● **Gemeentemuseum**, Stadhouderslaan 41. Tel: (070) 338 1111.
● **Museum Meermanno-Westreenianum**, Prinsessegracht 30. Tel: (070) 346 2700.

SHOPPING

The area in and around Denneweg known as *de buurtschap* is the antiques quarter at the heart of the city.

Along Denneweg, look out for:
Ivory and porcelain from the east, in particular pieces from the early 17th century, are the speciality of **John Brand** at No 69A. **English Interiors**, at No 57, deals in early 19th-century English furniture as well as vintage wristwatches from Switzerland. **Neeltje Twiss** (No 10) is a family-run business that specializes in "modern antiques". They also have furniture from the 18th century and earlier and stylish *objets d'art* from the 1920s.

AUCTION HOUSES

Glerum Kunst en Antiek Veilingen, Westeinde 14. Tel: (070) 356 0165.
Van Stockum Antique and Auction House (Veilingen), Prinsengracht 15. Tel: (070) 364 9840.

WHERE TO EAT AND DRINK
Lodewieck
Denneweg 5
Tel: (070) 346 8819
Try the decadent desserts in this unpretentious lunchroom in the heart of the antiques quarter.

Le Bistroquet
98 Lange Voorhout
Tel: (070) 360 1170
The menu at this cosy bistro, conveniently close to the twice-weekly antiques market, features house-smoked salmon and Zeeland oysters.

WHERE TO STAY
Carlton Ambassador
2 Sophialaan
Tel: (070) 363 0363; Fax: (070) 360 0535
In the quiet, historic Mesdag quarter near the museums, the Carlton's late-19th century rooms are furnished in Old Dutch and English styles.

Inter-Continental des Indes
54–56 Lange Voorhout
Tel: (070) 361 2345; Fax: (070) 361 2350
Built as a palace in the 1850s and once the haunt of Mata Hari and Anna Pavlova, it is now famous for its attentive service and luxurious rooms.

Restaurant-Hotel Savelberg
14 Oosteinde, Voorburg
Tel: 070-387 2081; Fax: 070-387 7715
This early 18th-century manor house is in a small village just 15 minutes' drive from the city centre.

IN THE AREA

Leiden, north of The Hague, is a picturesque old university town, once an important market centre. The Rijksmuseum van Oudheden (Rapenburg 28) houses a renowned collection, including masterpieces from Egypt, Greece, the Far East and Holland's own rich past. On the outskirts of the town, at Oegstgeest, is **Antiekboerderij Almondhoeve**, an unusual "antiques farmhouse" with a large collection of antique furniture and high-quality replicas.

Skating on The Hofvijver

DELFT

The charm of Delft's pottery extends to the whole of this beautifully preserved and deeply historic old Dutch water town.

Dutch Delft punchbowl, c.1710

THE PICTURESQUE TOWN OF DELFT has changed very little since Jan Vermeer painted his *View of Delft* in 1661. Delft was a rich mercantile town, and its wide variety of building styles has been carefully preserved. Today the medieval structure of the historic centre houses many interesting shops, galleries, cafés and restaurants. It is a visual feast – charming canals with their arched bridges, stately mansions, courtyards, church towers, narrow alleys and the beautiful market square.

The name of Delft, however, remains synonymous the world over for the distinctive tin-glazed earthenware to which it has given its name.

HISTORY REVISITED

THE STORY OF DELFT

Chinese porcelain was introduced to Europe in the early 1600s and a century later Europe learned the secret of its manufacture (see page 135). The Dutch East India Company grew rich on importing the sought-after blue-and-white ware for those who could afford them. When war in China broke out in 1644 and cut off supplies, Dutch potteries fulfilled demand by adopting the colours and chinoiserie patterns for their own tin-glazed ware. Delft, one of the home ports of the East India Company, became the leading centre and gave its name to similar products that came to be produced in Britain and Ireland (see page 68). Beer-making was in decline and the expanding potteries took over breweries, and some of their names reflected this early association: De Dobbelde Shenckan (The Double Tankard), 1659, for example.

Early Dutch earthenware had often been multi-coloured, and from the beginning of the 1700s the Delft repertoire expanded. Domestic flower and landscape images became popular alongside the Ming-inspired Oriental scenes.

The heyday of Delftware lasted until the end of the 1700s, but production continues to this day. The showroom at **Koninklijke Porcelyne Fles** traces the development of Delft through the centuries.

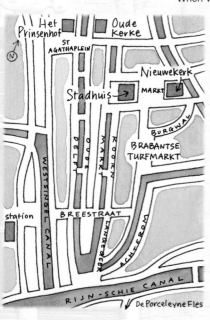

Many fakes of old Delftware were made, especially in the late 1800s. Fakes lack the simplicity of real 17th- and 18th-century Delft and look too fussy. Beware if anything looks too good: old pieces were used, and you should expect small chips. Early Delft pieces were seldom marked, so check marks against a reputable list.

● **Koninklijke Porcelyne Fles**, Rotterdamseweg 196. Tel: (015) 256 9214.

WHERE TO EAT AND DRINK

Le Vieux Jean
Heilige Geestkerkhof 3
Tel: (015) 213 0433
This charming restaurant celebrated its 25th anniversary in 1999. The menu is classic French with a modern touch and changes seasonally. The house speciality – sweetbreads with lobster sauce – is available all year around.

Stads Pannekoeckhuys
Oude Delft 113–115
Tel: (015) 213 0193
This family restaurant has been serving over 90 different kinds of pancake – both sweet and savoury – in an Oude Delft ambience for nearly 30 years. Closed Mondays.

WHERE TO STAY

Delft Museum Hotel & Residence
Oude Delft 189
Tel: (015) 214 0930; Fax: (015) 214 0935l
Situated on Delft's oldest canal and alongside Het Prinsenhof (see below), this hotel is a complex of 17th- and 18th-century monuments and stately canalside houses which has been filled with art and antiques.

Hotel de Ark
Koornmarkt 65
Tel: (015) 215 7999; Fax: (015) 214 4997
The De Ark occupies four 17th-century canalside houses in the old city centre. The rooms are spacious with all the modern amenities. The hotel also owns apartments in similar houses nearby.

Vermeer's View of Delft, *now in the Mauritshuis, The Hague (see pages 140–41)*

PLACES TO VISIT

The VVV (tourist office) has initiated "Talking Walls". These special audio tours provide a walk through the town to let the visitor experience a little of Delft's unique history, explaining the past of various historical buildings as you pass them.

The **Lambert van Meerten Museum** in the old town is worth a visit for its exhibitions of ebony-veneered furniture and earthenware. You will also find a collection of tiles, some of them very early and rare.

Originally built as a convent, **Het Prinsenhof** was given to William of Orange by the government of the new Dutch Republic in 1572. The Prince's Court became the monarch's home; it was also the site of his assassination. From 1932 to 1951, the rooms were transformed into a museum dedicated to the history of the Dutch Republic.

Delft has two churches. The **Oude Kerk**, founded in 1200, houses the largest carillon bell in the Netherlands and is used on state occasions. The **Nieuwe Kerk** (built between 1383 and 1510) is the resting place of many members of the House of Orange, including William of Orange. You will find beautiful stained glass in this church as well as

paintings and an exquisite collection of memorabilia associated with the Dutch royal family. Both churches can be visited using the same ticket, and in summer it is worth climbing the tower of the Nieuwe Kerk, which affords views as far as The Hague.

● **Lambert van Meerten Museum**, Oude Delft 199. Tel: (015) 260 2358.
● **Het Prinsenhof**, St Agathaplein 1. Tel:(015) 260 2358. Closed Mon.
● **Oude Kerk**, Heilige Geestkerkhof. Tel: (015) 212 3015.
● **Nieuwe Kerk**, Markt. Tel: (015) 212 3025.

SHOPPING

There are a number of interesting antique and ceramic shops and art galleries throughout Delft's historic city centre. Must-see streets include Vrouwe Jutteland, Vrouwenregt, Kerkstraat and Voorstraat.

A collection of old Delftware

Look out for:
Koos Rozenburg Antiek (Markt 32) specializes in Delftware from the 17th and 18th centuries.

Van Geenen Antiek (Voldersgracht 26) and **De Porcelijne Lampetkan**, (Vrouwenregt 5) are two family businesses that specialize in tiles and ceramics (including Delft) from the 17th and 18th centuries, as well as furniture from the mid-19th century.

De Jutter (Vrouw Jutteland 18) is run by a mother and daughter. Principally, they stock glassware from Leerdam and ceramic objects from Maastricht from the 1880s.

De Delftse Pauw (Delftweg 133) has a series of pottery factories that produce high-quality contemporary pieces.

FAIRS AND MARKETS

You can find a flea market on the banks of the many canals in Delft's town centre every Saturday throughout the summer.

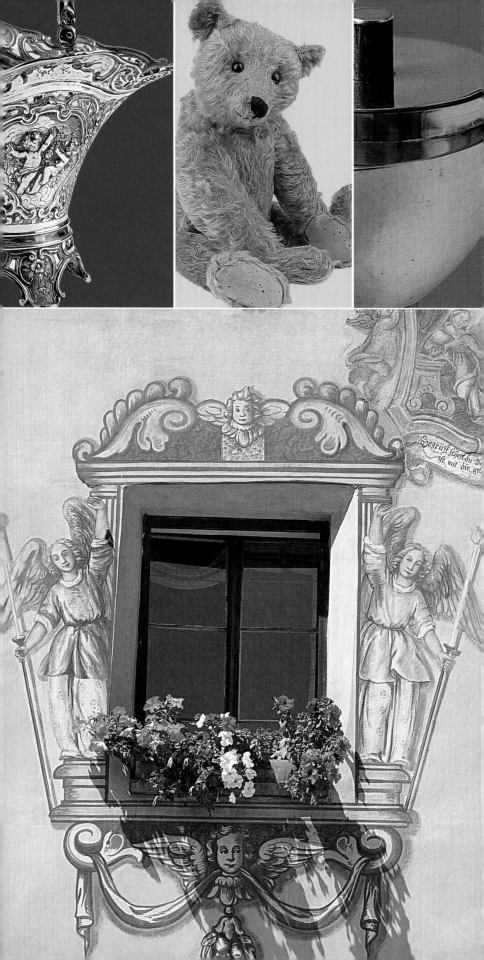

GERMANY, AUSTRIA & SWITZERLAND

THE ANTIQUES LANDSCAPE

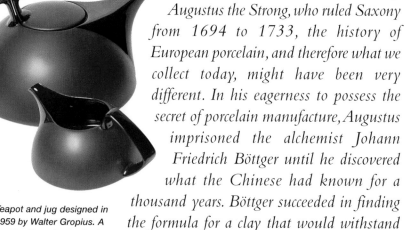

Teapot and jug designed in 1959 by Walter Gropius. A leading figure in the Bauhaus Movement, his designs are still in production today.

If it hadn't been for the obsession of Augustus the Strong, who ruled Saxony from 1694 to 1733, the history of European porcelain, and therefore what we collect today, might have been very different. In his eagerness to possess the secret of porcelain manufacture, Augustus imprisoned the alchemist Johann Friedrich Böttger until he discovered what the Chinese had known for a thousand years. Böttger succeeded in finding the formula for a clay that would withstand the high temperatures required to produce the fine, translucent porcelain that everyone who could afford it wanted on their table. Production started at the Meissen factory in about 1707 (see page 153).

Of course, what we know today as Germany, Austria and Switzerland were, until the late 19th century, a peppering of duchies, principalities, margraviates, landgraviates and bishoprics, all nominally under the control of the Holy Roman Empire and the Habsburgs. Most powerful were Austria, Saxony and Bavaria, under the Wittelsbachs, and the rising power of Brandenburg/Prussia under the Hohenzollerns. With natural rivalry for wealth and power came an urge to outdo one's neighbours. In their pursuit of such excellence, individual nation states specialized in furniture and glass-making, in art and architecture, producing designs and workmanship of the very highest standards. As a result, the whole region shares a legacy of impressively endowed castles and palaces, each embodying a succession of style developments that influenced the whole of Europe at different eras – from Neo-classicism in Berlin and Baroque in Bavaria to Jugendstil in Vienna.

Always worth looking out for are pieces of Biedermeier furniture and there are some excellent examples to be had – not just high-quality pieces from the prolific furniture centres of the mid-18th century, but also more recent provincial copies.

In antiques markets throughout Germany and Austria you are likely to find a huge variety of glass of all kinds. Coloured examples from Bohemia – formerly part of Bavaria and Lower Saxony – and enamelled and gilded pieces are worth buying.

In the classic 1940s film, The Third Man, Orson Welles, as Harry Lime, sums up Switzerland's only achievement as "the cuckoo clock". It makes a memorable quote but, in fact, Switzerland's clockmakers, like their jewellers, have always been the envy of the world. That same expertise has a tradition that extends to music boxes, automata and mechanical musical instruments, sought by collectors the world over.

Germany, Austria and Switzerland continued to be at the forefront of artistic endeavour in the 20th century, enjoying great periods of cultural development with the Jugendstil and Bauhaus movements. Look out for pieces originating from the Wiener Werkstätte, particularly those by Koloman Moser and Josef Hoffmann (see page 164). The range of collectable Bauhaus pieces is vast and includes furniture by Marcel Breuer, Gerhard Marcks' pottery, and textiles by Georg Muche (see page 149).

Following the reunification of Germany in 1989 the possibilities for antiques hunting have opened up massively – I once heard an antiques dealer who frequently buys on the continent describe Germany as "the new France".

Musical automaton c. 1920. Restoring such pieces requires great skill and can command high prices.

BERLIN

Lively flea markets, upmarket antiques dealers and some of the world's classiest museums: with the demolition of the infamous wall, Berlin is a city reborn.

A striking example of old Berlin's socialist art

AFTER WORLD WAR II, Berlin was partitioned into zones and the American, British and French areas gradually merged to become West Berlin. The Soviet zone in the east remained separate, culminating in the building of the wall in 1961. For nearly 30 years Berlin was a city split in two by a great concrete wall – on one side an island of western democracy and on the other a hardline communist state.

This is just one episode in Berlin's relatively recent history as a major city – first as capital of both pre-imperial Prussia and unified Germany under the Hohenzollern dynasty and, later, of the Weimar Republic which then made way for Hitler's Third Reich. Over time Berlin has become a sprawling city and is now almost five times the size of Paris. Comprised of 23 boroughs it is a place with a diverse cultural past and an impressive architectural make-up.

Berlin will fascinate antiques lovers. Many streets near Wittenbergplatz and Nollendorf-platz are lined with antiques shops, and there are several weekend flea markets. There is even a disused U-bahn station where stalls are set up in old subway cars.

For a glimpse of the magnificence of the pre-war capital, head to the historic eastern town with its spectacular architecture, grand avenues and wealth of museums. A visit to the new Stadtmitte, with Potsdamer Platz at its heart, will give you a vision of how it will look.

German travel poster depicting Berlin, c.1930s

HISTORY REVISITED

THE WEIMAR YEARS

With the close of World War I came an end to Germany's monarchy, with Kaiser Wilhelm II abdicating to make way for the Weimar Republic (1918–33). What followed was a period of cultural regeneration – often referred to as the "golden age" or the "Roaring Twenties" – a time of renewed interest in the arts against a background of political and social unrest.

Berlin became recognized as a capital of decadence and hedonism, where an avant-garde elite developed, embracing artists, painters and

Art Deco façade of Hackesche Höfe, a complex of apartments, a theatre, restaurants and shops

writers. Their work was reactionary, reflecting the times with a new degree of reality and resulted in such triumphs as film-maker Fritz Lang's *Metropolis*, the paintings of Otto

Items from a tea service designed by Walter Gropius

Dix, George Grosz and Max Beckmann, and Kurt Weill's and Bertolt Brecht's well-loved *Dreigroschenoper* (*The Threepenny Opera*).

Possibly the most significant cultural movement of the interwar period was the establishment of the Bauhaus school of art, architecture and design, founded by the architect Walter Gropius. His intention was to bridge the gap between the technical and creative aspects of design in order to produce furniture, ceramics, art and sculpture on a mass-market scale which, although aesthetically pleasing, were also functional. Berlin's **Bauhaus Archiv-Museum**, designed by Gropius, is dedicated to the school's short lifespan (1919–33) and includes works by artists Paul Klee and Wassily Kandinsky, designer Marcel Breuer and architect Ludwig Mies van der Rohe.

- **Bauhaus Archiv-Museum**, Klingelhöferstr. 13–14. Tel: (030) 254 0020. Closed Tues.

PLACES TO VISIT

Museuminsel's unique island complex of four museums includes **Alte Nationalgalerie**, which reopened in 2001; it has a truly superb collection of paintings and sculptures, with works by Auguste Rodin, Paul Cézanne, Edgar Degas and Max Liebermann, Berlin's famous portrait painter. Then the **Altes Museum**, an austere Neoclassical building, contains antique sculptures and bronze art. Also in the complex are the **Pergamonmuseum**, dedicated to the art of the ancient world, and one of the world's greatest museums, and the **Bodemuseum**, which has an unparalleled collection

Brandenburg Gate, currently undergoing restoration

of Byzantine and Egyptian relics.

The **Kulturforum** is a unique collection of museums, galleries, libraries and the city's philharmonic hall. Here you will find the **Gemäldegalerie**, one of Germany's finest galleries, with European paintings ranging from the 1200s to the 1700s. Close by is the **Kunstbibliothek**, containing art posters, costumes and a commercial art collection. The glass and steel **Neue Nationalgalerie** was designed by Mies van der Rohe and built in the 1960s. It houses mainly 19th-century works.

In Alexanderplatz, the showpiece of former East Berlin, you will find the **Fernsehturm**. At 400m (1300ft), this TV tower is among the tallest buildings in the city, with a spectacular view from the top.

- **Museuminsel**, Am Kupfergraben. Tel: (030) 209050. Closed Mon (Pergamon open Thurs 10am–10pm).
- **Kulturforum**, Matthäikirchpl. 8. Tel: (030) 2090 5555 (for all state museums in Berlin).
- **Fernsehturm**, Alexanderpl. Tel: (030) 242 3333.

Berlin porcelain solitaire set c.1890

SHOPPING

The greatest concentrations of antiques shops are around the old Nollendorfplatz station in Schöneberg for furniture, household goods and lamps, and around Savignyplatz in Charlottenburg for furniture, jewellery and local collectables. On Bergmannstrasse in Kreuzberg, there's funky clothing, accessories and decorative arts, and along Husemann-strasse in Prenslauer Berg, you'll find former-GDR memorabilia, furniture and books.

Look out for:
Jörg Schwandt (Keithstrasse 10) has 20th-century Danish silverware. Two doors away **Hannelore Plötz-Peters** has porcelain, miniatures and portrait paintings.

A variety of Art Deco specialists can be found in Schöneberg: **Antiquitäten Denk** at Kurfürstendamm 202, and **Echte Alte Lampen** at Pfalzburger Str. 12, which deals with lamps of this era. Paintings of the Berlin Secession, 1800s' furniture, glass from the Jugendstil period (see page 154) and 19th-century silver and gold items are stocked at **Ulrich Gronert** (Giesebrechtstr. 10).

A variety of collectables in Strasse des 17 Juni flea market

FAIRS AND MARKETS
The **Berliner Antik und Flohmarkt** is one of the largest, more established and expensive areas dealing in antique art. Under the tracks at Friedrichstrasse station there are other shops selling furniture, jewellery, and paintings.

The best flea market in town is held at weekends in the **Strasse des 17 Juni** in Charlottenburg, specializing in vintage clothing and second-hand items. During the week (except Tuesdays) try the flea market in the old **Nollendorfplatz** station.

AUCTION HOUSES

Christie's, Giesebrechtstr. 10. Tel: (030) 885 6950.
Sotheby's, Palais am Festungsgraben, Unter den Linden. Tel: (030) 204 4119.
Prinz-Dunst, Schlüterstr. 16. Tel (030) 313 5965.
Dannenberg, Wiesbadener Str. 82. Tel: (030) 821 6979.
Altus, Kalkreuthstr. 4–5. Tel: (030) 218 1818.

Paintings in Strasse des 17 Juni flea market

WHERE TO EAT AND DRINK

Ermelerhaus
Märkisches Ufer 10, Mitte
Tel: (030) 24 06 20
In a building that dates back to 1567, Ermelerhaus is decorated in the high Rococo style it acquired in the 18th century. On the menu are light variations of German favourites. Closed Sun/Mon.

Wintergarten im Literaturhaus
Fasanenstrasse 23, Charlottenburg
Tel: (030) 882 5414
Spy on Berlin's literary elite as they come and go to lectures and readings. You can enjoy breakfast, snacks and desserts in the basement café, or sit out in the conservatory-like winter garden.

Zur Letzten Instanz
Waisenstrasse 14–16, Mitte
Tel: (030) 242 55 28
This claims to be the oldest inn in Berlin, founded by a knight in 1621 and originally called the Glockenspiel. The food is hearty German fare.

WHERE TO STAY

Hotel Künstlerheim Luise
Luisenstrasse 19, Mitte
Tel: (030) 284480; Fax: (030) 28448 4480
Each room in this 1820s' hotel is decorated by a different local artist.

Hotel Astoria
Fasanenstrasse 2
Tel: (030) 312 4067; Fax: (030) 312 5027
Enjoy a traditional stay at this lovely, late 19th-century hotel.

Grand Hyatt
Marlene Dietrich-Platz 2
Tel: (030) 2553 1234; Fax: (030) 25531235
Berlin's avant-garde tradition is epitomized in this brand new, modern, state-of-the-art designer hotel with minimalist architecture. Huge bathrooms and there's a pool on the top floor.

IN THE AREA

Frederick the Great spent much of his time at **Sanssouci** near Potsdam, just 20 km (12 miles) south-west of Berlin. The land was used for cultivating fruit and vines until Frederick decided to build his summer residence here in 1745. Additional buildings were added over subsequent years, and it is now one of Berlin's most popular attractions. The **Bildergalerie** is close by and contains Frederick's collection of 17th-century Dutch and Italian paintings, with works by Peter Paul Rubens and Caravaggio.
● **Sanssouci**, Potsdam. Tel: (0331) 969 4206.
● **Bildergalerie**. Tel: (0331) 969 4181. Open summer only.

Bavaria's cosmopolitan capital is full of art, culture and *joie de vivre*, and is a hugely rewarding place to shop for antiques.

City coat of arms, featuring a monk, from which München gets its name

MUNICH IS SPECIAL. A long line of Wittelsbach rulers – the royal dynasty that reigned over southern Germany for almost 750 years until 1918 – have left their mark. Ludwig I and Maximilian II created monumental buildings and magnificent squares. Yet the city has a southern European feel with its Greek columns, Italian Baroque façades and French stucco. It is a superb city of contrasts: stunning Rococo court buildings amid space-age factories; soaring late-Gothic churches and smoky beer cellars; an air of affluence alongside the everyday.

A stoneware Kugelbauchkrug, c.1691

"A German heaven on earth" is how the American writer Thomas Wolfe described Munich. It is a place of differing interests, too – from the noisy camaraderie of the beer halls to the refinement and sophistication of the city's exceptional museums and art galleries, the state opera house and a range of shops, restaurants and attractions to suit all budgets and tastes.

With its vast green parks, gardens and forests on a river spanned by graceful bridges, Munich is a favourite with the Germans themselves, and shopping is hugely varied. For antiques hunters, the most exclusive shops are in the Stadtmitte, along and around Prannerstrasse, while the best flea markets can be found near Arnulfstrasse, along the northern side of the Hauptbahnhof.

ANTIQUES IN CONTEXT

Munich is a city with plenty to offer. Start at Marienplatz, with the Mariensäule built by Maximilian I, wait for the carillon to sound its famous melody in the Town Hall tower, then set off on your search.

NYMPHENBURG PORCELAIN

Conspicuously marked with a Bavarian shield, Nyphenburg porcelain was produced in Neudeck, on the outskirts of Munich, from 1747, before the factory moved to **Schloss Nymphenburg** in 1761.

If you are hunting for antique pieces, the best examples are from the early period until 1770. The most common wares are tea and coffee services, plates, tankards, cachepots and cylindrical food warmers. The finest and most popular decoration represents birds in trees or loose bouquets of flowers.

Today 60 master craftsmen work much as they always have – in the naturally lit studios of the factory built in the palace grounds. Every item is traditionally hand crafted, from throwing and forming to glazing and painting. More than 30,000 of the original 18th-century moulds and sketches are preserved here.

Nymphenburg has not remained in the past. With the advent of the 21st century, a trio of contemporary artists were invited to create new designs, so alongside the famous figurines and floral pieces, designs by Konstantin Greic, Ted Muehling and Bodo Sperlein have a collectability of their own.

In the palace, don't miss the Banqueting Hall, a Rococo masterpiece, the 100 portraits of women in the Gallery

Grand Marble Hall of Schloss Nymphenburg

of Beauties, the carriage museum and the porcelain gallery, exhibiting various pieces produced from 1747 to the 1920s.

The Nymphenburg shop looks like the palace's drawing room, with dove-grey furnishings and delicate porcelain in bow-fronted cabinets. You can also buy direct from the factory at the castle.

● **Schloss Nymphenburg**, Amalienburg. Tel: (089) 177494. closed Mon. Factory shop, Tel: (089) 129 1888)
● **Nymphenburg shops**, Odeonspl. and Briennerstr. Tel: (089) 282428)

Nymphenburg porcelain plate painted by J. Zachenberger, c.1760

MUNICH REVISITED

EARLY MUNICH

When Ludwig the Bavarian chose Munich as his seat of power in 1255, he built the **Residenz**,

Glockenspiel, installed in 1904 on the Neues Rathaus: it chimes daily at 11am and noon

probably Europe's first permanent royal palace, although it was only used as such for the next 50 years. A huge building was added, c.1580, and, for five centuries, alterations and additions were made so that Renaissance, Baroque, Rococo and Neo-classical architecture mingle to form one of Europe's great palace complexes.

The **Bayerisches Nationalmuseum** holds an extensive collection of Bavarian and other German art from medieval and Renaissance wood carvings to tapestries, arms and armour.

Munich's first city hall, the **Altes Rathaus**, built in 1474, has an atmospheric tower housing a lovely toy museum at the top of winding stairs.

● **Residenz**, Max-Josephpl. 3. Tel: (089) 290671.Open until 8pm Thurs in summer.
● **Bayerisches Nationalmuseum**, Prinzregentenstr. 3. Tel: (089) 2112401.
● **Altes Rathaus**, Marienpl. 15. Tel: (089) 23300.

SHOPPING

AROUND PRANNERSTRASSE

Within the last few years, Prannerstrasse has developed into the "Antique Mile" of Munich.

Look out for:
Gerhard Röbbig (Prannerstr. 3) stocks 18th-century German porcelain as well as French furniture from the Louis XV and Louis XVI eras.

Georg Urban (Prannerstr. 5) sells religious art from medieval times to Baroque and Rococo and has lots of interesting pieces, including items from houses in the Bavarian countryside (a style known as Irschenberg). **Galerie-Kunsthaus Trost** at the same address specializes in furniture of the Baroque and Neo-classical eras.

Metz de Benito (Prannerstr. 7) has a mix of furniture, sculptures, paintings, faience and religious and folk art.

Sisters **Anna-Maria Wager** and **E. Helga Ahrend** (Prannerstr. 4) specialize in miniature paintings and exclusive jewellery from the 18th century to Art Deco. They also stock some fine French furniture from the 18th and 19th centuries.

Clemens von Halem has a wonderful selection of antique clocks, mainly French, from the 17th-century until the First Empire. His shop, **Antike Uhren Schley** is in Montegelas Palais, Kardinal-Faulhaber-Str. 14a, and also includes a workshop from which he operates his own clock and watch restoration business.

Porcelain figures, c.1925, from the Bavarian Rosenthal factory in Selb

Antike Uhren Eder (Prannerstr. 4) also sells clocks, and usually has some high-quality antique German clocks in stock.

A huge choice of faience and stoneware is available from **Peter Vogt** (Marienpl. 8, with the entrance on Landschaftsstrasse).

Galerie von Spaeth (Theresienstr. 19A) is a specialist in glass from the 17th to the 20th centuries. You will find the shop's entrance on Fürstenstrasse. Here you can buy rare Baroque pieces from the 1700s, as well as many objects from the Italian masters based at Murano (see Venice, page 256) during the 20th century: from the 1920s and 1930s by Ercole Barovier and from the 1950s by Flavio Poii and Fulvio Bianconi.

You can find German art and furniture from the 19th century at **Axel Schlapka**, whose shop is at Gabelsbergerstr. 9.

> **MEISSEN**
> Founded at Meissen Castle in the early 1700s, the **Royal Saxon Porcelain Factory** produced the first hard-paste porcelain in Europe. Early Meissen pieces were strongly influenced by Chinese and Japanese styles. No identifying marks appear on the earliest Meissen, and many pieces are split or torn where they dried out too soon. For Meissen and Dresden porcelain, visit **Kunstring Meissen**, Briennerstrasse 4. Tel: (089) 281532.

SCHWABING

Once regarded as the bohemian quarter of Munich, home to the city's artists, Schwabing has developed into a popular shopping area.

Look out for:
At Schackstrasse 5 is **Herbert M. Ritter** who specializes in silver. At Seestrasse 4 you will find **Galerie Christel Reuther** which is not only a rich hunting ground for frames and mirrors, but also for furniture. Items from the 18th-century Munich court can be found here, as well as vases, urns and small sculptures.

FAIRS AND MARKETS

For those who find flea markets irresistible, there is one every weekend beneath the Donnersberger railway bridge on Arnulfstrasse (on the north side of the Hauptbahnhof). There is always an interesting selection of cheap antiques among the assorted junk from all over eastern Europe.

AUCTION HOUSES
Kunstauktionshaus Hugo Ruef, Gabelsbergerstr. 28. Tel: (089) 524084. For modern and traditional art.
Karl & Faber, Amirapl. 3. Tel: (089) 221865. Specializes in 19th-century art and sculpture.
Neumeister Kunstauktionen, Barer Str. 37. Tel: (089) 2317100. Specializes in 18th- and 19th-century and modern paintings, sculptures, furniture, silver and porcelain.

A Hyalith vase, imitation marble, c.1850

Copper and silver teapot by Mariane Brandt, c.1924, in the geometric style of the Bauhaus (see page 149)

JUGENDSTIL

At the beginning of the 19th century, Munich had a growing reputation in the art world, and it was here that Jugendstil – Germany's answer to Art Nouveau – was born. In 1892 a group of young artists left the Munich Artists' Association to form the Munich Society of Visual Artists, whose first exhibition included paint-

German cabinet, 1880, typical of the Jugendstil

ings by two key exhibitors: Franz von Stuck and Otto Eckmann. Stuck built a magnificent house – the **Villa Stuck** – for which he designed the furniture, furnishings, friezes and light fittings. Eckmann also turned to design, producing Japanese-inspired woodcut prints for the magazine *Die Jugend*, which gave its name to Jugendstil. Eckmann designed textiles, ceramics, metalware and furniture; his Five Swans tapestry became an icon of its genre.

Other artists emerged, such as August Endell and Hermann Obrist. Obrist was known for his embroideries and Endell for designing the Elvira Studio. Both designed furniture with similar metalwork decoration. A former artist, Richard Riemerschmid, was commissioned to design a service for the Meissen porcelain factory. His brother-in-law, Karl Schmidt, founded the Dresden workshops and built a garden city for his workers, with a training school and theatre. He broke with the movement's precepts by introducing standardized components, combining machine and hand techniques. This development signalled the renaissance of German folk art, with artists such as Bruno Paul and Peter Behrens making the transition from Jugendstil to functionalism. Art Nouveau became art for everyday life.

● **Museum Villa Stuck**, Prinzregentenstr. 60. Tel: (089) 4555 5125.

Electroplated silver Art Nouveau fruit bowl, c.1910 from the leading metalware factory, WMF

WHERE TO EAT AND DRINK

Lenbach
Ottostrasse 6
Tel: (089) 549 1300
Booking is a must in this spectacularly redesigned 100-year-old city palace, where guests enter along a floor-lit catwalk.

Dukatz
Salvatorplatz 1
Tel: (089) 291 9600
A converted 19th-century city mansion, Dukatz is where the literary crowd gather to hear book readings and to enjoy German cuisine with a modern, light touch.

Hundskügel
Hotterstrasse 18
Tel: (089) 264272
Munich's oldest tavern dates from the 15th century and is dripping with history from its crooked walls.

Boettner's
Theatinerstrasse 9
Tel: (089) 221210
This elegant restaurant has been in business since 1901. It's a good place at which to enjoy traditional German and French haute cuisine in

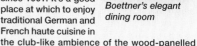

Boettner's elegant dining room

the club-like ambience of the wood-panelled dining room.

WHERE TO STAY

Mandarin Oriental Munich
Neuturmstrasse 1
Tel: (089) 290980; Fax: (089) 222539
The most luxurious hotel in the city is in a beautifully renovated Neo-Renaissance building that was originally built in the late 1800s as a high-society ballroom. The individually furnished rooms are all extravagantly and beautifully decorated.

Torbräu
Tal 41
Tel: (089) 242340; Fax: (089) 2423 4235
The same family has run this historic hotel, in the lea of the 14th-century Isartor gate, for several hundred years. Open since 1490, it is decorated in an Italian style and is in a good location for sightseeing and shopping.

Gästehaus am Englischen Garten
Liebergesellstrasse. 8
Tel: (089) 383 9410; Fax: (089) 3839 4133
As its name implies, this guesthouse is beside the English Gardens. Over 200 years old, it was once a water mill and is in a delightful location.

IN THE AREA

Landshut, 65km (40 miles) north-east of Munich, is an undiscovered gem. Every four years for three weeks in summer the Landshut Wedding is celebrated (the next one is 2005). The festival commemorates the marriage in 1475 of Prince George of Bavaria-Landshut, son of Ludwig the Rich, to Princess Hedwig, daughter of the King of Poland. Inside its ancient walls the whole town takes part. You can visit two Wittelsbach homes: the 13th-century **Burg Trausnitz**, where the dukes lived until 1503, and the Italian Renaissance **Stadt-residenz** in the Old Town. The cobbled market street is one of the most beautiful in Germany.

The Baroque city of Würzburg, on Germany's Romantic Road, and the historic little town of Bamberg have another, more recent, claim to fame: they form the antiques centre of East Franconia.

Detail of the staircase in the Archbishop's Palace, Würzburg

KNOWN AS THE PEARL OF THE ROMANTIC ROAD, Würzburg dates from the 10th century, when it was ruled by powerful and rich prince-bishops. This beautiful town stands at the junction of ancient trade routes with vineyard-covered hills as a backdrop. The present city is actually an impressive restoration, for it was all but destroyed at the end of World War II. Those who knew it before say the heart of the city has been recaptured and is as impressive as it always was.

Bamberg, 80 km (50 miles) to the east, is one of Germany's great historic towns. It rose to prominence in the 11th century under the Holy Roman Emperor Heinrich II, who proclaimed it capital of his empire. His cathedral still dominates the town. Bamberg's historic centre is on a small island in the River Regnitz, a delightful setting for its half-timbered gabled houses, formal 18th-century mansions and the brightly coloured row of fishermen's houses in Klein Venedig (Little Venice).

WÜRZBURG & BAMBERG

Bamberg's quaint Rathaus overlooking the River Regnitz, and, above, map of Würzburg

PLACES TO VISIT

Würzburg's fortress, the **Marienburg Festung**, was the original home of the ruling prince-bishops, and some parts of the building date from before AD700. Several Renaissance and Baroque apartments are open to the public, and the **Mainfrankisches Museum** within the fortress has a remarkable collection of art treasures recalling Würzburg's rich and varied history. There is a fascinating gallery devoted to sculptor Tilman Riemenschneider (1460–1531), who was born in the city. Along with paintings and porcelain exhibits, the collections of firearms, antique toys and ancient Greek and Roman art and artefacts are also worth a visit.

The **Residenz** in Würzburg is a wonderful Baroque palace designed by architect Balthasar Neumann and built between 1719 and 1753. Most of the interior work was created by the Italian stuccoist Bossi and the Venetian master, Giovanni Battista Tiepolo.

Bamberg's **Neue Residenz** is an immense Baroque palace, once home to the prince-electors. The palace also houses the state library, with thousands of books and illuminated manuscripts. The great **Dom** in Bamberg is one of the country's most important cathedrals and has played various roles throughout Germany's history. It was here, with the cathedral only half-completed, that Heinrich II was crowned Holy Roman Emperor in 1014. Inside the cathedral is one of Germany's most impressive collections of art treasures and monuments.

● **Marienburg Fortress** and the **Mainfrankisches Museum**, Würzburg. Tel: (0931) 43016. Closed Mon.
● **Residenz**, Residenzpl., Würzburg. Tel: (0931) 355 1712.

The Residenz, Würzburg: magificently Baroque

● **Neue Residenz**, Dompl., Bamberg. Tel: (0951) 56351.
● **Dom**, Dompl., Bamberg. Tel: (0951) 502330.

SHOPPING

Some of the finest Frankonian wines, in their distinctive green, flagon-shaped bottles, come from the vineyards surrounding Würzburg, but one of the principal draws of the city itself is some of the finest antiques in the area.

In Würzburg's main pedestrian area of Schönbornstrasse, there are many upmarket shops selling a wide range of items as well as a number of cafés, where you can sip your drink and consider your purchases.

Look out for:
Barbara Rummel (Textorstr. 13–15) offers an unusual selection, ranging from mid-19th century sculptures to antiquarian books. **Manfred Giolda** (Kardinal-Faulhaber-Pl. 4) specializes in silverware and furniture from the early 19th century.

MORE THAN JUST TOYS

Dolls were among the earliest toys, existing in the most primitive and the most sophisticated civilizations, and provide a fascinating record of social history. The great majority of antique dolls found today were made in the 19th and 20th centuries. Changing ideals of beauty are illustrated in their shape, form and clothes – from the rare primitive adult figures of the 17th and 18th centuries to the idealized children of the 19th century, on to the German character dolls and caricature Kewpie and Googly dolls of the 20th century. Thuringia, just north of Würzburg, was a centre for German porcelain and many factories became involved in doll-making. German character dolls, their faces modelled on real people, are now the rarest and most sought after today.

Bears are a relatively new phenomenon. Modern jointed bear appeared in the early 1900s in Germany when Margarete Steiff first modelled her toy on performing animals. Although other companies imitated her style, hers are the most valuable.

Open-mouth doll from Germany, c.1905;
Brown Steiff teddy, c.1909

For anyone who has an interest in the interior decoration of the 18th-century courts, try **Kunsthandel Albrecht Neuhaus** (Hainestr 9) who has a fine stock of items from this era.

Franz Xaver Muller's Kunsthandlung Antiquariat (Kardinal-Faulhaber Pl. 2) has many stunning paintings and fine art.

Bamberg is a great place for antiques hunting; you can find a wide variety of antique shops in and around Karolinenstrasse.

Look out for:
You will find good-quality furniture, paintings and kitchen antiques, at

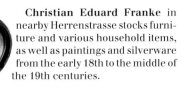

Late 16th-century Schnelle, or tall tankard, from Siegburg

Kunsthandel Senger (Karolinenstr. 8–10) and **Kunsthandel Hurtl** (Karolinenstr. 9). Porcelain lovers should walk further down the street to Istvan Csonth's **Bamberget Tassenkabinett** at No. 22, which is a paradise of a shop specializing in tea, coffee and chocolate cups from the 18th and 19th centuries.

Also in Karolinenstrasse you will find **M. Wenzel Kunsthandel**, **Peter Loblein** and **Strohlein Antiquitäten**, who all carry a varied stock of antique clocks, jewellery and household accessories.

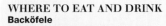

Pretty hard-paste Meissen figure, "Autumn", c.1810

Christian Eduard Franke in nearby Herrenstrasse stocks furniture and various household items, as well as paintings and silverware from the early 18th to the middle of the 19th centuries.

FAIRS AND MARKETS
As part of the annual **Bayreuther Wagnerfestspiele**, the Wagner Festival held each July/August, is the **Antiquitätenwoche** (antiques week). Check the tourist office (see Useful Addresses at the end of the book) for dates and details.

AUCTION HOUSES
The following are all in Bamberg:
Badum Auktionshaus, Karolinenstr. 11. Tel: (0951) 519 1492.
Sebök, Untere Königstr. 21. Tel: (0951) 202593.
Most, Karolinenstr. 1. Tel: (0951) 57565.

IN THE AREA

Coburg, 50km (30miles) north of Bamberg, is a little-known treasure. Founded in the 11th century, it was owned by the Saxe-Coburg dukes until 1918. The main attraction is the fortress on a hill above the town, which houses several museums. **Neustadt**, a little further on, is a centre for toy- and doll-making and has a museum showing toymaking through the ages.

Rothenburg-ob-der-Tauber, an hour south of Würzburg, is a wonderfully preserved medieval town, with numerous half-timbered buildings, as well as fountains and flowers, set against a backdrop of towers and turrets.

WHERE TO EAT AND DRINK
Backöfele
Ursulinergasse 2, Würzburg
Tel: (0931) 59059
This 400-year-old tavern serves good local dishes.

Brauereiausschank Schlenkerla
Dominikanerstr. 6, Bamberg
Tel: (0951) 56060
This old tavern (1516), with its black furniture and wood panelling, is a former monastery. Good Franconian specialties and locally brewed beer.

WHERE TO STAY
Hotel Walfischl
Am Pleidenturm 5, Würzburg
Tel: (0931) 35200; Fax: (0931) 3520500
Furnished in solid Franconian style behind a traditional façade, the Walfischl has been run by the Schwarzmeiers for three generations. It's in a good location with great views of the fortress.

Romantik Hotel Weinhaus Messerschmitt
Lange Strasse 41, Bamberg
Tel: (0951) 27866; Fax: (0951) 26141
A beautiful Baroque house where the famous aviator grew up, this has been a family hotel since

1832. Presidents, chancellors and the aristocracy have all stayed here.

Frankischer Hotelgasthof zur Stadt Mainz
Semmelstrasse 39, Würzburg
Tel: (0931) 53155; Fax: (0931) 58510
This inn dates back to the 15th century and has a good restaurant. Rooms are comfortable with traditional touches.

Wald und Schlosshotel
Friedrichsruhe-Zweiflingen, Baden-Württemberg
Tel: (07941) 60870; Fax: (07941) 61468
Once the summer palace and hunting lodge of the Hohenlohe-Oehringen princes, this hotel still

belongs to the family and is furnished with many original antiques. It is now a retreat for politicians and captains of industry. Its gourmet restaurant specializes in fish and game, and the Verrenburg wine is grown on the estate.

Wald und Schlosshotel

COLOGNE

Cologne, once a place of pilgrimage, is now a centre of art and fashion and the base of some of Germany's smartest antiques dealers.

Berlin plaque, painted on porcelain, c.1880–90

FAMOUS THE WORLD OVER FOR EAU DE COLOGNE, first produced in the early 1700s, Cologne is the largest city on the Rhine. A centre of power since Roman times, it was a member of the powerful Hanseatic League (see page 160) in the Middle Ages and became more important for European trade and commerce than Paris or London. In the early 1900s it was a major economic centre but, like many German cities, had to be extensively rebuilt after 1945. Only the magnificent Gothic cathedral, Germany's largest and finest, remained relatively untouched, and today it is the most visited building in Germany.

The old town, encircled by streets that follow the medieval city walls, has been pedestrianized and is now the cultural centre of the city. The major sights and shopping streets are here and can be covered comfortably on foot.

Today Cologne is a world-class centre for art and trade fairs, as well as a key business centre in western Europe. It is a vital, charming city in which commerce and culture blend well. During the summer, street festivals and fairs abound.

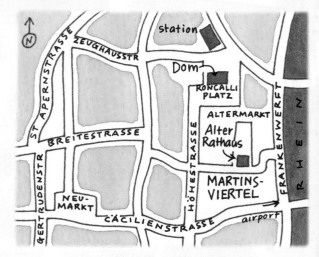

HISTORY REVISITED

FROM ANCIENT ROME TO ROMANESQUE

Cologne was first settled by the Romans in 38BC and for nearly 100 years it developed slowly until a local noblewoman, Julia Agrippina, daughter of the Roman general Germanicus, married the Roman Emperor Claudius. Her birthplace was elevated to the rank of a Roman city and given the name of Colonia Claudia Arae Agrippinensis, and for the next 300 years it flourished.

There is still plenty of evidence of the Roman connection, particularly in the Roman-German museum. In the 9th century, Charlemagne, the first Holy Roman Emperor, restored the city's fortunes and appointed the city's first archbishop. The ecclesiastical legacy is demonstrated by its Romanesque churches and its awe-inspiring Gothic cathedral whose twin spires dominate the skyline.

PLACES TO VISIT

The **Dom**, Cologne's cathedral, was begun in 1320 but not completed for 550 years. When finished, the two west towers, at 157m (515ft) tall, were the world's tallest buildings. The cathedral was built to house what were believed to be the holy relics of the three Magi. The other great treasure is the Gero Cross, a huge oak crucifix dating from AD97. There are also beautiful 14th-century stained glass, a magnificent altarpiece and intricate choir screens.

Constructed in the 1970s to house Cologne's Romano-Germanic artifact collection, the **Römisch-Germanisches Museum** surrounds the famous mosaic that was found during the building of a war-time air raid shelter. Over 90m (295ft) square, the mosaic illustrates the adventures of Dionysus, the Greek god of wine.

Experts regard **St Gereon's** as one of the most important medieval buildings still in existence. The church stands on the site of a Roman burial ground and Roman masonry forms part of its structure.

At **Glockengasse 4711**, you can visit the house (decorated in the style of the time) where Italian chemist Giovanni-Maria Farina first created eau de Cologne in the early 1700s.

- **Dom**, Domplatz. Tel: (0221) 135130.
- **Römisch-Germanisches Museum**, Roncalliplatz 4. Tel: (0221) 221 24438.
- **St Gereon's**, Gereonshof 4. Tel: (0221) 134922.
- **Glockengasse 4711**. Tel: (0221) 925 0450.

SHOPPING

Cologne is a haven for antiques lovers. German collectors are keen on 20th-century pieces (particularly Jugendstil; see page 154) and fine design.

Look out for:

St Apern-Strasse is full of interesting shops. **H.G. Klein** (No 2) specializes in antiques and old art. You can find furniture from the 1700s, tapestries, sculptures and antique wallpapers at **Benedikt Korth** (No 7). Eduard Rotmann's **Galerie Rotmann** (No 11) sells Fabergé, Russian silverware from 1600 to 1900, antique jewellery and 15th- to 19th-century icons.

One of the best places for Greek and Roman art in Germany is **Axel G. Weber** (Gertrudenstr. 29). For original Art Deco objects try specialists **Galerie Claud** (Deutzer Freiheit 103). They restore items, and have artifacts by Printz, Lambert-Rucki and Le Corbusier. A collectors' market of 20th-century items takes place each October.

Pierced openwork German silver basket, c.1890

WHERE TO EAT AND DRINK

Le Moissonnier
Krefelder Strasse 25
Tel: (0221) 729479; Fax: (0221) 732 5461
Possibly the best restaurant in the city with warm, welcoming, late 19th-century bistro décor and wonderful food.

Früh am Dom
Am Hof 12–14
Tel: (0221) 258 0389
The vaulted ceilings in this former brewery are painted with bold frescoes. Good German food.

WHERE TO STAY

Dom-Hotel
Domkloster 2A
Tel: (0221) 20240; Fax: (0221) 202 4444
Stunning location next to the cathedral, this late 19th-century hotel is brimming with antiques and each room is individually decorated.

Chelsea
Jülicherstrasse 1
Tel: (0221) 207150; Fax: (0221) 239137
A contemporary designer hotel that is much favoured by artists and art dealers.

IN THE AREA

Roman legions came to **Aachen**, some 70km (40 miles) west of Cologne, for the healing properties of its springs – the Elisenbrunnen – which still attract visitors. Some of its buildings with their distinctive three-windowed façades date back to the era when Charlemagne made the town a great centre of the Holy Roman Empire, in the 9th century. The cathedral contains Charlemagne's marble throne and the greatest collection of Carolingian art and architecture in Europe. Charlemagne is buried here in a golden shrine, and over 30 later Holy Roman Emperors were later crowned here, each donating a lavish gift to the cathedral.

Cologne cathedral, once a pilgrimage centre to rival Rome

HAMBURG

International trade – from Spain to the steppes of Russia in medieval times, and later with America and the Indies – brought wealth and a taste for fine living to Hamburg.

Biedermeier chair, c.1820

FOUNDED IN 810 BY CHARLEMAGNE, for centuries Hamburg was a walled city with huge fortifications. As a former member of the Hanseatic League, which dominated commercial interests in Europe from the 13th to 15th centuries, Hamburg became a tremendously influential port in the 1800s, playing host to some of the world's fastest ships and largest shipping fleets.

The Great Fire of 1842 destroyed most of the original city and, in World War II, over half the city was levelled. But with

careful planning, Hamburg recaptured its pre-war grandeur and elegance; its fine architecture includes good examples of Jugendstil buildings, and there are some interesting 14th-century houses in the old residential part of the city.

Central Hamburg – with its unique skyline of six spires – boasts elegant hotels, shops and cafés with parks while, to the east of the city, the district of St Georg is home to a growing community of antique dealers.

HISTORY REVISITED

THE HANSEATIC LEAGUE

Hamburg's official title as *Freie und Hansestadt* dates from the creation of the Hanseatic League, founded in the 13th century to protect the trading rights of north German merchant cities – its history is recorded at the **Museum für Hambürgisches Geschichte**.

A visit to **Speicherstadt**, Hamburg's 19th-century warehouse district is also worthwhile for its streets of gable-fronted buildings, and don't miss the **Kontorhausviertel** district, with its huge 1920s' red-brick buildings, between Steinstrasse and Messberg.

● **Museum für Hambürgisches Geschichte**, Holstenwall 24. Tel: (040) 4284 12380. Closed Mon am.

German antique till

PLACES TO VISIT

The **Krameramtswohnungen** are Shop-keepers' Guild houses. Half-timbered, with distinctive chimneys and decorative brick façades, they date from the 1620s and were built for members' widows. One of them, the house marked C, is open to the public.

A visit to Hamburg would not be complete without a trip to the city's piers – the **Landungsbrücken** – and a tour of the harbour by boat.

● **Krameramtswohnungen**, Krayenkamp 10. Tel: (040) 3110 2624.
● **Landungsbrücken**. Tel: (040) 3195 959.

SHOPPING

The St Georg area is especially good for antiques shops, particularly the 40 or so shops in the **Antik Center** in Klosterwall. **Waltraud Basedau**'s shop (Harvestehuder Weg 59) is a must for anyone with an interest in old walking sticks. For a variety of lamps and light fittings, try **Winfried Bobsien** (Alter Fischmarkt 11).

German porcelain and ormolu tureen with cover, c.1860

Sculpture and furniture from the 18th and 19th centuries can be picked up at **Otteni Kunsthandel** (Elbchaussee 264), and **Edmund J. Kratz** (Dockenhudener Str. 25) offers not only furniture from Baroque to Biedermeier, but also French bronzes and picture wallpaper.

For small art objects, visit **Erika Jacobs** (Johnsweg 2). For mainly 18th- and 19th-century antiques, go to **Urs. S. Niederoest** (Hohe Bleichen 22).

AUCTION HOUSES

Schopmann, Hohe Bleichen 22. Tel: (040) 3232390.
Hauswedell & Nolte, Poseldorfer Weg 1. Tel: (040) 404132100. Specialize in books, sculpture, autographs and non-European art.

IN THE AREA

The quaint Fischmarkt and carefully preserved streets of half-timbered merchants' houses in **Stade**, 60 km (35 miles) north of Hamburg, help to give a picture of what Hamburg must have been like in the 17th and 18th centuries. A Dutch influence can be seen in the Altstadt where the Rathaus, built in 1667, displays traces of Dutch Renaissance architecture. Once a Hanseatic port, Stade fell under Swedish rule for much of the 17th century, and the local history museum is housed in a warehouse called the Schwedenspeicher.

WHERE TO EAT AND DRINK

Deichgraf
Deichstrasse 23
Tel: (040) 36 42 08
One of several eating places on this historic street, this canal-side restaurant serves fish dishes of the highest quality. Filled with 19th-century antiques, it captures the charm of a classic Hanseatic merchant house.

Landhaus Scherrer
Elbchaussee 130, Altona
Tel: (040) 880 1325
Once an old brewery, this restaurant on the banks of the Elbe serves local dishes created by one of the region's most innovative chefs. Recipes are based on local produce which include freshwater crabs and north sea fish.

WHERE TO STAY

Vier Jahreszeiten
Neuer Jungfernstieg 9-14
Tel: (040) 34940; Fax: (040) 3494 2600
Said to be Germany's best hotel, this 19th-century town house is full of antiques and rare tapestries. The Jahreszeiten-Grill has been refurbished in Art Deco style.

Kempinski Atlantic Hotel
An der Alster 72–79
Tel: (040) 28880; Fax: (040) 247129
Overlooking the Alster in central Hamburg, this luxury hotel with its early 20th-century gabled façade is a local landmark.

Hotel Prem
An der Alster 9
Tel: (040) 2483 4040; Fax: (040) 280 3851
In this quiet gem of a hotel, established in 1912, no two rooms are furnished alike.

Restored warehouses along Deichstrasse

VIENNA

From the glittering empire of the Habsburgs and the Holy Roman Empire, Vienna inherited a culture and style that appreciates the best of the past.

The Anker Clock in Hoher Markt

ONCE THE CAPITAL OF THE HOLY ROMAN EMPIRE, Vienna is a city of great historical and cultural wealth. It was once said that "the streets of Vienna are covered with culture as the streets of other cities are covered in asphalt". In spite of a reputation for being rather formal, the Viennese have a passion for good music and culture. They may visit the opera two or three times a week rather than go to a trendy bar or nightclub. This city has even turned the ball into an art form, with some 300 of them hosted each year. Its famous Opera Ball attracts Hollywood stars, aristocrats and statesmen from all over the world.

Architecturally, Vienna's old and new buildings are reminders of the city's past and its present. The old town, its skyline dominated by the Hofburg, the Stephansdom and the Karlskirche, is still very much the heart of the city with newer, more modern developments radiating out from its centre.

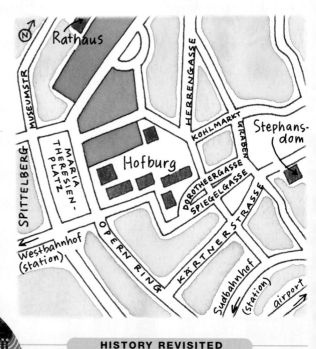

HISTORY REVISITED

SECESSIONISM

Inspired by the Munich avant-garde, Joseph Hoffman, Koloman Moser and Joseph Olbrich declared themselves Secessionists in 1897 to found the Association of Austrian Artists. They rebelled against the exclusive organization which controlled the arts in Vienna decreeing that all "foreign" art was suspect. Their early exhibitions introduced European art to Vienna and included artists such as Gustav Klimt. They wanted to raise the standards of Viennese craftsmanship, relating it to modern interiors and promoting an urban ideal of decorative art. Biedermeier furniture was an example.

Majolikahaus façade by Otto Wagner

ANTIQUES IN CONTEXT

The Ringstrasse which encloses the city is home to some of the most impressive buildings in the world. The place has a majestic aura with architectural and cultural treasures ranging from the **Hofburg** (the Imperial Palace of the Habsburgs) to the coffee houses for which Vienna is famous.

The **Hofburg** – centrepiece of Imperial Vienna – was the residence of the Dukes of Austria's Bakenburg family from the 13th century onwards, then, when the Habsburgs began their rule, the Hofburg became the seat of the German monarchy. From the 15th century, for almost 400 years, it was the centre of administration for the Holy Roman Empire. From 1804 to 1918, the palace was the residence of the emperors of Austria, who were also kings of Hungary, Bohemia, Croatia and Galicia.

Nationalbibliothek in the Hofburg

The palace was constantly being rebuilt with almost every monarch making his mark according to the architectural fashion of the time. The complex has 18 wings enclosing 19 courtyards in styles from Baroque to Gothic to Renaissance to Biedermeier. Hundreds of rooms are open to the public, including the Kaiserappartements (State Apartments), the Schatzkämmer (Treasuries), the Spanische Reitschule (Spanish Riding School) with the world-famous Lipizzaner stallions, the Burgkapelle (Chapel, home to Vienna Boys' Choir), the Imperial Porcelain and Silver Collection and Austria's national library.

A Viennese landmark: the Baroque Karlskirche

PLACES TO VISIT

The **Museum für Angewandte Kunst** has superb collections of Austrian furniture, porcelain, *objets d'art* and priceless Oriental carpets. There is a display devoted to Jugendstil and Joseph Hoffman and his followers (see next page and page 154.)

Set aside an entire day to see the **Kunsthistorisches Museum** which houses the immense fine art collection amassed by the Habsburgs.

With its towering Gothic spires and brightly coloured tiled roof the **Stephansdom** dominates the city's skyline, and from its south tower you get a magnificent view over the city. The oldest part of the church dates back to the 13th century, but along with the rest of the city it was refashioned in Gothic style in the 14th century. In 1683 the Turks laid seige to Vienna and although they failed to take the city they caused severe damage to the Stephansdom, which had to be largely rebuilt, this time in splendidly Baroque style.

Beethoven's piano collection in the Kunsthistorisches Museum

The **Siegmund-Freud-Museum** is housed in the apartment where Freud treated his first patients and developed modern psychiatry. It has a replica of his couch (the original is in London).

Vienna's giant ferris wheel, the **Riesenrad**, built by an Englishman, Walter Basset in 1897, was featured in the classic film of the city's underworld *The Third Man*. The wheel towers more than 60m (200ft) over the city, offering great views from its wooden cabins.

- **Hofburg**, centred on Neue Burg palace. Tel: (01) 533 8570.
- **Museum für Angewandte Kunst**, Stubenring 5. Tel: (01) 711360. Closed Mon; open Tues until midnight.
- **Kunsthistorisches Museum**, Maria-Theresien Pl. Tel: (01) 525 24401. Closed Mon.
- **Stephansdom**, Stephanspl. Tel: (01) 515 52 3526. Closed Mon.
- **Sigmund-Freud-Museum**, Bergg. 19. Tel: (01) 319 1596.
- **Riesenrad**, Prater Park. Tel: (01) 512 8314. Variable operating times according to time of year.

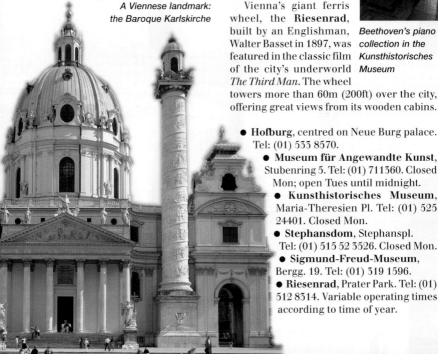

VIENNESE DESIGN

The **Wiener Werkstätte** studios, founded in 1903 by the Secessionists Josef Hoffmann and Koloman Moser, specialized in the production of metalwork, jewellery, furniture, textiles and leather articles. Although made for a wide public, they were too expensive for most ordinary people. A mainly mechanized process was used, although some items were handmade to order.

From the early 1900s Hoffman's designs took the form of starkly geometric, pierced fretwork desk-stands, vases and candlesticks in silver or painted metal, but from around 1910 his silver or brass bowls and dishes were more organic in inspiration, with lobed and fluted or ribbed sides and smooth surfaces.

Moser designed small, decorative items such as cylindrical or sphere-shaped vases decorated with smooth surfaces and hardstones. Both Moser and Hoffman were influenced by the geometric style of Charles Rennie Mackintosh (see page 62).

Kunsthistorisches Museum hall

Michael Thonet (1796–1871) was a pioneer of the bentwood technique and became one of the major figures in the development of Austrian Art Nouveau furniture. He steamed solid or laminated wood to bend it into shape, replacing angular corner joints by gentle curves. Several of his chairs have become classics. The first catalogue of bentwood furniture was produced by Gebrüder Thonet in 1859.

The sinuous pieces became associated with Art Nouveau, and one of the factory's major designers was Josef Hoffmann.

VIENNA PORCELAIN

Claudius du Paquier founded his factory in Vienna in 1718, at which time it was the only competitor of Meissen, Europe's first porcelain maker (see page 153). The solid shapes of Vienna's porcelain contrasted with more delicate Oriental-type decoration, but each piece reflected the ornate Baroque style of Vienna itself.

By the mid-1700s the factory, now under State management, produced many figurines but they lacked character. By 1784 the Rococo style had fallen out of fashion in favour of Neoclassical shapes using dark coloured grounds and elegant gilt scrollwork. The factory eventually closed in 1864.

Cutlery designed by Josef Hoffmann, c. 1925

SHOPPING

Vienna is an exciting place to shop, whether you want high-profile designer stores, small antiques shops in the old city or the uncertainty and fun of flea markets and fairs.

Look out for:
Lobmeyer (Kärntnerstr. 26) has been owned by the same family for five generations. It produces very beautiful drinking glasses and crystal chandeliers and has many prestigious clients. It is renowned for its exquisite *Musselinglas* (it almost bends at a touch). At **Glasgalerie Michael Kovacek** (Spielg. 12), you will find a superb collection of glass with examples from 16th-century Venice, through Baroque, Biedermeier to Art Nouveau and Tiffany. There are also pieces from the 1950s and '60s. **Galerie Asboth**, along the sme street at No 19, specializes in antiquities of East Asia.

For a good selection of all types of art, look in on **Kunsthandel Antoine Bauernfeind** (Dorotheerg. 9). **Bel Etage** (Wolfgang Bauer, Mahkerstr. 15) specializes in Art Nouveau and Art Deco furniture, as does **Kunsthandel Patrick Kovavacs** (Rechte Wienzeile 31). For modern Austrian classics, such as Oskar Kokoschka, visit **Galerie Richard Ruberl** (Himmelpfortg. 1) or **Wienerroither & Kohlbacher** (Strauchg. 2). **Galerie bei der Albertina** (Lobkowitzplatz 1) specializes in Art Nouveau, Art Deco and Wiener Werkstätte ceramics. At the showroom of world-renowned jewellery designer **Michaela Fray** (Lobkowitz Plaza 1) is work inspired by Klimt and Schiele. For fine silverware, search out **Antiquitäten Reisch** (Stallburgg. 4).

For fine antique furniture go to **Reinhold Hofstätter** (Bräunerstr.) or **Mario Perko** (Spiegelgasse). Or for the quirkily different on a small scale, go to **Frimmel** (Freisingerg. 1): a button shop to beat all others.

The classic Thonet chair, still produced

SHOPPER'S TIP

By the turn of the 19th century, the Thonet factories were turning out 4,000 pieces of furniture a day. The firm still flourishes in Austria, manufacturing some excellent modern furniture as well as its traditional bentwood pieces. The bentwood chairs with cane seats produced in various designs are readily available, but more collectable are the rarer large rocking chairs and recliners.

WHEN IN VIENNA...

Treat yourself to a musical interlude at one of the many churches that double as concert halls. The **Burgkapelle** at the Hofburg Palace is the home of the Vienna Boys' Choir and you can listen to them sing Mass (get tickets, available from a number of sources, beforehand). **Ruprechtskirche**, in Ruprechtspl. is the oldest church in Vienna, dating from the 11th century. It opens for classical concerts on evenings during the summer.

FAIRS AND MARKETS

The **Flohmarkt** (flea market) is open for business Monday to Saturday all year at the end of Naschmarkt. Beside the Danube Canal at Salztorbrücke you'll find the **Kunst und Antikmarkt**, which operates during the summer months. It offers a mixed selection including some high-quality items.

Plate in the Vienna style but made c.1870, shortly after the Vienna factory closed

AUCTION HOUSES

Dorotheum, Dorotheerg. 17. Tel: (01) 515600. And also at Baumkirchner Ring 4. Tel: (01) 22467.
Sotheby's, Singerstr. 16. Tel: (01) 5124 7720.
Christie's, Bankg. 1 & Herreng. 17. Tel: (01) 533 8812.

Shopping in Kärntnerstrasse

WHERE TO EAT AND DRINK

Demel Konditorei
Kohlmarkt 14
Tel: (01) 535 1717
One of Vienna's oldest tea and pastry shops (1888), this is a great place to indulge yourself as you sit and relax in wonderful surroundings.

Café Hawelka
Dorotheergasse 6
Tel: (01) 512 8230
One of the last art-café-literature houses. Run by the same couple since it opened 60 years ago.

Piaristenkeller
Piaristengasse 45
Tel: (01) 406 0193
The Piaristenkeller's cellars were once part of a monastery. Now, as well as the wine on which the restaurant prides itself, they unexpectedly contain a hat museum.

Hansen
Wipplingerstrasse 34
Tel: (01) 532 0542
Housed downstairs in the Börse (Vienna's stock exchange), this unique restaurant also houses an exotic, but expensive flower market.

WHERE TO STAY

Hotel Imperial
Kärntner Ring 16
Tel: (01) 501 100; Fax: (01) 501 10410
Elegant and private, this luxury hotel is as much a palace today as it was in 1873 when it was opened by Emperor Franz Josef. Some rooms have 9-m (30-ft) high ceilings complete with 19th-century oil paintings on the walls.

König von Ungarn
Schulerstrasse 10
Tel: (01) 515 840; Fax: (01) 515848
A charming hotel ("The King of Hungary"), built in the early 1800s, lies in the shadow of the cathedral. Comfortably furnished with country antiques and wooden panelling.

Regina
Rooseveltplatz 15
Tel: (01) 404 460; Fax: (01) 408 8392
This 19th-century hotel has a lovely view of the Sigmund Freud Park. High ceilings and attractive decor with elegant chandeliers and statues. Freud used to eat breakfast here every morning.

Austria
Wolfeng 3
Tel: (01) 515 230; Fax: (01) 515 23506
High-ceilinged rooms, Oriental carpets and a haven for art lovers: the hotel owns and displays the Mornington art collection. It has two wonderful restaurants, one with two Michelin stars.

IN THE AREA

On Vienna's outskirts, **Schloss Schönbrunn** (called the "Versailles of Vienna") was built for the Habsburgs between 1696 and 1713 as their summer residence. A splendid Baroque building with imposing formal gardens, it was used by Empress Maria Theresa, Napoleon and Kaiser Franz Joseph I (1852–1925), who was born and died here. Magnificent rooms, such as the Round Chinese Cabinet and the Great Gallery, are decorated in Rococo style. Within the grounds is Europe's oldest zoo (established in 1752 to amuse the court), as well as an exquisite Palm House, the Gloriette (a Neo-classical arcade) and a butterfly house.

SALZBURG

Salzburg's Goldgasse has become known as Antiques Mile, and the birthplace of Mozart is becoming as well known for its antiques as for its musical heritage.

Engraved goblet by Anton Kothgasser, c.1820

FOUNDED IN THE 7TH CENTURY, Salzburg was situated on an important military route connecting northern and southern Europe and has been an important administrative seat from Roman times. The city was ruled by independent archbishop-princes, who wielded political power from the late 13th century until 1803 when Napoleon made it an electorate. Twelve years later the emperor of Austria gained control.

Trade in salt – called "white gold" – had brought early prosperity to Salzburg and enabled the rulers to build a superb domed and spired city often referred to as the "Rome of the North", because of its Italian character, its many sacred buildings and its romantic atmosphere. Few other cities offer such a wealth of Baroque splendour. Many of the sights are recognizable from the The Sound of Music, the film that brought Salzburg worldwide fame.

Salzburg offers a cultural programme boasting more than 4,000 events throughout the year, and starts with Mozart Week in January, followed by Easter and Summer festivals. There are cultural days, a jazz festival in November and, in December, Advent Singing in the Mozarteum's great hall.

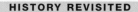

HISTORY REVISITED

WOLFGANG AMADEUS MOZART

The house where Mozart was born in 1756 is packed with Mozart memorabilia, and the house where he grew up is now the Mozart Audio and Film Museum. The **Mozarteum** is a regular venue for concerts and houses archives of his work; the courtyard here contains the summerhouse in which Mozart wrote *The Magic Flute*. Salzburg's busy musical calendar always features his work, even performances of his operas by marionettes, reaching a high point each January with Mozartwoche, a week devoted to Salzburg's musical genius.

● **Mozarts Geburtshaus**, Getreidegasse 9. Tel: (0662) 844313.
● **Mozarts-Wohnhaus**, Makartpl. 8. Tel: (0662) 87422740.
● **Mozarteum**, Schwartzstr. 26. Tel: (0662) 6198 4500.

The birthplace of the great composer

PLACES TO VISIT

The **Festung Hohensalzburg** is Salzburg's 11th-century fortress, set high above the town with spectacular views (take the funicular up, if climbing the steep Festunsgasse does not appeal). There are tours of the State Apartments and, in the basement, an exhibitionof historical marionettes, including characters in Mozart operas.

● **Festung Hohensalzburg**, Mönchsberg. Tel: (0662) 8424 3010.

SHOPPING

The best place to start shopping is in the old part, starting at Alter Markt – the centre of the old city. Walk along Getreidegasse, with its wrought-iron shop signs, and explore the interconnecting side alleys. On the other side of the river, there are more antiques shops in Platzl and Linzer Strasse, while Goldgasse has become the city's "antiques mile".

Look out for:
Deco Art (Wiener-Philharmoniker-Str.1) and **Schwaighofer** (Drei-fältigkeitsg. 9) stock Art Deco antiques, while examples of work by Gustav Klimt and Oskar Kokoschka can be found at **Rupertinum Moderne Galerie** at Wiener-Philharmoniker-Str. 9.

At Christian Sturm's **Dies und Das** in Schranengasse you can find everything from 20th-century jewellery to paintings, from furniture to mirrors, and from sculpture to exquisite tableware.

German bronze statuette of a gladiator, c.1910

If your interest is antique Austrian furniture or early 19th-century glass and porcelain, then visit **Katharina Baumgartner** (Goldg.). **Maria Pintar** (Dreifältigkeitsg. 4) specializes in Art Deco jewellery. Don't miss long-established goldsmith **Rautenberg** (Alter Markt).

Masterpieces from Vienna can be found at **Constanze Ilko** (Goldg. 13), who stocks furniture designed by Gustav Siegel and Marcel Kammerer, as well as vases and bowls from Zsolnay (see Budapest, page 178).

Gerhard Schöppel (Gestätteng. 5) and **Ilse Guggenberger** (Brodg. 11) specialize in rare Austrian items, **Karolina Schubert** (Bürgerspitalg. 2) in Meissen porcelain.

FAIRS AND MARKETS

There is an **Art, Antiques and Rarity Fair** every October. For details contact the tourist office (see Useful Addresses at the end of the book).

Dresden two-handled cabinet cup and trembleuse saucer, late 1800s

A tour party being guided through the Alter Markt in the heart of the old city

WHERE TO EAT AND DRINK

Zum Eulenspiegel
Hagenauerplatz 2
Tel: (0662) 843180; Fax: (0662) 8431 806
Full of quaint nooks and crannies, the Eulenspiegel (named after the medieval German folk-philosopher) is housed in a building that dates back to at least the beginning of the 15th century. Expect hearty traditional Austrian fare.

St Peter Stiftskeller
St Peter Bezirk 4
Tel: (0662) 848481
This is one of the oldest restaurants in Europe, perhaps over 1000 years old. The courtyard has stone archways and vine-trellised walls.

WHERE TO STAY

Bristol
Makartplatz 4
Tel: (0662) 873557; Fax: (0662) 873 5576
Built in 1890, this is a sumptuous hotel that has retained its 19th-century elegance. Great views over the river and the fortress.

Blaue Gans
Getreidegasse 43
Tel: (0662) 842 4910; Fax: (0662) 8424919
The 500-year-old "Blue Goose" has been run by the same family since 1918.

Schloss Fuschl
Hof bei Salzburg
Tel: (0662) 2922530; Fax: (0662) 292253531
Just outside the city, this 15th-century castle was built as a hunting lodge for the archbishop-princes of Salzburg.

IN THE AREA

Schloss Hellbrunn, built in 1613 by an eccentric archbishop, is just 5 km (3 miles) from Salzburg. The entertaining aquatic gardens are more of a focus than the palace. Here, water is the main element and comes from numerous springs in the nearby Hellbrunn Mountains.

There are mysterious grottoes, water-driven figures in the shape of animals or birds and concealed fountains. Don't be surprised if you are suddenly deluged by a shower of water while strolling through these bizarre grounds.

GENEVA

Geneva, in a spectacular lakeside setting at the foot of the Alps, is regarded as one of the world's foremost centres for antique watches and jewellery.

Musical automaton, c.1920

GENEVA COMBINES SWISS EFFICIENCY with French *savoir-faire*. Almost surrounded by France, it is little wonder that the city has such a French atmosphere. It has world-class museums of art and natural history, and the United Nations presence adds to Geneva's small population, making it a centre of European cultural life, with expensive shops and exclusive restaurants.

From the shores of Lake Geneva (known locally as Lac Léman), parks and esplanades give way to cobbled streets that wind up to the place du Bourg-de-Four, historic centre of the Vieille Ville. Here, behind quaint shopfronts, lie some of the world's most prestigious jewellers and watchmakers, while across the lake are auction houses whose dazzling sales are perhaps rivalled only by those of New York and London.

HISTORY REVISITED

A PLACE OF REFUGE

Since its formation in 1291, the Swiss Confederation has been a refuge for non-conformists. In the 16th century John Calvin established his Temple de l'Auditoire in Geneva, from where he taught the new religious doctrines, and the town has since provided a haven for many other thinkers and writers, including the French philosophers Voltaire and Jean-Jacques Rousseau and the Scottish religious reformer John Knox (see page 57). The Red Cross, founded here in 1863, has a museum that movingly records the organization's work.
● **Musée International de la Croix-Rouge et du Croissant-Rouge**, 17 avenue de la Paix. Tel: (022) 748 9511.

PLACES TO VISIT

In the **Musée de l'Horlogerie** are timepieces from every era – the chiming watches are particularly appealing. The **Musée Ariana** has a magnificent collection of ceramics, from early pottery to precious pieces of Nyon, Meissen and Sèvres porcelain.

- **Musée de l'Horlogerie**, 15 route deMalagnou. Tel: (022) 418 6470. Closed Tues.
- **Musée Ariana**, 10 avenue de la Paix. Tel: (022) 418 5450. Closed Tues.

SHOPPING

Geneva's picturesque old town, the Vieille Ville, has a great number of antiques shops, many in old town houses.

Look out for: **Ernst Schmitt & Co** (3 rue de l'Hôtel-de-Ville) has antique silver and 18th- and 19th-century English furniture, and **Au Vieux Canon** (40 Grand-rue) deals in English silver from the 19th and early 20th centuries. **Buchs** (34–36 Grand-rue) has restored picture frames. **Jadis** (21 Grand-rue) stocks a selection of antique jewellery and watches. **Ars Nova** (6 rue Jean-Calvin) is an excellent Art Deco emporium.

A 1922 Patek Philippe watch, auctioned in Geneva in 1999

FAIRS AND MARKETS

Every Wednesday and Saturday the **Grand Chapiteau Genevois de Brocante** is held in the Plaine de Plain-Palais. In the summer the arts and crafts market on the Place de la Fusterie is also worth a look.

AUCTION HOUSES

Antiquorum, 2 rue du Mont-Blanc. Tel: (022) 909 2850.
Christie's, 8 place de la Taconnerie. Tel: (022) 319 1766.
Sotheby's, 13 quai du Mont-Blanc. Tel: (022) 732 8585.

Bidding at the Antiquorum auction house, which handles jewellery, clocks and watches

Antiques shop in Geneva's old town

WHERE TO EAT AND DRINK

Le Lion d'Or
5 place Pierre-Gautier
Tel: (022) 736 4432; Fax: (022) 736 4422
Said to be one of the best restaurants in the city, it has stunning views and the interior decoration is in the style of Louis XV.

Les Armures
1 rue des Puits-St Pierre
Tel: (022) 310 9172
This 16th-century stone building, reputedly Geneva's oldest café, is a good place to enjoy fondue and rösti.

Au Pied de Cochon
4 place du Bourg-de-Four
Tel: (022) 310 4797
An old bistro which retains rustic beams and original zinc-top bar. It is crowded and lively.

WHERE TO STAY

Le Richemond
Jardin Brunswick
Tel: (022) 715 7000; Fax: (022) 715 7001
This thriving, lively, luxury hotel has been run by the same family since it opened in 1875.

Hôtel De La Cloche
6 rue de la Cloche
Tel: (022) 732 9481; Fax: (022) 738 1612
This small 19th-century hotel was once a luxurious apartment. Welcoming atmosphere.

Romantik Hotel Domaine de Chateauvieux
Peney-Dessus
Tel: (022) 753 1511; Fax: (022) 753 1924
Set amid the vineyards west of Geneva, this was once part of the 17th-century castle of Peney.

IN THE AREA

About 25km (15 miles) along the northern shore of Lake Geneva you'll find **Nyon**. The town can trace its history back to when Julius Caesar used the settlement as a military outpost, and has been a popular waterfront resort since the 19th century. In its ancient castle there are many examples of Nyon's delicate, almost translucent porcelain, made between 1781 and 1813. A little further on, in the small village of L'Auberson, is the **Musée Baud**, an eclectic collection of automata and music boxes, including rarities from the 18th century.

EASTERN EUROPE

THE ANTIQUES LANDSCAPE

Painted wooden coffer with bold, colourful decoration of floral and geometric motifs. Pieces such as this continue a long Eastern European tradition of furniture painting.

What we cavalierly group together as "Eastern Europe" is a huge, varied region, and understanding something of its history, its successive empires and shifting boundaries helps when looking at antiques. Bohemia, for example, ceased to exist in the 17th century, yet the term Bohemian glass has never died out, and you will find ornately enamelled, richly coloured examples originating from the Czech Republic, Slovakia and Germany. Medieval market towns as far east as Kiev and Novgorod were part of the Hanseatic League (see page 160), and an established trade route that ran east from what is now Belgium through Cologne and along the Main valley to Bamberg and Prague encouraged the exchange of crafts as well as commodities. Furniture made for aristocratic Russians and Habsburgs was extremely sophisticated, but provincial and folk art — love spoons, painted chests, small boxes, coffers and cupboards — is also highly desirable, although there are many modern reproductions.

For most of the 20th century travel behind the Iron Curtain was limited and difficult; thankfully this is no longer the case. Despite the relaxation in many border controls, however, rules regarding the export of antiques are strongly enforced. As the advice at the back of this book (see Useful Addresses) warns, regulations frequently change. A reputable dealer should be able to supply all the required paperwork — it is imperative to get full documentation, particularly if the item is of considerable age. Religious artifacts, icons in particular, can be extremely difficult to export. Past losses have had another effect, too. Many dealers scour far and wide for stock and an item you see in a shop in Prague or St Petersburg may actually have been sourced in Paris or Rome — and is unlikely to be a bargain. I knew someone who spotted some highly collectable costume jewellery in the window of an antiques shop in Prague. He was shocked to find that the Czech price was steeper than in London!

That said, there is much to look out for. The very mention of the name Fabergé conjures up images of jewelled eggs worth a fortune, and indeed the Fabergé creations in the Hermitage (see page 187) are priceless. But Fabergé was a big enterprise in St Petersburg and also had shops in Moscow (opened 1887) and Kiev (1905), which produced vast amounts of gold and silver "smalls". Much Russian silver is very collectable and it is still reasonably easy to find small examples such as teaspoons. Enamelled pieces are often beautiful, and a popular technique in the 19th century was tula work. (Elsewhere known as niello, this uses a black infill in incised silver, a type of decoration that began in ancient Egypt).

Much high quality porcelain was and is made throughout the area, from Herend and Zsolnay in Hungary (see page 178), to the 19th-century Neo-classical pieces of the Imperial factory of St Petersburg. After the Russian Revolution this became the State porcelain factory and then, in 1925, the Lomonosov porcelain factory. Today overtly Revolutionary wares are sought after, particularly those by members of the Suprematist art movement. The Gardner Factory, established by an Englishman in 1765 at Verbilki, near Moscow, is perhaps best known for the brightly coloured figures of tradespeople it made in the 19th century, although it also produced tea services.

The Royal Dux factory has produced exquisite porcelain figurines since it was founded in 1853.

PRAGUE

Prague is a magnificent medieval masterpiece and a city that is being rediscovered by increasing numbers of visitors attracted by its artistic heritage and fascinating shops.

Mid-19th-century gilded and enamelled Bohemian tankard

ONE OF EUROPE'S FINEST CITIES, Prague is a treasure trove of architectural delights because it is the only European capital that has been so completely untouched by war or disaster for over 600 years. Bisected by the River Vltava, which runs south to north through its centre, Prague's two halves are connected by numerous bridges; the oldest and most famous is Karlův most, the Charles Bridge. On the west, or left, bank, are the Hradčany, Prague's castle district and the Malá Strana, or little quarter. On the right bank is the Staré Město, the old town, dating from the 12th century; it incorporates the Josefov, Prague's old Jewish quarter and the Nové Město, the new town, some of which dates back to the 14th century.

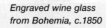

Long noted for its cultural heritage, Prague is especially famous for music and literature. Composers Antonin Dvořák, Bedrich Smetana and Leos Janáček are all celebrated in the annual Pražké jaro – Prague Spring – music festival during May and June, as are writers Franz Kafka, Jaroslav Haček and Rainer Maria Rilke.

The best areas for antiques are in the Staré Město, particularly around the Josefov where you will find Jewish artifacts and antiques, and in the Malá Strana. The flea market to the north, in Holesovice, is also worth a visit.

An ideal time to visit is from late November to March, when the city lives up to every expectation of the archetypal snow-bound central European city.

Engraved wine glass from Bohemia, c.1850

HISTORY REVISITED

A MEDIEVAL INHERITANCE

Prague is a city with an almost unspoilt medieval architectural heritage. The Hradčny district is dominated by the **Pražký Hrad**, Prague's castle. Founded in the 9th century, architectural additions have been made throughout the last 11 centuries. Highlights are the Main Hall of the Old Castle and St Vitus Cathedral, the largest church in the country. Work on the latter started in the late 1300s, but was not finished until 1929, resulting in a range of architectural and decorative styles.

Golden seal of Charles IV

Karlův most (The Charles Bridge), dating from 1357, links the two sides of the city, and is fortified at each end by picturesque medieval towers.

In Staré Město you'll find Prague's most spectacular square, **Staroměstské náměstí**. Star among the architectural treasures here is **Staroměstská radnice s orlojem**, the astronomical clock, which features the famous hourly mechanical performance of Christ and the Apostles. **Chrám Matky Božy před Týnem** (Church of Our Lady before Tyn), begun in the mid-1300s, is Prague's most impressive Gothic church. A source of considerable

Statue of King Wenceslas

national pride, it was commissioned during the reign of George of Poděbrady.

Josefov, the Old Jewish Quarter, dates back to the 13th century, alhough little is left of what was there prior to the "cleaning up" of the area around the turn of the 20th century, when a Parisian-style boulevard – Paňžká – was run through the middle of it. What does remain is the 13th-century **Staronová synagóga**, the oldest preserved synagogue in central Europe, still being used as a place of worship. Other surviving structures include the **Státni židovské muzeum** (State Jewish Museum), the **Židovniká radnice** (Jewish Town Hall) and the 15th-century **Stary židovský hřbitov** (Old Jewish Cemetery).

One of the largest glass collections in the world is in the nearby **Uměleckoprůmyslové muzeum** (Museum of Decorative Arts), which also has amazing collections of tapestries, furniture and clocks from all over Europe.

- **Pražký Hrad**. Tel: (02) 2437 3368.
- **Starom ěstská radnice s orlojem**, Staromestské nám. Tel: (02) 2448 2909.
- **Chrám Matky Božy př ed Týnem**, Celetná 5. Tel: (02) 232 2801.
- **Staronová synagóga**, Çervená 2. Tel: (02) 232 1954.
- **Státni židovské muzeum**, Tel: (02) 231 0681.
- **Uměleckoprůmyslové muzeum**, 17 listopadu 2. Tel: (02) 2421 8565.

BOHEMIAN GLASS AND PORCELAIN

Porcelain and glass are the two crafts most often associated with Bohemia (the old name for this region). High-quality decorative glassware has been made here since the 13th century. Especially notable is the cut, engraved glass in high Baroque style made from the mid-1600s (when a method of gem engraving was perfected) to about 1750. The originality of design and bold ornamentation made this glass the most sought after in Europe. Enamelling was also a popular method of decoration. *Zwischengoldglas* – a technique where a layer of engraved gold leaf was sealed between two layers of glass – was fashionable from 1730 to 1750. Another Bohemian method, from the 1800s, was "flashing", in which a clear glass object was dipped into coloured molten glass, the outer layer then engraved to reveal the clear glass. Alternatively, a ruby or yellow stain was brushed on, then scraped away. Two similar techniques (hyalith and lithyalin) were patented in the late 1800s, to produce a glass that imitated semi-precious stones.

The best-known porcelain is Royal Dux. Founded in 1860, the factory made figures, groups or figure-supported centrepieces decorated in matt colours with gold effects. Dux ware was very popular from 1880 to 1920; pieces from the 1930s to the 1950s are also desirable. Traditional designs are produced today.

Royal Dux figurine, 1930s

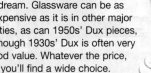

BUYER'S TIP

Although generally cheap by Western standards, Prague isn't necessarily a bargain-hunter's dream. Glassware can be as expensive as it is in other major cities, as can 1950s' Dux pieces, although 1930s' Dux is often very good value. Whatever the price, you'll find a wide choice.

SHOPPING

It is worth exploring different parts of the city for antiques shops in Prague as, unlike many cities, they are not concentrated in any one particular area. Expect to find plenty of Art Nouveau and Art Deco pieces, traditional costumes and relics from Prague's period as one of the fashion capitals of Europe in the 1920s and 1930s, as well as glassware and porcelain – albeit not always at the knock-down prices that might be expected (see page 173). All reputable dealers belong to a single assocation, The **Antiques Association for the Czech Republic** (see Useful Addresses at the end of the book).

Bric-a-brac stalls in the quaint Staroměstské naměsti, the heart of the Old Town

Look out for:
Alma (Valentinská 7) is a high-class shop with a good selection of porcelain and lace as well as costumes. **Antique** (Kaprova 12), a very expensive shop, has a fine collection of Art Deco watches. **Art Deco** (Michalská 21) is a reasonably priced shop that specializes in clothing and costume jewellery from Prague's period as eastern Europe's fashion centre. **Jan Hunek Starozitnosti**'s (Pařižká 1) wide range of expensive glassware dates from the 1700s to the 1930s.

Music Shop Antik-variát (Národní trida 25) is the place for music collectors, with vinyl from the 1920s onwards, including Eastern Bloc rarities.

Christian Dior 1950s collar necklace

Jan Pazdera obchod a opravna (Lucerna Passage, Vidockova 30) sells antique cameras and accessories.

More of a junk shop than an antiques store, **Judolf Spicák Vetesnictví** (Ostrivní 26) has an eclectic mix; there may be surprise finds here.

Jinohradsky bazárek (Mánesova 64) is full of reasonably priced high-class knick-knacks.

Marbled, or lithyalin, glass, c.1895

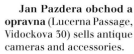

Vladimir Anderle Antique (Václavské náměstí 17) is a shop for the serious collector, with high-quality collections of glassware and men's and women's jewellery and watches, as well as art and Russian icons.

WHERE TO EAT AND DRINK
Obecni dům – Pleňská restaurace
Municipal House, Náměstí Republiky 5
Tel: (02) 2200 2780
A beautiful restored Art Nouveau restaurant serving good-quality traditional Czech food.

Parnas
Smetanovo nábř
Tel: (02) 2481 9268
International cuisine in a wonderful Art Deco interior, with a great view of the castle. Expensive.

U Medvídků
Na Perštýně 7
Tel: (02) 2421 1916
A traditional beer hall and pension with a history going back to 1466. Serves typical Czech fare.

WHERE TO STAY
The best-known hotel in Prague is the lovely Art Nouveau **Europa** on Wenceslas Square, but there are plenty of other options, including the following:

Radisson SAS Alcron Hotel
Stepanská 40
Tel: (02) 2282 0000; Fax: (02) 2282 0100
A luxurious but pricey renovated Art Deco palace in a quiet street off Wenceslas Square.

U tri pstrosu
Drazického náměstí 12
Tel: (02) 5753 2410; Fax: (02) 5733 3217
This restored 16th-century house is popular so it's worth booking well in advance. Many rooms still have their original Renaissance paintings.

IN THE AREA

The restored Renaissance chateau of **Zámek Častolovice** is 70km (45 miles) east of Prague. It was built between 1588 and 1664, and with 20 furnished rooms and a 40-ha (100-acre) park, it is a welcome break from the city's bustle. You can visit many historic towns in Bohemia on day trips from Prague, including the elegant 17th-century **České Budějovice** (home to Budvar beer) and the restored spa towns of **Mariánské Lázně** or **Karlovy Vary**, once frequented by the rich.
● **Zámek Častolovice**, Masarykova 1, Častolovice. Open Apr–Sept; appts at other times. Tel: (0444) 323646; Fax: (0444) 321034.

The antiques market has been longer established in Budapest than in many of its former eastern bloc neighbours, which makes it a joy for collectors.

As HOME TO A FIFTH of Hungary's population and the centre of its wealth, political power and cultural life, Budapest – the "Pearl of the Danube" – has, since the end of the Cold War, once again become one of Europe's most popular tourist destinations. It became a city in 1873, when the towns of Buda and Óbuda on the west bank of the Danube were merged with Pest on the east, becoming, with Vienna, one of the two capital cities of the Austro-Hungarian Empire and the second largest city in central Europe after Berlin. Until World War II Budapest had an ethnically mixed population – Germans, Greeks, Serbs and Jews made up half the population – and all have left their mark. With its rich cultural heritage, Art Nouveau cafés, numerous museums, art galleries and antiques dealers, Budapest has plenty to offer the discerning collector.

BUDAPEST

HISTORY REVISITED

HOT SPRINGS

Spring waters from the Buda Hills have been enjoyed since Roman times. Budapest's 100 *gyógyfürdő* (thermal baths) are modern but some 19th-century and early 20th-century baths are still used. Most imposing are those from the Ottoman era with 16th-century pools: **Rác Gyógyfürdő**, **Király Gyógyfürdő**, **Rudas Gyógyfürdő és Uszoda** and the Gellért Hotel (see panel, page 179). The tourist office (see Useful Addresses at end of book) has a leaflet.

● **Rác Gyógyfürdő**, Hadnagy u. 8–10. Tel: (01) 256 1010.
● **Király Gyógyfürdő**, Fő u. 82–84. Tel: (01) 201 4329.
● **Rudas Gyógyfürdő**, Razgonyi Piroska u. 2. Tel: (01) 388 9740.

Historic Király Baths

ANTIQUES IN CONTEXT

Full of relics from the Habsburg period and the legacy of its flourishing Art Nouveau scene in the early 20th century, Budapest is an antiques hunter's dream. Hungarian porcelain and ceramics are popular buys, especially wares from Herend and Zsolnay.

HEREND

Herend Porcelán was founded in 1839 and is based west of Budapest in Veszprém. It is a household name in Hungary, and its antique pieces are highly collectable. Most wares before 1840 are marked "Mayer in Herend". Classic Herend tableware sets, dating from 1850 onwards and typically for 12 people, can be found in many middle-class homes today and are used on special occasions. New sets are still a popular wedding gift. **Porcelanium**, the factory's visitor centre, was opened in 1999, and is well worth a visit if you want to watch porcelain manufacture at first hand. Its restaurant serves everything on Herend crockery. The museum of the factory's goods displays some prestigious pieces, especially those with a "Victoria" decoration, named after Queen Victoria, who commissioned the factory to supply her with porcelain.

Herend porcelain figurine

ZSOLNAY

Founded in 1862 in Pécs (200 km/120 miles from Budapest), **Zsolnay** still produces fine ceramic wares and has a museum you can visit. The style of early Zsolnay ware was inspired by Islamic art; however, from 1893, the company (encouraged by French designers) started producing wares in Art Nouveau style.

The best of these pieces, made until the 1920s, were very inventive, with low-relief moulded decoration growing out of the piece in sinuous forms and decorated with iridescent lustre on a green base. This decorative technique (called "eozin") was a huge hit at the 1900 World Exhibition in Paris. Larger items, such as 1-m (3-ft) high vases, are rarer and more sought after. Most Zsolnay pieces are marked so it's easy to identify them; the earliest mark was a ribbon and medallion featuring the five towers of Pécs, but there are many variations, some painted in underglaze and others impressed. Many public buildings throughout Hungary, especially those with Art Nouveau decoration, feature roof tiles and accessories in Zsolnay ceramics. In Budapest you will find them in such prominent places as the Museum of Applied Arts, the Grand Market Hall and Matthias Church.

Art Nouveau ceramic jardinière, Zsolnay, c.1905

● **Porcelanium**, Kossuth Lajos u. 140, Herend. Tel: (01) 88 261444.
● **Zsolnay Manufactúra Rt.**, Zsolnay Vilmos út 37, Pécs. Tel: (01) 72 325266.

PLACES TO VISIT

Buda, the more historic – and more visited – part of the city, is the first destination of most tourists. Here you'll find the **Királyi Palota**, the castle, **Szentháromság tér**, Holy Trinity Square and **Mátyás Templom**, the Neo-gothic Matthias Church, as well as the wildly fantastic **Halászbástya** (Fisherman's Bastion, pictured left), with its seven turrets commemorating the seven Magyar tribes who settled in the area. There is a fabulous view over the Danube towards the parliament building. Among the host of museums, the **Szépmuveszeti Múseum** (Museum of Fine Arts) on the monumental **Hősök tere** (Heroes' Square) is worth visiting for the Art Nouveau decoration alone.

● **Mátyás Templom**, Szentháromság tér 2. Tel: (01) 155 5657.
● **Szépmuveszeti Múseum**, Dósza György út 41. Tel: (01) 343 9759. Closed Mon, also usually Jan–March.

SHOPPING

Silver watering can marked
"Eli Meyer", c.1880

With numerous dealers all within walking distance of each other, the best streets for antiques hunting are Falk Miksa u. and Váci u., both in District V in Pest. In Buda, Frankel Leó út in District II is your best bet. It is well worth noting that many antiques shops are closed at weekends in the summer, with most taking a long break for the first three weeks of August.

Look out for:
Darius Régiségkereskedő Kft. (Falk Miksa u. 24–26) specializes in Biedermeier and Viennese Baroque furniture.

Moró Antik, (Falk Miksa u. 13) has a wide selection of militaria and artifacts from the East. At **Style Antique** (Király u. 25), you will find restored antique pine furniture.

Sziget Galéria (Váci u. 63) sells and buys 19th-century art, as well as books, graphic art, maps, etchings and engravings.

If textiles interest you then look out for Halas lace. Opened at the turn of the 20th century and still operating, **Czipkeház és Czipkemúseum** (the Halas Lace Factory and Museum at Kossuth u. 37/a) produced award-winning designs. Most sought-after pieces are those with Art Nouveau or Renaissance motifs.

Central Antique Shop (Múzeum krt. 13–14) has an excellent collection of books, engravings, postcards and other paper antiques. **BÁV** is a chain of antiques shops with outlets all over the city (one of the most central is Ferenciek ter. 12).

Ecseri piac, Budapest's flea market: especially good for bargains during the week

FAIRS AND MARKETS

A flea market – **Ecseri piac** (Nagikorösi út 156) – is open weekdays from 8am to 4pm and on Saturdays from 7am to 3pm. But be warned: although the Saturday market tends to have a wider range of goods, it is also about 20 per cent more expensive than during the week.

AUCTION HOUSES
● **Belvárosi Aukcióház**, Váci u. 36. Tel: (01) 266 8374.
● **Klapka Árverési Csarnok**, Vámház krt. 9. Tel: (01) 215 0212.
● **Nagházi Galéria és Auksiósház**, Balaton utca 8. Tel: (01) 312 5631.

WHERE TO EAT AND DRINK
Iréne Légrády Antique Restaurant
Bárczy István u. 3–5
Tel: (01) 266 4993
Exclusive antique furniture, Herend porcelain, intimate atmosphere, superb food. Closed Sun.

Gerbeaud
Vörösmarty tér 7
Tel: (01) 429 9000; Fax: (01) 429 9009
This coffee house, established in 1860, is renowned for its six-layer Dobos-torta.

Ruszwurm Cukrászda
Szentháromság u. 7
Tel: (01) 375 5284
A legendary establishment, dating from the 1820s, this café still has its original cherrywood furniture with mahogany marquetry.

WHERE TO STAY
Danubius Hotel Gellért
Szent Gellért tér 1
Tel: (01) 385 2200; Fax: (01) 466 6631
This charming, elegant, internationally renowned Art Nouveau hotel first opened in 1918. Hungary's oldest spa hotel, it has myriad treatments on offer.

Radisson SAS Béke Hotel
Teréz körút 43
Tel: (01) 301 1600; Fax: (01) 301 1615
Magnificent late 19th-century hotel with a café decorated in Zsolnay ceramics.

IN THE AREA

An hour from Budapest, where the Danube rushes through a narrow, twisting valley, is the picturesque riverside town of **Szentendre**. A haunt of artists since the 1920s, the town has a wealth of museums, art galleries and antique shops. Recommended are the Village Museum (with reconstructions of traditional villages) and the Margit Kovács Museum (showing the work of Hungary's greatest ceramicist). Two other towns further along the river are **Visegrád** (once a Roman encampment, it also has an impressive citadel) and **Estergom** (a former capital, it's the centre of Hungarian Catholicism and home of the country's largest basilica).

WARSAW

As Poland's capital since 1569, Warsaw has been destroyed and rebuilt three times. Aptly, the city's motto is *Contemnit Procellas*, "It defies the storms".

Satirical political poster from the communist era

WITH A HISTORY STRETCHING BACK a mere seven centuries, Warsaw may not be as ancient as other Polish cities, but since it became the seat of government in 1569 it has been the focal point of Polish culture. The city was almost completely destroyed in 1944 but many of the historic streets, buildings and churches in Stare Miasto, the old town, have been painstakingly recreated since the 1970s. The old town square – Rynek Starego Miasta – is home to the Warsaw Historical Museum as well as Zamek Królewski, the Renaissance royal castle, which was originally built by Sigismund III in the late 16th century. In recognition of the success of this restoration, Warsaw was added to the prestigious UNESCO World Heritage List in 1981.

HISTORY REVISITED

ROYAL WARSAW

Trakt Królewski (Royal Way) runs from the old town south to Palac Wilanów, taking in three former royal residences. **Zamek Królewski**, restored in the 1970s, houses the Castle Museum. **Łazienki Królewskie**, dating from the late 18th century, was torched in 1944 and restored in the 1960s; its park is one of the most beautiful places in the city. At the far end of the Royal Way lies the grandest of the palaces, **Palac Wilanów**, known as the "Polish Versailles".

● **Zamek Królewski**, Plac Zamkowy 4. Tel: (022) 657 2170. Tues–Sun.
● **Łazienki Królewskie**, ul. Agrykola 1. Tel: (022) 621 6241. Tues–Sat.
● **Palac Wilanów**, Potockiego 1. Closed Tues.

SHOPPING

The **Rynek Starego Miasta** is surrounded by merchants' houses, originally built between the 15th and 18th centuries, and lovingly reconstructed since 1945. You'll find a number of shops and stalls selling interesting artifacts. Flea markets can be found all over the city, and the latest details can be found in local English-language papers, such as *The Warsaw Voice*, *Welcome to Warsaw* and *Warsaw: What, Where, When.*

Look out for:
Both **Cepelia** (Pl. Konstytucji 5) and **Rynek Starego** (Miasta 10) specialize in folk arts and crafts. Among the traditional wares are wooden kitchen utensils, tapestries, textiles and silver and amber jewellery.

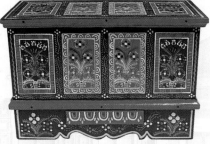
Wooden chest painted in traditional Polish style

Desa, at Rynek Starego Miasta 4–6 and Koszykowa 60–62, stock a fine selection of antiques; they are part of a chain of shops that used to be state run, but now operate under private ownership.

AUCTION HOUSES

Dom Aukcyjny, ul. Krakowskie Przedmiescie 4/6. Tel: (022) 826 4408.
Aukcyjny Salon Meblowy, ul. Senatorska 11. Tel: (022) 826 6009.
Aukcyjny Salon Sztuki Wspolczesnej, ul. Dobra 31. Tel: (022) 828 9560.

Restored houses in Rynek Starego Miasta that make up the historical museum

WHERE TO EAT AND DRINK
The Belvedere
Agrykola 1
Tel: (022) 827 0020
This superb restaurant is located in the 18th-century Orangery in Lazienki Park – particularly lovely at night. There are classic French dishes on the menu, but this is somewhere to try Polish specialities such as wild boar.

Fukier House
Rynek Starego Miasta 27
Tel: (022) 831 1013
One of the finest restaurants in Warsaw, Fukier House is situated on the ground floor of a 15th-century mansion with a Neo-classical façade and a cloistered courtyard.

WHERE TO STAY
Hotel Europejskiul
Krakowskie Przedmiescie 13
Tel: (022) 826 5051; Fax: (022) 826 1111
This hotel, dating from the late 19th century, had to be rebuilt after 1945. It has a fine Neo-classical exterior, a grand marble staircase and is home to one of Warsaw's best patisseries.

Le Royal Meridien Bristol
ul. Krakowskie Przedmiescie 42–44
Tel: (022) 625 2525; Fax: (022) 625 2577
This was one of the few hotels to escape destruction during World War II, and the 19th-century Secession-style façade is original.

IN THE AREA

Żelazowa Wola, 55km (35 miles) west of Warsaw, is the manor house in which the composer and pianist Fryderyck Chopin was born in 1810. Maintained in period style throughout, the building is now a museum devoted to Chopin, and a summer venue for piano recitals by top international pianists.

A couple of hours' drive south-east of Warsaw is **Lublin**. A wealthy trading centre in the Middle Ages, Lublin's old town is still being restored, but the ornamented merchants' houses around the main square give an idea of the town's medieval splendour.

182

KRAKOW

Krakow is a uniquely preserved medieval city. Once the capital of Poland, it is now rated one of the twelve great historic cities of the world.

The bugler who calls each hour at the Kościół Mariacki

FOR ANYONE WITH A PASSION for art, architecture or history, Krakow is a must. Miraculously, the city's medieval centre, with its fine towers, façades and churches, survived World War II.

Krakow was named after the legendary prince and dragon-slayer Krak, reputedly buried in one of the ancient mounds on the city's outskirts. The city walls were pulled down in the early 19th century, to be replaced by a ring of parkland – the Planty – which now encloses the old town. It is 1000 years since the installation of Krakow's bishopric, whose most famous modern incumbent, Karol Wojtyła, became Pope John Paul II in 1978. Krakow is the seat of Poland's oldest university and was the country's capital until 1596. In 2000 Krakow was named one of the European Cities of Culture.

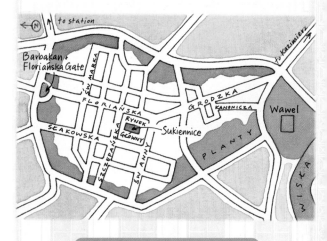

HISTORY REVISITED

CITY OF KINGS

For some 700 years from 1037, Poland was ruled from the castle on Wawel Hill. This ancient residence of Polish kings, with Romanesque elements and Gothic parts, acquired its present shape in the 16th century under two kings of the Jagiellonian dynasty: Alexander (1501–1506) and Sigismund I the Old (1506–48). It was built by master stone-mason Eberhard Rosemberger and decorated by three Florentine artists. The result was one of Europe's most spectacular monuments of Renaissance architecture. Only a part of the interior of Wawel Castle has survived and it now houses a collection of 138 tapestries (the castle's greatest treasure), which once belonged to Sigismund Augustus (1548–72).Visit the Royal Chambers and Treasury and Armoury and the Lost Wawel exhibition, as well as the Dragon's Cave.

● **Wawel Castle**. Tel:(012) 4225155. Free adm to exhibition on Sun.

PLACES TO VISIT

Krakow's university, established in 1364, is one of the oldest in Europe. Copernicus may have studied here and, in the oldest building, the **Collegium Maïus**, there is a display of astronomical instruments which includes a copper globe from 1510 – the first to show the Americas as they were known at the time.

Krakow has many Baroque churches including the **Kościół Mariacki** (Church of Our Lady) with its two towers of different heights. From the higher tower a bugle call rings out each hour, and breaks off on an abrupt note in commemoration of an unknown bugler, killed as he was calling the alarm to warn the city of an imminent Tartar attack in 1241. The main showpiece is a magnificent wooden altarpiece with more than 200 carved figures depicting medieval life.

- **Collegium Maïus**,
  ul. Jagiellonska 15.
  Tel: (012) 422 0549.

Exquisite amber necklace and ring

- **Kościół Mariacki**,
  Rynek Główny.
  Tel: (012) 422 0521.

SHOPPING

Beneath the Gothic arches of what used to be the old cloth hall – **Sukiennice** – in Rynek Główny are more than 50 stalls offering a wide variety of regional specialities. Look out for tooled leatherwork, such as slippers, bags and belts, embroidered felt or rabbit-skin slippers, and amber jewellery.

Look out for:
Those interested in military memorabilia should try **Arsenal** (ul. Floriańska 20), which specializes in Polish army uniforms, and **Gabinet Krakowski Numizmatyczny** (Rynek Główny 7), which stocks medals.

University Collegium Maïus, founded 1364

Art Deco (pl. Dominikanska 4) has a good selection of Art Deco furniture. **Antyki Bizuteria** (Rynek Główny 43) specializes in old jewellery, including Baltic amber, clocks and mantelpieces. **Desa** (ul. Mikołajska 10) stocks clocks, furniture and chandeliers. For old books, maps and prints head to **Silva Rerum** (ul. Stolarska 8) or to **Antykwariat** (ul. Sw. Toasza), an antiquarian book shop dating from 1869.

Shopping under the arches of the Sukiennice

IN THE AREA

The **Kosciuszko Mound**, a 300-m (1,000-ft) high hill, is located just west of Krakow. It is a memorial of Tadeusz Kosciuszko (1746–1817), the Polish revolutionary who fought against the British in the American War of Independence and against the Russians when they invaded Poland in 1792. From pagan times, mound-building was a tradition in Poland. According to legend, this mound (built in the 1820s) used earth from the sites of Kosciuszko's most famous battles. There is a wonderful view of the city from its summit, and a small museum.

WHERE TO EAT AND DRINK

Villa Decius
ul. 28 Lipca 17A
Tel: (012) 425 3390; Fax: (012) 425 3521
One of Kraków's finest restaurants, this villa was built for Justus Decius, who was historian and secretary to King Sigismund the Old in the 16th century.

Wierzynek
Rynek Główny 15
Tel: (012) 422 9896; Fax: (012) 422 1296
First established in 1334, this is supposedly where monarchs dined during their council in the 14th century. Great atmosphere, and very popular, so you will definitely need to book.

WHERE TO STAY

Pod Róza
ul. Florianska 14
Tel: (012) 4221244
Built in the 14th century, this is one of the city's oldest hotels: Tsar Alexander I once stayed here. It has been beautifully renovated and is right in the middle of town.

MOSCOW

Moscow is awakening to a new life. Everywhere there are new shops, restaurants and clubs, and the streets and squares are bustling with colour and trade.

Domes of St Basil's Cathedral in Red Square

MOSCOW TODAY IS IN THE THROES OF A RENAISSANCE. Many of its historic buildings are swathed in scaffolding as Russia tries to recapture its pre-Revolutionary past. The present, however, is very much in the forefront. Stark Socialist buildings display advertisements on electronic billboards, while close to Red Square an indoor shopping mall is being built. Shops and street sellers rival any modern city shopping centre. The Moscow Arts Theatre and the Bolshoi have been joined by smaller, innovative theatre companies. Now Orthodoxy is returning to Moscow as churches are refurbished. Many are open to the public, so anyone with an interest in architecture can tour one of the many monastery complexes or Baroque churches.

Typically gilded icon

RUSSIA'S SYMBOL OF POWER

Kremlin simply means 'fortress', but Moscow's **Kremlin** has been the symbol of Russia's mystery and power for almost five centuries, and through many dramatic changes has maintained its fascination. Behind walls 20m (65ft) high and 6m (20ft) thick, this is the oldest part of the city, much as it was after Moscow arose as the centre of a vast empire in the 15th century. It is truly a city within a city – several palaces form the Great Kremlin complex, and there are also three cathedrals, the Armoury and several museums within the walls.

● **The Kremlin**. Tel: (095) 202 3776 for info. Access varies.

SHOPPING

The main shopping districts are concentrated in the city centre, along Tverskaya ulitsa, the Arbat and Novy Arbat. At one end is the River Moskva, which you can cross to Kutuzovsky Prospekt; at the other is Arbat Square, which has been spruced up for tourists.

GUM, the State Department Store built at the end of the 1800s, has undergone extensive conversion since communist times. Three long passages with three storeys of shops run the length of the building. It's the nearest thing Moscow has to a shopping mall.

Gone are the days of frugality and plenty of shops now sell Russian – and Western – goods. In the old Kitai Gorod area, arts and crafts centres have opened in two former churches along Varvarka ulitsa. This is the place to look for work by talented local jewellers and ceramicists.

Look out for:
The Art Salon of the Arts Industry Institute (Povarskaya ul. 31) has an excellent selection of textiles, pottery and leather goods by its students and the teachers.

The Central Art Salon (Ukrainsky Bulvar 6) sells work by members of the Russian Union of Artists: nesting dolls, lacquered wood, ceramics, jewellery and Dagestani rugs.

Gardner's figurine of a glazier, c.1820

Gzhel (Petrovka ul. 22) sells blue-and-white Gzhel ceramic ware; visit **Sofrino** (Nikolskaya ul. 11) for religious memorabilia.

MARKETS

If you enjoy haggling, go to the flea market in Izmailovsky Park, a must for Soviet uniforms and handicrafts. Open weekends, but get there early as many booths are closed by midday.

Krestovaya Palaja anteroom in the beautiful Terem Palace (1635–37), within the Kremlin

Art on the Arbat: popular with tourists

WHERE TO EAT AND DRINK

Dining in Moscow can be a formal affair and it is always wise to book. Although casual dress is acceptable at most places, jacket and tie for men are expected at the restaurants of smart hotels.

Glazur
Smolensky bulvar 12
Tel: (095) 248 4438
This stylish 19th-century mansion in the Kropotkinskya district has a good choice of top-quality Russian delicacies.

TsDL
Povarskaya ulitsa 50
Tel: (095) 291 1515
The Soviet Writers' Union once met here. Its chandeliers and wood panelling recall the more elegant past of this 19th-century house. Good choice of specialities.

Dining room of the Hotel Metropol

WHERE TO STAY

Hotel Metropol
Teatralny Proyezd 1–4
Tel: (095) 927 6000; Fax: (095) 927 6010
Years of renovation have rescued one of the smartest hotels of pre-Revolutionary Moscow. Experience dining in the Art Nouveau elegance of its towering glass-roofed main restaurant.

Hotel National
Mokhovaya ulitsa 15/1
Tel: (095) 258 7000; Fax: (095) 258 7100
Art Nouveau at its most luxurious in this modern hotel that includes a rooftop swimming pool. A tendril-entwined staircase and stained-glass panels recall the early 1900s when it first opened.

IN THE AREA

About 25 km (15 miles) from Moscow, by the River Moskva, there is a striking group of buildings that blend into the landscape – the **Arkhangelskoye Estate Museum**. The French-designed main complex was built at the end of the 1700s for a Russian prince but it was sold to the director of the Hermitage Museum in St Petersburg in 1810. Restoration work has gone on for 80 years. Check whether it is open; if not, its French Park is full of great walks.

ST PETERSBURG

This fairytale city was built as the new capital of the Russian Empire, an elegant window on Europe. It is a treasury of the finest European decorative arts.

Miniature of the
Imperial regalia,
by Fabergé

LESS THAN 300 YEARS AGO Peter the Great planned St Petersburg as a rival to European cities. With over 100 islands and 60 rivers and canals, it is often compared to Venice. Its sparkling palaces and elegant riverside estates have seen wars and revolutions, culminating in the overthrow of the Romanovs and the city's demise as the nation's capital. Under its new name, Leningrad, the city withstood a 900-day siege in World War II and today, its original name restored, St Petersburg is again "the northern Venice". With over 100 museums, including the world-famous Hermitage and the Winter Palace, it is an impressive city of distinct seasons, from the cold light of a Russian winter to the enchantment of the White Nights in early summer. Visitors can marvel at the city that inspired the genius of musicians Tchaikovsky and Rakhmaninov and the writer Dostoyevsky.

HISTORY REVISITED

CATHERINE THE GREAT

This outstanding woman usurped the throne of her unpopular husband, Peter III, in a palace coup in 1762. Her expansionist foreign policy led to Russia's first naval victory and the annexation of the Crimea. She founded over 25 major academic institutions in Russia and recognized the importance of the great French Enlightenment philosophers Voltaire and Denis Diderot. Her passion for Neo-classical architecture inspired the Marble Palace and the Tauride Palace for two of her lovers: Grigory Orlov, who aided her coup, and the powerful army officer and statesman, Grigory Potemkin.

PLACES TO VISIT

No one can go to St Petersburg without visiting the **Hermitage**. One of the world's most famous museums, its vast collections occupy a number of buildings, including the **Winter Palace**, a stunning example of mid-18th-century Russian Baroque architecture. In the course of a decade in the late 1700s, Catherine the Great acquired over 2,500 paintings, 10,000 carved gems, 10,000 drawings and large amounts of porcelain and silver. There are also sections with Russian furniture, applied art, portraits and sumptuous clothing of the imperial family.

The beautifully proportioned **St Isaac's Cathedral**, with its enormous dome, is officially categorized as a museum. Its interior is lavishly decorated with precious stones and minerals, a stunning setting for the impressive 19th-century works of art it holds.

Vasilievsky Ostrov, the largest island in the Neva Delta and one of the city's oldest sections, is the heart of Peter the Great's original city. A popular residential area, it is now home to several academic institutions and the Stock Exchange.

● **The Hermitage/Winter Palace**, Dvortsovaya Naberezhnaya. Tel: (812) 311 3465. Closed Mon.

● **St Isaac's Cathedral**, Isaakievskaya Ploschod 1. Tel: (812) 315 9732. Closed Wed.

SHOPPING

St Petersburg has yet to catch up with the rest of Europe in developing a true antiques centre and, at the moment, the main attractions are arts and crafts. However, kiosks, tables on the street and impromptu markets are starting to take off, and are fun to rummage through – keep an eye out for antiques of the future such as art and good-quality local crafts.

Fabergé menthol holder, c.1900

Look out for:
Stroll along **Nevsky Prospekt** and halfway along the Gostinny Dvor centre, but beware of beggars. The **Guild of Masters** (Nevsky Prospekt 82) sells jewellery, ceramics and Russian native art made by members of the Russian Union of Artists.

The **Khudozhestvenny Salon** (Nevsky Prospekt 8) stocks ceramics, boxes, jewellery, paintings, dolls and a good selection of handicrafts. **Nasledie** (Nevsky Prospekt 116) carries different types of hand-painted lacquered wood, samovars, nesting dolls, amber and hand-painted trays.

The **Diaghilev Art Centre** (Nevsky Prospekt 20) sells the work of the best artists of St Petersburg, while **Palitra** (Nevsky Prospekt 166) specializes in the work of young Russian artists.

IN THE AREA

On a hill 25 km (15 miles) from St Petersburg is the royal summer residence of **Tsarskoje Selo**, an exquisite monument of Russian art and culture. In its 600ha (1,500 acres) of parkland, sprinkled with pavilions set around a central lake, is the Baroque-style, 18th-century Catherine Palace. Its precious art collection includes over 20,000 objects – bronzes, paintings, furniture, sculpture and porcelain from Russia and western Europe. Nearby is the Neo-classical palace and park of **Pavlovsk**.

The Cameron Rooms at Tsarskoje Selo

SCANDINAVIA

THE ANTIQUES
LANDSCAPE

Royal Copenhagen Christmas plate, 1929. The design, which has particularly good colour and definition, shows a church built to commemorate World War I.

The countries that make up Scandinavia were not among the empire-builders of the past two to three hundred years, so it often comes as quite a surprise – a pleasant one – to antiques collectors that such an amazing variety of "foreign" antiques have found their way here from the other side of the world. Scandinavian cobalt, however, was in great demand in the Far East and, in return, from the 18th century onwards, blue and white Chinese porcelain and other goods flooded into warehouses of such places as Copenhagen and Gothenburg. The extent of the influence of Chinese wares on Scandinavian life can be seen in the painted interiors of the houses in the Glomdalsmuseet in Elverum, Norway.

Another surprise is the fact that entire groups of antiques are relatively undervalued in their homeland. Even such big names in Swedish glass as Nils Landberg, Orrefors, Sven Palmqvist and Kosta can be found comparatively inexpensively. In Uppsala, just north of Stockholm, I picked up a very good late-1940s dusky grey vase designed by Per Lütken for Holmegaard of Denmark, and for a very low price. His is a distinctive style and later, mass-produced pieces are becoming very collectable (see page 202). Lighting is another highly underrated area, with designs by the Dane Poul Henningsen for Louis Poulsen, and terrific lampshades by Le Klint among the items you might find. Scandinavians are very good at embracing modern design, and pieces from the 1950s and 1960s are easily found.

Internationally renowned names such as the Danish silversmith Georg Jensen and the Finnish designer Alvar Aalto command high prices, of course, but keep an eye open for lesser known names, Anton Rosen or Johan Rohde, for instance. The Christmas plates produced by Royal Copenhagen each year (see page 202) are very collectable, especially for the years when production was scarce, such as during the wars, and the factory strike years of 1993 and 1995. Often unrecognized, but well worth seeking out are the wares of the small porcelain factory of Marieberg, near Stockholm, in operation from 1766 to 1787. Another Swedish name to look out for is Wilhelm Kåge whose designs include the Argenta range made while he was director of Gustavsberg porcelain works.

Provincial fairs and markets often reveal beautifully executed regional wares, some old, some not so old, based on early traditions. Touring round the little villages in the Telemark area of Norway I have found very pretty examples of painted folk art and country furniture. In Sweden, rural pieces, even 19th-century ones, still betray the enduring influence of Gustavian style (see page 196).

I have only concentrated in this section on Copenhagen, Stockholm and Oslo, but Scandinavia as a whole is still a relatively untapped market and, although distances may seem vast, travel from one area to another is easy. Bergen in Sweden has several antiques shops, as does Arhus in Denmark. Finland, Helsinki in particular, is gradually unearthing antiques dating from its time under Swedish and Russian rule that have, until now, been largely ignored.

The clean-cut lines of Mona Morales-Schildt's mirror-cut bowl, designed for Kosta in 1959, are typically Scandinavian.

OSLO

Artistic figures such as Edvard Munch and Gustav Vigeland have added to Oslo's rich history of trade and craft that began with the Vikings.

Vigeland's Wheel of Life *(1938) in Frognerparken*

OSLO HAS BEEN CAPITAL OF AN INDEPENDENT NORWAY for less than a century, but the original town was founded in 1048 by Harald Hardråde (half-brother of St Olav, Norway's patron saint), and the site had been a trading post since the 8th century AD.

In 1348 the Black Death claimed over half Oslo's population, and a debilitated Norway was reduced to a province of Denmark. Oslo was destroyed by fire in 1624, and the new city, rebuilt in the protective shadow of the Akershus fortress, was named Christiania after Renaissance King Christian IV. Norway was seceded to Sweden in 1814 but gained independence in 1905, with King Håkon VII, grandfather of the present monarch, as its monarch.

From the Royal Palace, Slottet, the pedestrianized Karl Johans Gate, named after the Swedish king who ruled Norway in the 19th century, runs downhill through the centre of the old town, where museums and an abundance of galleries (plus a magnificent new opera house under construction) mean there is plenty to see. The antiques trade in Oslo reflects the city's patchwork history, so alongside Royal Copenhagen porcelain, Swedish textiles and rustic furniture you will find Chinese porcelain, for which Scandinavia was an important market in the 18th century. The country has a high artistic tradition, with Munch, Grieg, Ibsen and Vigeland, whose free open-air sculpture park is a highlight of Oslo's popular Frognerparken.

HISTORY REVISITED

A replica of the Oseberg *in the Vikingskipshuset*

WARRIORS WITH WANDERLUST

In the turbulent 8th and 9th centuries AD the Vikings ruled the seas around Europe. From their Scandinavian homelands raiding parties harried the islands of Britain and Ireland, and high-prowed Viking ships voyaged up into the icy wastes of Iceland and Greenland, from where they reached out to the coast of America. But where they plundered they also settled and traded, and the Viking influence stretched from the Arctic Circle to the Mediterranean. In 1014 King Knut (Canute) ruled an area that encompassed the whole of modern Norway, Denmark, England and southern Sweden.

For these men of the sea, ships were a way of life and of death, and three magnificent longships used as Viking warrior tombs have been excavated in the Oslo area. Their finely carved oak hulls, together with the grave goods they contained, are on display at the **Vikingskipshuset**.

The Vikings' seamanship and their propensity for violence gave them a formidable reputation, but they were also farmers, craftsmen and traders, achievements which have been largely overlooked. In the **Historisk Museum** are displays of Viking jewellery, coins, artifacts and fascinating documentation on the customs and exploits of these remarkable people.

● **Vikingskipshuset**, Bygdøy. Tel: 22 43 83 79.
● **Historisk Museum**, Frederiks Gate 2. Tel: 22 85 99 12.
Free admission, but only open 3–4 hours a day. Closed Mon.

A traditional rural house in the Folkemuseum

PLACES TO VISIT

The Bygdøy peninsula is home to several notable museums, including the open-air **Norske Folkemuseum**, with its collection of over 150 old houses from around the country.

The **Akershus Fortress**, which celebrated its 700th anniversary in 1999, provides a vivid history lesson from medieval times to World War II and is surrounded by parkland.

Kunstindustrimuseet i Oslo, founded in 1876, is one of the earliest museums of decorative arts in Europe. The emphasis is on 18th-century silver, glass, enamels and furniture, but contemporary Scandinavian design and crafts are also well represented.

The painter Edvard Munch bequeathed his entire collection of his own works to the city, and the **Munch Museum** now houses over 5,000 paintings, prints and drawings. Oslo's **Nasjonalgalleriet** also has a large collection of Munch, including *The Scream*.

Playwright Henrik Ibsen's last residence, where he lived from 1895 until his death in 1906, has been restored to create the **Ibsen Museum** and is now open to the public.

A short drive from the city is the manor house of **Bogstad Gård**. Built 1760–80, it is rich in furniture, silver and works of art.

- **Norske Folkemuseum**, Museumveien 10. Tel: 22 12 37 00.
- **Akershus Fortress**. Tel: 23 09 39 17.
- **Kunstindustrimuseet i Oslo**, St Olavsgate 1. Tel: 22 03 65 40. Closed Mon.
- **Munch Museum**, Tøyengata 53. Tel: 23 24 14 00. Closed Mon.
- **Nasjonalgalleriet**, Universitetsgata 13. Tel: 22 20 04 04. Closed Tue.
- **Ibsen Museum**, Arbiensgate 1. Tel: 22 55 20 09. Access by guided tour only.
- **Bogstad Gård**, Sørkedalen 826.Tel: 22 06 52 00. Open May–Oct only: Sun pm and guided lunchtime tours Mon–Fri.

The 700-year-old Akershus Fortress

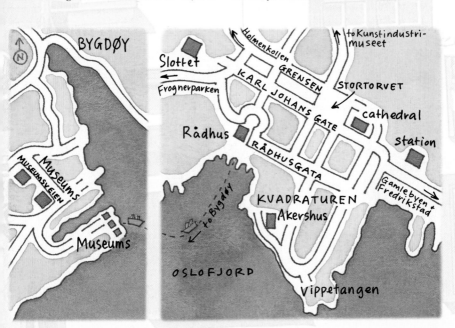

WHERE TO STAY

Holmenkollen Park Hotel Rica
Kongeveien 26
Tel: 22 92 20 00; Fax: 22 14 61 92
An elegant, luxurious hostelry since 1900, the Holmenkollen has been owned by the Brochmann family for four generations. Each room is individual in style and the Theatre Café attracts theatregoers from the Nationaltheatret opposite.

Gabelshus Hotel
Gabelsgate 16
Tel: 23 27 65 00; Fax: 23 27 65 60
This quaint gabled hotel in the Frogner district first opened its doors in 1912. Today, it offers modern comforts combined with historical furnishings, and has a fine restaurant.

Grand Hotel
Karl Johans Gate 31
Tel: 23 21 20 00; Fax: 23 21 21 00
Situated on Oslo's main thoroughfare since 1874, this imposing hotel has been the traditional location for many Nobel Prize celebrations and addresses by visiting heads of state.

Holmenkollen Park Hotel Rica

WHERE TO EAT AND DRINK

Engebret Café
Bankplassen 1
Tel: 22 82 25 25
Oslo's oldest restaurant building dates back to the 18th century, and is a charming place to enjoy a delightful smorgasbord.

Restaurant Magma
Bygdøy Allé 53
Tel: 22 55 99 00
Sonja Lee and Laurent Sur-Nille offer *cuisine rustique* in an art-filled setting. Opened in 2000.

SHOPPING

Oslo's antiques shops are mainly in the West End around Industrigate, the upmarket quarter of stately mansions, fashionable boutiques and restaurants.

Look out for:

The family-run **Kaare Berntsen** (Universitetsgate 12) is considered Oslo's premier antiques dealer. The 70-year-old shop is more like a private museum, with room upon room of Norwegian art, including works by Ludvig Karsten, Per Krohg, Frits Thaulow and Edvard Munch, as well as an impressive selection of 17th- and 18th-century furniture, clocks and unusual carved wooden items.

Traditional rustic pottery

Olav Skrindo, at Industrigate 60, specializes in rural furniture from the 18th and 19th centuries (which each region would paint and decorate in its own style), while **Bjørn Seim** at No 63 stocks a wide range of porcelain and glass.

For 19th-century French glass, from chandeliers to wine goblets, try **Galleri Ingelbrecht** (Ole Vigs Gate 12). Look out, too, for Chien Lung porcelain. Made for the European market in the 18th century, it was mainly bought by Danes and Swedes who at that time were wealthier than the Norwegians.

Japanese porcelain ewer (c.1700), of a type popular in 18th-century Scandinavia

At **Antik'n** (Hegdehaugsveien 36) Per and Brittmarie Nilsen have interesting pieces, ranging from furniture to Royal Copenhagen porcelain, Ming vases and charming tableware.

For antique items in copper, brass and pewter, try **Gamle Stua** (Frognerveien 4) or **Gard Antikviteter** (Schøningsgate 7).

FAIRS AND MARKETS

The **Njårdhallen** art and antiques fair is held during the first week of November at Sørkedalsveien 106 (Tel: 90 09 64 50).

Vestkanttorvet, a bric-a-brac market, is held at Amaldus Nielsens Plass in the Frogner district every Saturday.

AUCTION HOUSES

Blomqvist Kunsthandel, Tordenskidds Gate 5. Tel: 22 70 87 70.
Grev Wedels Plass, Gamle Logen, Grev Wedels Plass 2. Tel: 22 86 21 86.

IN THE AREA

Baerum Verk ironworks is about a 20-minute drive north of central Oslo. The foundry here opened in 1610, and the village of Baerum that developed around it is charming. The wooden cottages that once housed the foundry workers are now occupied by more than 60 shops and craft workshops, alongside a museum. The shops are open daily, but the workshops and galleries close on Mondays.

For dedicated antiques hunters, the **Johan Albert Mohn** auction house (Domkirkegate 7–9. Tel: 55 31 13 73) and **Bergen**'s excellent antiques dealers are just an hour's flight away.

Whether it's ceramics or glass, furniture or fine art, there's plenty to catch the eye of the antiques shopper in Sweden's "city by the water".

Traditional gabling in Gamla Stan, Stockholm's old town

BUILT ON 14 ISLANDS, STOCKHOLM is a wonderful melange of the fabulously cosmopolitan and the elegant charm of bygone times. With some 70 museums and over 700 restaurants, Stockholm has it all: exclusive shops, lively nightlife and a host of cultural attractions. The water that surrounds and divides Stockholm is revered by the city's inhabitants. In fact, it is so clean that you can actually swim and fish right outside the parliament buildings.

Most visitors are drawn first to Stadsholmen, the triangular island on which the Old Town, Gamla Stan, is situated. With its cobbled streets and narrow winding passageways, Gamla Stan is a beautifully preserved medieval enclave in the heart of the city. It's a wonderfully picturesque place, where the medieval nestles comfortably alongside the modern. Its well-trodden streets are lined with old-style coffee houses, second-hand bookshops, artisans' studios, cellar restaurants and a host of antiques shops guaranteed to inspire the ardent collector.

Deciding which museums and galleries to visit while in Stockholm can be difficult, and you will find yourself spoilt for choice. Most of the them can be found in Gamla Stan and include the Royal Palace and the Museum of Medieval Stockholm. The National Museum and the Museum of Mediterranean Antiquities are in Norrmalm, Stockholm's modern town centre. From here, a walk through the Kunsträgården will take you over a bridge and on to the island of Skeppsholmen. This island is a haven for culture vultures, and home to both the Museum of Modern Art and the Museum of Architecture.

STOCKHOLM

ANTIQUES IN CONTEXT

The avid antiques hunter will find Stockholm a veritable treasure trove. An overwhelming element of Swedish style is the influence of King Gustav III, whose legacy has placed Stockholm firmly on the antiques hunter's map.

Typically Gustavian interior: clean lines with Rococo-influenced gilding combined with comfort

GUSTAV, A ROYAL PATRON

Of the personalities who have shaped Stockholm's history, few can match the extravagance and flair for grandeur of the 18th-century monarch, Gustav III. His reign (1771–92) is seen as a golden age for Swedish culture, a time now known as the Gustavian Enlightenment.

A philosopher, actor and accomplished writer, King Gustav III was a man whose love of the arts and theatre became the driving force behind the establishment of a national Swedish culture. A great admirer of the French, the king was strongly influenced by their sense of style. The elaborate, sweeping lines characteristic of French Rococo were tempered to suit Swedish tastes, evolving into a simpler, cleaner form that became known as Gustavian style.

A pair of chairs in the unmistakable Gustavian style

Royal patronage fostered the cultivation of a uniquely Swedish style which can be observed in Stockholm's many royal residences. **Drottningholm Slott** was the king's home from 1771, as it still is for the present royal family. With its magnificent Baroque and Rococo gardens and Chinese Pavilion, the building was modelled on the Palace of Versailles. Its 17th-, 18th- and 19th-century interiors are magnificent and the perfectly preserved theatre, built in 1766, is the world's oldest. Don't miss Queen Hedvig Eleonora's lavish state bedroom.

Within the verdant oasis of Ekoparken (the world's first national city park) lie Royal Haga and the royal palaces of **Ulriksdal**, Haga and **Gustav III's Pavilion** – perhaps the finest example of late Gustavian style. If you stroll through Haga you can also see the copper tents, built in 1790 for the king's bodyguard, now housing the park museum.

Gustavian style made way for *europeiska empirstilen*, and an example of this is the **Rosendal Slott**, set in the royal park of Djurgården. This palace, built by Karl IV Johan from 1823 to 1827, has lavish interiors, furniture, textiles and artifacts that are very characteristic of this Empire style.

● **Drottningholm Slott**. Tel: (08) 402 6280. Open Sat/Sun 12–3.30pm.

● **Ulriksdal Slott/Gustav III's Pavilion**. Tel: (08) 402 6130. Opening hours subject to change.

● **Rosendal Slott**, Rosendalsvagen. Tel: (08) 402 6130. Closed Mon.

PLACES TO VISIT

Waldermarsudde was the palatial home of "painter prince" Prince Eugen, art collector and patron. **Strindbergmuseet**, dramatist August Strindberg's last home, has been reconstructed as it was when he died in 1912.

The world's oldest open-air museum, **Skansen**, opened in 1891. Over 150 buildings depict life before industrialization, and artisans demonstrate 19th-century skills.

● **Waldermarsudde**, Prins Eugens Våg 6.
Tel: (08) 781 1755. Closed Mon.

● **Strindbergmuseet**, Drottninggatan 85.
Tel: (08) 411 5354. Closed Mon.

● **Skansen**, Djurgårdsslatten 49.
Tel: (08) 442 8000.

SWEDISH GLASS

The Swedish art of glassmaking can be traced back to 1556, when King Gustav Vasa brought Venetian glassblowers to his court.

The most famous glassworks, those at Kosta and Orrefors, are located in the southern province of Småland, where the vast forests provided wood to power the furnaces. **Kosta** was founded in 1742 by two generals, Anders Koskull and Georg Bogislaus Stael von Holstein, who

A traditional Swedish house in Skansen

Kosta ornamental glass, 1960s

used the first two syllables of their surnames to name their glassworks. Over the years Kosta (now Kosta Boda) pioneered the production of lead crystal glass of the very finest quality.

Orrefors originally produced windowpanes and bottles. In 1913 the works were taken over by Johan Ekman, who brought in two artists whose designs transformed Orrefors beyond all recognition. This marriage of the aesthetic and glassblowing skills, honed and perfected over centuries, placed Sweden in the vanguard of 20th-century glass design.

HISTORY REVISITED

Stortorget, the main square in Gamla Stan

GAMLA STAN

This, the original site of the city, was founded some 750 years ago at the point where Lake Mälaren flows into the Baltic Sea. To protect the mainland from pirates and attack, the regent Birger Jarl built a fortress here from which to

control the waterways. The town that grew up around it became an important trading centre and eventually became the seat of the king, establishing Stockholm as Sweden's capital.

Gamla Stan is home to everything from a cannonball still embedded in a building in the main square to the remnants of its 16th-century city wall and elegant 17th-century town houses. Its crowning glory – the magnificent palace, **Kungliga Slott**, designed by Nicodemus Tessin the Younger in Italian Renaissance style – was completed in 1754.

No longer home to the Swedish royal family, much of the palace is open to the public. It has five museums, many notable works of art, original furnishings from the 1660s onwards, as well as its world-famous Swedish and Gobelins tapestries.

● **Kungliga Slott**.
Tel: (08) 402 6130. Closed Mon.

SHOPPING

Many of the 14 islands that make up Stockholm are divided into areas called *malms* (ore hills), each with its own unique charm. Each *malm* has a cluster of antique emporiums – a mecca for browsers and collectors. When it comes to shopping for antiques in Stockholm, those in the know make a beeline for Odengatan, whose parade of antiques shops is the perfect place to start.

NORRMALM

Afrodite Antik (Odengatan 92) has shelves of exclusive glassware and crystal by collectable names such as Orrefors and Kosta. Look out, too, for the delicate animal porcelain figures from Rörstrand. **Old Arthur**, next door, also offers a wonderful range of glassware and furniture from the Jugend (Sweden's Art Nouveau) period.

With barely room to swing the proverbial cat, **Vasakällaren Antik** (Odengatan 88) is a basement crammed with curios and 19th-century Swedish *Allmoge* – painted country furniture.

The city's largest collection of *Allmoge* furniture is at **Norrmalms Uppköpsaffär** (Roslagsgatan 19), one of Stockholm's oldest antique shops (dating from 1907).

Mästerby Antik (Roslagsgatan 9) has a vast collection of 18th- and 19th-century chandeliers and ceramics from Meissen, Rörstrand, Gustavsberg and Rosenthal.

Go to **Apollo Antik & Konsthandel** at Tegnérgatan 5 to find Sweden's largest and most exclusive collection of antique glassware from Kosta, Orrefors and Reijmyre, and porcelain from Gustavsberg, Rörstrand and Rosenthal. This exquisite shop also specializes in art and jewellery.

A collection of elegant Swedish glass

Två Sekler (Odengatan 94) has an excellent selection of furniture, lamps and other choice pieces from the 18th and 19th centuries. **Vita Valvet**. at No 90 specializes in 18th- and 19th-century chandeliers, ceramics, glass and porcelain. And for clothes, jewellery and curios go to **Epok** at No 83.

Art Deco Antik (Upplandsgatan 36) always has an interesting selection of Art Deco pieces, from Sweden and elsewhere.

Jugend vases, c.1900, from the Rörstrand pottery

ÖSTERMALM

The street to head for on Östermalm is Karlavågen. **Karla Antik & Inredning** at No 71 has classical pieces of furniture, chandeliers and decorative art, as well as originals and quality reproduction pieces from the Empire, Rococo and Gustavian periods.

For furniture dating from 1780 to the 1930s, as well as porcelain, chandeliers and paintings, visit **Antik & Möbelförmedlingen på Östermalm** at No 81. **Östermalms Fyndmarknad**, at No 89, has been a family business for 30 years and deals in glass, ceramics and furniture.

While in Östermalm, take a stroll along Arsenalsgatan, Kommandörsgatan and Sibyllegatan for a number of exclusive shops offering a diverse range of antiques.

GAMLA STAN

Stockholm's Old Town is rich in antiques shops as well as historic sights.

Look out for:

Antikaffären PHM (Storkyrkobrinken 10) has a broad range of glassware, china, ceramics and silverware.

Arångsunds-Boden Antik (Trångsund 10) has fine crystal by Kosta and Orrefors. Look out for signed work by Vicke Lindstrand, Gunnar Cyrén and Bertil Wallien. Also pay a visit to **Kreuter Antikhandel** (Köpmangatan 18) for Russian icons, chandeliers, furniture and military items from the 17th century onwards.

Hopareboden (Österlånggatan 31) has a varied collection of teddies, dolls and doll's house furniture, and **Fartygsmagasinet i Stockholm**, along the same street at No 19, specializes in antiques of a nautical flavour.

Art Deco Gustavberg vase

SHOPPER'S TIP

If you are in Stockholm in January, try to get along to the antiques fair at Stockholmsmässan, held every year. This **Antikmässan** (Tel: (08) 749 4100) is the largest in Scandinavia, with over 150 exhibitors, and an estimated 10,000 visitors. At other times of the year the Grand Hotel hosts a very prestigious fair each month. (Tel: (08) 660 8170 for details.)

WHEN IN STOCKHOLM...

... visit the "haunted palace" of **Spökslott**. It is said to have been haunted from 1840, when part of the garden caved in, revealing a coffin. Today the building is owned by Stockholm University and houses its collection of 360 paintings from the 16th to the 19th centuries, as well as the Hellner collection with 700 pieces of Orrefors glass.

● **Spökslott**, Drottninggatan 110. Tel: (08) 16 47 07 to arrange appointment.

Façade of an antiques shop in Gamla Stan

Löfgrens Antik (Storkyrkobrinken 3) is a dealer where you can expect to find Asian antiquities among the exclusive ceramics, and **Möbel-Hanson** at Storkyrkobrinken 6 has glassware, brass, copper and crystal.

In Kåkbrinken, **Medusa** at No 10 and **Fenix** at No 5 are also worth checking out, but are closed on Mondays (and Fenix opening times are sporadic).

SÖDERMALM

Katarina Kuriosa (Åsogatan 95) has a good selection of antiques and curios covering a variety of periods. **Din Antik**, at Hornsgatan 30, specializes in Baroque and Rococo chandeliers and **Albert & Herbert Antikbod** (29C) describes its stock as "a little bit of everything from 1800 to 1950".

Maria Antik (Torkel Knutssongatan 31) is more of a flea market than an antique shop.

AUCTION HOUSES

Stockholms Auktionsverk, Jacobsgatan 10, Gallerian. Tel: (08) 453 6700.

Lilla Bukowskis, Strandvägen 7A. Tel: (08) 614 0800.

WHERE TO EAT AND DRINK

Bistro Wasahof
Dalagatan 46
Tel: (08) 323440
A favourite haunt of Stockholm's literary elite, this late-19th-century bistro is the perfect place for dinner after a day's shopping on Odengatan. The seafood platters are excellent and impromptu operatic performances are not unheard of.

Operakällaren
Karl XII Torg
Tel: (08) 676 5800
Gustav III was once a regular at this 1900s' restaurant, set in Stockholm's magnificent opera house. Fine dining in a restaurant where old-world style and Swedish culinary tradition live on.

Ulriksdals Wärdshus
Solna
Tel: (08) 850815
No visit to the royal palace at Ulriksdal would be complete without stopping for a spot of lunch at this 17th-century inn – one of Sweden's oldest. The Smörgåsbord buffet is a must and the wine cellar has a marvellous selection of vintage wines.

Stallmästaregården
Nortull
Tel: (08) 610 1300; Fax: (08) 610 1340
Dating back to the 1660s, this restaurant offers a traditional Swedish gourmet experience in the beautiful surroundings of Haga Park.

WHERE TO STAY

Grand Hotel
S. Blasieholmshamnen 8
Tel: (08) 679 3500; Fax: (08) 611 8686
Built during the golden age of "great hotels" at the end of the 19th century, the Grand is a work of art in itself. Its 21 suites are furnished with a charming blend of modern and antique furniture. The Veranda restaurant overlooks Kungliga Slott, the parliament buildings and the opera house.

Clas på Hörnet
Surbrunnsgatan 20
Tel: (08) 612 5130; Fax: (08) 712 5315
Close to Odengatan, this classic Stockholm inn dating from 1731 is now a hotel with a restaurant that's well worth a visit. The interior is Gustavian in style and the 10 guest rooms are individually decorated with antiques from the period.

Victory Hotel
Lilla Nygatan 5
Tel: (08) 506 4000; Fax: (08) 506 4010
A hotel with a distinctly nautical flavour, in the heart of the Old Town. Among its memorabilia is an original letter from Admiral Nelson to his mistress, Lady Hamilton. Try the Swedish delicacies served up at Leijontornet, the restaurant next door.

IN THE AREA

Gripsholms Slott was once the home of medieval monarch Gustav Vasa. A fortress in the Renaissance-style, the castle is located near Mariefred on the shores of Lake Mälaren. Under the royal patronage of Gustav III the castle was made home to the National Portrait Gallery and now holds some 4,000 paintings.

Birka, on the island of Björkö, 30 km (20 miles) west of Stockholm, is the site of Sweden's first Viking town, founded towards the end of the 8th century on a sheltered shipping route. The museum (**Birkamuseet**) has an exhibition of the artifacts uncovered by archeological excavations of the town's burial grounds.

COPENHAGEN

Literally meaning "Merchants' Harbour", Copenhagen has been a centre of trade for centuries. The streets that run parallel to the long shopping street – the Strait – are lined with all manner of antiques shops.

A soldier on guard outside Christiansborg

THE DANISH CAPITAL IS A BUSTLING SEAPORT on the Øresund Strait, just across from Sweden, at the mouth of the Baltic Sea. It was a major commercial city even before the Bishop of Roskilde founded København in 1167.

Old Copenhagen is roughly defined as the area within the city's original, medieval ramparts. It is here that 16th- and 17th-century Nordic-style, half-timbered houses stand next to grander buildings of Dutch and Rococo design. Graceful and unimposing, many of these fine buildings are a legacy of the Danish Golden Age: a renaissance of art, philosophy and architecture from 1800 to 1850.

The city centre is a warren of winding streets, canals and public squares. Strøget, a pedestrian shopping mall, is the main thoroughfare. At one end is Rådhuspladsen, the town hall's large square, and the Tivoli Gardens. The square of Kongens Nytorv, with the Kongelige Teater and the Nyhavn restaurant district, is at the other. Across the harbour tourists can visit the picturesque maritime district of Christianshavn and the hippie-style Free City of Christiania.

For an aerial view of Copenhagen, climb the 17th-century Rundetårn in the old city. Traffic is restricted in much of the centre, so walking or cycling are the best ways to get about.

THE GOLDEN AGE

The first half of the 19th century was a period of great cultural activity within Denmark and is generally referred to as the country's Golden Age. Arts and sciences rose to new heights during this time, and Hans Christian Andersen, August Bournonville, Hans Christian Ørsted, C.W. Eckersberg, Søren Kierkegaard and Bertel Thorvaldsen are just some of the many artists and philosophers who lived and worked in Copenhagen during those years.

Preoccupied with ideas of the Danish people and with national origins, the city's artists and intellectuals persuaded King Frederick VII to introduce Denmark's first constitution in 1848. This, and those that followed it, are now re-garded as the foundation stones of modern Denmark.

Much of the architecture of the age still stands. The most notable architect of the period, C.F. Hansen, designed the 1730s chapel of **Christiansborg Slotskirke**. Beside it stands the colourful **Thorvaldsens Museum**, designed in 1848 by N.G. Bindesbøll. It is dedicated to Denmark's greatest sculptor, Bertel Thorvaldsen (1770–1844), who worked in Rome and made a celebrated return to the city in 1838.

Day by Danish sculptor Bertel Thorvaldsen

Recent years have witnessed a revival of the music from this period – both at home and abroad. Symphonies, opera, choral music and recitals from this era can be heard during Copenhagen's autumn/winter theatre season and may include gems such as Niels W. Gade's *The Elfin Shot* or J.P.E. Hartmann's *Little Kirsten*. The **Kongelige Teater** presents ballets by the Golden Age master, August Bournonville.

Danish Golden Age art has also acquired a new world status in the wake of several international exhibitions. For the best collections, visit the **Statens Museum for Kunst** and nearby **Hirschprungske Samling**. On exhibition are paintings by C.W. Eckersberg, Christen Købke and the major landscape artists, J.T. Lundbye and Louis Gurlitt.

The lively and attractive harbour of 18th-century Nyhavn

Certainly the most famous figure to emerge from the Danish Golden Age was author and storyteller Hans Christian Andersen (1805–75). Born to a poor shoemaker in the provincial town of Odense, Andersen found fame and fortune in Copenhagen. His literary works such as *The Little Mermaid* and *The Ugly Duckling* are still admired beyond their entertainment value as fairytales. A number of his original manuscripts can be seen on request at the **Kongelige Bibliotek**, Copenhagen's royal library.

Every two years there is a festival celebrating this era of Denmark's history. With a range of arts – exhibitions, concerts, ballet and drama – its aim is to revive the triumphs of the period and to relate them to the Denmark of today. The next **Golden Days in Copenhagen** festival will be in 2002.

- **Christiansborg Slotskirke**, Prins Jørgens Gård 1. Tel: (045) 3392 6300. Open Sun only, 12–4pm.
- **Thorvaldsens Museum**, Porthusgade 2. Tel: (045) 3332 1532. Closed Mon.
- **Kongelige Teater**, Kongens Nytorv. Tel: (045) 3369 6969. Closed Mon.
- **Statens Museum for Kunst**, Sølvgade 48–50. Tel: (045) 3374 8494. Closed Mon.
- **Hirschsprungske Samling**, Stockholmsgade 20. Tel: (045) 3542 0336. Closed Tues.
- **Kongelige Bibliotek**, Søren Kierkegaards plads 1. Tel: (045) 3347 4747. By appointment only.
- **Golden Days in Copenhagen**. Tel: (045) 3542 1432; Fax: (045) 3542 1491; www.goldendays.dk

The Little Mermaid

ANTIQUES IN CONTEXT

Copenhagen has produced a number of extremely talented designers and craftsmen. Areas of particular interest are 18th-century porcelain, 19th-century silver and 20th-century glass.

Bing and Grøndahl vase, c.1908

PORCELAIN

Initially founded by an apothecary in 1775, **Royal Copenhagen** was called the Den Kongelige Porcelains Fabrik until 1868. Its most famous product was the 1,602-piece *Flora Danica* table service commissioned by Catherine the Great of Russia in 1790. Each piece is decorated with botanical illustrations of Danish wild plants. The service is on display in Rosenborg Slot.

In 1908, the company began to produce an annual Christmas plate with a different design each year. Early 20th-century examples and any made during World War II are particularly sought after. Look out, too, for Royal Copenhagen porcelain figures made in the 1950s by the Georg Jensen silversmith, Henning Koppel.

SILVER

Georg Jensen founded his jewellery and silver firm in 1905. With the painter Johan Rohde, Jensen developed a style that combined elegance with excellent craftsmanship. His jewellery and some early silver are Art Nouveau in style, while later flatware, coffee and tea pots and other domestic ware are recognized by their clean outlines and sense of balance. Styles span Art Nouveau, classical Art Deco, Organic ("Free Form"), Modernism and Post-modernism. Although Jensen's designs have been

Copenhagen porcelain, 19th-century teacup and saucer

widely copied you can be sure your piece is genuine because, except for some early pieces, the silver marks are well documented.

The Georg Jensen flagship store at Amagertorv 4 sells antique silverwork and modern designs and the museum has a full range of exhibits from 1904 to 1940.

GLASS

Holmegaard was not well known outside Scandinavia until interest in Nordic design began in the 1950s. Founded in 1825, this glass factory is now Denmark's leading maker of modern tableware and hand-blown ornamental glass. From classic pieces to futuristic glass sculpture, Holmegaard is highly collectable and not overly expensive. Look for vases by Per Lütken (1940s to 1950s), especially elegant dusky blue and grey ones, which are rarer than those in dark green glass.

Take a day trip to the **Holmegaard Glasværk** at Næstved, two hours south of Copenhagen, to see glass being made by both hand-blowing and modern mechanized processes. There is also a very interesting glass museum and a shop that sells seconds.

● **Royal Copenhagen Porcelain Factory**, Smallegade 47. Tel: (045) 3814 9297.

● **Georg Jensen Museum**, Amagertorv 6. Tel: (045) 3314 0229.

● **Holmegaard Glasværk**, Glasværksvej 54. Tel: (045) 5554 5000.

Part of the Blossom range designed by Georg Jensen

The Baroque Great Hall of Rosenborg Slot

PLACES TO VISIT

Rosenborg Slot, the Royal Treasury, was built by King Christian IV in 1617 as his summer palace. Around two dozen of the palace's sumptuous rooms are open to visitors, and the paintings, fine furniture and art treasures accumulated by the royal family from the 16th to 19th centuries that are exhibited here are arranged in chronological order, which gives you a fascinating insight into changing styles and tastes in Danish art. The Rosenborg is also where the Danish crown jewels are on display to the public.

In the **Kunstindustri-museet** you can see applied arts, crafts and industrial design from the past 300 years ranging from ceramics, furniture and glass to silver and textiles.

Henning Koppel pillbox, 1950s

The **Arbejdermuseet** is devoted to the social history of the city's working classes and shows how they have lived from the late 19th century to the present day. Among various exhibitions are reconstructions of typical homes from the 1870s, the 1930s and the 1950s.

● **Rosenborg Slot**, Øster Voldgade 4A. Tel: (045) 3315 3286.
● **Kunstindustrimuseet**, Bredgade 68. Tel: (045) 3314 9452.
● **Arbejdermuseet**, Rømersgade 22. Tel: (045) 3393 2575.

ROYAL CONNECTIONS

Yellow buses and red commuter trains offer scenic and historic day trips up the Øresund coast. The first major stop is at Klampenborg, where you can walk, cycle or ride through vast tracts of forest and meadows – more than 2,000 free-roaming fallow deer live here. Near the entrance is **Bakken**. At 400 years old, it is the world's oldest amusement park.

A little further north lies Humlebæk, home to one of Europe's outstanding museums of modern art, the **Louisiana Museum for Moderne Kunst**. At the end of this coastal rail line is the bustling ferry port of Helsingør, known in English as Elsinore. Here stands **Kronborg Slot**, the legendary home of Hamlet. Although Shakespeare was not historically accurate, Kronborg's spires and mighty walls are an apt setting for the drama.

North Sealand, inland from the coast, offers gentle countryside and towns such as Hillerød. The castle in the centre is **Frederiksborg Slot**, a well-restored Renaissance palace that houses Denmark's **Nationalhistoriske Museum**. Less than half an hour by train west of Copenhagen is the ancient royal seat, Roskilde. In the **Domkirke** lie the remains of 38 Danish monarchs, and the crypts are open to the public. At the harbour sits the superb **Vikingeskibsmuseet**. On display are five Viking vessels raised from the bed of Roskilde fjord; another eight have recently been unearthed.

● **Bakken**, Dyrehavevej 62, Klampenborg. Tel: (045) 3963 7300. Closed late Aug–late March.
● **Louisiana Museum for Moderne Kunst**, Gammel Strandvej 13. Tel: (045) 4919 0719.
● **Kronborg Slot**, Kronborg 2c, Helsingør. Tel: (045) 4921 3078.
● **Frederiksborg Slot/Det Nationalhistoriske Museum**, Hillerød. Tel: (045) 4826 0439.
● **Roskilde Domkirke**, Domkirkestrade 10. Tel: (045) 4635 1624.
● **Vikingeskibsmuseet**, Strandengen, Roskilde. Tel: (045) 4630 0200.

TRY NOT TO MISS...

Amalienborg Slot is a four-winged square of Rococo mansions in old Copenhagen. The private living quarters of Queen Margrethe II and her family are here, but parts of the palace complex are open to the public. The **Amalienborg Palace Museum** shows ancestral private chambers and artifacts from the Danish monarchy. In **Christian VIII's Palace** you can see reconstructions of royal chambers spanning three generations, from 1863 to 1947.

Frederiksborg Slot

SHOPPING

Every high street in Copenhagen has its antiques shops and art galleries, and every Saturday there are flea markets. Begin browsing in the old city centre for the unique or classic antique.

STRØGET
Along here are the Royal Scandinavia group of stores: **Illum** (Østergade 52), a department store with a worthwhile antiques and collectables market on its third floor, and **Royal Copenhagen Antiques** (Amagertorv 6) with three of Denmark's most sought-after "brands": Royal Copenhagen porcelain, Georg Jensen silver and Holmegaard glass (see page 202). Midway along this bustling road, the street opens onto a vista of Christiansborg Slot, the seat of parliament, and the spire of the 17th-century stock exchange.

A strong Art Deco design for the Royal Copenhagen Christmas plate, 1929

THE STRAIT
For a day of browsing, concentrate on the cobbled side streets immediately south of Strøget towards the canal. Stroll down what the locals call the Strait, a long street that changes its name from Farvegade to Kompagnistræde and then Læderstræde.

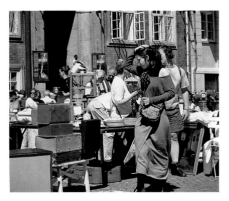

The ever-busy Gammel Strand flea market, which sets up every Friday and Saturday in summer

Pinnau (Kompagnistræde 27) specializes in antique toys, pictures and prints and has a wide choice. **Antique & Kunst** (Kompagnistræde 11) has a good selection of Royal Copenhagen's *Flora Danica*, as well as blue fluted porcelain.

From here on, the Strait is a series of antiques emporia side by side with trendy shops and cafés. **Inuit**, at Kompagnistræde 21, is something a little different, and separate sections of the shop are devoted to Russian icons, ethnographica and antiques from Greenland (which until 1979 was a province of Denmark). **Sølvkælderen**, at the corner of

the short street, Naboløs, is the largest antiques dealer in the city, and the place to go if you are looking for antique silver and plate.

BREDGADE
Resume browsing on the far side of Kongens Nytorv on the two parallel avenues of Bredgade and Store Kongensgade. Only very determined hunters get this far, but it is well worth the effort. Bredgade starts with Nyhavn, an 18th-century quay of restored wooden ships. Here antiques sellers are shoulder-to-shoulder with cafés, bars and excellent restaurants. If you can't find what you want here, try the side streets, which offer curio shops, maritime antiques and vintage books. For antique crystal and chandeliers, visit **Morgens & Angelo** (Bredgade 4). A little further along, at Bredgade 32, **Dansk Møbelkunst** stocks some of the finest examples of Danish furniture and classic Danish design. **Antique Moderne** (Bredgade 36A) specializes in 20th-century antiques as well as period furnishings.

Royal Copenhagen vase, c.1900

OTHER HUNTING GROUNDS
From any spot in the old centre of the city, a five-minute bus ride will take you to the "other" Copenhagen. Here you will discover the bustling communities that lie beyond the lakes and former city ramparts. These are called the "bridge" districts because you reach them by bridge. Antiques hunters should chart a course for the streets that are adjacent to Frederiskberg Allé, along the Ravnsborggade in the Nørrebro district, and Ryesgade in Østerbro – a collector's paradise.

SHOPPER'S TIP

Three former architects have dominated the Danish furniture industry since the late 1940s: Hans J. Wegner, Arne Jacobsen and Finn Juhl. All created elegant, stylized pieces, stressing comfort and functionality. The key designer of Danish modern lighting is Poul Henningsen, best known for his PH-5 lamp and his organic Artichoke of 1958. Several lines are still in production or reproduced as limited editions.

IN COPENHAGEN...

The internationally famous **Tivoli Gardens** were opened in 1889 on the rural edge of town as a novel way of entertaining the public. They are home to a host of cultural activities from ballets, pantomimes and the circus to fairground rides, shooting galleries and restaurants – there is even an open-air stage. A large market is held here at Christmas and there is ice skating on the lake. In spring the gardens are planted with 45,000 tulips.

Silverware at Sølvkaelderen, Copenhagen's largest antiques dealer

MARKETS AND FAIRS

On Fridays and Saturdays, May to September, walk down Naboløs towards the canal to find the **Gammel Strand flea market**, a big outdoor antiques market directly across the river from the Thorvaldsens Museum. On Saturdays, **Israels Plads**, just west of Nørreport Station, is a popular spot for seeking out hidden treasures.

The flea market in **Kongen Nytorv** is held on Saturdays between May and October, and is a good place to look for Danish design.

In November, some 130 antiques dealers, and a few dozen coin and stamp collectors, converge on the **Forum**, an exhibition hall on Rosenørns Allé.

AUCTION HOUSES

Bruun Rasmussen Auction House, Bredgade 33. Tel: (045) 3313 6911.
Christie's, Tværgade 10. Tel: (045) 3332 7075.
Ellekilde Auction House, Bredgade 25. Tel: (045) 3391 1121.
Kunsthallen Auction House, Gothersgade 9. Tel: (045) 3332 5200.

WHERE TO EAT AND DRINK

Krogs Fiskerestaurant
Gammel Strand 38
Tel: (045) 3315 8915; Fax: (045) 3315 8319
Established in 1910, this traditional canal-front restaurant faces the Thorvaldsens Museum and the Christiansborg Palace. Indulge in fine seafood but expect equally fine prices.

The elegant dining room of the Krogs Fiskerestaurant

Peder Oxe
Gråbrødretorv 11
Tel: (045) 3311 0077; Fax: (045) 3313 9086
A lively bistro that serves moderately priced pasta, meat and seafood dishes. It is housed in a superb 17th-century building and on its walls are 15th-century Portuguese tiles.

Café Sorgenfri
Brolæggerstræde 8
Tel: (045) 3311 5880
Genuine Danish cuisine with all the trimmings. Open sandwiches or entire platters, hot meat- or fish-and-potato dishes. This 150-year-old basement restaurant is next to the Strait with its many small antiques shops.

WHERE TO STAY

Hotel d'Angleterre
Kongens Nytorv 34
Tel: (045) 3337 0100; Fax: (045) 3312 1118
First opened in 1750, this is one of the oldest hotels in Copenhagen. The elegantly preserved building is steeped in history and stands facing the Royal Theatre and Nyhavn Quay. This five-star establishment is in the heart of the city's most exclusive shopping area, close to numerous art galleries and antiques shops.

Copenhagen Admiral
Toldbodgade 24–28
Tel: (045) 3374 1414; Fax: (045) 3374 1416
Converted from a 200-year-old granary at the harbour's edge, the Admiral has exposed beams and a maritime atmosphere. It is conveniently close to Nyhavn, with its many restaurants, and royal Amalienborg Slot.

Top Hebron
Helgolandsgade 4
Tel: (045) 3331 6906; Fax: (045) 3331 9067
Built in 1900, this is a quiet, modest hotel located near the central railway station, the Tivoli Gardens and Rådhuspladsen. All the rooms have recently been refurbished in contemporary and elegant Danish style.

IN THE AREA

Across the sea from Copenhagen lies Malmö, in Sweden, a lively seaport and market city and an ideal place for finding antiques. Malmö can be reached in 30 minutes by train via the new Øresund Bridge-Tunnel, or in 45 minutes by high-speed ferry. One of the recommended sights is the Malmöhus, a former royal castle dating from the 1500s, now home to the **Malmö Museer**. Another is the St Gertrud quarter, where many of the houses date back to the 16th and 17th centuries.

One of the oldest buildings is **St Petri Church**, founded in the early 14th century and full of beautiful, well-preserved treasures.

PORTUGAL
& SPAIN

THE ANTIQUES LANDSCAPE

All over the Iberian peninsula you find strong reminders, from architecture to textiles, of the long period of Moorish rule that ended 500 years ago (see page 223). But in subsequent centuries it was exploits abroad which brought prosperity to these lands. Spanish galleons and Portuguese carracks traded from the Far East to South America and the wealth they created was shared by the aristocracy and the merchant classes. Christopher Columbus's aim to find a western passage may not have succeeded, but the continent he claimed for Spain proved an undreamed of source of wealth. Indianos, Spaniards who prospered in colonies from Florida to Chile, returned to build retirement mansions, monuments to their wealth.

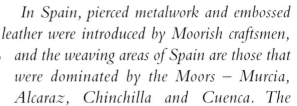

A Hand of Fatima doorknob is still a common sight on many doors in Andalucia.

In Spain, pierced metalwork and embossed leather were introduced by Moorish craftsmen, and the weaving areas of Spain are those that were dominated by the Moors – Murcia, Alcaraz, Chinchilla and Cuenca. The alpujarra, a rustic Andalucian bedspread with a linen warp and woollen weft, originates from the Sierra Nevada, the same mountains that provided the caliphs of Granada with snow to chill their sherbets.

It is probably in ceramics that you can best see the breadth and richness of the area's history, from the lustreware introduced by the Moors (see page 228) and 18th-century faience influenced by styles from France (especially Moustiers) to modern art pieces. Alcora (established 1727), just north of Valencia, made faience called loza fina; it soon became the foremost ceramic producer in Spain, and Valencia is still noted for its ceramics and furniture. In the 19th century many ceramics factories revived earlier designs, but quality can be variable, so it is worth studying original museum pieces to appreciate what to look out for. Spanish bric-a-brac markets — rastros — are prominently advertised. Some can be very large — I remember one in a small village inland from the Costa Blanca that stretched for a mile beside a river bank, with everything on offer from religious statuary and enormous sideboards to the junk from someone's cellar. Holiday areas are often written off for antiques hunting, but many dealer friends have come across great finds in the Costa del Sol and the Costa Blanca — usually pieces that are too large or too grand to accommodate when people move house.

In Portugal the Moorish influence can be seen in the continued appeal of azulejos, decorated painted tiles. "Carpet" tiles, which might entirely line a room, are reminiscent of the repeating patterns of Islamic rugs, while later pictorial designs recall the blue and white porcelain the carracks imported from the east. If you want to buy ceramics here, names to remember include Rato, the royal factory founded near Lisbon in 1767, and maiolica from Caldas da Rainha (see page 232).

I am always on the look out for the unusual. Portugal, particularly the area around Oporto, has a history of fine wood carving and you can find mirrors based on designs by Thomas Chippendale, many dating from the 19th and 20th centuries. And there are glass factories (such as La Granja de San Ildefonso, near Segovia) that produced domestic and decorative glass including a quirky piece like the almorratxa, a glass receptacle for sprinkling rosewater, based on a Moorish original. And don't forget to search around antiques markets in the Algrave — they're a great treasure trove.

Painted tiles, or azulejos, depicting King Alfonso II of Portugal, who reigned from 1211 to 1223.

MADRID

From the antiques shops of the Salamanca district to some of Europe's finest art collections, Madrid is a city of enormous appeal.

Late 17th-century dish from Talavera de la Reina

MADRID IS THE CAPITAL AND PIVOT of a country that, in a generation, has shaken off its repressive republican past, yet never lost its sense of history. The city came under siege during the Civil War of 1936–9 but that war, and Spain's isolation until General Franco's death in 1975, all seem a bad dream now for one of the liveliest and most enjoyable cities in Europe.

Madrileños are known as "night cats", and an evening stroll is perhaps the best way to enjoy old Madrid, with the beautiful arcaded square of the 17th-century Plaza Mayor at its heart. The square is famous for its bars and craft shops but is also fun for the more eccentric places where genuine cowboy boots

can be had or where the Guardia Civil buy their famous uniform hats. The Plaza de la Villa lit at night is a gem, as is the recently restored and pedestrianized Plaza de Oriente in front of the royal palace, and in Puerta del Sol – the theoretical centre of the city and of Spain – the New Year is seen in to enormous exuberance.

Antiques hunting in Madrid often unearths the unexpected for, as well as local ceramics and furniture, you may find items that originated in the Netherlands, which Spain once ruled, or Latin America.

Historical picture tiles on a restaurant wall depicting Madrileñas taking a carriage ride

Goya's Execution of the Defenders of Madrid, 3 May 1808, *painted in 1814*

ROYAL MADRID

Madrid's status as capital of Felipe II's newly united kingdom in 1561 was precarious for some time – between 1601 and 1606 there were plans to move the capital to Vallodolid. Nevertheless, Madrid grew steadily, and in 1734 Felipe V began reconstruction of his palace to reflect the power of the Borbón dynasty he had founded.

The scale and opulence of the **Palacio Real** is amazing, yet there is plenty that is fascinating and idiosyncratic, such as the armour collection, the porcelain room, entirely clothed in green and white Buen Retiro porcelain (see next page), and enough Stradivarius violins to supply a small

orchestra. The present king and queen live on the city's outskirts, but the palace is still used for state occasions.

Under Carlos III (*r.*1759–88), often referred to as "Madrid's best mayor", the city acquired some of its major sights, including the Prado (see page 213), the botanical gardens and the landmark fountain in Plaza de Cibeles.

The 19th century started with the French occupation and, as Napoleon and Wellington fought the Peninsular Wars – Guerra de Independencia to the Spanish – Madrid was caught up in the violence, and Goya produced some of his most powerful work in response.

The monarchy, rocked by the Carlist Wars of the 1830s and 1840s and later revolutions, ended when Alfonso XIII abdicated in 1931. Its revival after 44 years of republicanism, however, was an unexpected success, with the accession of Alfonso's grandson, Juan Carlos, in 1975.

● **Palacio Real**, Calle de Bailén. Tel: (091) 454 8800.

Buen Retiro chinoiserie figurine, c.1765

PLACES TO VISIT

Doña Juana, sister of Felipe II, founded the **Monasterio de las Descalzas Reales** in the 16th century. Despite the *descalzas* (barefoot) in the name, it is the *reales* (royal) that reflects how the aristocratic nuns lived. Their living quarters and chapel were richly endowed with Brussels tapestries, and paintings by Brueghel, Titian and Spanish artists Francisco de Zurbarán and Bartolomé Murillo.

The **Museo Nacional de Artes Decorativas** is famous for its rooms furnished to recreate different historical and regional styles – a highlight is the riotously coloured Valencian kitchen. The museum also has extensive collections, chronologically arranged, of pottery, porcelain and glass, as well as typically Spanish *cordobón*, or embossed leatherwork.

The **Museo Sorolla** is in the former home of this wonderful Spanish Impressionist painter and some of his most attractive and personal work is on display. The home of the writer Lazaro Galdiano is also a house-museum, with a fine art collection, including the best English work on show in Madrid.

Spain introduced chocolate to Europe from its American colonies, and chocolate con churros – a cup of rich, thick chocolate served with fingers of deep-fried dough – is an addict's dream. Find your way to **Chocolateria San Gines** to indulge in different varieties and blends.

● **Monasterio de las Descalzas Reales**, Plaza de las Descalzas. Tel: (091) 521 2779.

● **Museo Nacional de Artes Decorativas**, Calle de Montalban 12. Tel: (091) 532 6499.

● **Museo Sorolla**, Calle General Martinez Campas. Tel: (091) 310 1584.

● **Museo Lazaro Galdiano**, Calle Serrano 122. Tel: (091) 561 6084.

● **Chocolateria San Gines**, Pasadizo de San Gines (beside the church of the same name).

The studio where Joaquín Sorolla painted

SHOPPING

BUEN RETIRO PORCELAIN

The Palacio del Buen Retiro gave its name in the 18th century to a porcelain factory established by King Carlos III. He effectively moved the factory of Capodimonte from Italy to Spain (until 1759 Carlos had been King of Naples and Sicily), and 18th-century Buen Retiro porcelain is almost identical to that previously produced by the celebrated Neapolitan factory. However, when local clay began to be used in place of Italian materials, the character of Buen Retiro altered. Typical pieces from the 1780s and 1790s are Neo-classical Greek in style. Despite the discovery of local kaolin deposits, the factory did not survive the first decade of the 19th century.

Carlos III also imported Italian *pietre dure* craftsmen (see page 244), and Buen Retiro produced some fine pieces – there are some good examples of *piedra dura* table tops from the 1780s in the Prado.

Late 18th- or early 19th-century picture tiles (azulejos) from Talavera de la Reina

TALAVERA DE LA REINA

Tin-glazed earthenware has been made at Talavera de la Reina, on the Castilian plain south-west of Madrid, since the middle of the 16th century. The town's potteries were first renowned for their decorative tiles and picture panels – one factory alone was commissioned by Felipe II to produce almost 25,000 tiles for his palace at El Escorial. When the use of silver for domestic wares was restricted by law in 1601, the factories began to make bowls, drinking vessels and other tableware to take the place of table silver.

Pastoral and bullfighting scenes were popular for decoration, and many of the pieces produced today are in the style of these 17th-century pieces. Early work hardly ever carries a maker's mark.

Early 17th-century chest with carving typical of Spanish craftsmanship at the time – often using chestnut or mahogany

There are three main areas to shop for antiques in Madrid.

SALAMANCA

This fashionable area grew up in the 19th century, and Calle de Serrano is one of Madrid's smartest shopping streets. You'll find a number of antiques shops in the parallel streets of Claudio Coello and Lagasca.

Glass vase, 1930s, originating from Mexico

Look out for:

The 11 high-calibre shops within the **Centro Anticuarios de Lagasca** have stock varying from ceramics and paintings to quality furniture as well as startling religious statuary and objects which suggest the sacking of a couple of cathedrals. Among the antiques shops are art galleries covering the 18th century to the present day. **Lepina Portela** at Lagasca 36 has an excellent selection of fine porcelain, and **Bermondsey**, at Claudio Coello 16, stocks an amazing range of carpets and tapestries.

CALLE DEL PRADO

This used to be the centre of Madrid's antiques trade, but is losing out to the Salamanca district. Nevertheless, **Luis Morueco** at No 16 on its own justifies a visit. The large shop is filled with antiques from delicate 18th-century porcelain to heavy carved chairs and chests.

RASTRO

The Rastro area is near the Puerta de Toledo, one of the old city gates.

Look out for:

Galerias Piquer, at Riberia de Curtidores 29, is a complex of nearly 50 shops. There are specialists in chandeliers, Oriental objects and porcelain as well as an extensive range of furniture from the humble and agricultural to the most perfect Art Deco. There is an astonishing range of garden statuary; for example, I once found a bronze walrus there.

Nuevas Galerias at No 12 is similar, but more modest in scale and, at No 15, **Galerias**

WHEN IN MADRID...

...don't miss the stunning art collections. In the vicinity of Paseo del Prado are three of the greatest galleries in Europe. First, of course, is the **Museo del Prado** itself.

Its works by Velázquez and Goya are incomparable, but there are also first-class examples of Titian's most powerful work. Just opposite is the magnificent **Thyssen-Bornemisza** collection of Western art, from pre-Renaissance Italy to Lucien Freud.

The third part of the artistic triangle is the **Centro de Arte Reina Sofia**, named after the Queen of Spain, which covers 20th-century art. Picasso's *Guernica* is here.

La Infanta Margarita *in the Prado, by the great 17th-century court painter Diego de Velázquez*

Rivera is a gallery of shops where antiques and general "old stuff" mix. The **Nuevo Mercado** is a modern shopping precinct adjoining Puerta de Toledo metro station, and some brave and interesting antiques shops are moving in.

FAIRS AND MARKETS

If you go to the Rastro area on Sunday morning be prepared for a huge and lively street market selling mainly junk – but remember to keep a close watch on your valuables.

AUCTION HOUSES

Duran, Calle Serrano 12. Tel: (091) 577 6091. The most active of Madrid's auction houses, with monthly sales of art and antiques.

The Rastro flea market

WHERE TO STAY

A suite at the Wellington Hotel

Wellington
Velázquez 8
Tel: (091) 575 4400; Fax: (091) 576 4164
Rooms here have every modern amenity, but in the style of the days of empire. Ideal for the Salamanca district.

The Ritz
Plaza de la Lealtad 5
Tel: (091) 701 6767; Fax: (091) 701 6776
The Ritz was built at the instigation of Alfonso XIII and opened in 1910. The unadulterated luxury the king sought is still the hotel's hallmark – and it is also perfectly located next to the Prado.

Jardines De Recolletas
Calle Gil de Santivanes 6
Tel: (091) 781 1640; Fax: (091) 781 1841
A medium-priced, very attractive hotel whose prime appeal is in its location – in the heart of the Salamanca antiques district.

WHERE TO EAT AND DRINK

Botín and L'Hardy (founded 1830 and where Queen Isabella II was known to leave her underwear behind after dining with admirers in private rooms) appear in all the guides but more enjoyable might be:

Casa Lucio
Cava Baja 36
Tel: (091) 365 3252
One of the best of traditional Castilian inns, with heavy wood beams and barrel-vaulted ceilings and serving local dishes. The cellar-like rooms are noisy and packed with a mixture of locals and visitors. Booking is essential or check out others in the street.

La Opera de Madrid
Calle Amnistia 5
Tel: (091) 559 5092
Great value, and serves an excellent house red. There's an opera singer on weekend evenings, and its location is a good excuse to stroll around the Plaza de Oriente before or after dinner.

IN THE AREA

Historic towns and palaces lie scattered across the high Castilian plain: Philip II's austere palace-monastery of **El Escorial**, scholarly **Salamanca**, **Segovia**, with its breathtaking Roman aqueduct and fairytale *alcázar*, and, perhaps my favourite, **Toledo**, where El Greco lived until his death in 1614.

In the Middle Ages Toledo was renowned for its craftsmen: here were forged the world's finest swords, and exquisite examples of Mudéjar work (see page 223) survive. With its dramatically improved lighting, don't miss the cathedral's magnificent interior, or the *alcázar*, where the Republicans were besieged for 70 days in 1936.

BARCELONA

One of the most stylish cities in the world, Barcelona has so much to offer, from great museums and galleries to shops that have hardly changed in 100 years. Plus, of course, stunning *modernista* buildings.

Gaudí's unfinished Sagrada Família cathedral

BARCELONA IS A CITY WITH ENORMOUS CREATIVITY. When I am here, I always feel in touch with the arts, not just the traditional art of museums and galleries but the avant-garde that fuses fine art and architecture and design to make any walk through the city an exciting experience. Barcelona knows how to mix ancient with modern, to put breathtaking new buildings right up against beautiful old ones, like the Museum of Contemporary Art in the heart of the working district of El Raval.

El Raval is one half of the old town, the other half is the Barri Gòtic, and they are divided by La Rambla, one of the world's great thoroughfares, animated by florists and bird-stalls, mummers and musicians. The colourful pavement designed by Joan Miró in Plaça de la Boqueria, halfway along, is a reminder that this is the home town of some of the foremost names in 20th-century art and design.

The Barri Gòtic is an extraordinarily well-preserved medieval quarter (some streets carry one-way signs for horses and carts). Many of its old *bodegas* and shops have their original interiors, and it's an eye-opener to peek into cavernous workshops where furniture restorers carry on their trade. Ceramics are a tradition here as they are in much of Spain, so look out for traditional Catalan ceramic pots and tiles in green and brown, as well as the local porcelain from Lladró.

MEDIEVAL TO MODERNISTA

For more than 500 years, from AD878, an unbroken succession of counts of Barcelona ruled over the region of Catalonia, which had its own language, its own laws and customs. Today, as a semi-autonomous state within Spain, it still has its own government, the Generalitat. This is run from its quite stupendous Gothic building in Plaça de Sant Jaume (see page 220).

At its heart, Barcelona is a medieval city, and no stretch of the imagination is needed when you walk through the Barri Gòtic's shady alleys and lanes to know what it looked like half a millennium ago. Look at the tombs and gravestones in the cathedral and you will see there was no landed aristocracy, no titled rich; it was merchants and guildsmen who made this one of the great ports of the Mediterranean.

In the 13th century Catalonia expanded under Jaume the Conquerer, beginning Mediterranean conquests that would include the Balearic Islands, Sardinia and Sicily. By 1243 Barcelona's shipyards, the Drassanes, were constructing ships that established Catalonia as a major power at sea for over 400 years. Among the exhibits in the **Museu Marítim**, now housed in the Drassanes, is an imposing life-sized model of the ship that led the combined fleet of Spain and that other great Mediterranean power, Venice, to victory against the Turks at the Battle of Lepanto in 1571.

As Catalonia's territories expanded, so did Barcelona. The town had centred around the cathedral and Plaça de Sant Jaume, which had been the Roman forum. Now its walls were rebuilt to stretch down to the Llotja, the stock exchange (completed in 1380), and the port, while grand mansions were built down Carrer Montcada.

In 1494 Christopher Columbus was received by King Fernando and Queen Isabel in the magnificent Gothic hall, Saló de Tinell, in the **Palau Reial Major**, and the dozen native Americans he brought with him were baptized in the cathedral. Columbus's discoveries also brought a decline to the city,

Casa Lléo Morera, one of Barcelona's distinctive modernista *houses*

Late 16th-century maiolica albarello (pharmacy jar), possibly Catalan

as the New World poured South American gold into Spain's southern ports of Seville and Cádiz. But American cotton brought a revival in fortunes to Barcelona, and in the 18th and 19th centuries, with water power from the rivers coming down from the Pyrenees, it became the textile capital of Spain. This was where the industrial revolution on the Iberian peninsula began.

By the late 19th century, the old city was bursting out of its walls, spreading into the Eixample, the "expansion", where *modernista* architects were given free reign. In this power-house of creativity, universal exhibitions were launched, the first in 1888, the second in 1929, when the optimistic fantasies on the hill of Montjuïc were built. Here, alongside the huge exhibition halls, are the Palau Nacional, home of the Catalan art museum (see next page), the Teatre Grec and the **Poble Espanyol**. Created for the 1929 Exhibition, the Poble Espanyol is a generic Spanish village, made up of 116 replicas of architectural styles from all over Spain, created by leading architects of the time.

● **Museu Marítim**, Drassanes de Barcelona, Avinguda de les Drassanes. Tel: (093) 342 9920.
● **Palau Reial Major**, Plaça del Rei. Tel: (093) 315 1111.
● **Poble Espanyol**, Avinguda del Marqués de Comillas. Tel: (093) 508 6330.

One of over 100 examples of vernacular architecture reconstructed in the Poble Espanyol

ANTIQUES IN CONTEXT

From the alleys and lanes of the Barri Gòtic to the exhibition spaces of the hill of Montjuïc, you'll never be at a loss for something to look at in Barcelona. Vibrant with art and culture, it has some of the most exciting museums and galleries in Europe.

At the centre of Barcelona's old town is the cathedral and royal palace. The cathedral has a gloomy, Gothic look, so it is surprising to discover that its main façade was not built until the 19th century. Behind the cathedral wander down either Carrer Paradis (where you can step into the entrance of No 10 and see columns that were once part of a Roman temple), or down Carrer Bisbe, where a lovely Gothic bridge connects the Generalitat, the region's parliament, with the residence of the Catalan president.

A rainy-day blessing near here is the **Museu Frederic Marès**, entered via the orange-tree patio of the royal palace. It has a wonderfully eclectic collection, ranging from medieval religious sculptures, which fill the lower floors, to walking sticks, parasols, pipes and saucy postcards on the upper floors.

The houses in Carrer Montcada were built by the merchants who grew rich from trade

Cuboard designed by Gaspar Homar i Mesquida, 1901

Tiled interior of the modernista *Casa Navàs, showing the detailed design of the mosaic floor*

in the Middle Ages, and the street is the best example of what much of medieval Barcelona must have been like. One mansion is now the **Museu de Textil i d'Indumentària**, a legacy from this textile manufacturing town. Its collection includes designs by Mariano

Fortuny y Madrazo who, although he made his name in Venice (see page 257), was born in nearby Reus.
● **Museu Frederic Marès**, Plaça de Sat Iu 5. Tel: (093) 310 5800.
● **Museu de Textil i d'Indumentària**, Carrer Montcada 14. Tel: (093) 310 4516.

BARCELONA'S ARTISTS
Pablo Picasso was only 14 when his family arrived in Barcelona in 1895. His father taught in the art school that was then above the Llotja, the 14th-century stock exchange, and they lived nearby. So too did Joan Miró, who was 12 years younger than Picasso. Both painters have their own museums here, and Salvador Dalí has his own in nearby Figueres (see page 221).

The wonderful **Museu Picasso** is important not only to see what a precocious talent this young man had, but also because it gives you the opportunity to see inside three grand Gothic mansions in Carrer Montcada.

You can see the abundant talent of Catalonia's 20th-century painters, together with some fine *modernista* furniture from the city's grand houses, in the **Museu d'Art Modern** in the Parc de Ciutadella, a pleasant park colonized by parrots that have escaped from their cages in La Rambla.

The city's main art gallery, the **Museu Nacional d'Art de Catalunya**, has a fine Gothic collection and paintings by Spanish masters. In addition, the gallery houses the finest Romanesque art collection in Europe.
● **Fundació Joan Miró**, Parc de Montjuïc. Tel: (093) 329 1908.
● **Museu Picasso**, Carrer Montcada 15–23. Tel: (093) 319 6310. Closed Mon.
● **Museu d'Art Modern**, Parc de la Ciutadella. Tel: (093) 319 5023.
● **Museu Nacional d'Art de Catalunya**, Parc de Montjuïc. Tel. (093) 622 0375.

CASA NAVAS
Period domestic interiors are hard to find in Barcelona. To see the furnished interior of a *modernista* mansion, you can visit Domènech i Montaner's **Casa Navàs**, dating from 1901, at Reus, near Tarragona. The tiled main hall, decorated by Gaspar Homer i Mesquida, is typically grand.
● **Casa Navàs**, Plaça del Mercadel, Reus. Tel: (097) 734 5943. Open Thurs, Fri, Sat.

Hispano-Moresque copper lustre chargers, probably early 16th century

PEDRALBES

A small excursion to the western outskirts of the city leads to the Palau Reial de Pedralbes, belonging to the Güells and converted to a royal palace in 1919; Alfonso XIII stayed in it once before his exile. Its rooms fit for a king can still be visited, however, and, as the **Museu de les Arts Décoratives**, they provide an appropriate setting for furniture and art from all periods of Catalan history. The palace also houses the **Museu de Ceràmica**. This is the place to go to see one of Catalonia's great traditional crafts. Pots, bowls and dishes date back to the 15th century, and there are 20th-century ceramics by Picasso and Miró.

Make time to visit the 13th-century **Monestir de Pedralbes** nearby. Not long vacated, the monastery's refectory, hospital and cells are furnished as if in use, and the former dormitory contains part of the hugely impressive Thyssen-Bornemisza collection of religious art.

● **Museu de les Arts Décoratives**, Avinguda Diagonal 686. Tel: (093) 280 1364.

● **Monestir de Pedralbes**, Baixaida del Monestir 9. Tel: (093) 280 1439.

Decorative façade of a residence in the old town

INFLUENTIAL FIGURES

ANTONI GAUDI

Modernisme is Barcelona's own, very distinctive style of Art Nouveau. It flourished between the two great trade exhibitions held in 1880 and 1929. It is not an easy style to define: in Passeig de Gràcia its three great practitioners, Antoni Gaudí i Coronet, Josep Puig i Cadafalch and Luís Domènech i Montaner, have buildings virtually side by side and all are quite different. What is certain is that the most extravagant of the architects was Gaudí. Born in Reus near Tarragona in 1852, he met his wealthy (and main) patron, the Catalan philanthropist Eusebio Güell, shortly after graduating from architectural school in Barcelona. Among his many commissions from Güell was **Parc Güell**, which was to be a large *modernista* housing estate with 60 homes and an underground market. Only two were completed, one of which Gaudi lived in and is now the **Casa-Museu Gaudi**, containing some of the furniture he designed and his architectural plans. The covered market, with a belvedere above, has his hallmark of brightly coloured ceramic chips and exotic sculptures.

Other commissions in Barcelona included **Palau Güell**, the family's town house (completed in 1890), **Casa Milà**, known as La Pedrera (the stone quarry), which has a lovely stairwell, bizarre chimneys and an exhibition area, and **Casa Batlló**, among that trio of (unvisitable) buildings in the Passeig de Gràcia. The flowing lines that Gaudi

A blue chameleon made of ceramic mosaics in Gaudi's Parc Güell

favoured are evident in the stonework, as well as in details such as the railings, ironwork, glass and ceramics.

Gaudí's greatest legacy is without doubt the awe-inspiring **Temple Expiatori de la Sagrada Família**, which he took over in 1883 and worked on obsessively until his death in 1926. With only one façade completed, he left a great deal to be done. Efforts are being made to complete this icon of Barcelona, one of the most ambitious projects in Spain.

● **Casa-Museu Gaudí**, Carrer del Carmel 28. Tel: (093) 284 6446.

● **Palau Güell**, Carrer Nou de la Rambla 3. Tel: (093) 317 3974.

● **Casa Milà** (La Pedrera), Passeig de Gràcia 92. Tel: (093) 484 5980.

● **Temple Expiatori de la Sagrada Família**, Carrer Mallorca 401.

Chair by Gaudi, c.1902, in more classically Art Nouveau style

SHOPS OLD AND NEW

The city is divided into two distinct shopping areas: the old town of the Barri Gòtic and the stylish Eixample. To get a full flavour of what the city has to offer, you should visit both, but it's the old town where the more intriguing shops lie.

Half the fun of shopping in Barcelona is the contrast between the medieval old town and the chic Eixample, where style is everything. Add to this a tradition of pavement cafés and delicious *tapas* (*tapes* in Catalan), and the whole idea of shopping becomes a delight.

BARRI GOTIC

Many of the shops seem as if they have always been here, their flagstoned, cavernous interiors and old-fashioned lighting still preserved. The oldest, with a beautful decorated interior, is the candle shop **Subirà de Cera**, at Carrer Baixada Lliberteria 7, which opened as a fashion house in 1761. Many streets were once devoted to the sales of single items

17th-century jug in traditional Catalan green and terracotta

(candle-makers in Carrer de la Cera, jewellers in Carrer de la Boqueria, herbalists in Carrer de l'Hospital) and some of these shops still give the streets their flavours. There are also many old-style shops selling single items: hats, buttons, feathers, umbrellas, gloves, or traditional rope-soled shoes (see them being made at **La Manual Alpargetera**, Avinyó 7).

Antiques shops are found all over the Barri Gòtic, but some in the more touristy areas can be expensive. Many are in the Call, which used to be the Jewish quarter.

Escribà Pastisseries' 1902 shop front, La Rambla

Look out for:

Heavy furniture, gilded pieces and church statuary are typical of some of the shops' displays, such as **Borrajo Manin** at San Domènec del Call 9.

Items in some of the antiques shops in nearby Carrer Banys Nous look like museum pieces. **Gemma Pova** (No 5) has ceramics, wrought-iron and hand-blown glass. **Alberta Grasas** (No 14) has been run by the same family for three generations, and you'll find a wide-ranging stock here, covering European furniture, paintings, clocks, silver and porcelain. Ceramics from Catalonia and Valencia can be found at **Juan Sanchez e Hijo** at No 17; Catalan glass is also a speciality of **Sandval** at No 21. Take a break, if not a glass of wine, in El Portal, one of the city's famous old wine bars or *bodegas*.

SPANISH FURNITURE

Traditional Spanish furniture is, on the whole, heavy and robust, but in a country of many regions and poor communications, local influence has always been strong. In the south, the Moorish Mudéjar style left its mark (see page 223), while Catalan merchants preferred simpler forms. Castille was most influenced by foreign designs, especially French. In the early 19th century, Fernandino, a heavy, opulent style, evolved under Fernando VII, followed by Isabellino, a romantic Gothic look.

Typically Spanish items of furniture include four-poster beds with decorated headboards and heavy *caixa* wedding chests with drawers and compartments for both bride and groom. Iron embellishments, such as corner reinforcements or table stretchers, are common. Simple sideboards often have marble tops, and 19th-century *chineros* came in two parts: a desk of drawers below and panels, perhaps with mirrors, above, which would serve as a domestic altar.

Spanish giltmetal-mounted marquetry cabinet, 17th-century

Carrer de Ferran in the Barri Gòtic

Carrer Banys Nous leads into Carrer Palla, a curved lane that follows the old Roman wall. **Cervera** at No 9 has archeological objects, **Maria Ubach** at No 10 specializes in 17th- and 18th-century ceramics, and in the same building **Luis and Manuel Barbié**, in business since 1965, have paintings and sculptures. **Juan Chincho Campanera** at No 19 specializes in antique dolls, **Sabartes Tejero** at No 21 has a good line in decorative arts and **Enrique Estrada**'s wide selection of antiques at No 27 are mainly from the 19th century. Best known, perhaps, is the **Sala d'Art Artur Ramón** on three floors at Nos 23–25, run by the same family for four generations. Its prices reflect the high quality of the antiques and works of art on offer, from Romanesque caskets to Picasso bowls.

For hefty chestnut sideboards, terracotta pots or thin-backed antique nursing chairs (which look quite uncomfortable), try **Antiugüedades Boada** at 6 Plaça Oriol.

Antique books and print shops abound in this, the publishing capital of Spain. Around the royal palace, try **Librería Violén**, 1 Plaça del Rei, and **Grafique el Tinell**, at 1 Freneria, which specializes in old prints and lithographs, especially posters of blocks of the old guild (*gremis*) trades. **Libreria Selvaggio** at 12 Freneria is another stop for maps, prints and antiquarian books.

The street for art galleries is Carrer Peritxol, a little lane off Plaça del Pi, running parallel to La Rambla. The oldest art gallery here is **Sala Parés** at No 5, founded in 1840, where Picasso first exhibited in 1901, when he was 20. It still sells the best of contemporary works. **Art Peritxol** at No 8 specializes in 19th- and 20th-century Catalan paintings.

One shopping experience not to miss is the Mercat de Sant Josep, known as **La Boqueria**. This food market halfway down La Rambla is a 19th-century iron construction of railway station proportions where fresh fish, vegetables and mushrooms never looked more appetizing.

Spanish girandole earrings, c.1760

EL RAVAL

The district on the opposite side of La Rambla from the Barri Gòtic is not known for its antiques, but the shops of this working-class district are especially quaint. Those in Carrer de l'Hospital, by the old city hospital, specialize in leather goods and remedies. A particular favourite is **La Reina de las Flores**, at No 111, run by Francisco Bertrán who makes his own perfumes, and sells them in recycled old-fashioned bottles, while his soaps and toiletries, such as the shaving lotion with an evocative 1950s style label, fit in any luggage bag to take home.

EIXAMPLE

Eixample has some of the city's best antiques shops and prestigious galleries within the Quadrat d'Or, the *modernista* "golden square" above Plaça de Catalunya.

Look out for:

At 73 Passeig de Gràcia is the **Bulevard dels Antiquaris**, a mini-mall of some 70 antiques shops with a great range of art and antiques. **Acanto** specializes in clocks, **Arbeo** in ceramics, **Govarys** in porcelain dolls, **Nou-Cents** in 19th- and 20th-century Catalan paintings, **William** in glass. There is a small café here, too. Anyone interested in the design of household objects should also visit **Vinçon**, at No 96, on the corner of Carrer Rosselló. This store of household goods, in the magnificent home of the great Barcelona artist and caricaturist Ramon Casas (1866–1932), is at the cutting edge of Barcelona design and there are sometimes exhibitions here.

Water jugs in a style unchanged for centuries

SHOPPER'S TIP

La Bisbal is one of the most important craft centres in Catalonia, and has specialized in the production of ceramics since the 17th century. The centre of the town is lined with shops selling earthenware jugs, crockery, bottles and decorative plates based on traditional forms, and in the green, brown and yellow colours that have become a local trademark.

Another shop that should not be overlooked is **BD Ediciones de Disegno**. Housed in Casa Tomás, a beautiful three-storey building designed by Domènech i Montaner at 291 Carrer de Mallorca, it is a design shop of impeccable taste. Its products include reproductions of tables, chairs, mirrors and door furniture by Gaudí, as well as Dali "lobster" telephones and furniture by Charles Rennie Mackintosh (see page 62). There are also lamps by Fortuny, the Catalan-born artist and designer whose fashion creations can be seen in the Museu de Textil i d'Indumentària (see page 216).

Urbana, at 258 Carrer de Còrsega, deals in architectural salvage, taking advantage of the redevelopment in the city in recent years. It has gates, garden seats and fireplaces, some antique, some reproduction, and, in particular, some *modernisme* items.

BEYOND DIAGONAL
One or two streets on the far side of the Avinguda Diagonal have a handful of shops that sell quality antiques. **Antic**, at 190 Carrer Muntaner, specializes in French Empire furniture; in Via Augusta **Borras Mari** deals in 19th-century European furniture, bronzes and decorative arts; and at 92 Carrer Gran de Gràcia **Caoba** has English furniture and Art Deco.

MARKETS
Most of the regular antiques markets are in the Barri Gòtic. At weekends craft stalls are set up at the lower end of La Rambla. There are a couple of dozen regular stalls in the **Mercat Gòtic d'Antiquitats** outside the cathedral every Thursday, with a mix of items from tools and teacups to postcards and bobbins. On Thursday and Saturday stalls are set up in the attractive Plaça del Pi, but don't get too excited about the paintings for sale in the adjacent Plaça Oriol at the weekend.

On Sunday mornings there is a coin and stamp market in Plaça Reial, and a coin and book market in Mercat Sant Antoni, the big old market on the corner where Carrer de Tamarit meets Comte Urgell.

Another favourite Sunday spot is the Moll de Drassanes by the old port, which has an antiques and bric-a-brac market, while the Port Olímpic, with wall-to-wall restaurants, is a favourite spot

Restoration work being carried out on an exhibit in the Museu Marítim

Modernisme-style chair, Catalan School

for Sunday strollers, and craft and bric-a-brac sellers lay out their wares along the Passage Marítim behind.

The biggest flea market is **Els Encants** in Plaça de les Glòries. This is a vast hotch-potch of shops, stalls and pavement dealers. It takes the best part of a day to get around, but get there early for the bargains. There are some great local antiques to be rooted out among the more ordinary items. It opens Mondays, Wednesdays, Fridays and Saturdays, but there are some wholesalers in the neighbouring streets of Carrer Aragó and Carrer Dos de Maig open to the public all week.

FAIRS
Book and antiques fairs are regularly held in Barcelona. The biggest and most interesting fair of all is the **Antiquaris-Barcelona**. It is held in the Fira de Barcelona exhibition halls at the foot of Montjuïc in February.

AUCTION HOUSES
Castellana Subhastes Barcelona, Calle Diputació. Tel: (093) 496 1980.
Arce Subastas, Calle Santaló. Tel: (093) 202 1000.
Subhastes de Barcelona, Consell de Cent 278. Tel: (093) 487 0445. Specialists in manuscripts and antique maps.

Herara-style rustic walnut table, late 16th century

IN BARCELONA...

FESTA DE SANT JORDI
San Jordi, St George, is the city's patron saint, and his day, 21 April, is declared National Book Day. Book stalls line the pavements and girlfriends buy boyfriends books, who in return offer them a carnation. On this day, the Palau de la Generalitat, the parliament building, is open to the public – a rare opportunity to see the magnificent Gothic interior and famous orange-tree patio.

WHERE TO EAT AND DRINK

Eating *tapas*, small portions of elegantly presented food, is a fun way to spend an evening, and an excuse to stroll in the Barri Gòtic. There are many enticing *tapas* bars in Eixample, too, such as **Tapa-Tapa** at 44 Passeig de Gracia.

Set Portes
Passeig Isabel II, 14
Tel: (093) 319 2950
The city's oldest restaurant opened just after the completion of the Neo-classical Porxos arcade in 1836. Picasso, García Lorca and all the Spanish artistic greats have eaten here. Lovely old-world atmosphere, with piano. Rice dishes a speciality. Lunchtime set menus are excellent value.

Los Caracoles
Carrer dels Escudellers 14
Tel: (093) 302 3185
The most famous Barri Gòtic restaurant, and the most typical, made its name in the 1940s when the rich and famous came here. Now it's mostly tourists, but none the worst for that. Paella and spit-roast chicken are specialities.

Els Quatre Gats
Carrer Montsió 3 bis
Tel: (093) 302 4140; Fax: (093) 317 4033
Built in 1895 by Josep Puig i Cadafalch (see page 217), this is where the *modernista* artists hung out and, five years later, where Picasso showed his first impressive works. Restored to its original café in 1983, with walls full of pictures, it's an evocative place to stop for a coffee or a meal.

Café de la Opera
La Rambla 74
(no phone listed)
Have a coffee or hot chocolate in the splendour of a bygone age in this famous haunt opposite the Liceu opera house. Casanova drank here.

WHERE TO STAY

Claris
Pau Claris 150
Tel: (093) 487 6262; Fax: (093) 215 7970
It is a rare treat to be staying in a museum of Egyptology. Señor Jordi Clos i Llombart's small private collection is on the ground floor of this Eixample hotel in the 19th-century former Vedruna palace. The juxtaposition of antiquities and the startlingly modern, of European antique furniture and Eastern kilims, epitomizes the successful mix that characterizes Barcelona.

Oriente
La Rambla 45
Tel: (093) 302 2558; Fax: (093) 412 3819

Some of the rooms in this famous old hotel have balconies that overlook the animated Rambla – ask for one if you want to feel at the heart of the city and are happy to listen to the noises of the night. The building is the former friary of Sant Bona-ventura (1670) and its enclosed cloisters form the beautiful lounge.

España
Sant Pau 9
Tel: (093) 318 1758; Fax: (093) 317 1134
Moderate hotel with plain rooms but two wonderful *modernista* ground floor dining rooms decorated by Domènech i Muntaner (see page 217) in 1903.

Peninsular
Sant Pau 34
Tel: (093) 302 3138; Fax: (093) 412 3699
Inexpensive hotel in a monastery converted by *modernista* architects. Lovely interior patio.

IN THE AREA

Surrealist artist Salvador Dalí is celebrated at several venues in his native Alt Empordà, north of Barcelona. The **Dalí Teatre-Museu** in Figueres, where he was born in 1904, is one of the most visited museums in Spain, full of jokes and surprises. His house near Cadaques, 30km (20 miles) away, is also a museum, and **Casa-Museu Salvador-Dali** is one of the most pleasing of artist's houses to visit – full of creativity, yet a simple and beautiful home.

Peratallada is a medieval town with cobbled streets, an hour's drive north of Barcelona, near Girona. It has some fine artisans' shops, where you can buy wicker (try Antic, who also have antiques) and ceramics (try Manbel Art). There is a wonderful hotel, the Castell de Peratallada, which is an 11th-century castle with six large rooms. Restaurant Bonay is the place to eat, situated on Plaça les Voltes, with fresh fish brought from the coast just 15 minutes away.
● **Dalí Teatre-Museu**, Figueres.
Tel: (0972) 677500.
● **Casa-Museu Salvador-Dali**, Port-Lligat.
Tel: (0972) 258063.

The holy mountain of **Montserrat**, 55km (35 miles) north-west of the city, makes an invigorating day trip. More than 1,200m (4,000ft) up, its 19th-century basilica contains La Moreneta, the 12th-century Black Virgin who has become Catalonia's patron saint. Listen to the Escalonia, the famous boy choristers who sing in the basilica twice a day, and enjoy exploring the hermits' caves and chapels in this popular Sunday spot.

The mountain retreat of Montserrat

SEVILLE

Romans, Visigoths, Moors, Christians, Jews, and the riches of the Americas shaped the character of this beautiful city, in which browsing and shopping is such a pleasure.

Entrance to the gardens of the Reales Alcázares

After the Genoese navigator Christopher Columbus (Cristóbal Colón in Spanish) rediscovered the Americas for their Catholic Majesties Fernando and Isabel, Seville was awarded the monopoly on trade with the New World. Ships laden with silver and gold unloaded close to the Torre del Oro and Seville became the richest port in Europe. Magnificent churches and grand houses soon sprung up all over the city. But wars and the impoverishment of agriculture caused by the final expulsion of the Moors in 1609, contributed to a depletion of the city's wealth. By the 1680s the Guadalquivir river had silted up and the lucrative overseas trade passed to Cádiz.

Seville is a place to savour. Its narrow streets are packed with craft and antiques shops, and however much time I spend in the Barrio de Santa Cruz, I always find something new and memorable. It is also a city that engenders affection. After living for over 20 years in Castille, the early 20th-century Spanish poet, Antonio Machado, wrote of his native city:

My memories are a secluded patio in Seville
And a luminous orchard in which grows a lemon tree.

The nostalgic lines seem to encapsulate much of what makes Seville so special to its inhabitants and visitors. Despite being a large city, its *barrios* (quarters) retain the intimacy and charm of centuries gone by and the colourful legacy of many cultures.

HISTORY REVISITED

AL ANDALUS

In AD476, five centuries of Roman rule in Spain came to an end and the whole country came under the rule of the barbarian Visigoths. Although the Visigothic King Recared converted to Catholicism in 589, the Hispano-Roman population did not easily absorb the Germanic Visigoths, the Jews in particular being hostile to a Christian government. In 710 the Visigoths appealed to the North African Moors for help in their internal conflicts. This was a fatal move. Within ten years the Moors had conquered huge areas of Spain, the far north alone remaining under Christian control, and a succession of Arab dynasties would rule most of the peninsula for the next 700 years.

The Moors named their new conquest Al Andalus. In 1147 the Berber Almohads made Seville (at that time called Ixvillia) the capital of their empire and, before their defeat by the Christian armies of the north less than a century later, Seville underwent a renaissance. The *alcázar* was rebuilt (today it is the best-preserved Moorish fortress in Spain), and the main mosque was enlarged. Its towering minaret topped with bronze spheres took 12 years to construct and could be seen from miles around. The Torre del Oro (Golden Tower) constructed beside of the river Guadalquivir served as a surveillance point and formed part of the city's defences. Arab water engineers built *aljibes* and *acequías* (tanks and canals) and dug a system of wells, some of which are still working today, which irrigated this arid land and enabled them to cultivate exotic crops such as oranges, pomegranates and rice.

Orange trees in the heart of old Seville

Late 15th-century Hispano-moresque copper lustre armorial charger

The Reconquest, the gradual reclamation of Islamic Spain by Christian forces, wrested successive kingdoms from Moorish rule, and in 1248 Seville fell to the Christian monarch, Fernando III. Palaces and churches were built to proclaim the power of the Christian kings. Ironically, many of the local craftsmen who worked on these signs of Christian authority were Muslims or recent converts, called *mudéjares* – literally "those permitted to stay". A distinctive hybrid architectural style, which became known as Mudéjar, developed alongside Gothic and Baroque styles from northern Europe, and many buildings in Seville show these influences to some degree.

The most potent reminder of Moorish culture in Seville itself are the **Reales Alcázares**. This large and beautiful complex of palaces, pavilions, courtyards and gardens was the residence of both Moorish and Christian rulers. In 1364 Pedro I, The Cruel, built himself a palace which is regarded as one of the best examples of Mudéjar style. Another palace within the Alcázares, the Salón de Embajadores (built in 1427) has a dazzling dome made of carved and gilded wood. Throughout the Alcázares intricate fretwork and horseshoe arches recall North African architecture. Elegant *patios* covered in lacy plasterwork blend effortlessly with the gardens full of the fountains and rills beloved of desert nations.

When the last Moorish ruler, the Nasrid Boabdil of Granada, was expelled from Spain in 1492, "the cold breath of Fernando and Isabel", to quote the poet Federico García Lorca, settled over the country. The remaining Moors were forcibly converted or expelled, along with the Jews who had contributed so much to the cultural and economic development of the country, and much scientific and technical knowledge and artistry went with them.

● **Reales Alcázares**, Patio de Banderas. Tel: (095) 450 2324. Closed Mon.

The riverside watch-tower of the Torre del Oro

ANTIQUES IN CONTEXT

Seville's fascinating history is evident all over the city, from the atmospheric narrow streets of the Barrio de Santa Cruz, to churches filled with art treasures and the exuberant *azulejo*-decorated *pabellones* of the Parque de Maria Luisa.

ARABESQUES

At the heart of Seville's old town lies the Barrio de Santa Cruz, a maze of narrow streets where wrought-iron balconies cast shadows against white-washed walls and sun-bleached shutters. The *barrio* has many restaurants, small hotels and souvenir shops, yet it is an intensively lived-in district and there is still much evidence of the city's past.

This was Seville's Jewish quarter, and in some door-ways you can see mezuzahs, the containers for the tiny scrolls of the Torah that Jews touch as they pass the threshold. Elsewhere, a graceful brass hand of Fatima (see page 226) on the door suggests that the house had Muslim occupants.

The Moors had a great sense of privacy and tended to hide their riches and their lives behind tall walls. All over Seville, houses, whether palatial or modest, tend to follow a similar pattern. They usually have massive doors, often reinforced with elaborate iron tracery and large decorative nail heads as if to resist an impending siege. Some doors are plated with thin layers of copper fixed with iron nails and, over the years, the metal has acquired a rich patina. You'll also notice that it is common for windows looking onto the street to be small and generally protected by a *reja*, a decorative grille, while the windows that overlook the inner *patio* are much larger. You may need to peer through a momentarily opened door to catch a glimpse of one of these hidden courtyards. The *patios* overflow with lush greenery and pots of scented flowers, and there is the ever-present tinkling of water from fountains.

If you want to see a palatial Seville mansion and its garden in all its glory, you can visit the 15th-century **Casa de la Condesa Lebrija**. Only parts of this lovely house, with its mosaic floors and Mudéjar

Resplendent interior of the Archivo de Indias, founded 1785

Early 16th-century Hispano-moresque "winged" vase with lustre finish

plasterwork, are open, as it is still the private residence of the Countess Lebrija.

Reminders of Moorish rule are everywhere, even in the imposing Gothic cathedral, built in 1401. Despite being a statement of Christian supremacy, its builders incorporated rather than obliterated much of the elegant Islamic architectural detail of the mosque on whose site it was built. The cathedral's entrance, la Puerta del Perdón, is the original entrance to the mosque, and the gateway retains its original Moorish plasterwork and great doors faced with bronze. These lead into a courtyard filled with orange trees – the Patio de los Naranjos – which still contains the fountain where the faithful carried out their ritual ablutions before entering the mosque. The cathedral's tower, the Giralda, is one of the most remarkable examples of Islamic architecture. By the time of the Reconquest this minaret had become a

Gothic balustrades and Mudéjar decorations viewed from the Patio Principal of Casa de Pilatos

well-loved landmark and only the entreaties of the Sevillanos prevented its destruction, but it acquired a golden angel on top to show its Christian allegiance. The top of the Giralda is reached by a series of 35 gently inclined ramps and is well worth the climb as the views over the city are breathtaking.

● **Casa de la Condesa Lebrija**, Calle Cuna 8. Tel: (095) 421 8183. Open Mon & Sat 6–7pm.
● **Cathedral & Giralda**, Plaza Virgen de los Reyes. Tel: (095) 456 3321.

PLACES TO VISIT

Granted sole right of trading with the New World, Seville's 16th-century mercantile centre, the Lonja, was a mirror of the riches that were bought and sold there. It now houses the **Archivo de Indias**, a collection of literally millions of valuable documents, including letters from voyagers such as Christopher Colombus and Hernán Cortés. The correspondence is of great historical interest, but it is the early maps of Latin America that are especially fascinating.

The **Casa de Pilatos** is a real curiosity. Built in 1519 by the Marqués de Tarifa following his pilgrimage to Jerusalem, it was thought to be a copy of the house of Pontius Pilate, hence its name. In fact the marquess's aim was to combine Mudéjar and Gothic styles with the Renaissance architecture that he had admired on his travels. Muslim arches and expanses of *azulejos* blend harmoniously with the Italian Renaissance fountain and authentic Greek and Roman statues in the main courtyard, while the upper floors are filled with family portraits and antique furniture. The delightful gardens feature a romantic bower of palms, pavilions and an orange grove.

Early 20th-century Spanish chair in the modernista style

South of the Reales Alcázares and the busy Puerta de Jerez lies the shady green Parque de María Luisa. In 1929 this was the site for Spain's Exposición Ibero-americano and it is studded with a variety of *pabellones*, (pavilions, but actually large buildings), erected for the Exposition, fountains and fantastical *azulejo* creations. The Pabellón Mudéjar houses the **Museo de Artes y Costumbres Populares**, where you can see colourful flamenco and bullfighting costumes, and also exhibits that explain traditional Andalucian crafts such as *azulejo*-painting and leather embossing.

● **Archivo de Indias**, Avda de la Constitución. Tel: (095) 421 12 34. Open Mon–Fri 10am–1pm.
● **Casa de Pilatos**, Plaza de Pilatos. Tel: (095) 442 52 98. The first floor is still occupied by the owners, and can be seen by guided tour only.
● **Museo de Artes y Costumbres Populares**, Parque María Luisa. Tel: (095) 423 2576.

CÓRDOBA

Two thousand years ago the town of Córdoba, 140km (90 miles) east of Seville, was a Roman provincial capital, but its moment of glory was as the capital of Muslim Spain, when it became a centre for art, poetry and philosophy. At that time Christians, Muslims and Jews lived side

A 12th-century bronze lamp

by side in harmony and this rich, multicultural legacy can be seen all over the city in its monuments and buildings. Jewel among these is the great mosque, the **Mezquita**. Started in AD785 and added to over many centuries, it combines elements of Roman, Gothic Byzantine, Syrian and Persian architectural styles, and in the 16th century a huge Catholic cathedral was built inside. Despite this architectural mix, the Mezquita has lost none of its power to awe.

Art lovers should head for the **Museo de Bellas Artes** to see an impressive collection of paintings and sculptures by such Spanish masters as Joaquín Sorolla, Bartolomé Murillo and Francisco de Goya.

Shopping in Córdoba is a delight. The narrow cobbled streets of the Judería, the old Jewish quarter beside the Mezquita, have been left unchanged by the passing centuries. Here you will find many silversmiths and workshops producing crafts such as intricate filigree jewellery, handpainted ceramics and the embossed leatherwork named after the town: *cordobón*. Close to the Mezquita is a handicraft market, the Zoco Municipal de Artesanía.

● **Mezquita**, Calle Torrijos. Tel: (0957) 47 05 12.
● **Museo de Bellas Artes**, Plaza del Potro 1. Tel: (0957) 47 33 45.

Interior of the Mezuita, with its forest of more than 850 columns of granite, jasper and marble

SHOPPING IN SEVILLE

Seville has much to offer the discerning collector. Centuries of tile- and ceramic-making, and traditional craftwork such as embroidered shawls, fans, lace mantillas, filigree jewellery and leatherwork all speak of a diverse and colourful past.

Although Seville is quite a big city, the fourth largest in Spain, the areas for antiques shopping are mostly very central.

AROUND THE CATHEDRAL
This enchanting district, the centre of old Seville, has some very good antiques shops.

Alcora faience "blackamoor" candlestick, c.1750

Look out for:
El Bazar del Barrio, at Mateos Gago 24, is a specialist in antique *azulejos* and traditional Spanish ceramics. You'll also find modern studio pottery here. Just off Calle Mateo Gago, at Calle Rodrigo Caro 3, **Perfume Agua de Sevilla** sells jasmine-scented eau de toilette and fine soaps. **Centrartis**, at Calle Ximénez de Enciso 9, is an interesting place to look for antique jewellery and *objets d'art*.

Manuel Piñanes, at Alemanes 13, deals in paintings, chiefly by 19th- and 20th-century artists. **Enriqueta Anticuaria** (Calle Hernando Colón 35) has a little bit of everything, including porcelain and furniture. Just along the same street, at No 39, is the fine art dealer **Saavedra Montaño**. Among the 17th-century still-lifes you should find paintings of life in the Seville of yesteryear. **Casa Rodríguez** (Calle Francos 35) is one shop among many in Seville that deals in religious images.

Brass Hand of Fatima doorknob, 19th century

Antique Andalucian fan edged with lace

Montelongo Antigüedades, in Calle Muñoz y Pavón, stocks a variety of Spanish furniture, along with clocks, candlesticks, paintings and bronzes. Montelongo have another shop at Calle Alvarez Quintero 15, which runs north from the cathedral towards Plaza del Salvador.

Forming one edge of the Barrio de Santa Cruz is the Avenida de la Constitución. **Antigüedades Ortega**, at No 5, offers antique glass and ivory and some religious paintings, but their speciality is vintage bullfight posters. **Poster Félix**, at No 26 (next to the post office), also has a good choice of vintage posters; it is run by the uncle of the owner of **Antigüedades Félix e Hijos**, just down the road at No 20. Félix e Hijos specialize in classical antiquities, and everything they sell is authenticated by an archeological institute in Berlin. For tiles, paintings, shawls and lace mantillas as well as furniture, pop into **Lola Ortega** in Plaza del Cabildo. Around the corner, in Calle Arfe, **El Postigo** is an arts and crafts centre with a wide variety of handmade items.

Ana Abascal–Patricia Medina is an elegant antiques shop in Calle Fernández y González 15, which is between the cathedral and the Ayuntamiento (town hall). They have a selection of Spanish and French period furniture, lamps and *objets d'art*.

CALLE DE LAS SIERPES
The pedestrianized Calle de las Sierpes, which runs north from the Plaza de San Francisco, is synonymous with elegant shopping in Seville. It is also the place to see and be seen, especially at the evening *paseo*. Along with the parallel Calle Tetuán, it offers the best of modern Spanish design alongside traditional Andalucian crafts and antiques.

Look out for:
At Calle Sierpes 89, **Segundo** is an antiques shop specializing in 19th-century paintings and antique jewellery. A minute away, in Calle Alvarez Quintero (at No 7, on the first floor of Edificio Ciudad de Sevilla), is **Isbiliya**, a dealer in militaria. Among the specialist items stocked here are campaign medals, medieval helmets and 17th-century swords.

At Acetres 10, just the other side of the Casa de la Condesa Lebrija (see page 224), is the wonderful **Bastilippo**, which usually has a great selection of textiles for sale – mainly shawls and lace – as well as furniture and a variety of *objets d'art*.

If exhaustion threatens, **La Campana**, Seville's most famous *pastelería* is at the northern end of Calle de las Sierpes. A popular watering hole with Sevillanos, it offers cakes and ices which seem too beautiful to eat, and also sells gift-wrapped boxes of biscuits and sweetmeats. Founded in 1885, the shop features engraved mirrors which reflect the fine *azulejos* and gleaming brass fittings.

OTHER HUNTING GROUNDS

The area around Plaza de la Alfalfa, a little to the north of the Barrio de Santa Cruz, has a number of antiques shops (the square itself is the venue for a weekend pet market). **Antigüedades Carlos**, at Calle Pérez Galdós 34, is a tiny shop crammed with all manner of things, including furniture and paintings. **Fernández Antigüedades** (Calle Cuesta del Rosario 25) is run by the third generation of the same family. They deal in paintings, furniture and high-quality *objets d'art*. **Arcángel Antigüedades**, at Calle Cabeza del Rey Don Pedro 19, has a stock of English and Spanish furniture, the latter mostly from the 19th century; they also exhibit paintings by local painter Alfonso Grosso.

Classic Spanish furniture can be found at **Antigüedades Angel Luis Friazza**, at Calle Zaragoza 48. Friazza also deals in marble busts and bronzes and usually has a selection of religious antiques.

An 18th-century print of a performing horse of the Spanish Riding School, based in Jerez

---

SHOPPER'S TIP

A real taste of Seville can be found at the **Convento de San Leandro**, close to the Casa de Pilatos. Since the 18th century the nuns here have produced *yemas* – sweetmeats made from egg yolks. It is a closed order so you never see the nuns. Instead there is a drum in the wall into which you place your order and money. The drum turns and your sweets and change appear.

GRANADA

A narrow lane in Granada's colourful Alcaicería

Granada was the last outpost of Muslim rule in Spain. The Nasrid dynasty reigned from 1238 until Boabdil's defeat in 1492 at the hands of the troops of Fernando and Isabel. Inside the flamboyant Gothic Capilla Real, the royal chapel in Granada, you can see a relief which depicts the defeat of Boabdil as well as the marble mausoleums of the Catholic Monarchs.

The **Alhambra** is the impressive legacy of the Nasrid caliphs. It embodied their concept of paradise and the exquisite workmanship in the series of palaces and the beauty of the courtyards and gardens is enthralling.

When shopping in the town itself below the Alhambra, most people head first for the small shops in the Mercado Arabe of **La Alcaicería**. Look out for ceramics bearing a pomegranate motif; the fruit introduced by the Moors gave the city its name (*granada* is Spanish for pomegranate). **Francisco Rienda**, Cuesta del Chapiz 6, has a good selection of ceramics. Marquetry is still widely practised in Granada, and **Miguel Laguna** (Real de la Alhambra 30) makes and sell items on the premises. **Tienda la Victoria** (Calle Zacatín 21) has a superb collection of old prints, curios and furniture. Around the Gran Vía you will find *platerías* where beautiful silver is sold.

● **Alhambra and Generalife gardens**. Tel: (0958) 227527.

View of the Alhambra's fortress-like exterior, seen from the opposite hillside of El Albaicín

Azulejos in abundance in the Plaza de España

ANDALUCIAN CERAMICS

Pottery, in one form or another, has existed in Spain for over 4,000 years but it was the impact of Arab culture which changed the course of Spanish ceramic art, when the Moors introduced iridescent lustreware – the hallmark of Spanish ceramics. Málaga was producing this gleaming "golden pottery", as it was known, as early as the middle of the 13th century, but later it was made in centres all over Andalucia and up the coast into Murcia and Valencia. Málaga made a speciality of large ornamental vases, 1m (3ft) or more in height, with distinctive "wings" (see page 224). Very few survive.

Traditional glazed earthenware was painted in high-fired colours – bright green, brown, blue and ochre. In addition to tableware and pots in all shapes and sizes, local potters made *macetas*, the attractive plant containers that can be seen in every *patio* around the city, and *azulejos*. These decorative tiles were a highly practical wall and floor covering, easy to clean and cool under foot. Early patterns followed the Muslim restrictions about reproducing the human form and were generally highly intricate geometric designs or carried floral motifs. Later, pictorial scenes became fashionable, and towards the end of the 19th century *azulejo* panels became

Tiled façade of the Fábrica Cerámica Santa Ana

Ceramics and azulejo panels on display in a Triana shop

popular for street signs and shop fronts, and were also used like advertising billboards. One of the most renowned appeared in 1924 to advertise the new model of Studebaker – you can see it in Calle Tetuán.

Traditional and modern studio pieces can be found in abundance and in many places it is possible to watch the potters at work. One of the best places to buy ceramics or *azulejos* is **Cerámica Santa Ana**, Calle San Jorge 31, in the Triana district; another is **Antonio Campos**, at Calle Alfarería 22.

TRIANA

Triana was the traditional gypsy quarter, and generations of flamenco artists and famous bullfighters come from here. Not surprisingly, it is also a good place to go for extravagant flamenco dresses. **Juan Osete**, 12 Calle de Castilla, has a particularly stunning range. You will see Andalucians young and old in their traditional dress at every fiesta.

SEVILLE SILKS

Rich, figured silks, originally imported from the eastern Mediterranean but made in Spain from the 9th century onwards are particularly desirable. Early silks may have been woven

Don Quixote and Sancho Panza in azulejos

The best time to see Sevillanos in all their finery is during the **Feria de Abril**, held shortly after Easter. Families erect elegant marquees by the river and revellers dance into the night. During the day the young men and señoritas parade in traditional costume on superbly turned out horses.

Some flamenco you see can be rather tourist-orientated, but the gypsy bars of Triana often have impromptu performances – you will need to get there very late and be prepared to wait.

For first-class flamenco dancing and singing, attend the **Bienal de Arte Flamenco**, held in even years. Tel: (095) 450 5600 (town hall) for information.

Cristina Hoyos, one of Spain's most famous flamenco dancers

by craftsmen from Baghdad and look very similar to Syrian silks. Following the expulsion of the Moors, there was an influx of weavers from Italy, and later, in the 18th century, many French weavers and designers from Lyon (see page 107) set up workshops in Spain. Some Spanish silks dating from certain periods are quite difficult to distinguish from their Middle Eastern, Italian, and North African counterparts, but Spanish examples are characterized by highly detailed designs and motifs such as birds' wings.

FAIRS AND MARKETS

Look for coins and stamps in the Sunday market held in Plaza del Cabildo. There is also an antiques and bric-a-brac market held on Thursdays in Calle Feria in the northern Macarena district.

A *rastro* – flea market – takes place on Sunday mornings in La Alameda de Hércules. Here you will find anything from from old farm tools to brass ornaments and paintings. A larger *rastro* is held in the Parque Alcosa.

Each spring the **Salón Nacional de Antigüedades** is held in the Palacio de Exposiciones y Congresos. Tel: (095) 446 75140.

AUCTION HOUSE
Antigüedades y Subastas de Sevilla, Calle Carlos Cañal 7. Tel: (095) 421 4182.

Double-spouted vessel decorated with the bold brush strokes typical of Spanish earthenware

WHERE TO EAT AND DRINK
You can easily spend an evening indulging in *tapas*, those delicious small dishes served up with drinks. *Tapas* hot spots are the Barrio de Santa Cruz and Triana. **La Giralda** (Calle Mateos Gago 1) is especially interesting – its vaults are the remains of a Moorish bath. Others well worth a visit include: **Casa Omana** (Plaza Omana), **Bodega la Albariza** (Calle Betis 6) and **El Rinconcillo** (Calle Gerona 2).

Mesón Don Raimundo
Calle Argote de Molina 26
Tel: (095) 422 3355
A former 17th-century convent with antique furniture, tapestries and ceramics. On the menu is Andalucian food at its very best: wild duck, rabbit and partridge from the marshland of the Guadalquivir, and excellent seafood. In addition to "ordinary" wines it has is a list of remarkable *reserva* wines. Very popular, so booking essential.

La Albahaca
Plaza de Santa Cruz 12
Tel: (095) 422 0714
Situated in a 1920s house, the interior is furnished with 17th-century antiques. The food is modern Basque and seasonal. Booking advisable.

Stained-glass window in the Alfonso XIII hotel

Corral del Agua
Callejón del Agua 6
Tel: (095) 422 4841
In summer, tables are set around the fountain in the courtyard of this old Andalucian house. The excellent menu is seasonal and its position, in the heart of the Barrio de Santa Cruz, is ideal.

WHERE TO STAY
Alfonso XIII
San Fernando 2
Tel: (095) 422 2850; Fax: (095) 421 6033
This luxury hotel was built for King Alfonso XIII in 1929 in the Mudéjar style. It has a Moorish interior of stained glass windows and glazed tiles. Bedrooms are decorated in Moorish, Castillian and Classical Baroque styles. It has a typical Sevillian inner courtyard with a fountain.

San Gil
Calle Parras 28
Tel: (095) 490 6811; Fax: (095) 490 6939
This early 1900s mansion was restored with great care and consideration. The original tiled entrance is breathtaking. The bedrooms have charming wrought-iron furniture.

Murillo
Lope de Rueda 7 & 9
Tel: (095) 421 6095; Fax: (095) 421 9616
This antiques-filled town house hotel is situated in the heart of the Barrio de Santa Cruz and close to several antiques shops.

Las Casas de la Judería
Callejón de Dos Hermanas 7
Tel: (095) 441 5150; Fax: (095) 442 2170
This was the house of the Duque de Bejar in the 18th century, and is arranged around a typical inner *patio*. Ideal for the Barrio de Santa Cruz.

LISBON

A relatively small capital with richly decorated palaces and a cosmopolitan outlook, Lisbon introduced Europe to influences from all over the world.

Alfonso II (1211-1223) the third king of Portugal

DESPITE ITS HILLY, COBBLED STREETS, LISBON IS easy to get around. Lovely old wooden trams, a funicular railway and the wonderful *elevador* (vertical lift) that opened in 1902, take much of the legwork out of sightseeing. And there is certainly plenty to see, from the old Moorish quarter with its imposing castle and picturesque whitewashed houses, to the elegant Art Nouveau shops and cafés, and numerous churches, museums and galleries.

The Praça do Comércio beside the River Tagus (Tejo in Portuguese) is surely one of the grandest water gateways to any city, and it gives a hint of the multicultural nature of this former

capital of empire. The sight of Cape Verde women in the fish market brings Africa to mind; the smell of coffee is straight from Brazil; the tea salons a taste of China. Portuguese sailors travelled far and wide to bring back riches from its colonies and to trade with other countries. Huge quantities of porcelain were brought from China, Brazil provided exotic hardwoods as well as coffee and gold, while spices came from India. All these global influences are imbued in Lisbon's way of life, as is the sadness for those who sailed so far from home, recalled in the haunting *fado* songs traditionally sung in bars in the old town. But the city is also bold and exuberant, with great palaces and flamboyant Baroque mansions. Particularly striking are the *azulejos*, beautiful tiles that decorate the inside and outside of buildings; they remain one of the most enduring memories.

The massive Monument to the Discoveries, built in the 1960s

The Blue Room of the Palácio de Ajuda

The **Museu-Escola de Artes Decorativas** in the Palácio Azurra in the Alfama has furniture, silverware, ceramics and textiles spanning five centuries, while a little further east the **Museu Nacional do Azulejo**, in a former convent, has a wonderful collection of Spanish, Dutch and Portuguese tiles dating from the 15th to the 20th century. *Azulejos* are also the highlight of **São Roque**, in the Bairro Alto, the most decorated church in the city, which also has a small but delightful museum of religious art.

The city's grandest building, however, is undoubtedly the **Mosteiro dos Jerónimos** in Belém, begun in 1502, an enormous church built with profits from the pepper and spice trade with India.

PLACES TO VISIT

Lisbon is blessed with a number of good museums which are worth visiting for the grand buildings in which they are housed as much as for their collections.

The most fascinating domestic interiors can be seen in the **Palácio Nacional de Ajuda**, a former royal residence designed in 1802. Its fully furnished period rooms are decorated with original wall and ceiling panelling and fabrics, and there is a cabinet full of Meissen porcelain and a library of rare manuscripts.

The Manueline Mosteiro des Jerónimos

- **Palácio Nacional de Ajuda**, Calçada de Ajuda. Tel: (21) 363 70 95. Closed Wed.
- **Museu-Escola de Artes Decorativas** Largo das Portas do Sol 2. Tel: (21) 881 46 00.
- **Museu Nacional do Azulejo**, Rua de Madre de Deus 4. Tel: (21) 814 77 47.
- **Museu de São Roque**, Largo Trindade Coelho. Tel: (21) 323 50 50.
- **Mosteiro dos Jerónimos**, Praça do Império, Belém. Tel: (21) 362 00 34.

HISTORY REVISITED

A SEAFARING CITY

Most of Lisbon is less than 250 years old. It was almost entirely rebuilt under the energetic leadership of the Marquês de Pombal, chief minister to José I, after a devastating earthquake on 1 November 1755. Among other losses were records of this seafaring city, whose explorers, under Henry the Navigator (1394–1460), set out to discover the world. The few things that remain are kept in the **Museu de Marinha** in the Mosteiro Jerónimos in Belém. From here great navigators such as Vasco da Gama and Ferdinand Magellan set off on their voyages of discovery. By the time of Manuel I (1469–1521) Portugal was Europe's premier naval power. Even its own variety of Gothic architecture, Manueline, reflects nautical themes. Twisted ropes, coral, sea creatures and anchors were all incorporated into such buildings as the **Torre de Belém** and the Mosteiro Jerónimos where it reaches its apogee.

Portugal's influence straddled the world. First conquering the Azores, it went on to collect five African countries and enclaves in India (Goa) and China (Macau). Its colonies greatly influenced its culture, arts and drinking

habits – it brought tea (*chá*) and coffee to Europe. The city's history is told in the **Museu da Cidade** in the 18th-century Palácio Pimenta.

- **Museu de Marinha**, Praça do Império, Belém. Tel: (21) 362 00 10.
- **Torre de Belém**, Tel: (21) 362 00 34.
- **Museu da Cidade,** Campo Grande, 245 Tel: (21) 759 16 17.

The fortified 15th-century Torre de Belém

ANTIQUES IN CONTEXT

Lisbon's old town is spread across several districts, each with its own distinct character. Antiques hunters who enjoy the hustle and bustle of street markets should check out the area around the cathedral. For a more upmarket shops, head for the Bairro Alto.

BAIRRO ALTO

This is where you will find some of the best antiques, principally in Rua Dom Pedro V. **Antiguidades Moncada** at No 34 sells furniture, porcelain and glass; **Galerie da Arcada** at No 56 has religious carvings in stone and wood from the 15th to the 19th century; **Sola**, at Nos 68–70, specializes in *azulejos*; and **Xairel** at No 111 sells regional Portuguese antiques. Old prints, *gravuras*, are sold in second-hand bookshops such as **Livaria Olisipo**, Largo Trindade Coelho 7–8 and **Livraria Artes e Letras**, a few doors away at No 3. In the tiny **O Velho Sapateiro** at Travessa de Queimada 46, you will find bric-a-brac, prints, old postcards and collectables.

If you want to take home something with typically Portuguese flavour, look out for the maiolica wares modelled on fruit, vegetables, animals and sea-life that were made in abundance by the factory of Mafra and Son in the second half of the 19th century. These bold, colourful creations were inspired by the 16th-century ceramics of the Frenchman, Bernard Palissy. Wares are marked with the words "M. MAFRA CALDAS PORTUGAL".

Good quality antiques shops can be found in Rua São Bento near the national parliament, Palácio de São Bento. **Doll's**, at No 250, sells antique dolls and toys, as well as furniture from the 17th century onwards; **Ricardo Hogan** at No 281 has a range of tiles dating from the 16th century. **Brique-a-Bràque de São Bento** at No 342 stocks furniture, silverware and ceramics. Around the corner at Travessa de Santa

The Feira da Ladra and São Vicente

Chinese blue and white vase made for the Portuguese market, c.1552

Quitéria 2, **Baú** has furniture from the 17th to the 19th century and a selection of Art Deco lighting.

CHIADO

A disastrous fire in 1988 destroyed several major department stores, but Chiado remains an important shopping area. Rua de Alacrim is worth exploring for antiques. **Santa Anna**, at No 91, is a ceramics factory with a shop beneath dating from 1749. **Ouriversaria Aliança**, at Rua Garrett 50, has a fine selection of filigree jewellery. At Largo de Chiado 18, you can see Portugal's best-known porcelain, Vista Alegre, being made. Pop in to **Manuscritto Histórico** at Calçado da Sacramento 50, where you will find European manuscripts and prints dating from the 16th century.

ALFAMA

The oldest part of Lisbon, to the east of the Baixa, is centred on the castle and cathedral, or *Sé*. Among several antiques shops in the area are **Antiguidades Outra Era** at Largo Santo António de Sé 15, which specializes in religious art, and **Casa Domingues**, Rua de Santa Marinha 3, which sells silverware, glass and jewellery. Nearby is the Italianate church of São Vicente da Fora, which overlooks the Feira da Ladra (see Markets) and contains the tombs of most of Portugal's monarchs.

The azulejo panels that characterize Lisbon were revived as an art form in the early 20th century

WHEN IN LiSBON...

ARTISANAL WORK

Portugal has a strong regional crafts tradition, *artesanato*, involving wool, lace, gold and silver, as well as ceramics. **Arte Rustica**, Rua Aurea 246-8 in the Baixa and **Pais em Lisboa**, Rua do Reixeria in Bairro Alto are both good places to go for genuine handmade crafts. At Estoril, the main resort on the coast to the west, artisans come from all over the country for a craft fair in July and August.

BAIXA

The busy central district behind the Praço do Comércio is not noted for antiques, but most of its shops are decidedly antiquated, thanks to controlled rents which have kept the same owners and services going for years. Streets are named after their specialist trades – Rua da Prata for silversmiths, Ruo do Ouro for the goldsmiths and jewellers' shops. The many quaint Art Nouveau shopfronts and pavement cafés make it a pleasure just to wander and window-shop here.

FAIRS AND MARKETS

Feira da Ladra, the Thieves' Market, is held in Campo do Santa Clara on Tuesday mornings and Saturdays. There is a lot of junk, but there are bargains to be had here, too. The **Feira Numistica** in the Praço do Comércio is a Sunday morning stamp and coin market. The **Feira do Livro**, an antiquarian book fair, is held from May to June, in either Praço do Comércio or Parque Eduardo VII.

AUCTIONS

In Estrela, to the west of the city, an auction is held every Monday evening at **Cabral Moncada Leilões**, Rua Mag Lup 12l.

Typical Portugeuse ceramic bowls, handpainted with brightly coloured flowers

WHERE TO EAT AND DRINK
Tavarns
Rua Misericórdia 37
Tel: (21) 342 11 12
Dating from 1784, this glittering, gilt-edged restaurant is one of the oldest and most famous in Lisbon.

A Brasileira
Rua Garrett 120
Tel: (21) 346 95 41
Opened in 1895, this Chiado café has long been a favourite with artists and writers.

Tágide
Largo da Academia Nacional de Belas Artes 18–20
Tel: (21) 342 07 20
There's a great view of the river from this restaurant, which is decorated with beautiful 18th-century tiles and has a 17th-century fountain.

Solar do Vinho do Porto
Rua de São Pedro Alcantara 45
Tel: (21) 347 57 07
The venerated Port Institute's base in an 18th-century *solar* (mansion) in the Bairro Alto feels like a club and makes a good meeting place. More than 300 kinds of port can be bought by the glass.

WHERE TO STAY
As Janelas Verdes
Rua das Janelas Verdes 47
Tel: (21) 396 81 43; Fax: (21) 396 81 44
A small, popular hotel in an 18th-century palace, with a wonderful courtyard garden. The lounge is well furnished with antiques. There are only 18 rooms, so book well in advance.

York House
Rua das Janelas Verdes 32
Tel: (21) 396 24 35; Fax: (21) 397 27 93
This 17th-century converted convent has a wonderful atmosphere and is full of charm and character. The tiled restaurant serves good food.

Lapa Palace
Rua Pau de Bandeira 4
Tel: (21) 394 94 94; Fax: (21) 395 06 65
This palatial 19th-century town house in the exclusive Lapa residential district is equipped for business and pleasure and has a good restaurant. The grounds feature a pool and waterfall.

Casa de Quinta Nova da Conceição
Rua Cidade Rabat 5
Tel: (21) 778 00 91; Fax: (21) 772 47 65
A survivor of the 1755 earthquake, this wonderful family mansion is full of original antiques. It only has four rooms, so do book. Closed Aug.

IN THE AREA

Just to the west of the city is the 250-year-old **Palácio Nacional de Queluz**. This former royal palace is now a museum of decorative arts showing the evolution of Portuguese taste from the mid-17th to the early 19th century.

Also close by is the magnificent **Palácio Nacional de Vila de Sintra**, which was the royal summer residence for 600 years. One of the highlights is the profusion of glorious 15th- and 16th-century *azulejos*. The nearby 19th-century **Palácio Nacional de Pena**, is an amazing mock-Gothic fantasy. Inside, the rooms have been left as they were when the royal family fled on the eve of the 1910 revolution.

ITALY

THE ANTIQUES LANDSCAPE

Antiques hunters still get excited about the chance of coming across a little etching by Leonardo or a Botticelli sketchbook. The reality is, as usual, quite different, and hunters should beware of photographs that have been overpainted and even prints that have been photocopied and then slightly tea stained! This caveat apart, Italy is a formidable repository of art. The Renaissance that revolutionized art and architecture in the 15th century is generally agreed to have begun in Florence, and the florid Baroque style embraced by courts all over Europe in the 17th century had its origins here, too. Carlo Bugatti furniture, Gio Ponti ceramics for the Richard-Ginori pottery factory and Alessi lighting are 20th-century names to add to a long artistic tradition.

A 19-century medallion mosaic surrounds a painting of Florence's Piazza della Signoria.

In medieval times, artists and artisans in Italy flourished under the patronage of wealthy rulers who, while so often at war with neighbouring city-states, at home provided commissions that encouraged a flowering of all the arts, from painting and sculpture to pottery and glass. Faenza, one of the earliest pottery centres, gave its name to faience – tin-glazed earthenware or maiolica – and through the 15th and 16th centuries towns the length of the peninsula were producing their own distinct styles of faience in huge numbers. Names such as Cafaggiolo, Montelupo, Deruta (see page 250) and Naples were joined in the 18th century by Le Nove, Bassano, Turin, Milan and others. By the 19th century many factories were replicating early works – particularly esteemed are pieces from Le Nove and the Florentine factory of Cantagalli.

Italian collectables are often more highly regarded – and therefore more expensive – outside Italy, so look out for train sets by Elettren and Biaggi, Ingap's tinplate toys from the 1920s and Lenci dolls with their pressed-felt faces, especially those dressed in national costumes.

Italy offers antiques hunters far more than the few places I have included in this section: Milan and, especially, Turin, have a large number of antiques dealers, and Bologna, Modena and Ravenna in Emiglia-Romana are also thriving centres. If you are travelling between Venice and Florence, a small detour to Ferrara, with its castle that was once home to Lucrezia Borgia, is well worthwhile. Naples, in the southern region of Campania, is also a well-established antiques centre.

Also in the south, Calabria has one or two larger cities that are worth visiting – Reggio di Calabria and Cosenza. One advantage of this region, referred to as the toe of Italy's boot, is that it remains largely overlooked by tourism and has, so far, avoided the overcrowding suffered in so many other cities, where there are often long queues for famous buildings. In some cities you can avoid these by booking a local guide and asking for a visit before opening time or after hours; others offer advance ticket booking which, for a price, gets you in without queuing. And, just as hotel concierges can get you into any opera or top restaurant even if fully booked, they also often know where to find that special antique you are looking for. Yes, they do get commission, but look on this as part of the dealer's advertising budget; you don't pay any more.

Arlequino is the best recognized character from the Commedia dell'Arte, and a popular figure for reproducing in ceramics.

ROME

Mother of one of the world's great empires, Rome is a city where art and craftsmanship have always been prized.

A 16th-century istoriato maiolica plate from Urbino

TRADITION SAYS THAT ROME WAS FOUNDED by the twins Romulus and Remus in 753BC, but in fact the first settlement was here around 1200BC, and the Etruscan Tarquinius was ruling here in the 7th century BC. When the Etruscans were expelled in 509BC, the new Republic was founded, and by the beginning of the Christian era, Rome ruled over an empire stretching from Britain to North Africa and into Asia Minor. By the end of the 5th century, barbarians had brought the failing empire to its knees, but Rome's classical sites attract millions of tourists.

As traffic swirls around the massive Monumento Vittorio Emanuele II, dubbed the typewriter or the wedding cake, you may feel that life in Rome is frenetic, but Romans are skilled in the art of *far niente* (doing nothing), and some of the greatest pleasures in Rome are simply strolling the streets of the historic centre, or Trastevere, where "true" Romans are said to live.

Gold aureus (coin) of the Emperor Diocletian (c. AD284–305) and a Roman wine jug, 2nd–3rd century AD

CLASSICAL ROME

Despite centuries of abuse, Rome's ancient monuments are an irresistible draw. The **Foro Romano**, once the heart of Roman life, has been much built over, but he **Colosseum**, where 60,000 spectators flocked for lavish entertainments, is still awe-inspiring. Its name came, not directly from its size, but after a giant statue of Nero (c.AD54–68) that once stood here, part of the megalo-maniac emperor's fantastic golden house, **Domus Aurea**.

● **Colosseum**. (Tel: (06) 700 4261). **Foro Romano**: Closed Tues and Sun pm. **Domus Aurea**. (Tel: (06) 85 30 17 58). Closed Tues.

Restoring the frescoes of the Sistine Chapel

GOD'S ARTIST

As a boy Michelangelo Buonarotti (1475–1564) trained in Florence, but many of his greatest works, commissioned by a succession of popes, are in Rome. An early sculpture under papal patronage is the graceful Pietà that stands just inside St Peter's, created for the notorious Borgia Pope, Alexander VI. In San Pietro in Vincoli stand three huge statues he sculpted for the tomb of Julius II. Looking at the imperious Moses one can only guess at the memorial that Michelangelo envisaged for his patron; sadly, it was not finished.

The ceiling frescoes of the Vatican's Sistine Chapel, which Michelangelo began in 1508, had to be painted while he was lying on his back. Despite this difficulty he succeeded in conveying a concept that pervades his work: that the divine beauty of God is symbolized by the earthly beauty of the human body. His *Last Judgement* for the west wall, a powerful yet dark work reflecting the misery he saw in the world about him, was not completed until 1541. Now these masterpieces are restored, it's worth hiring a guide to get in before the crowds.

● **San Pietro in Vincoli**. Tel (06) 488 2865.
● **St. Peter's/Vatican Museums**: Tel: (06) 698 8333. Entrance to basilica free; museums open am only Nov–Apr. Closed Sun except last Sun of month when admission is free.

PLACES TO VISIT

As architect of St Peter's from 1629 on, and the most popular artist of his time, **Gianlorenzo Bernini** (1598–1680) transformed Rome. His churches, palaces and fountains can be seen all over the city, from the colonnades that ring the Piazza San Pietro in front of St Peter's to the ebullient Fontana dei Quattro Fiumi in Piazza Navona.

The **Villa Borghese**, built in 1613, was designed originally as a summer retreat for Cardinal Scipione Borghese, Bernini's patron. It houses many renowned sculptures, including Antonio Canova's semi-nude statue (1805–1807) of the infamous Pauline Borghese, Napoleon's scandal-prone sister.

Another great art collection belongs to the illustrious Doria-Pamphilj family, and in the privately owned **Galleria Pamphilj** you can see, among others, Tintorettos, Titians and Caravaggios. Velázquez's portrait of Pope Innocent X captures exactly his weak and suspicious nature –

Baroque figure in Fontana del Moro, Piazza Navona

Canova's elegant marble of Pauline Bonaparte Borghese as Venus

on seeing it the subject himself is supposed to have commented "too true, too true". Some rooms have particular themes: the Saletta Verde is Venetian in style and the Saletta Azzura is hung with 19th-century family portraits. It is worth paying for a tour which takes you into rooms normally closed to the public.

Of the many specialist collections in Rome, one of the most individual is the **Museo degli Strumenti Musicale**. Exhibits here cover musical instruments from every era, from ancient Greek *auloi* (whistles) to a rare early form of piano built by the harpsichord-maker Bartolomeo Cristofori in 1722. There are curiosities, too, such as travelling harps designed to stand on cobbles.

Rome's expatriate community of writers and artists is remembered in the **Museo Keats-Shelley**, a library and museum furnished as the romantic poets knew it. It was in this house that John Keats died on 23 January 1821, aged only 25.

● **Villa Borghese**, Piazzale Scipione Borghese 5. Tel: (06) 841 7645. Closed Mon. Advance reservation essential.
● **Galleria Pamphilj**, Piazza del Collegio Romano. Tel: (06) 679 7323. Closed Thurs.
● **Museo degli Strumenti Musicale**, Piazza Sta Croce. Tel: (06) 701 4796. Open am only.
● **Museo Keats-Shelley**, Piazza di Spagna. Tel: (06) 678 4235.

SHOPPING

Window of an antique shop in via dei Coronari

Two of the major areas for antiques shopping in Rome are the Centro Storico, between Piazza Navona and the river, and just east of via del Corso, between Piazza del Popolo and the Spanish Steps.

CENTRO STORICO

Now bisected by the broad and busy Corso Vittorio Emanuele II, the triangular historical centre is bounded on two sides by the River Tiber. Via dei Coronari and via Giulia and the streets between them are rewarding hunting grounds.

Look out for:
Antiqua Res (via dei Coronari 32) has a broad selection of furniture and paintings, as well as bronzes and porcelain. **Pietro Talone**, further along at No 135, stocks lights and lamps from ornate Baroque to angular Art Deco.

Art Deco and Stile Liberty (the Italian term for Art Nouveau) remain popular: check out **L'Art Nouveau** at No 221, and **Tempi Moderni** at via del Governo Vecchio 108.

For striking jewellery, the artisans' studios around via Giulia and Campo de'Fiori still turn out beautiful pieces. **Mosaicum**, at via della Scrofa 113, also has antique jewellery.

AROUND PIAZZA DI SPAGNA

In the 18th and 19th centuries, many artists and writers settled in the vicinity of Scalinata di Spagna, the Spanish Steps. Goethe, Lord Byron and John Keats all patronized the Caffè Greco (see Where to Eat and Drink opposite), and in the piazza itself are Babington's Tea Rooms, started by two English spinsters in 1896 and still going strong. This is the place to go when you need a good cup of tea and don't care what it costs.

As via Condotti and via Borgognana are to fashion, so **via del Babuino** and **via Margutta** are to antiques – the best. Minimalism prevails: with one simple artefact arranged elegantly in a dealer's window, window dressing becomes an art form, and window shopping like visiting a picture gallery. Along via del Babuino, which runs from Piazza di Spagna up to Piazza del Popolo, you will find the finest furniture, paintings and *objets d'art*.

Look out for:
Soligo (via del Babuino 161) specializes in military antiques and medals, such as those from Garibaldi's campaigns, while **Moretti**, at No 95, has beautiful antique scientific and astronomical instruments.

Dish designed by Piero Fornasetti (1913–88)

The parallel via Margutta is a narrow street where you will find a number of specialists in rugs and hangings, from Flemish tapestries to Oriental carpets. You will also find paintings here, including 19th-century oils and watercolours, and eastern art. **Galleria 1900**, at via Vittoria 37, is another good shop for Stile Liberty.

For jewellery, look in on **Petocchi** (Piazza di Spagna), which supplied members of Italy's royal family from 1861 to 1946. **Peroso** (via Sistina 29) was founded in 1891 and stocks classical antique jewellery.

SPECIALIST SHOPS

Several shops specialize in old and fine paper and associated objects; this is where to bring a valuable book if it needs rebinding. **Il Sigillo** (via Giulia 69) has paper, fine pens and a wide variety of objects covered in the typically Italian marbled papers, as does **Poggi** (via del Gesù 74). Go to **Casali** (piazza della Rotonda 81a) or **Nordecchia** (Piazza Navona 25) for old prints and engravings.

Carlo Bugatti chair (1902) with distinctive beaten copper detailing

---

SHOPPER'S TIP

Roman antiquities, both genuine and fake, are for sale everywhere in Rome. Prices, even for something you would expect to be rare and precious, such as a 2000-year-old Roman glass vase, are surprisingly reasonable, so don't assume that an affordable piece is necessarily a copy, but do get the necessary certification (see Useful Addresses at the end of the book).

TERME DI CARACALLA

In ancient Rome, citizens came not only to bathe in the public baths, but to relax and learn the latest news as they progressed through the *calidarium*, *tempidarium*, *frigidarium* and *natatio*. The most finely preserved today are the Caracalla Baths, completed AD217, which could accommodate more than 1,500 bathers at a time. Viale delle Termi di Caracalla. Tel: (06) 575 8302.

Unsurprisingly, the Eternal City of St Peter is noted for religious objects, from crucifixion paintings to Baroque carved Madonnas in search of a new home. The shops in the vicinity of the Vatican attract too many tourists for keen prices, so look instead in via di Porta Angelica (just outside the Vatican) and around the Pantheon in via del Cestari.

OTHER HUNTING GROUNDS

For maiolica, visit **Bottegantica** at via di San Simone 70. **Fantasia**, at via Barberini 69, is the place to go for a range of antiques, from furniture to silver and jewellery.

FAIRS AND MARKETS

The Sunday flea market at Porta Portese, in Trastevere, claims to be the largest in Europe. It attracts a wide range of dealers, although genuine antiques will have a high price tag.

AUCTION HOUSES

La Casa d'Aste Babuino, via dei Greci 2/a. Tel: (06) 361 1743.
Finarte: via Margutta 54. Tel: (06) 320 7679.
Gallerie L'Antonina: piazza Mignarelli 23. Tel: (06) 679 2064 or 679 4009.

A stall at the huge flea market which is held every weekend at Porta Portese

WHERE TO STAY

Being a city of pilgrimage adds to the problem of finding a reasonably priced hotel in Rome.

The elegance of the Aldrovandi Palace

Aldrovandi Palace
Via Aldrovandi 15
Tel: (06) 322 3993;
Fax: (06) 322 1435
This 19th-century *palazzo* is set in its own little park beside the Borghese Gardens. It has elegant antique furnishings – and a swimming pool.

Lord Byron
Via de Notaris 5
Tel: (06) 322 0404;
Fax: (06) 322 0405
Small and exclusive, this has a regular clientele who return faithfully, so book ahead. The rooms are full of antiques and its restaurant, Le Jardin, is renowned for Italian specialities.

Hassler-Villa Medici
Piazza Trinita dei Monti 6
Tel: (06) 678 2651; Fax: (06) 678 9991
One of Rome's best, and best-located, hotels, with a fantastic view of St Peter's from the rooftop restaurant. In fair weather the courtyard becomes a breakfast room and traditional afternoon tea is served in the cosy Salone Eva in winter.

WHERE TO EAT AND DRINK

Checchino dal 1887
Via Monte Testaccio 30
Tel: (06) 574 3816
You need a large appetite to do justice to the Roman cuisine of this Michelin-starred restaurant that, as its name records, has been running since 1887. Closed Sun and Mon.

Caffè Greco
Via Condotti 86
Tel: (06) 679 1700
This café opened in the early 1700s and was last redecorated in 1860. You don't come here for the overpriced food (or the snail-slow service) but to sit where Casanova flirted, Mad King Ludwig of Bavaria raved and Keats coughed. Closed Sun.

Antic Pesa
Via Garibaldi 18
Tel: (06) 580 9236
The Antic Pesa now serves traditional classical food, but it was orginally established, in what had been a convent in the 17th century, as a sort of soup kitchen providing basic sustenance for the many peasants who came to the Customs Office in nearby via Garibaldi. It has a wonderful indoor garden.

The **Villa d'Este** at Tivoli, about an hour's drive east of Rome, is lovely by day or night. The original gardens were laid out in 1550 by Cardinal Ippolito d'Este, son of Lucretia Borgia and the Duke of Ferrara, and provided the inspiration for the water gardens of many Roman villas. More than 3,000 fountains, some sculpted by Bernini, cool the air and the Avenue of 100 Fountains is fabulous.

Natural springs feed the pools and baths of the nearby **Villa Adriana**, built for Emperor Hadrian (AD76–138). The latest archeological finds from the extensive site are exhibited in the Antiquarium, which was recently renovated.

FLORENCE

With a cityscape that looks much as it did during the Renaissance, Florence remains one of Europe's greatest cultural destinations.

Painting of Piazza della Signoria within 19th-century mosaic tondo

FROM AN OBSCURE SETTLEMENT ON THE BANKS OF THE ARNO, Florentia grew in strength and, in 1125, defeated its rival, Fiesole. Further Tuscan towns fell in its path and in an era of shifting alliances, political intrigue (this was the birthplace of Niccolò Macchiavelli) and the rise and fall of city-states, Florence established itself as a rising star.

Bolstered by banking and manufacturing, the city grew in stature until the Florentine court became one of the most glittering and important in Europe. Patrician families such as the Albizzi, the Ricci and the Strozzi grew rich, and the Medici family climbed to supremacy to rule in one form or another from the 14th through to the middle of the 18th century.

In the 18th century it became the custom for well-to-do young men to take an extended Grand Tour of Europe. In Florence they found a pleasing lifestyle and a ruling class that greatly supported the arts. With Italian unification in the 19th century, it was the Florentine language as used by Dante that provided the model for modern Italian, which helped boost the city as a capital of culture.

Florence remains a treasury of art, and anyone visiting this city will be overwhelmed by its wealth of paintings, sculpture and architecture. It is also a city of great beauty. The skyline is dominated by Filippo Brunelleschi's dome, one of the greatest engineering feats of all time, which is best seen from the Piazzale Michelangelo in Oltrarno, amid a sea of red roof tiles.

The Florence skyline, unmistakably defined by Brunelleschi's magnificent dome

HISTORY REVISITED

THE MEDICI DYNASTY

The Medici ruled Florence and, later, Tuscany between 1434 and 1737, during which time they produced four popes (Leo X, Clement VII, Pius IV and Leon XI) and two French queens: Catherine and Marie.

Descendants of Tuscan peasants from Cafaggiolo in the Mugello, north of Florence, it was not until Giovanni di Bicci (1360–1429) inherited the family cloth-making and banking businesses that the Medici began to gain status. They became established members of Florentine nobility during the 13th and 14th centuries and remain possibly the greatest patrons of the arts the West has ever seen.

Giovanni's two sons – Cosimo the Elder, known as *il Vecchio* (1389–1464) and Lorenzo (1394–1440) – each became the head of a long line of Medici, among whom two stand out as remarkable.

Known as *il Magnifico*, Lorenzo II (1449–92), was the grandson of Cosimo *il Vecchio*. A poet and patron of many artists, Lorenzo was the epitome of the Renaissance in both his philosphy and in politics. He was responsible for a collection of

Secret journals of the Medici Bank, with medallions and florins

classical sculpture in the Medici Garden near San Marco, where pieces included works by Andrea de Verrocchio and Sandro Botticelli. Lorenzo II is buried in the **Cappelle Medicee**, commissioned in 1520 by his nephew Cardinal Giulio de' Medici. The work of Michelangelo, the chapels form part of the Medici family church, **San Lorenzo**, the interior of which was designed by Brunelleschi in the early 15th century.

Forty years after Lorenzo's death Florence saw another great Medici,

Cameos of Lorenzo Il Magnifico (left) and Cosimo I

Cosimo I (great-great-grandson to Lorenzo I). He came to power at the age of 17 in 1537, and it was under him that the Medici ruled over not just Florence, but most of Tuscany as well.

As a patron of the arts Cosimo I employed Giorgio Vasari to design a building to house all of government administration. These **Uffizi** (offices) are now home to the incredible Medici collection of art, with works by Titian, Botticelli, Leonardo da Vinci, Caravaggio, Fra Filippo Lippi and Paolo Uccello among many others.

In order to see the power and wealth of the family, visit the **Palazzo Pitti**. Originally built by the Pitti family in 1460, the palace was sold to Cosimo I in 1549. Among the collections within the palace building are many Medici treasures and several rooms remain almost intact.

● **Cappelle Medicee**, Piazza di Madonna degli Aldobrandini. Tel: (055) 238 8602. Closed 1st, 3rd, 5th Mon of each month.

● **San Lorenzo**, Piazza San Lorenzo. Tel: (055) 28 60 78.

● **Galleria degli Uffizi**, Piazzale degli Uffizi 6. Tel: (055) 23885. Closed Mon.

● **Palazzo Pitti**, Piazza Pitti. Tel: (055) 265171.

Europe's first soft-paste porcelain, known as Medici porcelain, was made c.1575–78. Only about 60 examples survive

ANTIQUES IN CONTEXT

Florence is credited as the birthplace of the Renaissance. Countless museums and churches are bursting with works from this remarkable era of creative excellence.

Small 17th-century cabinet decorated in pietre dure, gilt and ivory. The top recess is lined with bargello-patterned paper (see page 247)

THE RENAISSANCE

Literally meaning "rebirth", this movement in European art of the 15th and 16th centuries saw artists seeking to recreate classical ancient Roman and Greek forms. Among the first great Renaissance artists were three Florentines: the architect Brunelleschi, the sculptor Donatello and the artist Masaccio.

Filippo Brunelleschi (1377–1446) is best known for the dome of the **Duomo Santa Maria del Fiore** in the 1430s. The design defied all normal construction techniques and the cupola's story is recorded at the **Museo dell'Opera del Duomo**.

Donato di Betto Bardi (1386–1466), known as Donatello, the most accomplished and influential sculptor of his time; his bronze *David* (*c.*1430) was the first Renaissance free-standing nude. Among the statues in the Piazza della Signoria you can see his *Judith and Holofernes*, and he also sculpted the statues for the niches of the Duomo's belfry, designed by Giotto in 1334.

Masaccio (1401–28), whose real name was Tomaso Guidi, was among the first artists to

adopt Brunelleschi's theories on perspective. The **Brancacci Chapel** of the church of Santa Maria del Carmine has a famed series of frescoes, largely by Masaccio, which are some of the finest examples of depth of field and three-dimensionality in Renaissance art.

One of the most illustrious artists of the Renaissance was sculptor, goldsmith and writer Benvenuto Cellini (1500–71). Prosecuted for fighting and killing a rival goldsmith in Rome, in 1523, he was condemned to death, but was absolved by Pope Paul III. Unable to stay out of trouble, Cellini moved from Rome to Florence and back again. He even spent some time in prison.

Tuscan ceramic vase in the Museo del Bargello

When Cellini returned to Florence in the 1550s he was welcomed by Cosimo I and entrusted with commissions for sculpture. His best-known work is the bronze *Perseus* (1554) which stands in the **Loggia dei Lanzi** in the Piazza della Signoria.

Many of Florence's Renaissance treasures can be seen in the **Museo del Bargello** (built 1255), which in 1865 became one of Italy's first national museums. It has entire rooms dedicated to Italy's top sculptors: Donatello's *David* is here.

● **Museo dell'Opera del Duomo**, Piazza del Duomo 9. Tel: (055) 230 2885. Closed Sun.
● **Museo Nazionale del Bargello**, Via del Proconsolo 4. Tel: (055) 238 8606. Closed Mon.
● **Brancacci Chapel**, Piazza del Carmine. Tel: (055) 238 2195. Closed Tues.

PLACES TO VISIT

The Gothic church of Santa Maria Novella is part of a large complex of buildings. One of them, with its entrance in the large cloister, is the **Farmacia di Santa Maria Novella**, the pharmaceutical workshop set up by the Dominican friars who built the church from 1279 to 1357. Herbs were cultivated in the gardens here as early as 1381 and used to produce a range of medicinal remedies. The old pharmacy equipment is on display in cabinets in the original rooms.

Interior of the pharmacy of the Dominican friars of Santa Maria Novella

The **Museo dell'Opificio delle Pietre Dure** is dedicated to the Medici-funded factory, which produced mosaics and hard-stone furniture for the Dukes of Florence from 1588 to the end of the 19th century. The rooms demonstrate the tools and techniques used and house a collection of marble and precious stones dating from the Medici era.

Frederick Stibbert was an English traveller and collector who, on his death in 1906, left his treasure-filled villa to the city. The 60 rooms of the **Museo Stibbert** are redolent of the lands he visited and the breadth of his interests: 17th-century Flemish still-lifes and 18th-century carved Italian chests; eastern costumes, silver ewers used by Stibbert himself and lace collars. There are arms and armour from all periods and all origins, and in the Sala della Cavalcata is massed an entire cavalcade of European and more exotic knights on armoured horseback.

For anyone interested in Michelangelo, a trip to Florence would be incomplete without a visit to the **Galleria dell'Accademia**. You will find all of his most important works here, including – perhaps the most famous – his statue of *David* (1504), which brought him recognition as the leading sculptor of his time.

There is a copy of *David* in the Piazza della Signoria, where it joins several other works in an outdoor exhibition. Among the superb statues here are Cellini's *Perseus* and Donatello's *Il Marcozzo* (heraldic lion). Also in the square are the Loggia dei Lanzi and the **Palazzo Vecchio**. Originally built in 1322, the latter underwent considerable remodelling under the Grand Duke Cosimo I. Vasari undertook most of the work, and created

Cellini's Perseus, *looking out over Piazza della Signoria*

frescoes to celebrate Cosimo's victory over Tuscany.

While visiting Palazzo Pitti in Oltrarno (see page 243), don't miss the Renaissance **Giardino di Boboli**, open to all since 1766.

● **Farmacia di Santa Maria Novella**, Piazza del Santa Maria Novella. Tel: (055) 7216276.

● **Museo dell'Opificio delle Pietre Dure**, Via degli Alfani 78. Tel: (055) 2651357. Closes at 2pm except Tues.

● **Museo Stibbert**, Via F. Stibbert 26. Tel: (055) 475520.

● **Galleria dell'Accademia**, Via Ricasoli 60. Tel: (055) 215449. Closed Mon.

● **Palazzo Vecchio**, Piazza della Signora. Tel: (055) 276 8465. Closed Thurs. and Sun.

● **Giardino di Boboli**, Piazza de' Pitti. Tel: (055) 218741.

Some of varied armorial collection of the Villa Stibbert

FLORENTINE JEWELLERY

During Renaissance times, it was not unusual for artists also to be jewellers and goldsmiths. Cellini was both sculptor and goldsmith, as were Luca della Robbia and Sandro Botticelli in the generation before him. Florence produced some superb jewellery, particularly gold set with precious and semi-precious stones.

A Medici daughter sent abroad for a dynastic marriage would take with her a chest full of jewellery; finely worked pieces set with precious stones and designed to show off Florence's wealth and power. Aristocratic families would have cameo artists carve their portraits to be sent to foreign princes. At home, everyone wore impressive jewels, which can be seen in portraits in the city's galleries. The Treasury of the Palazzo Pitti has wonderful examples of Renaissance jewellery, such as a display of *galanterie*, tokens of esteem from gentlemen to ladies.

Reliquary pendant, c.1600

Red and pink were favourite colours, so rubies, coral and cameos were extremely popular. Florentine artists also perfected the art of *vermiculatum*, tiny mosaic scenes to be mounted on brooches and rings.

A 14th-century cameo in a jewelled gold setting

SHOPPING

It is customary in much of Florence for a workplace to occupy the ground floor of a building, with the family that runs the business to live above it. The buildings are exquisite and, when looking for antiques here, take time to look at the shops themselves. Many are of architectural interest and some are older than the goods they display.

THE PONTE VECCHIO

The most established antiques dealers are clustered around the **Ponte Vecchio**. When it was built in 1345, it was common for traders to set up their stalls on bridges – often the only access into a town and therefore a guarantee of good business. Trade has continued on the bridge one way or another since that time and today jewellery shops and goldsmiths are a particular feature, many of them having been here for centuries. The bridge has become a major tourist attraction, however, so be prepared for crowds.

Look out for:
Carlo Carnevali (Borgo San Jacopo 64) overlooks the Arno with a great view of the Ponte Vecchio. He stocks furniture, paintings and sculpture from the 16th to 18th centuries, as well as antique clothing and small *objets* in glass, amber and ivory that once graced *cabinets de curiosité*.

Luzzetti Antichita, (Borgo San Jacopo 28a) stocks art and has stupendous paintings on gold backgrounds. The shop itself is in an ancient tower dating from 1208.

Romanelli (Lungarno degli Acciamoli 72–78) once housed Lorenzo Ghiberti's workshops. The shop deals in marble statues, and has done so since 1860. The company owns thousands of antique plaster casts, and sells bronzes as well as smaller items in marble and semi-precious stones.

Doccia porcelain hunting scene, 18th century

Arlequino, from the Commedia dell'Arte tradition (Meissen, c.1739)

Antiquariato Teglia (Via dei Bardi 27) is in a 16th-century building with carved stone floors that betray its origins as a carriage house. Here Marco and Luca Teglia restore and sell furniture from the 17th to 19th centuries, as well as rare musical instruments.

Jazz figurines made in Milan, 1920s

Volterrani & Raddi (Piazza del Pesce 7) sells hand-crafted Florentine jewellery and silverware, and their specialities include gold engravings and semi-precious stones. **G. Ugolini** (Lungarno degli Acciaiuoli, 66–70) have received awards for their traditional Florentine mosaics and marble inlay. The shop, crowded with tools, finished pieces and boxes of semi-precious stones, is a delight. **Gimar di Bacci** (Via Lambertesca 22) specializes in Florentine antiques, including bronzes, Etruscan art, ceramics, lamps and marble.

AROUND VIA MAGGIO

Across the river in Oltrarno, this area is also a good place for antiques.

Look out for:
Antichità Chelini (Via Maggio 28a), specializes in 15th- and 16th-century antiques. The shop has impressive vaulted ceilings, terracotta tiled floors and Florentine greystone doorways.

Antichita G. Bartolozzi (Via Maggio 18a) was founded in 1887 by the great-grandfather of the present owner and every night the original wooden shutters are used to close up the shop. Here you will find furniture, pottery, tapestries, paintings and sculpture from the 14th to 18th centuries.

The 16th-century *palazzo* at Via Maggio 42 is used as a showroom for **Turchi-Oggetti Antichi**'s Oriental antiques; business is conducted a few doors away (Via Maggio 50). Eleonora and Bruno **Botticelli** (Via Maggio 45) deal in medieval and Renaissance statuary and 17th-century furniture.

Florence's bridge of shops, the Ponte Vecchio, which has spanned the Arno since the 14th century

OTHER HUNTING GROUNDS
The streets that radiate out from Piazza Carlo Goldoni – **Via dei Fossi** and **Borgo Ognissanti** – are excellent places to look for Tuscan-style furniture from the 16th to 18th centuries, including splendid paintings, chests and holy vessels.

Look out for:
Top-quality antiques can be found at **Neri** (Via Fosse 55–57). **Fallani Best** (Borgo Ognissanti 15) specializes in Art Nouveau and Art Deco.

Mid 18th-century cameo brooch

ANTIQUES FAIR
Every other autumn, in odd-numbered years, Florence hosts the **Mostra Mercato Internazionale Biennale dell'Antiquariato**. This is the oldest antiques fair in Italy, and the most important, and the event attracts prestigious antiques dealers from Italy and the rest of Europe, selling a splendid and wide variety of antiques. It is held in the marvellously opulent 17th- century Palazzo Corsini on Lungarno Corsini – Tel: (055) 282635 for information.

MARKET
On the last Sunday of each month the Piazza dei Ciompi is the site of a flea market that attracts more than 80 stallholders.

Marble-topped table in carved maple, 19th century

WHERE TO EAT AND DRINK
Enoteca Pinchiorri
Via Ghibellina 87
Tel: (055) 242777
This magnificent Renaissance *palazzo* is reputedly the most expensive restaurant in Florence and my favourite. Proprietor Giorgio Pinchiorri has 150,000 bottles in his cellar.

Dino
Via Ghibellina 51
Tel: (055) 241452
A charming restaurant with vaulted ceilings on this 14th-century square in Santa Croce. It is famous for a number of signature dishes and its well-stocked cellar.

La Mossacce
Via del Proconsolo 55
Tel: (055) 294361
Great for lunch after the Bargello. The restaurant has been here for one hundred years, and serves authentic Tuscan food.

WHERE TO STAY
Helvetia e Bristol
Via dei Pescioni 2
Tel: (055) 287814; Fax: (055) 288353
A dignified hotel with superb service, this 18th-century *palazzo* has retained many features, including a stained-glass dome.

Hotel Regency
Piazza Massimo d'Azeglio 3
Tel: (055) 245247; Fax: (055) 234 6735
When Florence was Italy's capital for a short time in the 1860s, this was one of the villas built as private residences for ministers. Now turned into a small luxury hotel, it is furnished with 19th-century antiques and has a private garden.

Grand Hotel Villa Medici
Via il Prato
Tel: (055) 238 1331;
Fax: (055) 238 1336
Once an 18th-century nobleman's palace, this hotel has the luxury, in this busy city, of being surrounded by its own gardens. There is a swimming pool and the elegant rooms are filled with antiques. Don't miss the superb ceilings.

Grand Hotel Villa Medici

Hotel Excelsior
Piazza d'Ognissanti 3
Tel: (055) 264201; Fax: (055) 210278
The main rooms of this early 19th-century former *palazzo* contain marble floors, statues, superb tapestries, stained glass and frescoes.

IN THE AREA

Before the rise of Rome, **Fiesole**, which is 8km (5 miles) north of Florence, was a major Etruscan town. In the 14th century, Franciscan friars built a convent here and began to amass what is today one of the most important collections of Chinese bronzes extant in Italy. You can see it in the Museo Missionario.

The **Villa San Michele** in Fiesole is the ultimate in luxury, but when the building was a monastery designed by Michelangelo, what do you expect? Listed as an Italian monument, it is a haven set in the middle of its park, with antiques furnishing every room. A shuttle bus goes into Florence. Tel: (055) 567 8200; Fax: (055) 567 8250.

TUSCANY & UMBRIA

From Puccini's house in Lucca to the monthly antiques market in Arezzo, this is a wonderful region for antiques lovers to explore, and home to much of Italy's maiolica.

Flag of a competing contrada at Siena's annual Palio

EVEN FOR THE FIRST-TIME VISITOR, the countryside of Tuscany and Umbria, punctuated by the dark verticals of poplars and terracotta-roofed hill towns, is familiar, for there are rural views here that haven't changed since Renaissance artists painted the landscape 500 years ago.

During the 5th and 7th centuries BC the Etruscans, who gave their name to Tuscany, flourished in the hills around what is now Florence, but their strongholds were gradually absorbed into the relentlessly expanding Roman Empire. So close to

San Gimignano depicted in a 16th-century fresco of towns under Medici control, on the walls of the Villa Medici, Rome

Rome itself, the region was at the heart of the Empire, but it was at Lake Trasimeno, on the borders of Tuscany and Umbria, that the Roman army suffered one of its worst defeats. In 217BC, Hannibal ambushed them here and 16,000 soldiers perished in Trasimeno's marshes.

The rulers of the medieval city-states that arose later were influential patrons of the arts. To help secure their place in heaven, they employed the best architects, sculptors, painters and mosaicists to build and decorate religious buildings. This was where Giotto di Bondone, Fra Angelico and Piero della Francesca all created their masterpieces. Drive along the coast and the "snow" you see on the mountain tops marks the quarries of Carrara. Sculptors from Michelangelo to Henry Moore used marble from here, and you can visit the mills and workshops.

Early 16th-century maiolica plate from Cafaggiola

Umbria is Tuscany's less frequented "gentler sister". Arezzo and the wine-making town of Orvieto, in particular, have become centres for antiques and are excellent places to look for the local ceramics for which the whole area is known.

Map showing Tuscany & Umbria region with locations: Arno, Tevere, GUBBIO, FIRENZE (FLORENCE), AREZZO, PERUGIA, ASSISI, CORTONA, DERUTA, Lago Trasimeno, SPOLETO, LUCCA, SIENA, TERNI, SAN GIMIGNANO, MONTEPULCIANO, ORVIETO, PISA, Rome, Lago di Bolsena

HISTORY REVISITED

EARLY TUSCANY AND UMBRIA

In the Middle Ages the Lombards, Germanic tribesmen from the Danube valley, descended in the wake of the Goths, and established a dukedom at Spoleto. Charlemagne annexed the area and installed margraves (military governors). Their rule enabled the church to gain power and build religious houses, laying foundations for a superb cultural heritage.

During the 13th and 14th centuries, the area was a battleground between the Guelphs (who supported the Pope) and the Ghibellines (for the Emperor). The last margrave, Countess Matilda, died in 1115. She left her vast estate to the papacy, which stirred up Guelph and Ghibelline factions. While the Ghibellines brooded behind castle walls, the Guelph party was made up of the rising middle class, who wanted greater control over public affairs. You can still tell from a wall's crenellations which faction a castle or town supported. Swallow tails (with curved V tops) signified Guelph territory, and squared-off teeth-like crenellations indicated Ghibelline support.

Florence was Guelph, so Siena and Pisa supported the Ghibellines, but in some towns, such as San Gimignano, loyalties were split between areas or even families. Being on the pilgrimage route to Rome and a centre of the Knights Templar, San Gimignano had become a prosperous town. During this era of civil strife the rival Guelph Ardingelli and Ghibelline Salvucci families built increasing numbers of fortified towers, each trying to outdo the other, and the town became known as San Gimignano delle Belle Torre. Thirteen of the original 80 towers still stand, giving the town its very distinctive skyline.

In 1299 Dante made an impassioned plea in San Gimignano for solidarity among the Guelph towns, but the families continued to build further towers and destroy each other's until, in 1311, the ruling body of the Podestà imposed a limit on the height of towers. Salvucci retaliated by building twin towers. Squabbles, plague and war sapped the town and its citizens petitioned Florence to take over.

As a result the Medici dominated much of the rest of the region from the 15th to the 18th century, with independent city-states gradually becoming absorbed into the Papal States until Italian unification in the 1860s.

Perugia, Orvieto, Siena and numerous smaller towns have fabulous churches and monasteries, with foundations from Roman times. They are all decorated by vivid fresco cycles, with a raised crypt containing relics of saints and martyrs, and showing elements of Gothic, Renaissance and Baroque styles all together. Many have Romanesque (11th–13th century) façades, divided into three tiers with rose windows arranged above arched portals.

Woodcut print of medieval Pisa, c.1493

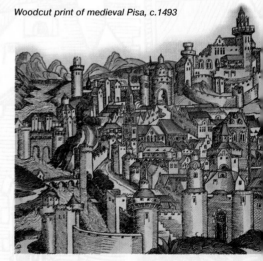

AROUND TUSCANY & UMBRIA

The region's historic towns have a shared tradition
for producing great artists, distinctive earthenware and
precious textiles such as gold-embroidered velvet.

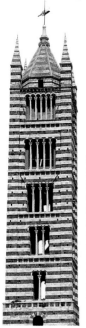

*Striped tower
of Siena's
Duomo*

SIENA

Tradition says that Siena was
founded by Senus and Aeschius,
sons of Remus, the legendary
founder of Rome. In the Middle
Ages the town grew wealthy
through its bankers, but when it
was finally conquered by its
bitter rival, Florence, in 1559 it
took 60 years for the town to
recover its financial standing.
The cities' fierce rivalry is celebrated annually in the colourful
pageantry of Siena's Palio.

The town's most famous
daughter is St Catherine, who
persuaded the Pope to return to
Rome from Avignon (see page
114). She was martyred in 1380 and her death
upon the wheel is obliquely remembered in
the Catherine wheel firework.

In the massive, shell-shaped **Piazza del
Campo** stands the cathedral, consecrated in
1258. The striped black and white façade is
matched inside by its "mint humbug" intarsia
paving – 56 panels of white marble picked out
in black stucco (1376–1547). Also in the
square, the elegant **Palazzo Pubblico** has
works by artists of the Siena school, including
Ambrogio Lorenzetti and Taddeo di Bartolo.

The Piazza del Campo is also the scene of
Siena's Palio, which goes back at least until

Oxen in Landscape, *a painting by Alberto Zardo
(1876–1959) that captures the Tuscan countryside*

the 13th century. By tradition rival districts,
contrade, would compete for the *palio*, the
banner awarded to the winner. The festival
takes place on 2 July and 16 August each year
and the highlight is a three-lap bareback horse
race around the Campo; celebrations continue
into the night.

Siena is known as a good place to buy
ceramics. At **Antica Siena** (Piazza del Campo
28) you will find locally produced pieces, most
commonly decorated in blue and yellow.

The **Piazza Mercato** holds a monthly
antiques and collectors' fair on the third
Sunday of every month.

● **Palazzo Pubblico**, Piazza del Campo.
Tel: (0577) 292263.

A CERAMIC TRADITION

Maiolica is thought to derive from Mallorca, having
been introduced to Italy via Moorish Spain.
Production in Italy dates from the 15th century with
major centres at Florence, Gubbio, Deruta, Urbino
and Orvieto. Traditional colours were blue, yellow,
red, green and purple, and highlights were
created using a white tin enamel.

Each centre had its own style of decoration.
Deruta, for example, favoured grotesque
characters while Montelupo used a
harlequin figure. Today, these plates
are rare and, therefore, expensive.

Names to look out for include
members of the Terchi family,
in particular Bartolomeo Terchi
(1650–1710) and also the Della
Robbia family.

*A 15th- or 16th-century pitcher, a blue
and gold lustre portrait dish, c.1525, from
Deruta and a Castel Durante dish, c.1540*

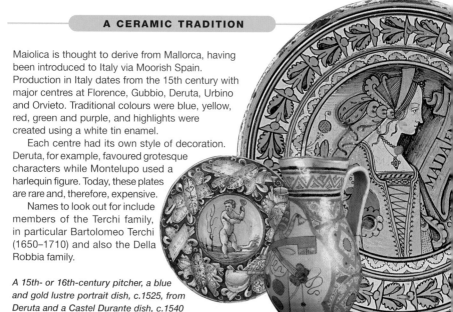

PISA

In the 12th century an appreciative Emperor Frederick Barbarossa rewarded loyal Pisa with extensive territory, but looking after this gift was a drain on the budget and, by 1284, Pisa had fallen to the Genoese. The town never recovered from this catastrophic defeat.

The centre of the town is Piazza dei Miracoli and each building in this walled square is worth visiting. Of world renown, of course, is the **Torre Pendente**, whose lean has been a concern ever since it was completed in 1350. Galileo Galilei, who conducted many of his experiments on the structure of the universe here, was born in nearby Via della Fortezza. Adjacent to the Leaning Tower is the cathedral (begun 1064), faced with variegated bands of marble to Buscheto's designs (his tomb is to the left of the main porch). The cemetery of **Camposanto**, surrounded by marble arcades, contains soil from the Holy Land.

Lucca's cathedral bell tower, with crenellations proclaiming its Guelph allegiance

In the 19th century Pisa had a large English colony, whom locals thought were mad: Lord Byron lived at Palazzo Lanfranchi with five carriages, nine horses and innumerable cats and dogs. Opposite lived fellow poet Percy Shelley with an adoring harem of women, while Charles Dickens and John Ruskin stayed round the corner at the Royal Victoria Hotel.

The Arno flows through Pisa and to the west, as the river flows out to sea, you can find the Marina di Pisa. The seaside resort has many sandy beaches and some beautiful Art Nouveau houses – well worth a visit if you have the time.

Tuscan oviform drug-jar, c.1500, with the portrait of a woman

If you fancy buying modern art, **Cagliostro Restaurant** (Via dei Castelletto 26) offers truffles with pasta, while you look at work by local artists.

● **Torre Pendente**, Campo dei Miracoli. Tel: (050) 560665
● **Camposanto**, Campo dei Miracoli. Tel: (050) 560547.

Around Campo dei Miracoli are souvenir shops filled with alabaster and marble figures in all shapes and sizes. Look down the side streets for the antiques shops with older, more attractive and sometimes cheaper versions.

Elsewhere in the town, try **Lenzi Ghino Giacomo** (Via Provinciale Vicarese 371) for Tuscan ceramics. For antiquarian books head for **Libreria Fogola** (Corso Italia 82). **Paolo Capri** (Via di Pratale 103) sells Florentine silverware.

LUCCA

Lucca's streets are laid out in their original Roman grid pattern within the town's 16th-century walls. The cathedral, with its principal façade squeezed in beside the campanile, is a beautiful 11th-century example of the Pisan-Romanesque style. The main entrance has 13th-century carvings by Nicola Pisano and Guidetto da Como.

The composer Giacomo Puccini was born in Lucca in 1858 and his house is now a museum with original manuscripts on display and, in the living room, the piano on which he composed *Turandot*.

In 1805 Napoleon gave the town of Lucca to his sister Elisa Baciocchi; she loved the area and lived at **Villa Reale** in nearby Marlia. Ironically, when Napoleon lost the Battle of the Nations in 1813, he was exiled to Elba, just off the coast. You might like to take the ferry over to the island and shop for antiques at **Cose Antiche** in Porto Azzorro.

In Lucca itself, the **Piazza San Martino** hosts a flea market on the third weekend of every month.

● **Museo della Casa Natale di Giacomo Puccini**, Corte San Lorenzo 9.
Tel: (0583) 584028.
● **Villa Reale**, Piazzale Verdi, Marlia.
Tel: (0583) 30108. Closed Dec-Feb.

Study in the corner of the living room of the house in Lucca where Puccini lived and died

The Umbrian town of Assisi, where St Francis, the patron saint of animals, was born

ASSISI

St Francis was born in this medieval town with its geranium-hung streets. Renouncing his privileged life he became a monk and was renowned for his rapport with birds and animals. A great reformer, he lived a holy life after receiving the stigmata, and founded the Franciscan Order. He died in 1226. His tomb is the centre of the **Basilica di San Francesco,** which dominates the town, a religious complex of a basilica with two superimposed churches – his body lies in the lower one. Ironically, for a man who led a life of simplicity and poverty, the basilica is one of opulence, decorated by Giovanni Cimabue, Simone Martini, Pietro Lorenzetti and Giotto di Bondone. Most of the damage inflicted from the earthquake in 1997 has been restored, and it receives a stream of pilgrims and visitors throughout the year.

● **Basilica di San Francesco,**
Piazza di San Francesco.
Tel: (075) 819001.

GUBBIO

Persevere past the mass of modern factories until you arrive at Gubbio's old town walls. Within, the Roman amphitheatre survives, as does much of the original Roman street pattern. Once the Romans left in the 5th century invaders destroyed the town, but the citizens rebuilt it on the original foundations. The Palazzo Ducale was built by the Duke of Urbino in the late 15th century when Gubbio rebelled against Papal rule and asked for protection.

When shopping, look out for locally made copies of Etruscan vases in black burnished *bucchera*. If you are a collector of antique weapons go to Ponte d'Assisi, where you will find the shops **Balestra** and **Medidevo**.

AREZZO

An important city under both Etruscan and Roman rule, Arezzo flourished as an economic centre, famous for its metalworkers and

The outdoor antiques market in Arezzo

craftsmen. The walls of 14th-century church of **San Francesco** are decorated with stunning frescoes by Piero della Francesca (*c.*1420–92).

Today the town is best known for its gold and clothing industries. It also has some fine antiques shops, many of them lining the Piazza Grande. On the first Sunday of each month the **Fiera dell'Antiquariato** is held in the square and attracts dealers and crowds from all over the area.

● **San Francesco**, Via Piero della Francesco. Tel: (0575) 20630.

Details of the fresco above the door of Orvieto Cathedral

PERUGIA

This is another Etruscan town protected by a Roman wall. In the Piazza IV Novembre is the **Fontana Maggiore**, a 13th-century fountain designed by Friar Bevignate, an expert on hydraulics, with Nicola and Giovanni Pisano's sculptures mixing Christian and pagan scenes. Locals say the **Palazzo dei Priori** containing the Umbrian National Gallery is the most beautiful public building in Italy.

● **Palazzo dei Priori**, Corso Vannucci 19.
Tel: (075) 574 1247.

Old Tuscan refectory tables are sought after by Italians

SPOLETO

Famous for its Festival dei Due Mondi in June and July, Spoleto is also noted for its 10,000 martyrs – the companions to St Abbondanza who were massacred in the amphitheatre here. Across the Ponte delle Torri, an aqueduct spanning Spoleto's precipitous gorge, is La Rocca, a 14th-century fortress used by popes to subjugate the region. It was used most recently as a prison for the would-be papal assassin in 1978, and is now a museum. The aqueduct provided water for the town and also served as an escape route in times of trouble.

Painted earthenware plate from Umbria with scene of tavern or inn, late 18th or early 19th century

ORVIETO

Perched on top of a volcanic crag, Orvieto has a superb cathedral and wonderful restaurants. From Orvieto Scala (the modern lower town) take the funicular railway up to the city where the impressive **Duomo**, probably one of Italy's finest Romanesque-Gothic gems, stands alone. Inside there are numerous treasures, including a wonderful 14th-century window.

The **Museo Claudio Faina** has on display a private collection of Etruscan artifacts, while the **Museo Archeologico** has ancient Greek artifacts. If you are feeling fit try tackling **Pozzo di San Patrizio**, a well dug at the orders of Pope Clement VII who took refuge in Orvieto in 1527. It took ten years to sink the 63-m (190-ft) shaft, which incorporated a double spiral staircase to allow pack horses to descend to collect water, and return up separate steps.

Orvieto has become a centre for antiques in Umbria. **Antichità Soliana** (Via Soliana 10) stocks furniture and clocks; and **Antichità Cavour** (Via San Leonardo) and **La Fornace** (Via della Cava 6–10) both specialize in furniture. At **L'Arte del Vasaio** (Via Pedota 3) you can find superb copies of ancient ceramics.

- **Duomo**, Piazza del Duomo. Tel: (0763) 341167.
- **Museo Claudio Faina**, Piazza del Duomo 29. Tel: (0763) 341511. Closed Mon.
- **Museo Archeologico**, Piazza del Duomo. Tel: (0763) 341039.
- **Pozzo di San Patrizio**, Via Sangallo. Tel: (0763) 343768.

A Tuscan table top, c.1700, in scagliola, a form of imitation stone used for highly polished surfaces

WHERE TO STAY

Elegant entrance to the Hotel Brufani

Hotel Brufani
Piazza d'Italia 12, Perugia
Tel. (075) 573 2541; Fax: (075) 572 0210
This 19th-century hotel sits on the highest hill in Perugia, and the rooms offer spectacular views of either the city itself or of the surrounding Umbrian countryside.

La Badia
La Badia, 5km (3 miles) south of Orvieto
Tel: (076) 330 1959; Fax: (076) 330 5455
Converted from a 13th-century monastery, La Badia has cloisters, 13th-century frescoes and a swimming pool. Excellent restaurant.

Hotel la Collegiata
Località Strada 27, San Gimignano
Tel: (0577) 943201; Fax: (0577) 94 05 66
Just outside town in a converted 1587 Franciscan convent. The top floor rooms have views of the town's 13 towers. Old Roman vaults have been converted into a dining room. Closed Dec–Feb.

Hotel Subasio
Via Frate Elia 2, Assisi
Tel: (075) 812206; Fax: (075) 81 66 91
Next to the Basilica, with wonderful views from many rooms. Charlie Chaplin stayed here.

Hotel Villa La Principessa
Via Nuova per Pisa, Lucca
Tel: (0583) 370037; Fax: (0583) 379136
Located in the hills that surround the city, La Principessa was once home and court to Castruccio Castracani (1281–1328), Lord and Duke of Lucca, and Machiavelli's model for the *Ideal Prince*. One of the most elegant hotels in Tuscany, it maintains the style of a 19th-century aristocratic Luccan villa.

WHERE TO EAT AND DRINK

La Buca di San Francesco
Via Brizi 1, Assisi
Tel: (075) 812204
At the heart of its historic centre, this restaurant is regarded as the best in Assisi for regional cuisine and fine wines. Dine outside in the stunning garden or in the atmospheric medieval cellars.

Al Marsili
Via del Castoro 3, Siena
Tel: (0577) 47154
Tuscan specialities are served in the brick-vaulted rooms of this 900-year-old wine cellar.

VENICE

Venice has been a tourist destination since the 19th century, and artists, art lovers and lovers come to marvel at its fragile beauty and wealth of culture.

A 1930s hotel luggage label

WHEN GOTHS SWEPT DOWN FROM THE NORTH 1500 years ago, locals in the Veneto sought refuge in the muddy islands offshore. Protected from the Adriatic by the sandbank of the Lido, a colony gradually established across the deep Rivo Alto, or Rialto. Builders drove piles deep into the heavy clay beneath the lagoon to support buildings, and a network of canals linked *campi*, or fields (which is why every Venetian square except San Marco is a *campo* and not a *piazza* as in the rest of Italy). Other cities may have more canals but only from Venice could Robert Benchley famously have cabled home: "Streets filled with water. Please advise."

Venice is prone to flooding, smelly backwaters and overcrowding, but it is also unique – ever since the Risorgimento led to the unification of Italy in the 1860s, Venice has viewed itself as a separate entity, a city-state with its own laws, customs and language. Traditionally, Venetians show allegiance to their city first, Italy second. Venice is also a city for people watching. Do as the locals do and saunter rather than scurry. Take time over a *caffè corretto* as the crowds parade by (Venetians will spend their last lira on dressing well) and venture beyond the bustle of San Marco to explore the bywaters of northern Castello and the quiet streets around Cannaregio.

Enamelled scent flask, atelier of Osvaldo Brussa, late 18th century

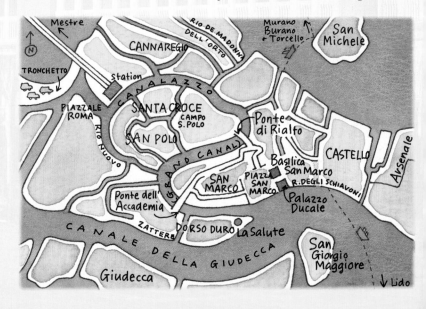

The Doge's Palace, largely unchanged since the 14th century

HISTORY REVISITED

THE SERENE REPUBLIC

What began as a temporary haven from the barbarian hordes was, by the 9th century, a flourishing town fiercely competing for trade around the Mediterranean. In AD997 the Venetians defeated the Dalmatian fleet, a victory still commemorated each May in the ceremonial Marriage of Venice to the Sea. Her defeat of the Genoese in 1380 made Venice truly Queen of the Adriatic, and the ships built in her formidable Arsenale ruled the eastern Mediterranean. Venice's maritime history is recorded in the **Museo Storico Navale**.

Leonardo Loredan, Doge 1501–21, from a tapestry in the Museo Correr

Poised between the bulk of Christian Europe and the infidel lands to the east, the city was swift to take advantage of its position. In 1204 Doge Enrico Dandolo diverted the forces of the Fourth Crusade to take Venice's great trading rival, Constantinople, seizing the riches of the Byzantine empire. In the Treasury of the **Basilica San Marco** lie just some of the precious objects acquired by the expanding Venetian empire, and in the small museum upstairs is the Quadriga, four finely wrought bronze horses brought from Constantinople itself (the horses that look out over the piazza are replicas). The entire basilica, with its jewel-studded *pala d'oro* and marvellous golden mosaics, announces the glory of Venice as much as the glory of God.

With the fall of Byzantium, the way east lay open and Venetian merchants, fuelled by Marco Polo's tales of Cathay, grew rich on silks and spices, jewels and slaves. Command of the trade routes gave Venice political power, and envoys from east and west would seek an audience at the **Palazzo Ducale**, the Doge's Palace. Since the 8th century Venice had been ruled, not by a hereditary monarch, but by a doge, elected by a machiavellian voting procedure by all patrician families in the Republic, whose names were recorded in the Golden Book. From the 14th century, however, true power lay in the hands of the Consiglio dei Dieci, the Council of Ten. The Serene Republic was kept in check via a sophisticated spy network, and it is no coincidence that the doors from the Sala del Consiglio dei Dieci in the Palace lead to the State Inquisitors' room and on to the prisons.

A tour of the Doge's Palace can be crowded and sometimes slow, but gives a vital insight into the seat of power. In the imposing Sala del Maggior Consiglio portraits of 76 doges form a frieze around the room. The obscured portrait is of Marin Falier, beheaded for plotting to become supreme ruler, but others have gone down in history with honour: Enrico Dandolo, blind and nearly 90 when he led the siege on Constantinople; Leonardo Loredan, diplomat and statesman for 20 years. In all 120 doges ruled Venice until Napoleon marched in, in 1797, bringing an end to La Serenissima, which had by then lost its hold on world trade and declined into a decadent pleasure dome.

- **Museo Storico Navale & Arsenale**, Castello. Tel: (041) 522 4951.
- **Basilica San Marco**, Piazza San Marco. Tel: (041) 522 5205.
- **Palazzo Ducale**, Piazza San Marco. Tel: (041) 520 4951.

WHEN IN VENICE...

IL CARNEVALE

Today, carnival denotes light-hearted fun, but the original revels had a more manic quality. They marked the last chance at jollity before Lent imposed a sombre mood and plain, meat-free diet – hence *carne vale*, or "farewell, meat". Venice's festivities, which died out in the 18th century, have been revived in the past 20 years to become a big draw each February, and masks and other carnival paraphernalia make attractive collectables. Most costumes are hired, but antique pieces, often family heirlooms, are highly valued.

ANTIQUES IN CONTEXT

The whole of Venice has been described as a living museum. Wander down any *calle*, pass through any *sottoportego*, and you will chance upon a scene that has changed little in three or four hundred years.

Late 17th-century Venetian gros point lace

VENETIAN LACE

Needle lace developed in Venice in the 16th century in two forms: flat and raised. The raised pattern, called *gros point de Venise*, was created by outlining the design and button-holing with a heavier thread, sometimes horsehair. The quality of workmanship made it popular with men and women across Europe, including Queen Elizabeth and James II in England; Van Dyke's sitters are often depicted proudly wearing Venetian lace collars. Fashions change, however, and this heavier lace fell out of favour during the 19th century, but was revived by Queen Marguerita of Italy, who in 1872 established a school on the island of Burano. Burano is home to the **Museo del Merletto**, where you can see fine examples of antique lace. A dwindling number of lace makers still sit outside their colourful houses, but be warned: real Venetian lace takes hours of work; what you see in shops is often made in the Far East.

● **Museo del Merletto**, Piazza Baldassare Galuppi, Burano. Tel: (041) 730 034.

VENETIAN GLASS

Glass furnaces from the 7th century have been discovered on the island of Torcello, and a guild for glassblowers was founded in 1224. By 1291 many in the trade had moved to the island of Murano (where they can still be seen), to be joined by

Venetian 17th-century tazza, showing detail of the latticino work

glassworkers fleeing Constantinople, from the Crusaders in 1204 and then the Ottomans in 1453.

Noted initially for *cristallo* (clear) glass, by the 16th century Venetian craftsmen had started to embellish their glass with colour, gilding and enamelling. At first there were severe penalties for anyone passing on their secrets, but the Medici Archduke Ferdinand and others eventually enticed glass masters to work for them (see page 243).

A Venetian winged goblet, early 17th century

Creativity was prized, and new techniques were developed, including *millefiori* (canes of coloured glass bonded together so a cross-section revealed a thousand multi-coloured "flower heads") and *latticino* (lines of opaque, usually white, glass used to create a fine tracery pattern). Glassblowers would also use massive pincers to mould glass while still malleable, producing elaborate "wings" and fluted stems with such heavy ornamentation that many drinking vessels would have been impossible to use.

A serpentine-fronted painted commode, mid-18th century

TRY NOT TO MISS...

Venice's glorious art collections: the **Accademia**, for masterpieces by Tiepolo, Carpaccio, Titian, Veronese and every other Venetian master; the Tintorettos treasured by his parish church, **Madonna dell'Orto**; the typically Venetian institutions of the *scuole*, repositories of great wealth in art; the **Museo Correr**, built by Napoleon, which today houses sculptures by Canova; Peggy **Guggenheim**'s curious unfinished *palazzo*, a homage to modern art.

Tools and techniques have remained unchanged for centuries, and you can still see glassblowers at work in many workshops behind San Marco and on Murano.

● **Museo Vetrario**, Palazzo Giustinian, Murano.
Tel: (041) 739 586.

PLACES TO VISIT

Palazzo translates as "palace", but although some Venetian *palazzi* are palatial

The Gothic Palazzo Giovanelli, overlooking the Grand Canal

inside, they are better described as the town houses of merchants and aristocrats. Venetians would use their houses for both business and family life and the layout was highly practical. Look at almost any *palazzo* along the Grand Canal and you will see a watergate (all too often rotting away), flanked by mooring posts; this gave access to a boat house and *fontego* or warehousing space and, via an inner courtyard, commercial offices. On the principal floor, the *piano nobile*, would be the *salone* and family rooms, with a loggia on the canal side. Above that were smaller private rooms and then servants' quarters on the top floor.

Many *palazzi* that have not been turned into hotels are now either divided into apartments or used as government offices, but **Ca' Rezzonico** survives with all its splendour intact. This great house is where the poet Robert Browning spent the last year of his life, dying here in 1889. Today it houses the Museo del Settocento and its rooms are furnished with the finest furniture and paintings from the 18th century: canvases by Guardi and Longhi, frescoes by Tiepolo, chandeliers from Murano, and a breathtaking ballroom that stretches the width of the house. On an upper floor is a marionette theatre.

For an insight into how a Venetian family lived during the last 400 years, visit the **Palazzo Querini Stampalia**, built in the 16th century. It has a wonderful collection of Venetian furniture, tapestries and glass, a vast library of nearly a quarter of a million books, and the Querini family's art collection that spans the greatest era of Venetian masters, from Giovanni Bellini (1430–1516) to Giambattista Tiepolo (1696–1770).

Tucked away between Campo Sant'Angelo and the Grand Canal is the *palazzo* where Mariano Fortuny y Madrazo lived and worked. Best known for his fine pleated silks, Fortuny settled here from his native Spain (see page 216) at the end of the 19th century, and here you can see examples of his textiles as well as some of his paintings and working tools.

Venice has always attracted artists and was a favourite stop on the Grand Tour. A trip down the Grand Canal will take you past *palazzi* where Lord Byron, Giuseppe Verdi, Henry James, Richard Wagner and others lived. An indulgent alternative to the *vaporetto* is a gondola (allow two hours at about £50 an hour for up to six people).

● **Ca' Rezzonico**, Fondamenta Rezzonico, Dorsoduro.
Tel: (041) 241 8506.
● **Palazzo Querini Stampalia**, Campo Santa Maria Formosa 52.
Tel: (041) 271 1411.
● **Museo Fortuny**, Campo San Benedetto, San Marco 3958.
Tel: (041) 520 0995.

Late 18th-century chair painted and gilded in typical north Italian style

The marionette theatre in Ca' Rezzonico

SHOPPING

Unlike many cities, Venice does not really divide itself into specialist shopping areas, so you can come across interesting shops all over the city. Below are some of the dealers in the main streets, but look down the little alleys for yet more fascinating shops.

SAN MARCO AND CASTELLO

Venetian glass perfume bottles, c.1870

The area around the popular Piazza San Marco is home to some of Venice's most prestigious shops and galleries.

Look out for:
On the east side of the square, in Casselleria di San Lio (No 5326), is **Rino Berengo**. This fascinating shop amassed a wonderful collection of brass door furniture from 1700 to the present; you will also find here a vast array of copper fish moulds. Just off the Piazza, in calle dell'Ascensione (No 1295), is the jeweller **Codognato** (a favourite of Jackie Kennedy) which always has a fine collection of 1920s pieces.

Head off from San Marco towards Dorsoduro (follow signs for Ponte dell'Accademia) and you will come to calle delle Botteghe, near the church of Santo Stefano. It is home to a number of antiques shops, including **Antiquus** (No 3131), a charming shop with a very good collection of old master paintings, silver and antique jewellery.

The **Kleine Galerie** (No 2972) is run by a father and son and deals mostly in antique books and prints; it also has a good stock of Italian maiolica and porcelain. Here you will also find **Galleria Rossella Junck** (No 3463), a stylish gallery specializing in antique Murano glass and contemporary art glass. The owner, Rossella Junck, also organizes exhibitions of both modern and antique glass at other galleries throughout Italy and abroad. She has two other premises in the San Marco area, one in calle delle Ostreghe and the other campo San Fantin, both near the site of the opera house La Fenice, which was so sadly destroyed by fire in 1996.

Heading west towards the Grand Canal you will come across the **Barovier Art Gallery** on Salizzada San Samuele (No 3216). The gallery's owner, Marina Barovier, is an expert on antique glass and she has written an authoritative book on the history of the Barovier family's involvement in the Murano glass industry: *L'Arte dei Barovier – Vetrai di Murano 1866–1972*.

Life-size Moors and Rococo ornaments for sale

SAN POLO

Across the Grand Canal is San Polo, the smallest district in Venice, which combines bustling market stalls, shops and bars with a maze of quiet backstreets and narrow passageways.

Venetian blue-painted lacca povera bureau decorated with coloured prints, probably 18th century

Look out for:
Cenerentola, on Rio Terrà dei Nomboli (No 2600), beside the Museo Goldoni, is a delightful shop with a great selection of antique lace and beautiful lampshades made from old fabrics. Nearby, on calle del Mandorlin (No 2862), just off campo San Tomà, you will find **Guarinoni**. This shop and restoration workshop houses a huge range of furnishings, some pieces dating from as early as the 16th century.

DORSODURO

Traditionally an area of artists and craftsmen, Venice's last remaining gondola workshop is in the Dorsoduro. After taking in the major sights of the area, including the Galleria dell'Accademia, it is worth wandering off the beaten track to explore the narrow alleyways and quiet, picturesque canals.

SHOPPER'S TIP

Many people disregard **Mestre**, the mainland area of Venice, but this can be a mistake. This modern town, where most Venetians now live, can be a great place to discover Venetian antiques without having to pay inflated tourist prices. Shops include: **Antichità al Pozzo** at 68 via Olivi, **Antichita Lugato** at 342 via Terraglio, and **Dolfin** at 35 via Spani.

Look out for:

Between the churches of San Barnaba and San Sebastiano runs calle lunga San Barnaba where **La Luna nel Pozzo** sells antiques and small ormamental objects. Stroll round the corner into Fondamenta San Basilio and you will come across workshops where you can see similar pieces being made. **Misterobuffo** specializes in carnival masks in pâpier maché, leather and ceramics. Nearby is **De Laurentis** where glassmakers produce vases, mirrors, art glass, cut crystal and chandeliers.

OTHER HUNTING GROUNDS

Cannaregio, in the north of the city, attracts fewer tourists, but is well worth a visit. Along Rio Terrà San Leonardo there are shops selling antique books and prints, and as you wander up towards the original ghetto you will find fascinating old craft shops and furniture restorers where you may pick up anything from a traditional Venetian lamp to an elaborate picture frame. Cannaregio is also home to the **Semenzato** auction house.

● **Semenzato**, Casa d'Aste.
Tel: (041) 721 811.

The "glassblowers" island of Murano

WHERE TO EAT AND DRINK

You will always pay a premium to eat near Piazza San Marco. This is where it pays to follow the locals; after a day's work the *gondolieri* head for restaurants serving fish and black pasta, or fegato (liver) alla Veneziana.

Antico Martin
Campo San Fantin, San Marco 1983
Tel: (041) 522 4121
Dating back to 1720, the restaurant is frequented by antiques dealers and also, because the Fenice theatre was nearby, by stage and opera stars. The menu includes regional specialities.

Caffè Florian
Piazza San Marco 56
Tel: (041) 528 5338
Opened in 1720, Florian's has long been a favourite with artists and writers – Rousseau and Byron are among its past patrons. Very pricey, especially when the resident orchestra is playing, but worth visiting for the wonderful decor.

Locanda Cipriani
Torcello
Tel: (041) 730 150
In the 1930s the wealthy hotelier Giuseppe Cipriani fell in love with the quiet island of Torcello and converted an oil and wine shop into a restaurant with rooms. Lunch begins as you take a boat to the island. Eat overlooking the vegetable garden where produce for the table is grown, with a backdrop of Torcello's 1,000-year-old cathedral. In summer you can eat under the vines and in winter enjoy locally shot water fowl. Closed Jan.

WHERE TO STAY

You won't find any featureless high rises here! Most of the hotels in the city are in beautiful old buildings brimming with character. There are also many self-catering apartments available (see Useful Addresses at the end of the book).

Hotel Danieli
Riva degli Schiavoni, Castello 4196
Tel: (041) 522 6480; Fax: (041) 520 0208
Built as a palace in the 14th century, and a hotel since 1822, the Danieli is a reminder of the enormous wealth of the Serene Republic. The lobby is a breathtaking expanse of marble. The terrace restaurant overlooks the lagoon.

Caffè Florian interior

Londra Palace
Riva degli Schiavoni, Castello 4171
Tel: (041) 520 0533;
Fax: (041) 522 5032
This luxurious waterfront hotel was built in 1860 and has been recently restored and refurbished with antique furnishings.

Hotel des Bains
Lungomare Marconi 17, Lido
Tel: (041) 526 5921; Fax: (041) 526 0113
Situated on the Lido, a cool retreat from the heat of the city, this elegant Art Deco hotel was the location for Visconti's *Death in Venice*. It has its own beach and is surrounded by private gardens.

IN THE AREA

Antonio Canova (1757–1822) was a great exponent of Neo-classicism, but is best remembered in Italy for his semi-naked statue of Napoleon's sister that scandalized Roman society (see page 239). His first major commission, *Daedalus and Icarus*, was so life-like he was accused of making casts from live models. His studio in Possagno near Treviso is now open to the public. The plaster casts are amazing – thousands of nails were hammered in so that students could take measurements and make exact copies of the master's work. On top of the hill is the Tempio, designed by Canova as his burial place.

The architect Andrea Palladio (1508–80) set a classical style copied in many parts of the world and many of his villas in the Veneto can be visited, including **La Malcontenta** on the banks of the Brenta canal, **Villa Barbaro** in the village of Maser and **La Rotonda** in Vicenza.

PALERMO

One-time Greek outpost, Norman stronghold and Arab capital, Palermo is a heady mix of art, culture and tradition from all over Europe.

Twelfth-century mosaic in the Cappella Palatina

IN AD553 SICILY BECAME PART OF THE BYZANTINE EMPIRE and its people converted to Christianity. Palermo became the capital of a Saracen emirate in AD831, and was subsequently invaded and conquered by the Normans in 1061. From 1415 to 1759 the island was subject to Spanish rule and, for a brief period in the early 19th century, it fell under British protection. Today the diverse influences of this rich history can be seen in the city's architecture where Muslim motifs are found in the Palatina chapel and where the Norman façade of San Cataldo bears inscriptions from the Koran, while lavishly decorated churches and aristocratic palaces betray the city's past wealth.

HISTORY REVISITED

OPERA DEI PUPI

Pupi (puppets) and puppet theatres are part of local life. The origins of the stories, often adapted to the modern day, go back to the times of Spanish chivalry, and such heroes as Orlando and Rinaldo who battled against the Saracens. With over 3,000 exhibits, the **Museo Internazionale delle Marionette** has the largest collection of puppets, marionettes and shadow puppets in the world. Performances are held here, and the museum hosts an annual *Festival di Morgana* of international puppets shows (October).

● **Museo Internazionale delle Marionette**, Via Butera 1. Tel: (091) 328060.

Rustic exhibits at Museo Etnografico Pitrè

PLACES TO VISIT

A jewel among Palermo's sights is the **Palazzo dei Normanni**, still outstanding despite having only one of its four great 12th-century towers remaining. Much of the complex dates from alterations made in the 16th and 17th centuries, including the arcaded Maqueda courtyard, built in 1600.

The Sala di Ruggero and the delicate Byzantine-style mosaics of the Cappella Palatina, King Ruggero II's private chapel, have survived since the 1130s. The chapel's wooden ceiling was produced by Muslim craftsmen still active in Norman Sicily and, along with the Biblical scenes that decorate the walls, contributes to the unique Arab-Norman style of this fine interior.

● **Palazzo dei Normanni**, Piazza Independenza. Tel: (091) 705 1111.

Merchant selling an eclectic mix of statues

Sicily has a long tradition of highly decorative carts drawn by equally ornate horses

SHOPPING

Palermo has a good number of antiques shops, with many of them specializing in maiolica and Sicilian furniture.

Look out for:
Antonello Governale (Via Libertà 102A) sells 15th- and 17th-century Sicilian maiolica. He also stocks 17th-century furniture. **Athena** (Via Libertà 6) specializes in maiolica, silverware and furniture. **Savoca**, in Via Milano, and **Di Carlo**, in Via Zara, deal in antique guns and hunting goods, while **La Bottega delle Stampe Antiche di Buffa** (Via Principe di Palagonia) is a haven for collectors of old and rare stamps. **Corimbo** (Via Principe di Belmonte) has large 19th-century furniture, jewellery and timepieces. You will find top-quality furniture, silverware and ceramics at **Trionfante** (Via Alto Fonte 80). **Antiqua Domus** (Via Wagner 11/B) sells everything from maiolica and porcelain to furniture and fine art.

FLEA MARKET

A **mercantino dell' antiquariato** is held daily by the Porta Uzeda.

WHERE TO EAT AND DRINK

A'Cuccagna
Via Principe di Granatelli 21/A
Tel: (091) 587267; Fax (091) 584575
In the heart of Palermo's historic centre, this restaurant has become a meeting place for artists and intellectuals. Specialities include excellent fish dishes and local cuisine.

Dei Vecchi Monsù
Via G. Turrisi Colonna 4
Tel: (091) 611 8523; Fax: (091) 588705
This fine restaurant in the Hotel Principe di Villafranca is filled with wonderful Sicilian antiques and local crafts. Excellent Sicilian food.

WHERE TO STAY

Grand Hotel Villa Igiea
Via Salita Belmonte 43
Tel: (091) 543744; Fax: (091) 547654
Overlooking the bay of Palermo with splendid terraced gardens, the villa was designed in 1908 by Ernesto Basile. It has elegant Art Nouveau furniture, and look for the typical Sicilian frescoes on the entrance floor.

Grand Hotel et des Palmes
Via Roma 398
Tel: (091) 602 8211; Fax: (091) 331545
Built in 1874, this hotel is typical of late 19th-century Liberty style, and is complete with a stunning inlaid ceiling in the Fireplace Hall. Wagner is said to have completed *Parsifal* here.

IN THE AREA

For breathtaking mosaics, visit **Monreale Cathedral**, 16km (10 miles) south-west of Palermo. A Norman-Arab masterpiece founded by William II in 1172 and containing his white marble tomb, the church has a mosaic cycle (1182) showing scenes from the Old Testament and the Gospels. There are also superb bronze door panels by Bonanno da Pisa (1185).

The **Museo Etnografico Pitrè** in Cidello, 8km (5 miles) north-west of Palermo, is also well worth a visit. Here you will find a comprehensive collection documenting the history of Sicilian tradition and crafts. Among some 4,000 exhibits are fine examples of regional textiles and costumes, ceramics, glass and puppets.

A maiolica pharmacy vase, or albarello, 1580

TURKEY

THE ANTIQUES LANDSCAPE

Prayer rugs can be distinguished by the representation of a mihrab or prayer niche in the design.

Turkey has only a toehold in Europe, but Istanbul is such a terrific place to shop that I had to include it. Turkey's capital may be Ankara, but it is Istanbul that is the hub of Turkish commerce. For almost 1,000 years, as Byzantium, then Constantinople, it was the richest city in Christendom. The Ottomans took Constantinople in 1453, and, under Suleiman the Magnificent (1520–66) their empire stretched to the gates of Vienna. Ottoman territory slowly diminished through the 19th century and in 1922 the independent republic of Turkey was created, with Thrace on the European side of the Bosphorus and the much larger Anatolia in Asia.

You will often come across mention of Iznik ceramics and glass. Many of the beautiful tiles in mosques and palaces came from here (see page 269), and the town was known for its enamelled glass as early as the 13th century. Iznik – Nicea in ancient times – is one of several towns well worth visiting. Another is Bursa, renowned for its bustling covered bazaar and for its rugs, now rather rare, woven from locally produced silk.

Some traders will try to persuade you that their rugs are antique but most sold in markets are relatively new. Usually silk rugs are better quality and more expensive, but very early rugs, produced in Ushak and Constantinople before 1700, were wool pile on a wool foundation. Other rug centres were Hereke and, further south, Ghiordes and Konya. Turkish crafts can be also seen in highly decorative metalware, jewellery and wooden carvings. Whatever you are buying, do barter at all times.

Istanbul boasts the world's largest covered bazaar – the Kapali Çarşi   a heady complex of thousands of stalls laden with rugs, jewellery and traditional Turkish crafts.

Clock from the Dolmabahçe Palace

ISTANBUL IS GEOGRAPHICALLY SPLIT by the Bosphorus, with half in Europe, and half in Asia. To the north is the Black Sea, and to the south, the Mediterranean, while Istanbul straddles the Golden Horn, an inlet of the Bosphorus. Historically, the city has been the capital of the two most significant and diverse powers of their time, the Byzantine and Ottoman Empires.

In AD 324, Byzantium became the seat of the Roman Empire under Constantine the Great. As Constantinople, it continued to be the capital of the Byzantine Empire until 1453 when Sultan Mehmet II conquered the city and began what became a 500-year rule by the Ottomans.

A walk in Istanbul today reveals the tremendous influence these two great powers had on the city, for it is a fantastic jumble of churches, mosques, museums and bazaars. Remnants of the great 4th-century palace built by Constantine the Great and the 6th-century Christian Aya Sophia sit in a city dominated by the minarets of some of the world's most impressive mosques. Built in the 15th and 16th centuries, the sound of their call to prayer fills the streets five times a day.

Ottoman silver coffee cups, 1883

A centre for trade for almost 16 centuries, Istanbul is a haven for antiques hunters. The Bazaar district is dominated by the enormous Kapali Çarşi where vendors ply shoppers with thick sweet coffee as a part of the bartering ritual. Here you will find everything from religious icons to hand-woven textiles, and from bright copperware to traditional ceramics. Not far away is the Misir Çarşi, the Eyptian Bazaar, with its wonderful display of herbs and spices.

Süleymaniye Camii, Istanbul's most important mosque

ISTANBUL

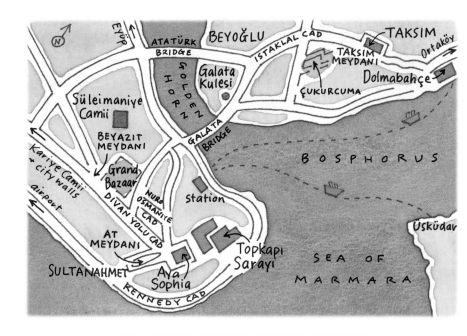

SINAN, MASTER ARCHITECT

The architect Mimar Koca Sinan (c.1491–1588) is perhaps best remembered for the **Süleymaniye Camii**. Constructed in the 1550s for Suleiman I, The Magnificent, it is Istanbul's most important mosque. Once built, it was not only a place of worship but also became a charitable foundation, providing food for the hungry.

Iznik tiles from the Rustem Pasa Camii

Sinan's body of work totals 131 mosques and 200 other buildings. His interiors reflect a creative sense of space, often combined with astounding geometrical and architectural details. His work is considered as close as Turkey gets to Renaissance architecture, and other master-pieces include: **Şehzade Camii**, the Prince's Mosque (1548), which is very decorative and has an elegant porticoed inner courtyard; **Rustem Pasa Camii** (1561), above the hustle and bustle of the Spice Bazaar, with a stunning Iznik tile interior; **Sokollu Mehmet Pasa Camii** (1571), one of Sinan's greatest accomplishments, erected on an incline and housing a gleaming wall of green and blue Iznik tiles; and **Azap Kapi Camii** (1577), one of his most attractive mosques, with an unusual stairwell entrance and lavish Baroque fountain.

- **Süleymaniye Camii**, Prof Siddik Sami Onar Caddesi, Vefa. Tel: (0212) 514 0139.
- **Sehzade Camii**, Sehzade Basi Caddesi 70, Saraçhane.
- **Rustem Pasa Camii**, Hasiicilar Caddesi, Eminönü.
- **Sokollu Mehmet Pasa Camii**, Sehit Çesmesi Sokak, Sultanahmet.
- **Azap Kapi Camii**, Tersane Caddesi, Azapkapi. Visitors at prayer times only.

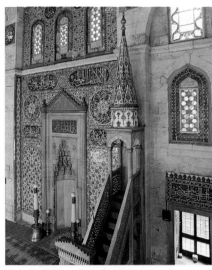

Sokullu Mehmet Pasa Camii

THE ASIAN SIDE

Two of Sinan's mosques are in this part of Istanbul. **Atik Valide Camii** (1583), which translates as "the old mosque of the Sultan's mother", was his last major work. On a hill above Üsküdar, a major feature is the marble *mihrab* surrounded by beautiful Iznik tiles. The **Şemsi Pasa Camii**, close to the waterfront, was built by Sinan in 1580, and is one of the smallest mosques in Istanbul. An unusual feature of the mosque is the adjoining tomb of Şemsi Ahmet, a 16th-century Grand Vizier.

ANTIQUES IN CONTEXT

With its rich cultural history, Istanbul has no shortage of mosques, museums and palaces. Each displays the tremendous wealth enjoyed in the city during an impressive sixteen centuries as the imperial capital.

Stunning interior of the Blue Mosque

PLACES TO VISIT

Topkapi Palace offers a fascinating insight into life during the Ottoman Empire. It was the royal residence of the sultans from the 1450s to the 1850s, undergoing structural changes and additions with each one. The now vast complex has been a museum since 1924, and houses a variety of exhibitions, including a large collection of Chinese and Japanese porcelain – much of which inspired the designs of Istanbul's Iznik tiles – and some fascinating examples of Ottoman manuscripts and calligraphy. The Harem, with more than 400 rooms, is well worth a visit, and do not miss the Treasury of the empire's riches, including among heaps of loose gems such precious items as a bejewelled throne and a dagger studded with emeralds and diamonds.

Next to Topkapi Palace is the **Arkeloloji Müzesi**, Istanbul's archeological museum. This enormous complex was built for archeologist Osman Hamdi Bey at the end of the 19th century, and contains exhibits spanning more than 5,000 years.

SULTANAHMET

Aya Sophia or Haghia Sophia has been both church and mosque, and still has many of its original 6th-century mosaics. It is its cavernous interior that is overwhelming, though, beneath the great dome more than 55m (180ft) above.

Turkish shadow puppets from an exhibition at Topkapi Palace

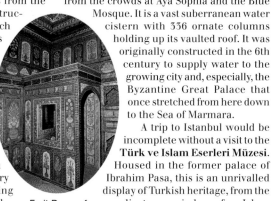

Late 18th-century Egyptian vase for the Turkish market

Less historic but more beautiful is the nearby **Sultan Ahmet Camii**. It is also called the Blue Mosque because of the colour of the Iznik tiles used for much of the interior, which give it a particularly calm and luminous quality. Dating from the beginning of the 17th century, it was built for Sultan Ahmet I. This mosque is unique in having six minarets where most have two or four. For the best view of it, look towards the domed rooftops as you stand next to the Ablutions Fountain in the courtyard.

The **Yerebatan Sarayi**, tucked around a corner in a quiet street, is a welcome respite from the crowds at Aya Sophia and the Blue Mosque. It is a vast suberranean water cistern with 336 ornate columns holding up its vaulted roof. It was originally constructed in the 6th century to supply water to the growing city and, especially, the Byzantine Great Palace that once stretched from here down to the Sea of Marmara.

A trip to Istanbul would be incomplete without a visit to the **Türk ve Islam Eserleri Müzesi**. Housed in the former palace of Ibrahim Pasa, this is an unrivalled display of Turkish heritage, from the earliest period of Islam (AD661–750) through to modern times. The rooms' exhibits are arranged either chronologically or geographically. Don't miss the museum's fascinating collection of rugs.

Fruit Room of Ahmet III, Topkapi Palace harem

● **Topkapi Palace**, Babihümayun Caddesi, Sultanahmet. Tel: (0212) 512 0480.
● **Arkeloloji Müzesi**, Osman Hamdi Bey Yok. Tel: (0212) 520 7740.
● **Aya Sophia**, Ayasophia Meydani, Sultanahmet. Tel: (0212) 522 1750. Closed Mon.
● **Sultan Ahmet Camii**, Sultanahmet Meydani. Tel: (0212) 518 1319.
● **Yerebatan Sarayi**, 13 Yerebatan Caddesi, Sultanahmet. Tel: (0212) 522 1259.
● **Türk ve Islam Eserleri Müzesi**, Atmeydani Sokak, Sultanahmet. Tel: (0212) 518 1805. Closed Mon.

SHOPPING

BEYOĞLU

A steep hill north of the Golden Horn, Beyoğlu runs either side of Istiklal Caddesi, Istanbul's pedestrianized main street, and is a hotspot for art galleries and cafés. In the heart of the district is Çukurcuma, an area where warehouses have been converted into boutiques. Here you can find delicate furnishings and hand-embroidered Ottoman fabrics.

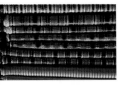

Coloured rugs in the Kapali Çarşi

Look out for:
Antikarnas (Faik Paşa Yok. 15), **Antikhane** (Faik Paşa Yok. 41) and **Asli Gunsiray** (Çukurcuma Cad. 74) are all worth a visit, particularly if you are looking specifically for Turkish or Islamic items.

Librairie de Pera (Galip Dede Cad. 22) is an antiquarian bookshop also selling postcards and prints. Music lovers should try **Filateli Pul Galerisi** (Galip Dede Cad. 45) and **Kamer Pul Evi** on (Galip Dede Cad. 51) for both old and new musical instruments.

MARKETS AND FAIRS

You'll need a full day to explore the **Kapali Çarşi** – the maze of streets that make up the Grand Bazaar – the largest covered market in the world. Offerings range from gold and amber jewellery to woven cushions to copper pots. The streets in the centre sell the more valuable goods. The market is open from Monday to Saturday.

On Sundays there is a flea market in **Ortaköy**, on the upper Bosphorus. Starting from the main square, stalls spread into the surrounding streets. Likely finds here are coins, glassware and Turkoman jewellery.

Silk prayer rug, c.1890, from the Bursa region

KILIMS

Turkey is famous for its variety of weaving and, in particular, for the bold-coloured kilims. Literally meaning "woven material", *kilim* is used to describe the flat-woven rugs which originated in this part of Europe as long ago as 6500BC.

Traditionally, kilims are handmade by women, with the skill passing from mother to daughter. These rugs are usually highly colourful and, while many are bold and abstract in design, others contain strong tribal images. Recurring features include columnar motifs, animal figures, bold hooked shapes, geometric designs and ram's horns. A typical feature of Turkish kilims is for such elements to be outlined in threads of a different colour.

Many Turkish kilims are also prayer mats, and can be distinguished by the motif of the *mihrab* – the prayer niche in a mosque which indicates the direction of Mecca.

Reverse of a solid siver mirror showing Ottoman craftsmanship; a steel Turkish jambiya with walrus ivory hilt, c.1825

AUCTION HOUSE

KÜSAV, Has Firin Cad 305, Beşiktaş

SHOPPER'S TIP

In most shops, particularly in the Grand Bazaar, you will be invited to barter for everything, from the smallest copper pot to the largest Turkish rug. It can be quite a challenge. I usually start at half the asking price but have been told that a quarter is nearer the mark. If you haven't left the shop and been pursued down the street at least twice you have probably paid too much!

Istanbul's famed Grand Bazaar: Kapali Çarşi

ECHOES OF THE PAST

Reward yourself after a day's hard sightseeing in Beyoğlu and stop in for a drink at the atmospheric bar of the Pera Palas Hotel. Agatha Christie was among celebrated guests in the past, and it is thought that she wrote *Murder on the Orient Express* while staying here.

Lobby of the Pera Palace Hotel

IZNIK TILES

By the time the Ottomans came to power in 1453, the town of Iznik, some 80km (50 miles) south-east of Istanbul, was already producing ceramics. It was during the next hundred years, however, that production increased significantly, owing to commissions from the Ottoman palaces for ceramic jars and bowls.

Although the area also produced the blue and white tiles so characteristic of Istanbul's finest buildings, they were not made in large quantities until the architect Sinan used them for his stunning mosques during the 16th century (see page 266).

The tiles, made from soft grey clay, are covered in a thin white slip and finished with a transparent glaze. Many of them combine Islamic designs with motifs from the Chinese ceramics that inspired them, which had been imported to Turkey from the 14th century.

There is a comprehensive collection of Iznik ceramics, and the 17th-century Küthaya ceramics that followed, at the Çinili Pavilion.

● **Çinili Pavilion**, Arkeoloji Müzesi, Osman Hamdi Bey Yok. Tel: (0212) 520 7740.

Brass inkwell and pen holder

WHERE TO EAT AND DRINK

Karafaki
Mesrutiyet Caddesi 100–102, Tepebasi
Tel: (0212) 243 0505
An evocative restaurant in the basement of the renowned Pera Palas Hotel. Built in 1892, primarily to accommodate travellers on the Orient Express, the restaurant still has many of its period features. The menu reflects an Aegean influence, with an emphasis on seafood.

Konyalı
Topkapi Palace, Sultanahmet
Tel: (0212) 513 9696
Having first opened in 1897, Konyalı is one of Istanbul's oldest restaurants. Situated in the grounds of Topkapi Palace, this popular restaurant has spectacular views over the Sea of Marmara. Serves Turkish and international food.

Darüzziyafe
Şifahane Caddesi 6, Beyazıt
Tel: (0212) 511 8414
A stylish restaurant in what used to be the kitchens of the 16th-century Süleymaniye Camii. The food is Ottoman-inspired and, in summer, is served in the adjoining courtyard. Note that this restaurant does not serve alcohol.

WHERE TO STAY

The Four Seasons
Tevkifhane Sokak 1, Sultanahmet
Tel: (0212) 638 8200; Fax: (0212) 638 8210
Within walking distance of the Blue Mosque and the Aya Sophia, this striking hotel was once a 19th-century prison. Beautiful gardens surround the hotel, and there is a stunning inner courtyard.

Yesil Ev
Kabasakal Caddesi 5, Sultanahmet
Tel: (0212) 517 6785; Fax: (0212) 517 6780

Yesil Ev (see left) – the Green House – is a 19th-century house nestled in a quiet spot around the corner from Aya Sophia. Antiques lovers will relish the Ottoman-style furnishings that adorn the rooms. The hotel has a formal and elegant restaurant that serves superb food – Turkish as well as international cuisine.

Obelisk
Amiral Tafdil Sokak 17–19, Sultanahmet
Tel: (0212) 517 7173; Fax: (0212) 516 8282
Overlooking the Sea of Marmara, this 19th-century wooden mansion house is furnished throughout in Ottoman style.

Turkish Maritime Lines organize round-trips on the **Bosphorus**, where passengers can alight at piers along the way. This is a great way to see some of the more outlying areas of Istanbul, and offers stunning views of the city itself. Among the highlights as you travel up towards the Black Sea are the **Dolmabahçe**

Sarayi – an extravagant Ottoman palace from 1856, with some stunning interiors; **Rumeli Hisari**, the Fortress of Europe, built in 1452 by Mehmet II, before his invasion of Constantinople; and the **Paşabahçe Glassworks**, the largest in Turkey, producing fine vases with blue and white stripes and gilded glassware.

USEFUL ADDRESSES

AUSTRIA

When phoning or faxing Austria from abroad, dial +43 and omit the first '0' of the regional code.

TOURIST OFFICES

VIENNA
Austrian National Tourist Office
Margaretenstrasse 1, A–1040 Wien
Tel: (01) 588 660. Fax: (01) 558 6620

Vienna Tourist Board
Obere Angartenstrasse 40, A–1025 Wien
Tel: (01) 211 14 222. Fax: (01) 216 84 92
Email: info@info.wien.at

SALZBURG
Salzburg City Tourist Office
Auerspergstrasse 7, A-5020 Salzburg
Tel: (0662) 889 870. Fax: (0662) 889 8732
Web site: www.salzburginfo.at
Email: tourist@salzburginfo.at

AUSTRIAN NATIONAL TOURIST OFFICE IN LONDON
14 Cork Street, London W1S 3NS
Tel: (020) 7629 0461. Fax: (020) 7499 6038
Web site: www.austria-tourism.at
Email: info@anto.co.uk

ANTIQUES DEALERS' ASSOCIATION

Osterreichische Kunst- und Antiquitäten handeler die der C.I.N.O.A angehoren
Wiedner Hauptstrasse 63, PF440, A-1045 Wien
Tel: (01) 50105 3331. Fax: (01) 50105 3043

OTHER USEFUL GROUPS

VIENNA WALKS AND TALKS
Wiethestrasze 69/1, A-1228 Wien
Tel: (01) 774 8901. Fax: (01) 774 8933
Web site: www.viennawalks.tix.at
Email: info@viennawalks.tix.at

SHOPPING INFORMATION

Shops are generally open Mon–Fri 8am to 6.00 or 6.30 pm (some are closed one or two hours for lunch), Sat: 8am to 12 midday or 1pm to 5pm.

EXPORTING ANTIQUES

Anything below the monetary limit of ATS 690.000 (which is applied to some antiques such as books more than 50 or 100 years old) does not need an export licence. Antiques over this value may need permission of the Bundesdenkmalamt (Office of Federal Monuments) to leave the country; this is something a dealer would tell you.

BUYING ANTIQUES TO BRING HOME

What countries define as an antique varies; the two most important considerations are usually age and value. Often there is no problem with exporting antiques, but serious antiques buying requires expert advice. It is always good practice to ask a dealer to include details of an antique on the recipt and to provide other documentation about its age or history. Always make a list of any antiques bought to show at customs, with any documentation including receipts.

BELGIUM

When phoning or faxing Belgium from abroad, dial +32 and omit the first '0' of the regional code.

TOURIST OFFICES

BRUSSELS
Belgian Tourist Board,
63 Rue du Marché-aux-herbes, 1000 Brussels
Tel: (02) 504 03 90. Fax: (02) 504 02 70

Brussels Tourist Office, Hotel de Ville de Bruxelles, Grand Place, 1000 Brussels
Tel: (02) 513 8940. Fax: (02) 513 8320
Web site: www.tib.be
Email: tourism.brussels@tib.be

BRUGES
Toerisme Brugge, Burg II, B – 8000, Brugge.
This office offers a free Guide on Art and Antiques listing 23 of the members of the arts, antiques and decorative objects association.
Tel: (050) 44 86 86. Fax: (050) 44 86 00
Website: www.visitbelgium.com

ANTWERP
Tourist Information Office
Grote Markt 15, B-2000 Antwerpen
Tel: (03) 232 0103. Fax: (03) 231 1936
Email: Toerisme@Antwerpen.be

BELGIAN TOURIST OFFICES IN LONDON
225 Marsh Wall, London E14 9FW
Tel: (020) 7531 0391.
Fax: (020) 7531 0393
Web site: www.belgium-tourism.net
Email: info@belgium-tourism.org

Tourism Flanders Brussels,
31 Pepper Street, London E14 9RW
Tel: (020) 77867 0311
24-hour brochure line: 09001 887799
Email: info@flanders-tourism.org

OTHER USEFUL GROUPS

ANTIQUES WORLD
General information about Belgian antiques dealers, markets and places to visit
Antiques World Belgium, 2 Rue Ernest-Allard, 1000 Brussels.
Tel: (02) 511 3161. Fax: (02) 503 0826
Web site: www.antiques-world.com
Email: antiques.world@pophost.eunet.be

INTERNET FLANDERS AND BRUSSELS
Web site: www.toervl.be
Email: info@toerismevlaanderen.be

INTERNET WALLONIE AND BRUSSELS
Web site: www.belgium.tourism.net
Email: info@opt.be

Information on antiques can also be found at: www.visitbelgium.com/antique.htm
Details of the Bruges international antique fair (held in November) www.publigil.be

ANTIQUES DEALERS' ASSOCIATIONS

Chambre Royale des Antiquaires de Belgique
32 Rue Ernest-Allard, B-1000 Brussels
Tel: (02) 513 4831.
Fax: (02) 502 0686

**Koninklijke Gilde van de Vlaamse Antiquaires
(Guilde Royale des Antiquaires de Flandres)**
Huis Asselman Coorevits,
Vlazendaalstraat 55, 1700 Dilbeek, Belgium
Tel/Fax: (02) 567 0838

SHOPPING INFORMATION

Opening times for shops are generally:
Mon–Sat, 10am to 6.30pm or 7pm. Antiques
shops and auction rooms are usually open
Sunday mornings for viewing.

EXPORTING ANTIQUES

As with all members of the EU, there is free
transport of goods for non-trade purposes in
Belgium. A special rate of VAT applies to antiques
(items over 100 years old) which may be varied in
some cases if buys are shipped out of the country.

CZECH REPUBLIC

When phoning or faxing the Czech Republic from
abroad dial +420 and omit the first '0' of the
regional code.

TOURIST OFFICES

PRAGUE INFORMATION SERVICE
Betlemske namesti 2, 116 98 Praha 1
Tel: (02) 54 12 444
Web site: www.pis.cz
Email: tourinfo@pis.cz

**TOURIST OFFICE IN LONDON
Czech Tourist Authority**
95 Great Portland Street, London W1N 5RA
Tel: (020) 7291 9925.
Fax: (020) 7436 8300
24-hour brochure line (calls cost 60p a minute)
09063640641
Web site: www.antor.com
Email: ctainfo@czechcentre.org.uk

ANTIQUES DEALERS' ASSOCIATIONS

The Antiques Association for the Czech Republic,
is the only association for dealers and collectors
and it also runs most of the main antiques fairs.
Asociace staroz itniku CR, Valentinská 7, Praha 1.
Tel and Fax: (02) 232 5875
Email: asocstar@iol.cz

OTHER USEFUL GROUPS

PRAGUE SIGHTSEEING TOURS
Praha 1, Klimentská 52
Tel: (02) 231 4661. **Fax:** (02) 231 80 17
Web site: www.vol.cz/pst
Email: pst@mbox.vol.cz

PRAGOTUR
2a Poricskov branou 7, 18650 Praha 8
Tel: (02) 171 4136. **Fax:** (02) 171 4127

SHOPPING INFORMATION

Most shops are open Mon-Fri 10am to 6pm.
Times for Saturday vary, but shops generally open
from 10 or 11am and close at 4 or 5pm.

EXPORTING ANTIQUES

There are no special regulations. You are advised
to obtain a bill of sale which gives details of the
antique. You may be asked to show receipts on
leaving the country.

DENMARK

When phoning or faxing Denmark from abroad,
dial +45 and then the number.

TOURIST OFFICES

DANISH TOURIST BOARD HEAD OFFICE
Vesterbrogade 6D, 1620 København V.
Tel: 33 11 14 15. **Fax:** 33 93 14 16. **Email:** dt@dt.dt

WONDERFUL COPENHAGEN OFFICE
Bernstorffsgade 1, DK–1577 København V
Tel: 70 22 24 42. **Fax:** 70 22 24 52
Web site: www.woco.dk
Email: touristinfo@woco.dk

DANISH TOURIST BOARD IN LONDON
55 Sloane Street, London SW1X 9SY
Tel: (020) 7259 5959 (Monday to Friday, 10am to
3pm only) **Web site:** www.visitdenmark.com
Email: dtb.london@dt.dk

ANTIQUES DEALERS' ASSOCIATIONS

DAU – Dansk Kunst og Antikvitetshandler Union
Toldbodgade 5, 1253 København
Tel: 33 11 46 36

KUNST- & ANTIKVITETS HANDLER RINGEN
Lindegaardsvej 14, 3520 Farum
Tel: 44 99 41 11. **Fax:** 44 95 32 26
Web site: www.antikringen.dk (includes list of
members and what they specialize in)
Email: post@antikringen.dk

OTHER USEFUL GROUPS

Buy a Copenhagen Card to give you free entry to
over 60 museums, unlimited train and bus travel.
Information **web site:** www.woco.dk

SHOPPING INFORMATION

Mon–Thurs, 9.30am to 5.30pm; Fri, 9.30am to
6pm; Sat, 9.30am to 1pm or to 3pm on the first
Saturday of each month.
Danish VAT is steep (25%) so it is particularly
worth non-EU visitors claiming the refund.

EXPORTING ANTIQUES

An antique must have an export licence (supplied
by the dealer) before it can leave the country.

FRANCE

When phoning or faxing France from abroad, dial
+33 and omit the first '0' of the regional code.
NB: France's regional codes cover a wide area.

TOURIST OFFICES

**PARIS
L'Office de Tourisme de Paris**
127 avenue des Champs-Elysées, 75008 Paris
Tel: (0) 83 668 3112 recorded information in French
and English. **Fax:** (01) 49 52 53 00
Web site: www.paris-touristoffice.com
Email: info@paris-touristoffice.com

**NORMANDY
Official Normandy Tourist Board**
14 rue Charles Corbeau, F27000 Evreux
Tel: (02) 32 33 79 00. **Fax:** (02) 32 31 19 04
Web site: www.normandy-tourism.org
Email: normandy@imaginet.fr

HOTEL GROUPS IN EUROPE

Relais-du-Silence Hotels,
direct booking: tel +33 (01) 44 49 90 00; fax +33 (01) 44 49 79 01; web site www.relais-du-silence.com or www.silencehotel.com

Romantik Hotels & Restaurants,
web site www.romantikhotels.de

Grand Heritage Hotels,
tel: +44 (020) 7244 6699; fax: +44 (020) 7244 7799 web site: www.grandheritage.com

Kernpinski hotels and resorts,
web site www.grandhotel-europe.com

Sheraton International
web site www.sheraton.com

Bayeux Office de Tourisme, 3 rue St Jean, 14400
Tel: (02) 31 51 28 28. **Fax:** (02) 31 51 28 29

Caen Office de Tourisme, 12 Place St Pierre, 1400
Tel: (02) 31 27 14 14. **Fax:** (02) 31 27 14 18

Honfleur Office de Tourisme
Quai le Paulmier, 14600 Honfleur
Tel: (02) 31 89 23 30. **Fax:** (02) 31 89 31 82
Email: office-du-tourisme-honfleur@wanadoo.fr

BORDEAUX
Office de Tourisme, 12 cours du 30 juillet, 33000 Bordeaux
Tel: (05) 56 00 66 00. **Fax:** (05) 56 00 66 01
Web site: www.bordeaux.com
Email: otb@bordeaux-tourisme.com

BIARRITZ
Office de Tourisme, 1 Square Ixelles, 64200 Biarritz
Tel: (05) 59 22 37 00. **Fax:** (05) 59 24 14 19
Web site: www.tourisme.fr/biarritz
Email: Biarritz.Tourisme@biarritz.tm.fr

DORDOGNE
Office de Tourisme, 25 rue Wilson, BP 2063, 24002 Périgueux
Tel: (05) 53 35 50 24. **Fax:** (05) 53 09 51 41
Web site: www.perigord.tm.fr
Email: dordogne.perigord.tourisme@wanadoo.fr

LOT ET GARONNE
Office de Tourisme, 4 rue André Chénier, BP 158, 47005 Agen
Tel: (05) 53 66 14 14. **Fax:** (05) 53 68 25 42
Web site: www.lot-et-garonne.com
Email: cdt@wanadoo.fr

LYON
Office de Tourisme, Pavillion de Tourisme, Place Bellecour, BP 2254-69214, Lyon Cedex 02
Tel: (04) 72 77 69 69. **Fax:** (04) 78 42 04 32
The office sells the Lyon city card, valid for one, two or three days, which gives unlimited public transport including some boat trips and entry to many museums.

MARSEILLE
Office de Tourisme, 2 rue Beauvau, 13001 Marseille
Tel: (04) 91 13 89 00. **Fax:** (04) 91 13 89 20
Web site: www.marseille-tourisme.com
Email: acceuil@marseille-tourisme.com

PROVENCE
Office de Tourisme, place de la Liberté, 84800 L'Isle sur la Sorgue
Tel: (04) 90 38 04 78. **Fax:** (04) 90 38 35 43
Office Touristique du Pays de Gorges
Salle des Gardes, Gordes
Tel: (04) 90 72 02 75. **Fax:** (04) 90 72 02 26

Office Municipal de Tourisme, 2 place du général de Gaulle, BP 160, 13605 Aix-en-Provence
Tel: (04) 42 16 11 61. **Fax:** (04) 42 16 11 62
Web site: www.aixenprovencetourism.com
Email: infos@aixenprovencetourism.com

TOURIST OFFICE IN LONDON
French Travel Centre,178 Piccadilly, London W1J 9AL
Information line (8.30am–8pm) 09068 244123 (calls cost 60p a minute)
Web site: www.franceguide.com
Email:info@mdlf.co.uk

ANTIQUES DEALERS' ASSOCIATIONS
The following organizations can offer help and advice as well as estimations and information about trustworthy dealers:

SFEP – SYNDICAT FRANÇAIS DES EXPERTS PROESSIONNELS EN OEUVRES D'ART ET OBJECTS DE COLLECTION
1 rue Rossini, 75009 Paris
Tel: (01) 40 22 91 14. **Fax:** (01) 40 22 91 34
Web site: www.franceantiq.fr/sfep
Email: experts1@club-internet.fr

CNES – CHAMBRES NATIONALE DES EXPERTS SPECIALISES EN OBJETS D'ART DE COLLECTION
48 rue Duranton, 75015 Paris
Tel: (01) 45 58 18 00. **Fax:** (01) 45 58 18 08
Web site: www.franceantiq.fr/cnes
Email: experts-cnes@wanadoo.fr

SNA – SYNDICAT NATIONAL DES ANTIQUAIRES
17 boulevard Malesherbes, 75008 Paris
Tel: (01) 44 51 74 74. **Fax:** (01) 44 51 74 75
Web site: www.franceantiq.fr/sna/sna_fr.htm
Email: syndicat@antiquaires-sna.com

SYNDICAT NATIONAL DES ANTIQUAIRES, NEGOCIANTS EN OBJECTS D'ART, TABLEAUX ANCIENS ET MODERNES
1 bis, rue Clément-Marot, 75008 Paris
Tel: (01) 47 20 31 87. **Fax:** (01) 47 23 51 83

CHAMBRE SYNDICALE DES ANTIQUAIRES ET BROCANTEURS DE BORDEAUX ET LA GIRONDE
15 rue Bouffard, 33000 Bordeaux
Tel: (05) 56 44 26 64

GROUPEMENT DES ANTIQUAIRES ET BROCANTEURS DU ROUSSILLON
56 bis, chemin Etang Long 66380 PIA
Tel: (04) 68 63 06 39

SYNDICAT DES ANTIQUAIRES, BROCANTEURS & GALERIES D'ART DE MARSEILLE & LA REGION
3 rue Fortia, 13001 Marseille
Tel: (04) 91 33 06 81

OTHER USEFUL GROUPS

Les Deux Chineurs provides a guide and translation service for auctions, antiques fairs and flea markets, in Paris or the provinces.
Tel: (06) 62 71 42 78.
Email: kyle@chineurs.com

Châteaux & Hôtels de France (manor houses of outstanding character)
Central booking, **tel:** (01) 40 07 00 20; fax: (01) 40 07 00 30
Web site: www.chateauhotels.com

"Paris Hotels Association Guide" and "Le Guide des hôtels-restaurants Logis de France" are available free from French tourist offices. You must book the accommodation yourself.

SHOPPING INFORMATION

Most shops are open from 10am to 7pm, Monday to Saturday. In the provinces, most shops are closed all day Monday and at lunchtime, from 12 midday to 2pm or from 1pm to 3pm.

EXPORTING ANTIQUES

No restrictions are imposed on exporting antiques from France but obtain a certificate of provenance for them if you can.

GERMANY

When phoning or faxing Germany from abroad dial +49 and omit the first '0' of the regional code.

TOURIST OFFICES

BERLIN
Berlin Tourismus, Europa-center, Budapester Strasse; also Brandenberger Tor, Pariser Platz. Also Am Karlsbad 11, 10785 Berlin
CallCentre (from UK): (01805) 75 40 40
CallCentre (in Germany): 0190 016316
Fax: (030) 25 00 24 24
Web site: www.berlin-tourism.de

MUNICH
Tourismusverband München-Oberbayern, Bodenseestr. 113, 81243 München.
Tel: (089) 82 92 18 30. **Fax:** (089) 82 92 18 28
Web site: www.btl.de/oberbayern/
Email: tourismus@oberbayern.btl.de

WÜRZBURG
Tourist-Information, Am Congress Centrum, 97070, Würzburg.
Tel: (0931) 37 2335. **Fax:** (0931) 37 3652
Web site: www.wuerzburg.de
Email: tourismus@fraenkisches-weinland.btl.de

BAMBERG
Geyerswörthstr. 3, 96047 Bamberg
Tel: (0951) 87 11 61. **Fax:** (0951) 87 19 60
Web site: www.bamberg.de
Email: touristinfo@bamberg.de

COLOGNE
Köln Tourismus Office, Unter Fettenhennen 19, 50667 Köln.
Tel: (0221) 221 33345. **Fax:** (0221) 221 23320
Web site: www.koeln.de
Email: koelntourismus@koeln.org

HAMBURG
Tourism-Zentrale Hamburg, Steinstrasse 7, 20095 Hamburg.
Tel: (040) 300 51 300. **Fax:** (040) 300 51 333
Web site: www.hamburg-tourism.de
Email: info@hamburg-tourism.de

GERMAN NATIONAL TOURIST OFFICE IN LONDON
PO Box 2695, London W1A 3TN
Tel: (020) 7317 0908. **Fax:** (020) 7495 6129
24-hour info and brochure line (UK): 09001 600 100 (calls cost 50p a minute)
Web site: www.germany-tourism.de
Email: gntoln@d-z-t.com

ANTIQUES DEALERS' ASSOCIATION

BDKA – Bundersverband des Deutschen Kunst- und Antiquitätenhandels e.V
Im Bauernholz 3, D-12179 Drestedt
Tel: (041) 8688 9595. **Fax:** (041) 86 666

OTHER USEFUL GROUPS

ANTIQUES AND COLLECTABLES – GERMANY
Internet information about dealers, shops and locations in Germany
Web site: www.acguide.com/SL-Germany.html

THE HISTORIC HIGHLIGHTS OF GERMANY
Tourist Information, Bahnhofstr. 49, D-69181, Leiman-Heidelberg
Tel: (06224) 92 64 43. **Fax:** (06224) 92 64 69

THE MUNICH SERVICE TEAM
Offers information about Munich – tours, hotels, tourist information
Tel: (089) 540 98 60. **Fax:** (089) 540 98 811
Web site: www.munich-specials.de

BERLIN AND MUNICH WALKING TOURS
Web site: www.berlinwalks.com

INSIDE COLOGNE CITY TOURS
Bismarckstr. 70, DD-50672 Köln
Tel: (0700) 24 89 87. **Fax:** (0221) 52 8667
Web site: www.insidecologne.de
Email: tours@insidecologne.de

SHOPPING INFORMATION

Most shops open Mon-Fri 9am to 6pm; Thursday closing is 8.30pm. Saturday opening times are 9am to 2pm. On the first Saturday in each month shops open until 6pm (summer) and 4pm (winter).

EXPORTING ANTIQUES

Generally, export transactions are not complicated. Dealers know that items designated as antiques should have a licence of sale for export.

GREAT BRITAIN & NORTHERN IRELAND

When phoning or faxing Great Britain or Northern Ireland from abroad, dial +44 and omit the first '0' of the regional code.

TOURIST OFFICES

BRITISH TOURIST AUTHORITY
Thames Tower, Black's Road, London W6 9EL
Tel: (020) 8846 9000. **Fax:** (020) 8563 0302
Web sites: www.britishtouristauthority.org and www.visitbritain.com

SCOTTISH BORDERS
Scottish Borders Tourist Board, Shepherds Mill, Whinfield Road, Selkirk TD7 5DT
Tel: (01750) 20555. **Fax:** (01750) 21886
Web site: www.scot-borders.co.uk
Email: sbtb@scot-borders.co.uk

LONDON
Tourist Information Service Tel: (020) 7370 7744

BRIGHTON
Visitor Information Service, Bartholomew Square, Brighton; and Church Road, Hove.
Tel: 0906 711 22 55 (calls cost 50p a minute). For an accommodation guide, call (0345) 573512 (local rate, 24 hours).
Web site: www.brighton.co.uk

YORK
York Tourist Information, De Grey Rooms, Exhibition Square, York YO1 7HB.
Tel: (01904) 621756. **Fax:** (01904) 639986.
Web site: www.york-tourism.co.uk
Email: tic@york-tourism.co.uk

HARROGATE
Harrogate Tourist Information Centre
Royal Baths, Crescent Road, Harrogate HG1 2RR
Tel: (01423) 537300. Fax: (01423) 537305.
Web site: www.harrogate.gov.uk/tourism
Email: tic@harrogate.gov.uk

MANCHESTER
Manchester Visitor Centre, Town Hall
Extension, Lloyd Street, Manchester M60 2LA
Tel: (0161) 234 3157. Fax: (0161) 238 990
24-hour brochure line (calls cost 60p a minute):
0906 871 5533

BATH
Abbey Chambers, Abbey Churchyard, Bath BA1 1LY
Tel: (01225) 477 101
Email: tourism@bathnes.gov.uk

BRISTOL
Bristol Tourist Information Centre, The Annexe,
Wildscreen Walk, Harbourside, Bristol.
Tel: (0117) 926 0767. Fax: (0117) 915 7340
Web site: www.visitbristol.co.uk

COTSWOLDS
Hollis House, The Square, Stow-on-the-Wold,
Gloucestershire GL54 1AF
Tel: (01451) 831082. Fax: (01451) 870083

EDINBURGH
Edinburgh and Lothian Tourist Board,
4 Rothesay Terrace, Edinburgh EH3 7RY
Web site: www.edinburgh.org
Email: ESIC@Edinburgh & Lothians Tourist Board

GLASGOW
**Greater Glasgow and Clyde Valley Tourist
Board**
11 George Square, Glasgow G2 1DY
Tel: (0141) 204 4480. Fax: (0141) 204 4772
Web site: www.seeglasgow.com

SCOTTISH TOURIST BOARD
19 Cockspur Street, London SW1Y 5BL
Tel: (020) 7930 8661
Web site: www.visitscotland.com

NORTHERN IRELAND
The Belfast Welcome Centre
35 Donegall Place, Belfast BT15AD
Tel: (028) 9024 6609. Fax: (028) 9031 2424
Web site: www.gotobelfast.com
Email: info@belfastvisitor.com

The Northern Ireland Information Centre
59 North Street, Belfast BT1 1NB
Tel: (028) 9023 1221. Fax: (028) 9024 096
Web site: www.discovernorthernireland.com
Email: info@nitb.com

ANTIQUES DEALERS' ASSOCIATIONS

BADA – The British Antiques Dealers' Association
20 Rutland Gate, London SW7 1BD
Tel: (020) 7589 4128. Fax: (020) 7581 9083
Web site: www.bada.org
Email: enquiry@bada.demon.co.uk

**LAPADA – The Association of Art and Antique
Dealers**
535 Kings Road, Chelsea, London, SW10 0SW
Tel: (0207) 823 3511. Fax: (0207) 823 3522
Web site: www.lapada.co.uk

CADA – Cotswold Antique Dealers' Association
Broadwell House, Sheep Street, Stow on the
Wold, Gloucestershire GL54 1JS
Tel: (01451) 830053. Fax: (01451) 870028

Web site: www.cotswolds-antiques-art.com
Email: info@cotswolds-antiques-art.com

**BABAADA – Bath and Bradford on Avon
Antique Dealers' Association**
London Road, Bath, BA1 6PL
Tel: (01225) 442215. Fax: (01225) 448196
Web site: www.babaada.com
Email: go@babaada.com

OTHER USEFUL GROUPS

THE ORIGINAL LONDON WALKS
PO Box 1708, London NW6 4LW
Tel: (020) 7624 3978
Recorded Information: (020) 7624 9255
Fax: (0207) 625 1932
Web site: http://www.walks.com
Email: london@walks.com

LONDON TRAVEL INFORMATION
Tel: (020) 7222 1234 (24 hours)
Web site: www.londontransport.co.uk

THE NATIONAL TRUST
36 Queen Anne's Gate, London SW1H 9AS
Tel: (020) 7222 9251. Fax: (0207) 222 5097
Web site: www.nationaltrust.org.uk
For National Trust holiday information:
NT Enterprises, The Stable Block, Heywood
House, Westbury, Wiltshire BA13 4NA
Tel: (01373) 858787. Fax: (01373) 827575

THE LANDMARK TRUST
(restores historic buildings and makes them
available for short lets)
Shottesbrooke, Maidenhead, Berkshire SL6 3SW
Tel: (01628) 825925. Fax: (01628) 825417
Web site: www.landmarktrust.co.uk
Email: bookings@landmarktrust.co.uk

ENGLISH HERITAGE
Customer Services Department, PO Box 569,
Swindon SN2 2YP
Tel: (01793) 414910. Fax: 01793 414926
Web site: www.english-heritage.org.uk

HISTORIC HOUSES ASSOCIATION
2 Chester Street, London SW1X 7BB
Tel: (020) 7259 5688. Fax: (020) 7259 5590
Web site: www.historic-houses-assn.org
Email: hha@compuserve.com

BAILEY'S HISTORICAL PUB WALKS
Two-and-a-half-hour treks visiting Belfast pubs
and discovering the city's history.
Tel: (028) 9268 3665

SHOPPING INFORMATION

Opening hours: Generally 9am to 5pm or 6pm
Monday to Saturday (often later in London). Many
shops now open Sundays – times may vary, but
usually 10am to 4pm.

EXPORTING ANTIQUES

Antiques over 100 years old are free of customs
and excise duty, but numismatic items, postage
and revenue stamps over 100 years old may
attract some VAT.

Antiques IMPORTED in your baggage when
returning to the UK are free of duty and tax if they
are your own property, are not for sale and their
value is within the duty and tax free allowances.
Antiques shipped or couriered into the UK must
be accompanied by a written declaration of the
age of the item/s or a certificate of evidence of
age (provided by the seller). The item/s must have
an entry form C88 with different codes for goods
from outside the EU and inside the EU.

HUNGARY

When phoning or faxing Hungary from abroad dial +36 and omit the first '0' of the regional code.

TOURIST OFFICES

BUDAPEST
Tourism Office of Budapest
1364 Budapest, Pf. 215
Tel: (01) 266 0479. **Fax:** (01) 266 7477
Email: info@budapesttourist.hu

HUNGARIAN NATIONAL TOURIST OFFICE IN LONDON
46 Eaton Place, London SW1X 8AL
Tel: (020) 7823 1032. **Fax:** (020) 7823 1459
Web site: www.hungarytourism.hu
Email: htlondon@btinternet.com

ANTIQUES DEALERS' ASSOCIATIONS

There is no national association as such. However dealers are licensed by the state and should display their accreditation. The Hungarian Government strongly advises visitors not to purchase anything from unlicensed vendors.

OTHER USEFUL GROUPS

Go to an Information Bureau to obtain a copy of a folder in English featuring events, collections and exhibitions, opening hours of galleries, regular auctions and rules of exporting works of art. A Budapest Card gives free entry to most museums (English guides provided).

SHOPPING INFORMATION

Centres are open every day all week from 10am to 6pm (some department stores stay open until 8pm on Thursdays). Markets are generally open only on Saturdays and Sundays, from about 7am to 5pm. Keep all receipts to apply for a tax refund. A cash refund is given only in local currency (forints); if you have bought by credit card fill in a refund form and make sure customs stamps your receipts before you leave Hungary.

EXPORTING ANTIQUES

No antique over 100 years old can be exported. Certain art pieces are "protected": if you buy one of these you will need a special permit to present to customs on leaving. Licences are issued by the National Gallery (Hungarian items): Magyar Nemzeti Galéria, The Royal Palace, Building B, C, D, 2 Szent György Square, Budapest (tel: (01) 175 7533); or Museum of Applied Arts (foreign-made items): Iparművészeti Múzeum, H-1091 Budapest 1X, Üllői út 33-37 (tel: (01) 217 5222). Both museums are closed on Mondays. Licensed art dealers know the procedure. The cost of the licence will be a percentage of the officially certified value of the antique.

IRELAND

When phoning or faxing Ireland from abroad dial +353 and omit the first '0' of the regional code.

TOURIST OFFICES

DUBLIN
Dublin Tourism Centre, Suffolk Street, Dublin 2
24-hour brochure line (01) 605 7792
Fax: (01) 605 7725
Web site: www.visitdublin.com
Email: reservations@dublintourism.ie
or information@dublintourism.ie

IRISH TOURIST BOARD IN LONDON
Irish Desk, Britain Visitor Centre,
1 Lower Regent Street, London SW1Y 4XT
Tel: 08000 397 000. **Fax:** (020) 7493 9065
Web site: ireland.travel.ie
Email: info@gulliver.ie

ANTIQUES DEALERS' ASSOCIATION

IADA – Irish Antiques Dealers' Association
Ian Haslam, Hon. Secretary
The Silver Shop, Powerscourt Centre, South William Street, Dublin 2.
Tel: (01) 679 4147. **Fax:** (01) 679 4147
Email: irantda@eircom.net
George Stacpoole, President,
Main Street, Adare, Co. Limerick, Ireland.
Tel: (061) 396 409. **Fax:** (061) 396 733
Email: stacpool@iol.ie

OTHER USEFUL GROUPS

For information on up-market B&Bs and private houses that offer accommodation with food, often in historic buildings, contact:
The Hidden Ireland, PO Box 31, Westport, Co. Mayo
Tel: (01) 662 7166. **Fax:** (01) 662 7144
Web site: www.hidden-ireland.com/index.html
Email: info@hidden-ireland.com

For information on tour guides contact:
FIGI Association of Approved Tour Guides
11 Skeen Road, Off Naven Road, Dublin 7.
Tel: (01) 838 5279

SHOPPING INFORMATION

Mon–Sat, 9am to 5.30pm (later on Thursdays) Most towns close half day on one day a week (this day is different from town to town). Small shops tend to close at lunchtime.

EXPORTING ANTIQUES

There are no restrictions. Dealers should provide a normal bill of sale with details of the antique.

ITALY

When phoning or faxing Italy from abroad, dial +39 and include the first '0' of the regional code.

TOURIST OFFICES

ROME TOURIST BOARD
Via 20 Settembre 26, 00187 Roma
Tel: (06) 42 13 81. **Fax:** (06) 421 38 22

FLORENCE
Via Manzoni 16, 50121 Firenze
Tel: (055) 23320. **Fax:** (055) 2346286

TUSCANY AND UMBRIA
A P T, Piazza del Comune, 06081 Assisi
Tel: (075) 812450. **Fax:** (075) 813727
Email: info@iat.assisi.pg.it
A P T, Via Mazzini 6, 06100 Perugia
Tel: (0755) 729842. **Fax:** (0755) 739386
Email: info@perugia.it
A P T, Via B. Croce 24/26, 56125 Pisa
Tel: (050) 40096. **Fax:** (050) 40903
A P T, Centro Servizi Informazioni Turistiche, Piazza del Campo 56, 53100 Siena
Tel: (0577) 289551. **Fax:** (0577) 270676
Email: aptsiena@siena.turismo.toscana.it

VENICE
A P T, Castello 4421, 30122 Venezia
Tel: (041) 529 8711. **Fax:** (041) 523 0399
Web site: www.turismovenezia.it
Email: apt-06@mail.regione.veneto.it

PALERMO
A A P I T, Piazza Castelnuovo 35, 90141 Palermo
Tel: (091) 605 8111. Fax: (091) 331854
Web site: www.aapit.pa.it
Email: aapit@gestelnet.it

ITALIAN STATE TOURIST BOARD IN LONDON (ENIT)
1 Princes Street, London W1R 8AY
Tel: (020) 7408 1254 (Mon–Fri 9am to 4pm).
24-hour brochure line: (09001) 600 280 (calls cost £1 a minute). Fax: (020) 7493 6695
Web site: www.enit.com
Email: enitlond@globalnet.co.uk

ANTIQUES DEALERS' ASSOCIATIONS
Sindacato Antiquari di Firenze e Provincia
6 via Strozziaodro 1-50123 Firenze
Tel: (05) 526 4031

Associazione Antiquari d'Italia
Piazza Strozzi 1, 50123 Firenze
Tel: (05) 528 2283. Fax: (05) 521 4831

Sindacato Romano Antiquari
227 via Coronari, 00186 Roma
Tel: (06) 687 5384

OTHER USEFUL GROUPS
TOURIST GUIDES IN VENICE
Ass. Guide Turistiche
Tel: (041) 523 9038

Guide Turistiche Autorizzate
Tel: (041) 520 9038. Fax: (041) 521 0762

SHOPPING INFORMATION
Shops are generally open Mon–Sat from 9.30am to 1pm and from 3.30pm or 4pm to 7.30pm. On Sundays some shops may open after lunch.

EXPORTING ANTIQUES
Sellers of antiques (that is, items more than 50 years old) should have received the permission of the Government's Fine Arts Department to arrange export by courier. Small antiques (books, prints) should be carried by you. Keep your receipts as proof of purchase on arrival home.

THE NETHERLANDS

When phoning or faxing the Netherlands from abroad dial +31 and omit the first '0' of the regional code.

TOURIST OFFICES
AMSTERDAM
VVV Amsterdam Tourist Office Stadionplein Argonautenstraat 98, 1076 KV Amsterdam
Tel: (020) 551 25 25
Email: info@amsterdamtourist.nl

THE HAGUE TOURIST OFFICES
VVV Den Haag/centre, Kon Julianaplein 30
PO Box 85456, 2508 CD Den Haag
VVV Den Haag/Scheveningen, Gevers Deynootweg 1134, PO Box 85456, 2508 CD Den Haag
Tel: (070)361 8888. Fax: (070) 347 2102 and (070) 352 0426
Web site: www.denhaag.com
Email: info@denhaag.com

DELFT TOURIST OFFICE
VW Delft, Markt 83 85, 2611 GS Delft
Tel: (0150) 213 0100. Fax: (0150) 215 8695

NETHERLANDS BOARD OF TOURISM IN LONDON
PO Box 523, London SW1E 6NT
24-hour brochure/info line: 0906 871 7777 (calls cost 60p a minute). Fax: (020) 7828 7941
Web site: www.holland.com/uk
Email: hollandinfo-uk@nbt.nl

ANTIQUES DEALERS' ASSOCIATION
VEREENIGING VAN HANDELAREN IN OUDE KUNST IN NEDERLAND
Keisersgracht 207, 1016 DS Amstersam
Tel: (020) 623 8904. Fax: (020) 623 8680

OTHER USEFUL GROUPS
BELGIUM AND HOLLAND ANTIQUES ONLINE
Information about dealers and antiques fairs, guided buying tours.
Web site: www.belgiumantiques.com

SHOPPING INFORMATION
Mon-Fri 8.30 or 9am to 5.30 or 6pm; Sat 8.30 or 9am to 4 or 5pm. Most cities have late night shopping on Thursdays and Fridays. In tourist resorts many shops are open at night and on Sundays. In Amsterdam department stores and other stores may be closed on Sundays and on Monday morning.

EXPORTING ANTIQUES
No restrictions apply when buying antiques in the Netherlands. The bill of sale should record details of the item you are buying.

NORWAY

When phoning or faxing Norway from abroad, dial +47 followed by the number.

TOURIST OFFICES
Norges Turistrad, PO Box 2893 Solli
N–0230 Oslo
Tel: 22 92 52 00. Fax: 22 56 05 05
Email: norway@ntr.no

NORWEGIAN TOURIST BOARD IN LONDON
5th Floor, Charles House, 5 Lower Regent Street, London SW1Y 4LR
Tel: (020) 7839 2650. Fax: (020) 7207 839 6014
Web site: www.visitnorway.com
Email: infouk@ntr.no

ANTIQUES DEALERS' ASSOCIATION
Norges Kunst- og Antikvitetshandleres Forening
Elisenbergveien 7, N-0265, Oslo
Tel: (022) 44 45 33. Fax: (022) 43 11 10

OTHER USEFUL GROUPS
Buy an Oslo Card (24, 28 or 72 hours) from the tourist office which gives free entrance to museums and travel on tram, bus and tube.

SHOPPING INFORMATION
The usual shopping hours during the week are 9am to 5pm. On Saturdays the hours are shorter: 10 am to 2 or 3pm. Shops are closed Sunday.

EXPORTING ANTIQUES
To export an antique over 100 years old you must apply to the Museum of Fine Art in Oslo; this is usually done for you by the dealer and it can take up to a week. There is no tax if your purchase is being shipped out of the country. If you are taking it with you may have to pay the 24% VAT and reclaim it back at the airport when leaving.

POLAND

When phoning or faxing Poland from abroad dial +48 followed by the number.

TOURIST OFFICES

POLISH TOURISM ORGANIZATION
Aleje Jerozolimskie 54, Central Railway Station
00-24 Warsaw
Tel: 22 36 50 55.
Web site: www.infolinia.pl
Email: lkukfit@pol.pl

WARSAW INFORMATION CENTRE
Informator Turystyczny
Plac Zamkowy 1/13, 00-262 Warsaw
Tel: 22 635 1881. Fax: 22 310464
Email: mit@supermedia.pl

WARSAW TOURIST OFFICE
00-336 Warsaw, ul. M Kopernika 30
Tel: 22 826 0788. Fax: 22 826 0798
Web site: www.warsawtour.pl
Email: info@warsawtour.pl

POLISH NATIONAL TOURIST OFFICE IN LONDON
First Floor, Remo House, 310-312 Regent Street, London W1B 3AX
Tel: (020) 7580 8811 (brochure request line)
Fax: (020) 7580 8866
Web site: www.pnto.dial.pipex.com
Email: pnto@dial.pipex.com

ANTIQUES DEALERS' ASSOCIATION

ASP – Antique Dealer's Association of Poland
ul Grodzka 6, 31-006 Kraków
Tel and Fax: 12 0602 62 0202

OTHER USEFUL GROUPS

The Ostoya Antiques House conducts auctions in Warsaw. **Tel:** 22 831 26 95. **Fax:** 22 635 55 78
Web site: www.auction-ostoya.art.pl
Auctions are also held at the Royal Meridien Bristol Hotel in Warsaw.

The former state-run **Orbis**, now independent, has hotels throughout Poland and arranges guided tours. Most city tours start from an Orbis hotel. Orbis, Ulica Marszalkowska 142, Warsaw.
Tel: 22 27 36 73.

SHOPPING INFORMATION

The old system was to open at 11am and shut at 7pm and some stores still do this while others such as department stores and kiosks open earlier.

EXPORTING ANTIQUES

When buying antiques in Poland, you should note that, because of the wholesale plundering of the country during World War II, the export of any piece (including books) dating from before 1945 requires a government permit. Antiques that can't be exported may have a pink label. Any purchase that you are thinking of making must be eligible for an export licence (arranged by the dealer). When you buy ask whether any special documentation is required (this is important as regulations change frequently). Warsaw Customs Headquarters, ul. Swietokrzyska 12 (tel: 22 694 3194).

PORTUGAL

When phoning or faxing Portugal from abroad, dial +351 followed by the number given.

TOURIST OFFICES

LISBON TOURIST OFFICE
Associação de Turismo de Lisboa
Rua da Junqueira 39 -1°, 1300-037 Lisboa
Tel: (21) 361 0350. Fax: (21) 361 0359
Web site: www.atl-turismolisboa.pt
Email: atl@atl-turismolisboa.pt

PORTUGUESE TOURISM OFFICE IN LONDON
23–25a Sackville Street, London W1S 3LY
24-hour brochure line: 09063 640 610 (calls cost 60p per minute). Fax: (020) 7494 1868
Web site: www.portugalinsite.pt
Email: tourisminfo@portugaloffice.org.uk

ANTIQUES DEALERS' ASSOCIATION

Associacão Portuguesa Antiquários
Rua do Alecrim 47, 4°C, 1200 Lisboa
Tel: 1 347 4571. Fax: 1 347 4572

OTHER USEFUL GROUPS

Pousadas and private manors, mansions and quintas (farms) where you can stay are found in historic areas. Pousadas bookings **tel** (UK): (020) 8876 1352 or **web site** www.pousadas.pt

Private houses booking **tel** (Portugal): 00351 258 835 065 or **web site** www.manorhouses.com

In Lisbon, buy a Lisboa Card from Carris kiosks giving free entry to 26 museums and free public transport for one, two or three days.

SHOPPING INFORMATION

Most shops are open Mon–Sat from 9 or 10 am to 1pm and from 3pm to 7pm; large shopping centres open daily from 10am to 11pm Not all shops open Sundays. Museums mostly close on Mondays.

EXPORTING ANTIQUES

Sellers should provide a bill of sale with details of the antique. There are no restrictions on what can be exported from Portugal.

RUSSIA

When phoning or faxing Russia from abroad, dial +7 and omit the first '0' of the regional code.

TOURIST OFFICES

COMMITTEE FOR TOURISM
(Moscow City Government)
15 Novy Arbat, Moscow 121019
Tel: (095) 290 2062. Fax: (095) 290 2062

ST PETERSBURG TOURIST INFORMATION CENTRE
Tel: (0812) 276 1642
Email: sad@cfea.ecc.spb.su

RUSSIAN TRAVEL CENTRE IN LONDON
70 Piccadilly, London W1J 8HP
Tel: (020) 7495 7570. Fax: (020) 7495 8555
Web site: www.inntel-moscow.co.uk
Email: inntelmoscow@inntel-moscow.co.uk

ANTIQUES DEALERS' ASSOCIATION

No association as such. Visitors to Russia are recommended to buy from antiques shops rather than street traders.

OTHER USEFUL GROUPS

Committee for tourism and development of resorts, Nevsky pr. 41, St Petersburg
Tel: 812 3122541. **Fax:** 812 3159796
Web site: www.guide.spb.ru
Email: travel@mail.wplus.net

KTS (Moscow accommodation, transfers, guides)
11 Chistoprudny, Moscow 121248
Tel: (095) 924 2166. **Fax:** (095) 924 8266

Kempinski hotels and resorts (Grand Hotel, St Petersburg); **tel** (book direct): 812 329 6000;
fax: 812 329 6001; **email:** dos@ghe.spb.ru
Sheraton Nevskij Palace (St Petersburg), **tel** (book direct): 812 275 2001, **fax** 812 301 7323

SHOPPING INFORMATION

Shops are generally open on Mon–Fri 10am to 7pm. Saturdays sometimes have shorter opening hours (until 5pm). If shops open on Sundays the hours may be 10am to 4pm.

EXPORTING ANTIQUES

You will receive a customs declaration on arrival to be completed on departure. Be careful about your purchases as souvenirs are subject to a 600% duty upon leaving the country.

If you buy in antiques shops, make sure that the price includes all necessary customs' documentation. You are advised not to purchase items more than 100 years old unless you can obtain written consent, in effect a licence from the Russian president, which the dealer would arrange. Generally, pieces of art and antiques produced before 1945 cannot be exported unless cleared for export at the St Petersburg Customs Administration: 10, The Line, Vasilyevskiy Island 4. Tel: 350 6374. This process will take at least a week and you will need photographs of the item.

SPAIN

When phoning Spain from abroad, dial +34 and omit the first '0' of the regional code.

TOURIST OFFICES

MADRID
O.T. Madrid, Plaza Mayor 3, 38012 Madrid
Tel: (091) 588 16 36. **Fax:** (091) 366 54 77

BARCELONA
O.T. Barcelona, Plaza de Catalunya 17, 8002 Barcelona
Tel: (093) 304 3135/304 31 34. **Fax:** (093) 304 3155
Email: turisme.bcn@bcn.servicom.es

SEVILLE
O.T. Sevilla, Avenida de la Constitución 21-B, 41001 Sevilla
Tel: (0954) 2214 04. **Fax:** (0954) 22 97 53
Email: ot.sevilla@turismo-andaluz.com

CORDOBA
O.T. Cordoba, Plaza Judá Leví,14003 Cordoba
Tel: (0957) 20 05 20. **Fax:** (0957) 20 02 77
Email: turismoaix@ayuncordoba.es

GRANADA
O.T. Granada, Plaza de Mariana Pineda 12 bajo, 18009 Granada
Tel: (0958) 22 6688. **Fax:** (0958) 22 8916
Email: turismo@dipgra.es

SPANISH TOURIST OFFICE IN LONDON
22-23 Manchester Square, London WIM 5AP
Tel: (020) 7486 8077. **Fax:** (020) 7486 8034
24-hour brochure request line: 0906 3640 630
(calls cost 50p a minute within the UK)

ANTIQUES DEALERS' ASSOCIATIONS

Asociación de Brocantes de Madrid,
6 Conde de Aranda, 28001 Madrid
Tel: (091) 435 4973
Visitors can obtain a list of the antiques shops of Madrid: the Guia De Anticuarios De Madrid. A medallion symbol showing Carlos III's profile indicates that the shop is a member of the Association.

Asociación de Empresarios de Almonedas y Antigüedades de Madrid y Su Provincia
16 calle Prado (Casa Morueco), 1. °1a, 28014 Madrid
Tel: (091) 429 3659

Asociación Profesional de Brocanters de Catalunya
4-2° 1 plaza Sant Josep Oriol, 08002 Barcelona
Tel: (093) 317 1996

Gremi d'Antiquaris de Catalunya
Rosellón 233, 3°, 2a, 08008 Barcelona
Tel: (093) 237 9656. **Fax:** (093) 237 3846
Email: lluc@gna.es

Gremio d'Anticuarios de Sevilla
7 calle Rodrigo Caro, 41004 Sevilla
Tel: (095) 421 6558

OTHER USEFUL GROUPS

Web site: www.tourspain.es

Paradores de Turismo
Central booking (Madrid), **tel:** 0034 91 516 6666;
fax: 0034 91 516 66 57. **Web site:** www.parador.es
Central booking (London), **tel:** 0044 (020) 7616 0300; **fax:** 0044 (020) 7616 0317.
Email:paradores@keytel.co.uk

SHOPPING INFORMATION

Shopping hours can have a genteel casualness. Antique shops will be open by 11am, but close at 2pm, opening again at 5pm until 8pm. Many shops are closed for a day and a half a week, usually Saturday afternoons and Sundays.

Typical opening hours for museums and other public places are Tuesdays to Saturdays from 9am or 10am to 7pm or 9pm. On Sundays and holidays, attractions are open only in the morning, from 9am until 2pm. Some smaller places will have shorter hours.

EXPORTING ANTIQUES

Generally no problems or restrictions. Obtain a bill of sale with details of your purchase.

SWEDEN

When phoning or faxing Sweden from abroad, dial +46 and omit the first '0' of the regional code.

TOURIST OFFICES

TOURIST CENTRE IN STOCKHOLM
Sverigehuset, Hamngatan 27 (Kungsträdgården), Box 7542, 10393 Stockholm
Tel: (08) 789 24 00. **Fax:** (08) 789 24 50
Web site: www.stockholmtown.com
Email: info@stoinfo.se

RECLAIMING TAXES

In EU countries, tax-free shopping is available to non-EU residents who can reclaim the VAT (value added tax) on purchases before leaving the country. The EU countries are: Austria, Belgium, Denmark, Finland, France, Germany, Greece, Ireland, Italy, Luxembourg, Netherlands, Portugal, Spain (not the Canary Islands), Sweden and the UK (Great Britain and Northern Ireland). Usually you need a refund form and the claim is either made through the store itself or at the airport (the method varies between countries). Refunds can be made through your credit card. EU residents can claim a refund in non-EU countries through shops or at the airport.

TOURIST OFFICE IN LONDON
Swedish Travel & Tourism Council
11 Montague Place, London W1H 2AL
Tel: (020) 7870 5606. **Fax:** (020) 7724 5872
Web site: www.visit-sweden.com
Email: info@swetourism.org.uk

ANTIQUES DEALERS' ASSOCIATION
Sveriges Konst- och Antikhandlarförening
Box 5818, 102 48 Stockholm
Tel: (08) 661 1241. **Fax:** (08) 662 0510
President Bo Knutsson Tel: (07)0346 6077

OTHER USEFUL GROUPS
A Stockholm Card (*Stockholmkortet*) for 24, 48 or 72 hours gives free entry to over 70 museums, free travel on underground, buses and trains, free car parking, free sightseeing (in summer).
Web site: www.stockholmtown.com

SHOPPING INFORMATION
Opening hours are generally: Mon-Fri 10.00am to 6.00pm, Sat 10.00am to 1.00pm, Sun closed.

EXPORTING ANTIQUES
You need a special permit to export antiques over 50 years old and this should be arranged by the seller. Your receipt should be stamped by customs before leaving the country.

SWITZERLAND

When phoning or faxing Switzerland from abroad dial +41 and omit the first '0' of the regional code.

TOURIST OFFICES
GENEVA TOURISM BOARD
Rue de Mont-Blanc 18, case Poshcla 1602,
CH-1211 Genève 1
Tel: (022) 909 7000. **Fax:** (022) 909 7075
Email: info@geneve-tourisme.ch

TOURIST OFFICE IN LONDON
Swiss Centre, 10 Wardour Street, London W1D 6QF
Tel: (020) 7841 1700. **Fax:** 020 7851 1720
Web site: www.MySwitzerland.com
Email: stlondon@switzerlandvacation.ch

ANTIQUES DEALERS' ASSOCIATIONS
Association Genèvoise des Antiquaires et Commerçants d'Art
5 place du Bourg de Four, 1200 Genève
Tel: (022) 310 7824
Web site: www.broc-antic.com

VSAK– Verband Schweizerishcher Antiquare & Kunsthandler,
Schachenstrasse 23, CH-4562 Biberist
Tel: (032) 672 4250

OTHER USEFUL GROUPS
Antiques and Collectables Guide to Switzerland internet site for antiques shops and dealers: www.acguide.com/SL-Switzerland.html

SHOPPING INFORMATION
Mon–Fri: shops open between 8am and 10am and close between 6pm and 10pm. On Saturdays they close between 4pm and 5pm. Evening shopping once a week (until 9pm) varies, in Zurich and Geneva it is Thursday. Many shops close on Sunday, but some large shopping centres open seven days a week, from 8am to 8pm.

EXPORTING ANTIQUES
There are no restrictions on what antiques can be exported, but an invoice or receipt is required, declaring the value of the goods. If antiques are valued at more than CHF 500, an export declaration is required which should be stamped at Swiss customs.

TURKEY

When phoning or faxing Turkey from abroad, dial +90 and then the number.

TOURIST OFFICES
ISTANBUL TOURIST CENTRES
Sultanahmet: **tel** 212 518 87 54; **fax** 212 518 18 02
Beyoglu: **tel** 212 243 37 31; **fax** 212 252 43 46
Taksim: **tel** 212 245 68 76

TURKISH TOURIST OFFICE IN LONDON
1st Floor, Egyptian House, 170-173 Piccadilly, London W1J 9EJ
Tel: (020) 7629 7771. **Fax:** (020) 7491 0773
24-hour brochure line: 0901 887755 (calls cost 60p a minute in UK)
Web site: www.tourist-offices.org.uk/turkey
Email: tto@turkishtourism.demon.co.uk

ANTIQUES DEALERS' ASSOCIATIONS
No association found. Visitors are recommended to deal only with licensed antiques sellers.

SHOPPING INFORMATION
Shops are generally open every day from 9 or 9.30am to 7pm (the bazaar opens at 8am). Some shops may shut at lunchtime in summer months.

EXPORTING ANTIQUES
Strict rules apply. If you buy what is described as an antique take it to the nearest museum for expert advice. If it is authentic and able to be exported you will be given a certificate (no charge) to show customs on leaving the country.

PUBLISHER'S NOTE

All information included in this guide was correct at time of going to press.
Opening times of shops and museums can vary so please telephone ahead before making a special trip.

INDEX

Acknowledgements

We would like to say a special thank you to the staff of the Tourist Offices in all the cities featured in this book, especially Krystyna Rees at the Polish Tourist Board, London, and Cristina Valentini, Italian Tourist Board, Venice. To our researchers Caterina Boselli, Victoria Cookson, Richard Elman, Georgina Fox, Giovanna Freanchina, Sonia Harvey, Ben Horslen, Astrid de Kerangal, Sandra Lacey, Cara Miller, Mark Mobsby, Eve Norris, Andrew Robinson, George Stacpoole, Kate Stuart-Cox, Gillian Thompson, Nathalie de Vries. To Anne Fisher, Caroline Hill, Sandra Horth, Paul Montague, Daniel Goodman and Carole Wood for their help in producing the book.

Key to the abreviations used in this list

A&J A&J Photographic AJ Andy Johnson AL Andrew Lineham ART Artemis BAL The Bridgeman Art Library BC Bonhams, Chelsea BD Barry Davies BK Bonhams, Knightsbridge C&C Cohen & Cohen CC/ME Clive Corless/ Marshall Editions Christo Christobal CI Christie's CK Caroline de Kerangal, Antiquites le Grand Mare, Brittany CL Chris Linton DN Drewitt Neate FC Furniture Cave FL Fay Lucas FORZA Forza G&G Guest & Gray GACT Gallery of Antique Costume & Textiles GR Graham Rae H&W Haslam & Whiteway JH Jeanette Hayhurst JJ John Jesse JM Jill Metcalf KB Karl Bartley L Legacy LA Lunn Antiques LB Linda Bee MA Manic Attic MG Michael German MN Mike Newton Morris Morris & Co NC New Century PB Philip de Bay PC Private Collection PG Pruskin Gallery RA Rare Art RR Rogers de Rin SA Somervale Antiques SAS Special Auction Services SC Sandra Cronan SF The Silver Fund Com SJP S.J. Phillips Ltd SPL Sotheby's Picture Library ST Steve Tanner TC Tim Clinch V&A V&A Picture Library VH Valerie Howard YW York Whiting Zeit Zeitgeist

1 t V&A; 1 b CI; 3 tl Chelsea Antique Rug Gallery/CL; 3 bl Bizzare/CL; 3 r CI; 4 Michael Jenner; 5 l DN/ A&J; 5 r AJ; 6 tl GR; 6 bl AL/A&J; 6 r PC/A&J; 8 tl SPL; 8 tc Sotheby's/A&J; 8 tr CI/A&J; 8-9 b David Towersey; 10 CI/A&J; 11 PC/A &J; 12 t Scottish Borders Tourist Office; 12 bl Scottish Borders Tourist Office; 12 b Scottish Borders Tourist Office; 13 c SJP/ST; 14-15 The Travel Library/ John Lawrence; 14 t Alan Copson Pictures; 14 b Michael Jenner; 15 c CI/A&J ; 15 b CI; 16 t Antiquarius, King's Road, London; 16 c Jellicoe/PB; 16 b YW/A&J; 17 t CC/ME; 17 tc Lots Road Gallery/www.lotsroad.com; 17 bc Sandra Cronan/CL; 17 bl Christo/GR; 17 br PC/GR; 18 tl Michael Jenner; 18 tr JH/A&J; 18 c DN/A&J; 18 b Alan Copson Pictures; 19 t DN/MN; 19 cl BK/ST; 19 cr Alan Copson Pictures; 19 b The Travel Library/John Lawrence; 20 t Michael Jenner; 20 c David Towersey/courtesy Gray's Antique Market; 20 bl C&C/CL; 20 b BK/ST; 21 t CC/ME; 21 c FC/D. Loveday/A&J; 21 b Michael Jenner; 22 t AL/CL; 22 cl Alan Copson Pictures; 22 cr The Travel Library/Alan Copson; 22 bl Paul Rennie/CL; 22 br MA/CL; 23 t Corbis/Jeremy Horner; 23 c CC/ME; 23 bl The Travel Library/John Lawrence; 23 br Alan Copson Pictures; 24 t Michael Jenner; 24 tc RA/ST; 24 bc RA/ST; 24 b Alan Copson Pictures; 25 tl Paul Rennie/CL; 25 tr SC/CL; 25 cl RR/CL; 25 cr CI; 25 b Michael Jenner; 26 tl Powerstock Zefa; 26 tr Paul Rennie/CL; 26 c JJ/A&J; 26 b L/CL; 27 t Michael Jenner; 27 tc PC/CL; 27 bc Michael Jenner; 27 bl The Travel Library/John Lawrence; 27 br Corbis/Martin Jones; 28 tl Quality Chop House; 28 tr Hazlitt's; 28 bl The Ritz Hotel; 28 br Dukes Hotel; 29 tl RR/CL; 29 tr National Trust Picture Library/ Andreas von Einsiedel; 29 c H&W/A&J; 29 b Alan Copson Pictures; 30-31 BG Britain on View; 30 T Incorporated Arts Ltd/D.I. Freeman; 31 T Britain on View; 31 C Robert Harding Picture Library; 31 B Corbis/Eye Ubiquitous/David Cumming; 32 T Robert Harding Picture Library/Andrew Robinson; 32 CL AL/CL; 32 CR Sotheby's/A&J; 32 BL CC/ME; 32 BR Britain on View; 33 T Michael Jenner; 33 B Robert Harding Picture Library; 34-35 BG Robert Harding Picture Library/Roy Rainford; 34 T Dean & Chapter of York; 34 B Michael Jenner; 35 T Corbis/Richard T. Nowitz; 35 C York Castle Museum; 35 B Robert Harding Picture Library/Michael Jenner; 36 T Robert Harding Picture Library/Adam Woolfitt; 36 B PC/A&J; 37 T York Civic Trust, Fairfax House, York; 37 CL CC/ME; 37 TCR CC/ME; 37 BCR Robert Harding Picture Library/Roy Rainford; 37 B Corbis/Patrick Ward; 38-39 Robert Harding Picture Library/Roy Rainford; 38 T Collections/Roger Scruton.; 38 B CC/ME; 39 T Robert Harding Picture Library; 39 B Robert Harding Picture Library/Roy Rainford; 40-41 Robert Harding Picture Library/Nelly Boyd; 40 T CC/ME; 41 T The National Trust Photographic Library/Stephen Robson; 41 C MPG/A&J; 41 B Robert Harding Picture Library/Nelly Boyd; 42-43 Robert Harding Picture Library/Roy Rainford.; 42 T CK/A&J; 42 C Michael Jenner; 43 T Robert Harding Picture Library/Nigel Francis; 43 B Robert Harding Picture Library/David Beatty; 44 T Robert Harding Picture Library/Adam Woolfitt; 44 CL Sotheby's/A&J; 44 CR CI/A&J; 44 B Robert Harding Picture Library/Roy Rainford.; 45 T Sotheby's/A&J; 45 C AL/A&J; 45 B Robert Harding Picture Library/Roy Rainford.; 46 T Robert Harding Picture Library/David Hunter; 46 B JM/GR; 47 B-G Robert Harding Picture Library/Julia Bayne; 47 T Michael Jenner; 48 TL JH/A&J; 48 TR Robert Harding Picture Library/Julia Bayne; 48 C Jonathan Home/GR; 48 B Michael Jenner; 49 T Robert Harding Picture Library/Rob Cousins; 49 C SPL; 49 B SA/Martin Norris; 50-51 BG David Towersey; 50 T David Towersey; 50 C David Towersey; 51 L Oxford Scientific Films/Martin Chillmaid; 51 R David Towersey; 52 T David Towersey; 52 CL David Towersey; 52 CR PC/ST; 52 B Sotheby's/A&J; 53 T Witney Antiques, Witney, Oxon; 53 C David Towersey; 53 BL Oxford Scientific Films/Bob Gibbons; 53 BR John Glover; 54 T Corbis/Adam Woolfitt; 54 C CC/ME; 54 BL David Towersey; 54 BR CI; 55 T Sotheby's/KB; 55 B David Towersey; 56-57; 56 t Britain on View/Adam Woolfitt; 56 c Robert Harding Picture Library/Guy Thouvenin; 56 b Corbis/Ecoscene/John Farmar; 57 t Michael Jenner; 57 b Phillips; 58 tl Michael Jenner; 58 tr CC/ME; 58 b Britain on View; 59 t Michael Jenner; 59 b CC/ME; 60-61; 60 t MG/CL; 60 c Phillips; 60 b Robert Harding Picture Library/Michael Jenner; 61 t Michael Jenner; 61 b Phillips; 62 t Robert Harding Picture Library/Adam Woolfitt; 62 c NC/MN; 62 bl CI; 62 br JJ/A&J; 63 t SAS/ST; 63 c Robert Harding Picture Library/Naomi Peck; 63 b Britain on View; 64-65 BSK Photo Library/Brian Kelly; 64 t BAL/V&A; 64 b Ulster Folk & Transport Museum, Cultra Manor, Holywood, Co. Down; 65 t Robert Harding Picture Library/E. Simanor; 65 c DN/Martin Norris; 65 b BSK Photo Library/Brian Kelly; 66-67 Robert Harding Picture Library/Philip Craven; 66 t Robert Harding Picture Library/Fraser Hall; 66 b CI; 67 t The Art Archive; 67 b Robert Harding Picture Library; 68 t JH/A&J; 68 c Number Twenty Nine, Dublin; 68 b BAL/Partridge Fine Arts, London; 69 tr BSK Photo Library/Brian Kelly; 69 tl BAL/National Museum of Ireland, Dublin; 69 bl CI/A&J; 69 bc CC/ME; 69 br Hulton Getty; 70 t Phil Voon; 70 c CC/ME; 70 bl CI; 70 br Robert Harding Picture Library/Philip Craven; 71 t Robert Opie Collection; 71 c Phil Voon; 71 b Corbis/Michael St. Maur Sheil; 72-73 GACT/ST; 72 tl G&G/CL; 72 tc ART/A&J; 72 tr YW/A&J; 74 AL/CL; 75 CK/A&J; 76-77 John Brunton; 76 t BAL/Musee Carnavalet/ Peter Willi,Paris; 76 bl John Brunton; 76 br BAL/Musee Marmottan,Paris; 77 c Paul Rennie/CL; 77 b CK/A&J; 78 tl Michael Jenner; 78 tr LB/CL; 78 bl Robert Harding Picture Library/Explorer/Guy Touvenin; 78 br John Brunton; 79 t BAL/Musee Jacquemart-Andre,Paris; 79 c SAS/MN; 79 bl CI; 79 br CK/A&J; 80 tl Corbis/Leonard de Selva; 80 tr SC/CL; 80 cl Michael Jenner; 80 cr PG/A&J; 80 b SC/CL; 81 t AL/CL; 81 cl Lalique; 81 cr ART/A&J; 81 bl John Brunton; 81 br SF/GR; 82 t Robert Harding Picture Library/C. Bowman; 82 c CK/A&J; 82 bl John Brunton; 82 br CK/A&J; 83 t Corbis/Philip Gould; 83 c CI; 83 b CC/ME; 84 t John Brunton; 84 c AL/CL; 84 bl Michael Jenner; 84 br John Brunton; 85 t Corbis/Owen Franken; 85 c Alexander von Moltke/MN; 85 bl John Brunton; 85 br Michael Jenner; 86 t Corbis/Stefano Bianchetti; 86 c CC/ME; 86 b Images Colour Library; 87 t John Brunton; 87 c John Brunton; 87 bl John Brunton; 87 br Alexander von Moltke/MN; 88 tl John Brunton; 88 tr John Brunton; 88 b John Brunton; 89 t Corbis/Harald A, Jahn, Viennaslide Photoagency; 89 c Hotel du Jeu de Paume, Paris; 89 b Corbis/Owen Franken; 90 t Corbis/Yann Arthus-Bertrand; 90 c GACT/ST; 90 b CI; 91 b/g Corbis/Gianni Dagli Orti; 91 t Corbis/Brian Harding, Eye Ubiquitous; 91 b Corbis/Gianni Dagli Orti; 92 c Robert Harding Picture Library/Explorer; 92 b Norman Brand; 93 tl Michael Jenner; 93 tr Corbis/Farrell Grehan; 93 c Alexander von Moltke/MN; 93 b Corbis/by kind permission of the National Gallery Collection, London; 94 t Robert Harding Picture Library/Explorer; 94 c CI; 94 b Corbis/Gianni Dagli Orti; 95 t VH/CL; 95 c Travel Ink/Peter Devenish; 95 b Corbis/Owen Franken; 96-97 Robert Harding Picture Library/Explorer; 96 t PC/ST; 96 b Robert Harding Picture Library/Explorer; 97 t VH/CL; 97 c Robert Harding Picture Library/Explorer; 97 b Robert Harding Picture Library/Explorer; 98-99 Robert Harding Picture Library/Nelly Boyd; 98 t AL/CL; 98 b CC/ME; 99 t Robert Harding Picture Library/Nelly Boyd; 99 c Alexander von Moltke/MN; 100-101 Michael Busselle's Photo Library; 100 t Corbis/Eye Ubiquitous; 101 t Michael Busselle's Photo Library; 101 c AL/CL; 101 b The Travel Library; 102 tl The Travel Library/Roger Howard; 102 tr CC/ME; 102 b DN/A&J; 103 t Corbis/Owen Franken; 103 c CC/ME; 103 b Michael Busselle's Photo Library; 104 t CI; 104 c CC/ME; 104 b The Travel Library/Philip Enticknap; 105 t Michael Busselle's Photo Library; 105 ct CC/ME; 105 cb GR; 105 b Michael Busselle's Photo Library; 106-107 Robert Harding Picture Library/Explorer; 106 t CI; 107 t Robert Harding Picture Library/Explorer; 107 c Corbis/Adam Woolfitt; 107 b Robert Harding Picture Library/Explorer; 108 t AL/CL; 108 c Robert Harding Picture Library/Explorer; 108 b AJ; 109 t Robert Harding Picture Library/Explorer; 109 c Robert Harding Picture Library/Explorer; 109 b Robert Harding Picture Library/Michael Jenner; 110-111 G&G/CL; 110 t CI; 110 b The Art Archive/Dagli Orti; 111 t G&G/CL; 111 tc VH/CL; 111 c Robert Harding Picture Library/Explorer; 111 b Ace Photo Agency/Vladimir Pcholkin; 112-113 Robert Harding Picture Library; 112 t CI; 112 c Carol Wood/www.french-treasures.com; 113 Robert Harding Picture Library; 114 t Corbis/Gail Mooney; 114 bl Corbis/Richard Bickel; 114-115 b Robert Harding Picture Library; 115 t Robert Harding Picture Library/Explorer; 115 c CI; 115 br Robert Harding Picture Library; 116 t Corbis/Gail Mooney; 116 tc Robert Harding Picture Library/Jean Brooks; 116 cl CI; 116 b Robert Harding Picture Library/Explorer; 117 t Corbis/Gail Mooney; 117 c Robert Harding Picture Library/Explorer; 117 b AL/CL; 118 tl Corbis/Gail Mooney; 118 tr Corbis/Leonard de Selva; 118 cl CI; 118 br CK/A&J; 119 t A.J. Phillips Ltd/ ST; 119 c Robert Harding Picture Library; 120-121 Robert Harding Picture Library/Rob Cousins; 120 tl BD/A&J; 120 tc LA/ST; 120 tr CC/ME; 122 V&A; 123 BAL/Ferrers Gallery, London; 124-125 Britstock-IFA/Chris Cheadle; 124 t Michael Jenner; 124 b Britstock-IFA/Gunter Graefenhain; 125 c Robert Harding Picture Library/Christopher Rennie; 125 b Robert Harding Picture Library/ Roy Rainford; 126 tl CI; 126 tr Zeit/PB; 126 b Robert Harding Picture Library/Explorer; 127 t Robert Harding Picture Library; 127 tc Robert Harding Picture

Library/ Louis-Yves Loirat; 127 b b/g Britstock-IFA/Chris Cheadle; 127 c Robert Harding Picture Library; 127 bc Christo/GR;

127 b Robert Harding Picture Library/K. Gillham; 128 t Robert Harding Picture Library; 128 c BAL; 128 bl BAL/Ferrers Gallery, London; 128 br Britstock-IFA/Chris Cheadle; 129 tl Robert Harding Picture Library/Explorer; 129 tr Robert Harding Picture Library/ Ken Straiton; 129 bl BAL/Musees Royaux des Beaux-Arts de Belgique, Brussels; 129 br Robert Harding Picture Library/ Julian Y Pottage; 130-131 Britstock-IFA/Chris Cheadle; 130 t Robert Harding Picture Library; 130 c BAL/Geffrye Museum, London; 131 t Robert Harding Picture Library/Explorer; 131 c Michael Jenner; 131 b LA/ST; 132 t Robert Harding Picture Library/Explorer; 132 c Corbis/Michelle Garrett; 132 b Toerisme Brugge; 133 t CC/ME; 133 c Robert Harding Picture Library/K. Gillham; 133 b Relais et Chateaux; 134-135 Robert Harding Picture Library/Nigel Francis; 134 t Robert Harding Picture Library; 135 t Images Colour Library; 135 c C&C/CL; 135 b Robert Harding Picture Library; 136 t Photo: Amsterdam Historical Museum; 136 c BD/A&J; 136 b Michael Jenner; 137 t V&A; 137 c Corbis; 137 cl BAL/Rijksmuseum, Amsterdam; 137 b Robert Harding Picture Library/Nigel Francis; 138 tl Michael Jenner; 138 c FORZA/MN; 138 b CI; 138-139 SAS/MN; 139 tr Restaurant Dorrius, Amsterdam; 139 c Robert Harding Picture Library/Adam Woolfitt; 139 b Robert Harding Picture Library/Nigel Francis; 140-141 Robert Harding Picture Library/Nigel Francis; 140 t BAL/Musee de la Revolution Francaise, Vizille, France; 141 tl CC/ME; 141 tr G.W. Dijsselhof, Gemeentemuseum, Den Haag 2000, c/o Beeldrecht Amstelveen; 141 b b en u International Picture Service; 142-143 Robert Harding Picture Library/Nigel Francis; 142 t CC/ME; 142-143 br DN/A&J; 143 t BAL/Maritshuis, The Hague, The Netherlands; 143 b Corbis/Kelly-Mooney Photography; 144 tl SF/GR; 144 tc BC/ST; 144 Cl; 144-145 Robert Harding Picture Library/ Phil Craven; 146 Morris/CL; 147 PC/CL; 148-149 Michael Jenner; 148 t Michael Jenner; 148 c Robert Opie Collection; 149 tl Michael Jenner; 149 tr Morris/CL; 149 c Michael Jenner; 149 b SPL; 150 t Michael Jenner; 150 b Michael Jenner; 151 b/g John Brunton; 151 t John Brunton; 151 b SPL; 152 t Robert Harding Picture Library/K. Gillham; 152 b Robert Harding Picture Library/Bildagentur Schuster; 153 t CI; 153 cl CL; 153 cr SA/MN; 153 b CI; 154 t Wilde/A&J; 154 c Restaurant Konigshof, Munchen; 154 b B. Adams/AJ; 155 b/g John Brunton; 155 t Robert Harding Picture Library/Adam Woolfitt; 155 br Robert Harding Picture Library/Bildagentur Schuster; 156 t Robert Harding Picture Library; 156 bl BC/MN; 156 br BC/ST; 157 t KB/Sotheby's; 157 c KB/Sotheby's; 157 b Wald und Schlosshotel; 158-159 Robert Harding Picture Library; 158 t CC/ME; 158 b Pruskin Gallery/A&J; 159 t SF/GR; 159 b Robert Harding Picture Library; 160-161 Robert Harding Picture Library/MPH; 160 t BAL/Bethnal Green Museum, London; 160 b Britstock-IFA/Goedel; 161 c CL; 161 b Robert Harding Picture Library/MPH; 162-163 Images Colour Library; 162 t Robert Harding Picture Library/Adam Woolfitt; 162 b Robert Harding Picture Library/Adam Woolfitt; 163 t Robert Harding Picture Library/Explorer; 163 c Robert Harding Picture Library/Adam Woolfitt; 163 b Images Colour Library; 164 t SPL; 164 c Robert Harding Picture Library/Adam Woolfitt; 164 b YW/MN; 165 t CC/ME; 165 b Robert Harding Picture Library/Rolf Richardson; 166-167 Images Colour Library; 166 t Glasgalerie Michael Kovacek, Spiegelgasse 12, 1010 Vienna; 166 b Powerstock/Zefa/Janicek; 167 t Travel Ink/Ken Gibson; 167 c CC/ME; 167 b DN/MN; 168-169 Robert Harding Picture Library/Explorer; 168 t PC/CL; 169 t Robert Harding Picture Library/P. Wysocki; 169 c Antiquorum, Geneva; 169 b Antiquorum, Geneva; 170-171 Michael Jenner; 170 tl AL/A&J; 170 tc CL; 170 tr Alan Copson Pictures; 172 CL; 173 B. Adams/A&J; 174-175 Alan Copson Pictures; 174 t AL/A&J; 174 c AL/A&J; 175 t BAL/State Archives, Vienna; 175 c Alan Copson Pictures; 175 b B. Adams/A&J; 176 t AL/CL; 176 c Robert Harding Picture Library/Christopher Rennie; 176 b GR; 177 b/g Robert Harding Picture Library/Ellen Rooney; 177 t Robert Harding Picture Library; 177 b Robert Harding Picture Library/Adam Woolfitt; 178 t CL; 178 c CL; 178 b Robert Harding Picture Library/Ellen Rooney; 179 t SF/GR; 179 b Robert Harding Picture Library/Maurice Joseph; 180-181 Robert Harding Picture Library/Adina Tovy; 180 CL; 181 t CL; 181 b Robert Harding Picture Library/Adina Tovy; 182-183 Robert Harding Picture Library/Adina Tovy; 182 Michael Jenner; 183 tl CL; 183 tr Robert Harding Picture Library/K. Gillham; 183 b Robert Harding Picture Library/Christopher Rennie; 184-185 Robert Harding Picture Library; 184 t Michael Jenner; 184 b Alan Copson Pictures; 185 t Alan Copson Pictures; 185 cl BAL/Hermitage, St. Petersburg; 185 cr Alan Copson Pictures; 185 b Corbis/Archivo Iconografico S.A.; 186-187 Robert Harding Picture Library; 186 t BAL/Forbes Magazine Collection, New York; 187 t Robert Harding Picture Library/E. Rooney; 187 c BK/ST; 187 b Robert Harding Picture Library/Adam Woolfitt; 188 tl CL; 188 c TC; 188 tr FL/CL; 188-189 GettyOne Stone; 190 M/MN; 191 JH/AJ; 192-193 Robert Harding Picture Library/K. Gillham; 192 t Robert Harding Picture Library/K. Gillham; 192 b Robert Harding Picture Library/R. Richardson; 193 t Robert Harding Picture Library/K. Gillham; 193 c Corbis/Richard T. Nowitz; 194 t Robert Harding Picture Library/K. Gillham; 194 c Robert Harding Picture Library/Adam Woolfitt; 194 b SAS/ST; 195 b/g Robert Harding Picture Library/K. Gillham; 195 t Robert Harding Picture Library/K. Gillham; 196 t Interior Archive/Fritz von der Schulenburg; 196 c TC; 196-197 b Robert Harding Picture Library; 197 t Robert Harding Picture Library/Christopher Rennie; 197 ct JH/AJ; 197 cb Robert Harding Picture Library/Paul van Riel; 198 t CI; 198 tc CL; 198 cl Michael Jenner; 198 cr CL; 198 b Robert Harding Picture Library/K. Gillham; 199 Corbis/Macduff Everton; 200-201 Robert Harding Picture Library/K. Gillham; 200 Michael Jenner; 201 t Corbis/Massimo Listri; 201 c Robert Harding Picture Library/Gavin Hellier; 201 b Robert Harding Picture Library/Kim Hart; 202 t JJ/A&J; 202 c SAS/MN; 202 b SF/GR; 203 t Corbis/Archivo Iconografico S.A.; 203 c FL/CL; 203 bl Robert Harding Picture Library/K. Gillham; 203 br Robert Harding Picture Library/Adina Tovy; 204 t French Metal Works/MN; 204 cl Cees v. Roeden; 204 cr CL; 204 b Robert Harding Picture Library/K. Gillham; 205 l Wonderful Copenhagen; 205 r Krogs Fiskerestaurant; 206 tl BAL/V&A; 206 tc CC/ME; 206 tr SC/CL; 206-207 Michael Busselle's Photo Library; 208 Robert Harding Picture Library/Robert Frerck/Odyssey/Chicago; 209 Corbis/TonyArruza; 210-211 Robert Harding Picture Library/ James Strachan; 210 t BAL/V&A; 210 b Robert Harding Picture Library/James Strachan; 211 t BAL/Prado, Madrid; 211 c CI; 211 b Robert Harding Picture Library/James Strachan; 212 t JH/AJ; 212 c CI; 212 b CC/ME; 213 t Wellington Hotel, Madrid; 213 c Michael Jenner; 213 b Corbis/Nik Wheeler; 214-215 Robert Harding Picture Library/Robert Frerck; 214 Alan Copson Pictures; 215 t Robert Harding Picture Library/Norma Joseph; 215 c BAL/V&A; 215 b Robert Harding Picture Library/ Jeremy Bright; 216 t Archivo Iconografico S.A.; 216 b Archivo Iconografico S.A.; 217 t CI; 217 tc Robert Harding Picture Library/Robert Frerck; 217 bc Alan Copson Pictures; 217 b CI; 218 t BAL/PC; 218 c Robert Harding Picture Library; 218 b CI; 219 t Robert Harding Picture Library; 219 tc SC/CL; 219 bc Robert Harding Picture Library/Robert Frerck; 219 b Robert Harding Picture Library/Robert Frerck; 220 t Archivo Iconografico S.A.; 220 c BAL/Talavera Antiques; 220 b Robert Harding Picture Library/Adam Woolfitt; 221 t Robert Harding Picture Library/Robert Frerck; 221 b Robert Harding Picture Library; 222-223 Robert Harding Picture Library/James Strachan; 222 t Alan Copson Pictures; 223 t Robert Harding Picture Library/K. Gillham; 223 c CI; 223 b Alan Copson Pictures; 224 tl Robert Harding Picture Library/Robert Frerck; 224 tr BAL/V&A; 224 b Robert Harding Picture Library/Explorer; 225 t Archivo Iconografico S.A.; 225 c Archivo Iconografico S.A.; 225 b Alan Copson Pictures; 226 t CI; 226 c Robert Harding Picture Library/Robert Frerck/Odyssey/Chicago; 226 b Corbis/Patrick Ward; 227 t Alan Copson Pictures; 227 c Robert Harding Picture Library; 227 bl Robert Harding Pi cture Library/James Strachan; 227 br Alan Copson Pictures; 228 t Alan Copson Pictures; 228 tc Robert Harding Picture Library/ Robert Frerck; 228 bc Alan Copson Pictures; 228 b Robert Harding Picture Library/James Strachan; 229 t Corbis/Elke Stolzenberg; 229 c Michael Jenner; 229 b BAL/PC; 230-231 Robert Harding Picture Library; 230 t Corbis/TonyArruza; 230 b Alan Copson Pictures; 231 t BAL/ Palacio de Ajuda, Lisbon; 231 c Alan Copson Pictures; 231 b Robert Harding Picture Library/Adina Tovy; 232 t Robert Harding Picture Library; 232 c BAL/Bonham's, London; 232 b Robert Harding Picture Library; 233 t Michael Jenner; 233 b Robert Harding Picture Library; 234-235 b National Trust Photographic Library/ John Hammond; 234 tl CI; 234 tc CI; 234 tr BAL/PC; 236 Corbis/Arte & Immagini srl; 237 CI; 238-239 Travel Ink/Ronald Badkin; 238 t SPL; 238 bl JH/AJ; 238 br BAL/PC; 239 t Corbis/Vittoriano Rastelli; 239 c The Travel Library/Philip Enticknap; 239 b Scala/Galleria Borghese, Rome; 240 t Corbis/Franz-Marc Frei; 240 c Paul Rennie/CL; 240 bl Bizarre/CL; 240 br Travel Ink/Ronald Badkin; 241 t Aldrovandi Palace Hotel, Rome; 241 b Corbis/Franz-Marc Frei; 242-243 Alan Copson Pictures; 242 t Corbis/Arte & Immagini srl; 243 t Alan Copson Pictures; 243 tc Corbis/Massimo Listri; 243 bc Corbis/Ted Spiegel; 243 b V&A; 244 t CI; 244 c Corbis/Arte & Immagini srl; 244 b Corbis/Massimo Listri; 245 t Scala/Loggia dei Lanzi/ Florence; 245 c Corbis/Massimo Listri; 245 bl The Art Archive/Bargello Museum/Dagli Orti; 245 br CI; 246 t Archivo Iconografico; 246 tc CI; 246 bc Archivo Iconografico S.A.; 246 b Alan Copson Pictures; 247 t Alan Copson Pictures; 247 c Sandra Cronan/ Chris Linton; 247 bl Corbis/Massimo Listri; 247 br Sina Hotels; 248-249 Corbis/Historical Picture Archive; 248 t Corbis/Owen Franken; 248 c BAL/Villa Medici, Rome; 248 b V&A; 249 Corbis/Historical Picture Archive; 250 tl The Travel Library/Philip Enticknap; 250 tr BAL/Phillips; 250 bl CI; 250 cb Corbis/Arte & Immagini srl; 250 br CI; 251 t The Travel Library/Philip Enticknap; 251 c CI; 251 b Corbis/Massimo Listri; 252 t The Travel Library/Philip Enticknap; 252 ct Corbis/Dennis Marsico; 252 cb The Travel Library/Philip Enticknap; 252 b CI; 253 t The Art Archive; 253 c CI; 253 b Sina Hotels; 254-255 John Brunton; 254 t Robert Opie Collection; 254 c CI; 255 t John Brunton; 255 c BAL/Museo Correr, Venice; 255 b John Brunton; 256 tl LA/ST; 256 tr CI; 256 c CI; 256 bl CI; 256 br John Brunton; 257 c CI; 257 b Scala/Ca' Rezzonico, Venice; 258 tl Trio/ Chris Linton; 258 tr Corbis/Arne Hodalic; 258 c CI; 258 b John Brunton; 259 t Robert Harding Picture Library/Tony Gervis; 259 b Michael Jenner; 260-261 Corbis/Hulton-Deutsch Collection; 260 t Robert Harding Picture Library; 260 b Scala/Museo Etnografico Siciliano Pitre'; 261 t Corbis/Jonathan Blair; 261 c Corbis/Hulton-Deutsch Collection; 261 b Bazaat/A&J; 262-263 b Michael Jenner; 262 tl Chelsea Antique Rug Gallery/ Chris Linton; 262 tc Robert Harding Picture Library/Robert Frerck; 262 tr Chelsea Antique Rug Gallery/CL; 264 Chelsea Antique Rug Gallery/CL; 265 b/g Michael Jenner; 265 t Robert Harding Picture Library/J.H.C. Wilson; 265 c Chelsea Antique Rug Gallery/CL; 265 b Robert Harding Picture Library/Nigel Francis; 266 t Robert Harding Picture Library/Robert Frerck; 266 bl Michael Jenner; 266 br Robert Harding Picture Library/Robert Frerck; 267 tl Robert Harding Picture Library/J.H.C. Wilson; 267 tr Chelsea Antique Rug Gallery/CL; 267 c Robert Harding Picture Library/Robert Frerck; 267 bl Robert Harding Picture Library/Robert Frerck; 267 br Robert Harding Picture Library/Robert Frerck; 268 tl Robert Harding Picture Library/Robert Frerck; 268 tr Chelsea Antique Rug Gallery/CL; 268 cl CC/ME; 268 cr Chelsea Antique Rug Gallery/CL; 268 bl Michael Jenner; 268 br Michael Jenner; 269 t Robert Harding Picture Library/Adam Woolfitt; 269 c Robert Harding Picture Library/Adam Woolfitt; 269 b Chelsea Antique Rug Gallery/CL.